To Richard
for his 84th
birthday

Nigel Fenner

CAMBRIDGE SPORT
IN FENNER'S HANDS

By
Nigel Fenner

who dedicates this book to his dad,
another Frank Fenner (1926-2016).

To request permissions, contact the author at

nigel@cambridgesportstours.co.uk

Hardcover/Paperback: 978-1-7393304-0-8

First edition: March 2023

Self-published by Cambridge Sports Tours

BOOK REVIEWS

Cambridge Sport: In Fenner's Hands (1st edition)

Derek Pringle (former Cambridge University, Essex and England cricketer, today journalist and author of "Pushing the Boundaries - Cricket in the 80s")

> *Driven by its famous university Cambridge is an acknowledged leader in art and science, yet who knew its role as the crucible for so many of today's sports and games? By turning his fascinating walking tour on the subject into a book, Nigel Fenner has written a step-by-step account (as you'd expect from a devout footslogger) of how this sporting prowess evolved and how much of it can be linked to his relative the Victorian cricketer, entrepreneur and Cambridge denizen, Frank Fenner. Rich with detail, 'In Fenner's Hands,' like the weathered appendages themselves, points, ushers and guides us through modern sport's birth and adolescence.*

Mike Petty MBE (Cambridgeshire Researcher, Lecturer & Historian)

> *A well-written and well-illustrated addition to Cambridge's history..... and a worthy tribute to Frank Fenner and Cambridge's sporting legacy.*

Richard Lawrence (Reviews Editor - The Association of Cricket Statisticians and Historians)

> *This account of Frank Fenner and his legacy in Cambridge is a most unusual book, which I very much enjoyed. Running through it, like a golden thread, is the character of Fenner, but this is more than a conventional biography, as it also embraces the history of the city and university of Cambridge, their impact on the sporting world, and in particular the man who played such a large part in the development of this sporting tradition.*

CONTENTS

The above chapter headings are also mapped as a route from north to south Cambridge – see next page.

MAP OF CAMBRIDGE

in c1836 when Frank Fenner was 25 years old.

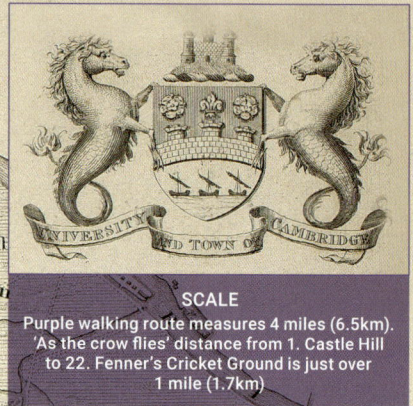

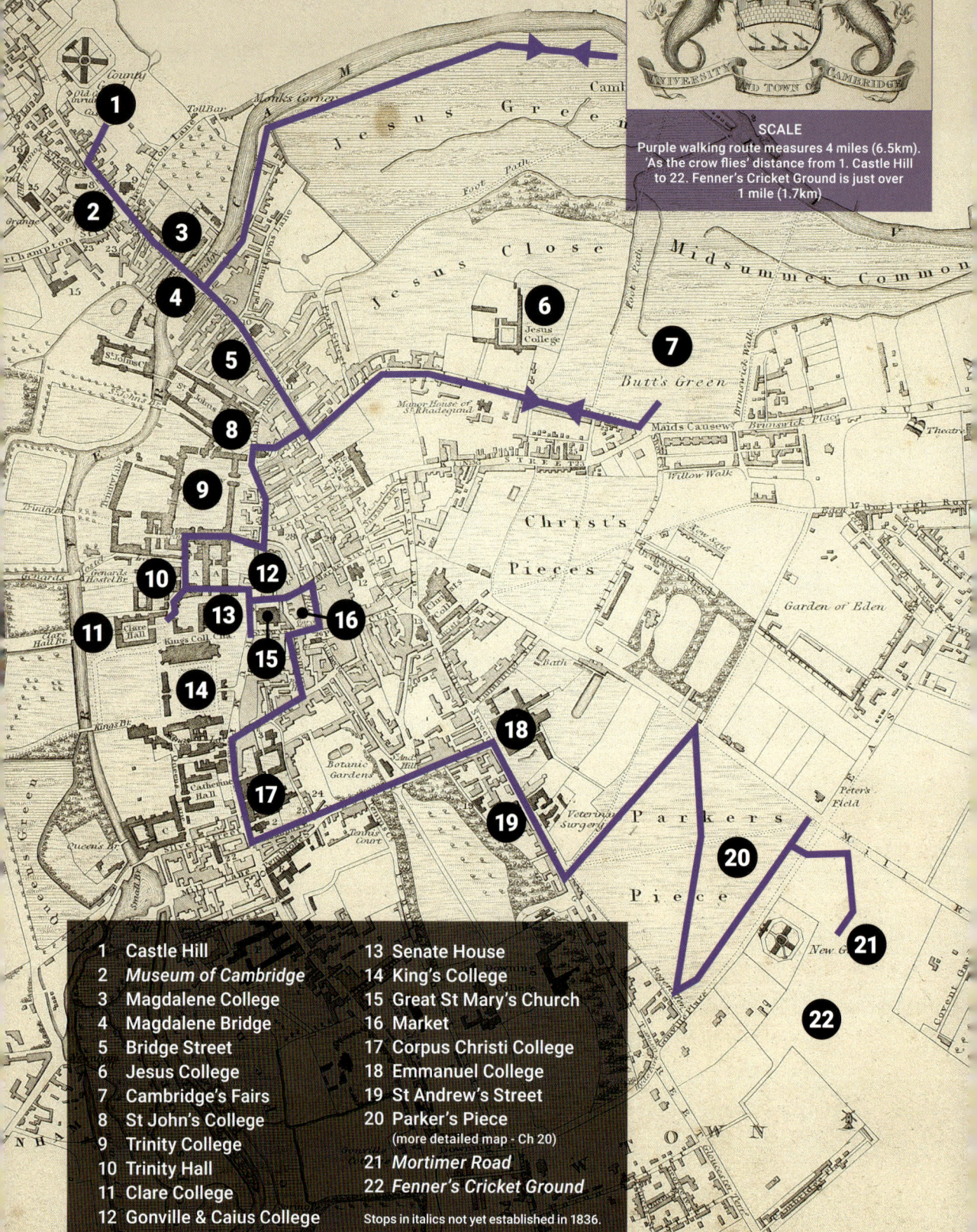

SCALE
Purple walking route measures 4 miles (6.5km).
'As the crow flies' distance from 1. Castle Hill
to 22. Fenner's Cricket Ground is just over
1 mile (1.7km)

1 Castle Hill
2 *Museum of Cambridge*
3 Magdalene College
4 Magdalene Bridge
5 Bridge Street
6 Jesus College
7 Cambridge's Fairs
8 St John's College
9 Trinity College
10 Trinity Hall
11 Clare College
12 Gonville & Caius College
13 Senate House
14 King's College
15 Great St Mary's Church
16 Market
17 Corpus Christi College
18 Emmanuel College
19 St Andrew's Street
20 Parker's Piece
    (more detailed map - Ch 20)
21 *Mortimer Road*
22 *Fenner's Cricket Ground*

Stops in italics not yet established in 1836.

Map provided by Cambridge Antiquarian Society and modified to display walking route,
and stops as chapter headings.

PREFACE

A few years before Frank Fenner died in 1896, aged 86, his hands were described as:

> worthy of preservation in a glass case in the pavilion at Lord's, like Galileo's at Florence, as trophies of his sufferings and glory. Broken, distorted, mutilated, half nailless, they resemble the hoof of a rhinoceros almost as much as a human hand.[1]

To make such a comparison with Galileo is extraordinary, implying the writer saw, and perhaps felt in Frank's hands evidence of his 'sufferings and glory', beyond the obvious physical damage that playing cricket will have wrought.

I grew up being only notionally aware of my relationship to Frank Fenner. In my childhood there was a large black and white print of an old cricket match in the family's attic that suffered from the damp and being walked over and torn.

Frank Fenner's own copy of W.H. Mason's 1849 print of 'a cricket match between Sussex and Kent, at Brighton'.

It was only when my father later shared the very sad story of the print being all that remained of a unique and very rare collection of his relative's cricket memorabilia that I began to take an interest. For a start the large print, belonging to Frank Fenner and featuring him aged 38 in 1849, standing front left, was restored and framed as a Christmas gift to hang in my family home.

When my father went away to fight in the Second World War, his mother, having also just lost her husband, gave all the remaining cricket memorabilia away believing it to be junk; for whatever reason the above print was stored elsewhere, and so was saved. It is all that remains.

Apparently, the collection was very impressive, seen by a journalist interviewing Frank in 1893 and reported as 'the many relics of [his] cricketing days',[2] and later by my father, who with some bitterness and sadness recalled some items being unique, that 'even Lord's Cricket Ground did not have', such as the original key to the above print.

In the absence of the insights this collection may well have provided, maybe *Cambridge Sport: in Fenner's Hands* compensates for this loss, and sets Frank's story in the context of the sporting revolution in England he lived through, and perhaps shaped, and yet was wounded by.

Book structure

The book follows a walking tour (full map on page 6 – mirroring exactly the chapter headings listed in the book's contents on pages 4 and 5) starting at stop 1, or chapter 1, on the top of Castle Hill overlooking Cambridge, providing opportunity to explore what makes the area unique, including the character and spirit of its people, shaped in part by the nearby Fens.

After Castle Hill the tour takes in the Museum of Cambridge, with its emphasis on local life, before visiting a number of the colleges of the University that largely dominate the heart of the Town (it became a city in 1951).

Each of the ten colleges on the tour are dealt with mostly in the same way, covering

- the college's history,
- sport before the nineteenth century,
- any interaction the college might have had across the middle of the nineteenth century with the town, and
- any other significant contributions the college, through present and past students (alumni) might have made towards England's sporting revolution across the nineteenth and early twentieth centuries.

In addition to the colleges the tour takes in the river, a variety of stops along two of Cambridge's streets (Bridge Street and St Andrew's Street), Midsummer Common, the Market Square and Parker's Piece, before finishing at Fenner's Cricket Ground. Some of these locations have been chosen because of a direct or indirect association with a particular sport or theme, which are listed in the table of Contents.

After the last stop at Fenner's Cricket Ground, chapter 23 follows Frank's move away from Cambridge to the west country for the last third of his life, with chapter 24 reviewing his life through his 'sufferings and glory', including his legacy. Chapter 25 ends the book with a review of the evidence accumulated across the tour to determine what role Cambridge might have had in England's sporting revolution.

The value of a walking tour

One way of understanding the growth of modern sport is through the 'penetration of neighbourhood, workplace, town'[3], which is why this book is structured as a walking tour.

Cambridge, compared to many other towns and cities in England, is fortunate to have retained many of its buildings, streets and parks as Frank Fenner would have experienced them.

If this book is to explore *Cambridge Sport: in Fenner's Hands*, then we would do well to heed Robert Macfarlane's advice (local best-selling author of *Landmarks*[4]) of 'scrutinising the parochial … the close-at-hand', if for no other reason than to explore how 'Fenner's' (the cricket ground) has somehow entered the local consciousness, even amongst those who know little about cricket, despite so little being known about him.

Sometimes understanding an individual, the life they led, and the world they shaped, and that shaped them, can best be understood through pilgrimage,[5] a journey visiting where they lived, worked and played.

Usually sports pilgrimages are associated with visiting stadia (such as Wembley, Twickenham or Wimbledon) for the 'pilgrim' to 'experience a strong sense of place, often becoming mixed with their sense of identity and an underlying sense of belonging'.[6] W.H. Auden refers to this as 'topophilia', or 'place-love',[7] where what is to be explored are the patina or the accumulated 'value-giving age signs or imprints…of those who have shared in its past…that help construct personal biographies or collective discourses linking different generations'.[8]

Cambridge Sport: in Fenner's Hands therefore endeavours to share Frank's personal biography, in the context of the sporting revolution he lived through and contributed toward, providing a collective discourse, certainly enriching the author, and hopefully the reader too.

Material used

The majority of the material used to write this book has been secured from other books, newspapers and reputable internet sources, which is why there are nearly 900 references. These references are listed at the end of each chapter.

Sometimes in the text a [square bracket] or a footnote (labelled with a letter of the alphabet and listed at the bottom of the page) are used to define a term or word, or add a further explanation.

Understandably, given the breadth of material, there will naturally be gaps and possibly errors for which the author apologises, asking that feedback on these be shared using the 'contact' facility on the *Cambridge Sports Tours* website (www.cambridgesportstours.co.uk) – thank you.

Nigel Fenner

1   W.K.R. Bedford in 'A chat about cricket' in *The English Illustrated Magazine* v 10. Oct 1892 – Sept 1893. Page 680.

2   A Veteran Cricketer article on Frank Fenner in the *Sketch* 1893.

3   Huggins in James Mangan (2006). *A Sport-Loving Society : Victorian and Edwardian Middle-Class England at Play*. Page 5.

4   Robert Macfarlane (2016). *Landmarks*. Penguin. Pages 63, 73 and 74.

5   Gammon, S (2004). 'Secular pilgrimage and sports tourism', in Richie and Adair (eds). *Sports Tourism: interrelationships, Impacts and Issues*.

6   'Places that Make Us' (2017). National Trust Research Report.

7   Robert Macfarlane (2016). *Landmarks*. Penguin. Page 323.

8   Richard Giulianotti (2011). *Sport: A Critical Sociology*. Pages 122 and 123.

ACKNOWLEDGEMENTS

Having never written a book before, had I known over four years ago I would have to rely on so many people for help, as well as the patience and understanding of those closest to me, I am not sure I would have started.

It is not just the significant time taken up in researching, reading, writing, re-writing that tells on your close family, but the changes to any author as they invest more and more of themselves into what is being created. This is particularly true when this book's focus is on a family member, who had his fair share of achievements and challenges, and who also lived where my family lives now – in Cambridge. So, thank you Diane, and our children, Tom and Rachel and their families Becca, Sebastian and Ralph, and James for your support and patience.

Another key member of our family is Margaret (God parent to our children) who as a *critical friend* read my first draft of this book, encouraging me to keep going, fed by the best cooked breakfasts anyone could wish for.

Next, I want to thank Carly Linghorn who picked up the editing reins, and knocked this book into shape, with that gift of suggesting changes, based on her sound experience and knowledge, whilst respecting my style and purpose for the book. This was not easy when my brief was to produce a biography, set in a challenging social context, and the beginnings of a sporting revolution, and structure it as a walking tour. Remember all this was also achieved in very challenging COVID times, so I am so very grateful to her.

Let me now flag the vital and special role Willie Sugg has had in making this book happen. He has been for many years the fountain of all knowledge in relation to the history of local cricket in Cambridgeshire up to the end of the nineteenth century; this included Willie publishing three booklets, one entitled *Fenner's Men*, liberally used as a reference throughout my book. When I first met Willie, he was planning to produce a book on Frank Fenner, but selflessly shared his extensive knowledge and wisdom with me, and more recently acted as my proofreader for *Cambridge Sport: in Fenner's Hands*, so I am so indebted to him.

When faced with the prospect of writing this book I felt the need for some guidance and, thanks to Jo Wroe (a good friend, now a best-selling author), I enrolled on the *Creative writing: an introduction to life* writing course run by the Institute of Continuing Education, University of Cambridge, and through interacting with other budding writers supported by Midge Gillies, the excellent course tutor, I was better prepared to embark on my quest.

As far as tracking down and using the content (information and images) is concerned I have a long list of individuals and organisations to acknowledge, given *Cambridge Sport: in Fenner's Hands* covers a lot of topics, many I knew very little about when I started. What has impressed me most of all about these encounters has been the generosity of people, sometimes leading to further insights, so thank you so much to:

BBC Radio Cambridgeshire - Steve Jackson, British Newspaper Archive, Cambridge Association for Local History - Kathryn Coles, Cambridge University Athletics Club - Chris Thorne, Cambridge University Cricket Club - Anthony Hyde, Cambridgeshire Collection at Cambridge Central Library - Mary Burgess and Ruth Long, Stephen Chalke, Downing College archives – Jenny Ulph, Mary Evans Picture Library, David Gent, Roger Gibbons, Girton College archives - Hannah Westall, Grays of Cambridge (International) Ltd - Richard Gray, Jesus College archives - Robert Athol and Rob Payne, Knights Auctioneers - Tim Knight, Lost Cambridge – Antony Carpen, Roger Mann, MCC / Lord's Cricket Ground archives - Robert Curphey, Friends of Mill Road Cemetery - Claire Martinsen and Mary Naylor, Museum of Cambridge / Capturing Cambridge website - Roger Lilley and Aimee Flack, Mike Petty MBE, Eric Southworth, Trinity College archives - Kevin McGeoghegan and Diana Smith, University of Cambridge Sports - Ashley Edwards and Nick Brooking, Sporting Landmarks - Ian Volans, and Adrian Wykes.

Many of these individuals / organisations are also thanked for providing specific images, as recorded alongside many of the 150 images the book contains.

In searching for a publisher I sought counsel from a number of individuals and organisations, and want to record a special thank you to Stephen Chalke (who also unearthed some vital information on Frank Fenner), Jeremy Lonsdale, Paul Smith and Chris Saunders. Jeremy's feedback was especially helpful encouraging me to persevere, including exploring the self-publishing route. This led to fruitful dialogue with Adrian Reith (now sadly no longer with us), John Dewhirst, and Nicholas Chrimes, the result being the self-publication of *Cambridge Sport: in Fenner's Hands*.

Whilst the self-publishing pathway brings with it the advantage of being in control of the whole process, I have had to learn quickly about designing and printing, and later when the book is printed about marketing too. I am grateful to Katy Etherington who has provided the best possible design, enriched along the way by helpful advice and ideas from Peter Bone and Paul Allitt. Thanks also to Ian Whitelegg (Prime Impressions) for providing guidance over a number of years resulting in *Cambridge Sport: in Fenner's Hands* being so expertly printed.

Finally I want to acknowledge the informal support and encouragement I have received from friends and my extended family such as Mike Croker, Dan Kunkle, Simon Sharpe, Roy Stoner, Mark Szymanski (now sadly not with us), and others in my cycling group of friends, plus those who have attended my talks and tours such as Mike Clenshaw (also now sadly not with us), Geoff Hack, Phil Hadridge, Pete Halasovski, and members of my village, Fen Drayton.

Thank you to you all, as well as those I might have failed to mention.

Front cover photograph: **Pole vault competition at Fenner's 1932.**
Photo by Hudson/Topical Press Agency via Getty Images.

Back cover photograph: **Frank Fenner aged 82 in 1893.**
Source: 'A Veteran Cricketer' article *The Sketch* 13 Sept 1893 Page 361.
© Illustrated London News/Mary Evans Picture Library.

CAST LIST FOR CAMBRIDGE SPORT: IN FENNER'S HANDS

The following is a cast list of those individuals in Cambridge who contributed to the rise in status of sport locally, many of whom Frank Fenner knew directly or was perhaps influenced by.

A limited cross selection of others that followed Frank historically are also listed.

Frank Fenner

Francis Phillips Fenner (or Frank as he was commonly known) was born in Cambridge in 1811 where he lived, worked and played until the early 1860s when he moved to Cheltenham, then in relatively quick succession to Weston-super-Mare, and Bath, where he died in 1896, aged 85.

It is not known where he lived as a child, nor where he was educated, although this was probably at home.

His working life when in Cambridge was as a tobacconist (in at least four 'shops'), combined with being a professional cricket player, coach and equipment retailer. He played cricket for All-England and was instrumental in Cambridge Town and County Cricket Club being one of the best sides in the country, thanks in no small part to his ability to bring Town and Gown players together.

Given cricket's popularity on the public grounds in Cambridge, Frank also created a dedicated ground which came to be named after him, and was also used very successfully for athletics and community events. This was taken up by the University, but not by the Town, leading to the start of the relative demise of local cricket. This coincided with Frank leaving Cambridge to start a new life in the West Country as a hotel proprietor, but this did not dent his enthusiasm for establishing new cricket grounds, and county teams.

Mary Fenner (nee Smith)

Mary Williams Smith was from Chatteris (a town in the Cambridgeshire Fens), marrying Frank Fenner in 1836. Together they had 12 children, six dying within 2 years of being born, one as a 12 year old, with the other 5 reaching adulthood (over 40). Mary died in 1892 aged 79, after 56 years of marriage, and was buried with Frank in Bath Abbey Cemetery.

Chroniclers of life in Cambridge

Josiah Chater started a diary aged 16 from 1844 to 1883. His perspective was initially as an apprentice in William Eaden Lilley's drapery shop, then setting up his own drapery business, first on Sidney Street, then on Market Hill.

Josiah also included entries on the arrival of the railway in Cambridge, royal visits, Town and Gown disturbances, the Volunteers Rifle Corps and the Working Men's College, all directly relevant to Frank Fenner.

Other chroniclers include Eglantyne Jebb who led research on the poverty and inequality between town and gown, publishing her findings in 1906.

Local cricketers

Daniel Hayward (1807 – 1852) played cricket for Chatteris with Frank Fenner in 1830, both later moving back to Cambridge which is where Daniel, living just behind Fenner's Cricket Ground probably used his groundsmanship skills to help in its creation. Daniel was father and grandfather to two of England's greatest cricketers (Thomas and Tom respectively), and another son, also called Daniel (the younger) who over a period of 40 years, more than anyone else locally, followed Frank Fenner's lead on providing sports facilities and equipment.

Other Fenner's groundsmen. Once Fenner's was established, Tom Parmenter was the first groundsman, succeeded by Walter Watts in 1861 who served for 47 years before handing over to Daniel Martin Hayward (grandson of Daniel Hayward) in 1908, then Cyril Coote in 1936 who retired 44 years later.

Town cricketers. Those who played with Frank, or that he had some responsibility for coaching, include Charles Arnold, Frederick Bell, Billy Buttress, Robert Carpenter, A.J. ('Ducky') Diver, Israel Haggis, and George Tarrant. Seven of these players were buried in Mill Road Cemetery, the whereabouts of six being unknown. Others that later followed include Tom Hayward, Sir Jack Hobbs and Ranjitsinhji, who before establishing himself in the University cricket team played on Parker's Piece with local town teams.

University cricketers. There were at least thirty University cricketers across the middle of the nineteenth century who either played for Cambridge Town and County Cricket Club alongside Frank Fenner, or took an active interest in its success, including the welfare of its players. These included Thomas Anchitel Anson, William Hammersley, Arthur Malortie Hoare, Robert Turner King, John Morley Lee, Oliver Pell, Henry Perkins, William Pickering, Frederick Ponsonby, Charles George Taylor, Fred Thackeray, Thomas M Townley and John Walker.

Other local sporting entrepreneurs

Henry John Gray (1836 – 1915) may be considered the most successful sports entrepreneur from Cambridge. He was born largely into poverty, starting his career aged 11 at the University Arms Hotel learning to be a racquets professional (also becoming world champion), prompting him to found his own business. Harry then became 'court keeper' at St John's College for 25 years before opening his first shop in Cambridge. Harry was also an accomplished cricketer, for example playing for Cambridge against an All-England XI in 1859, in a match organised by Frank Fenner.

Grays International (known for its iconic Gray–Nicholls cricket bats) today has an annual turnover of £25 million.

Elevating the importance of sport within 'the University'

Over many centuries, the University restricted any activity that might cause a distraction to studying. Even when sport was establishing a toe-hold, it was the students who led this initiative. This was taken up by a number of individual teaching staff in the last third of the nineteenth century: Emily Davies, Edmund Morgan, Henry Morgan, Leslie Stephen and Arthur Ward.

Promoters of sport from the university – with a global impact

- John Graham Chambers (rules of boxing, and promoting many other sports)
- Thomas Hughes (Author of *Tom Brown's Schooldays*, and past student at University of Oxford)
- Charles Kingsley (Muscular Christianity)
- Arthur Kinnaird (Association Football)
- Ranjitsinhji (Cricket)
- Edward Thring (education)
- John Charles Thring (Association Football – rules)
- Cecil Earle Tyndale-Briscoe (sporting evangelist)
- Rowland Williams (sporting evangelist)
- Max Woosnam (sporting allrounder).

Of course, there were very many others.

CHAPTER 1
Castle Hill

Shire Hall (left) **and Castle Hill** (right)

EARLY HISTORY AND SETTLERS

Over many hundreds of years, individuals have used Castle Hill as a vantage-point over Cambridge and the largely flat countryside and 'waterside' surrounding it.

This probably included Frank Fenner, who would have seen 'no fairer and certainly no more interesting prospect in England'.[1]

Painting of 'Cambridge from the Castle Hill - 1840' by James Ward RA
Displayed in Museum of Cambridge, image provided by Ann Miles.

Evidence has been found of a 3,500-year-old farmstead nearby, and later, during the Iron Age, a settlement located on Castle Hill itself.

Since then, Cambridge has been occupied by five different invaders. First were the Romans, who built a fortified town here, followed by the Anglo Saxons, responsible for building 'the Great Bridge' across the river Cam at the bottom of Castle Hill, giving Cambridge its name. The Danes followed, invading twice, then the Normans, who in about 1068 built a raised mound as a motte on the hill, later rebuilt by Edward I, who stayed there in 1293. Meanwhile, in 1209, students fleeing from Oxford University 'invaded', and have remained to this day.[2]

Cambridge has been located for many centuries at the convergence of both land and river routes, with relatively easy access to Europe, so providing the foundation for an 'economically precocious and religiously radical area',[3] which we look at in more detail next.

LOCAL CHARACTER AND SPIRIT

For many centuries local prosperity was driven by merchants, in the absence of any great local 'manors'. Reliance was on the river Cam (until the arrival of the railways in the mid-nineteenth century) to transport corn, fish, coal, local agricultural produce and stone to build the colleges of the University, as well as ferry wares and passengers to Stourbridge (formerly Sturbridge) Fair, the largest in Europe for many centuries.

Cambridge has been referred to as the 'Treasure Island of the Fens'[4] so it is no surprise its coat of arms, granted in 1575, prominently display ships and seahorses, in recognition of this close relationship to water.

Life was harsh in the Fens, so it was necessary to adapt and innovate in response to the unique surroundings. For the individual to navigate the Fens it was also common to use skates in winter, and stilts or 'stretches' in summer, 'to straddle high above the reeds … and the quaking bogs', which is why local people were sometimes known as 'Cambridgeshire Camels'.[5]

This way of life was threatened in the seventeenth century when Charles I planned to convert wetland into farmland through the draining of the Fens. It was because of their opposition, that local people earned the nick name of 'slodgers', or 'Fen Tigers', as featured in the Fen flag.

Sometimes, a game of camp ball (the popular local version of folk football) was advertised as a cover for bringing large numbers of people together to destroy the new drainage ditches, resulting in restrictions by the authorities not just of camp ball, but many other sports/public gatherings too.

Cambridge's Coat of Arms
Permission from Cambridge City Council.

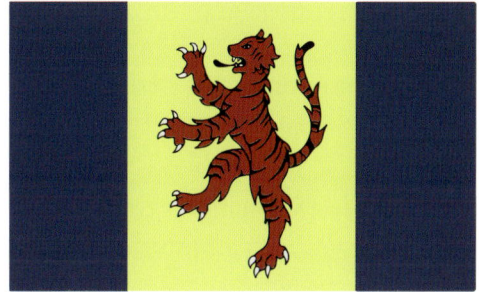

The Fen flag
Permission from James Bowman.

Religiously radical

In turn the Fens have been referred to as the 'Holy Land of the English' on account of the significant monastic foundations and cathedrals at Ely and Peterborough, with Castle Hill playing a very small part. In 695, according to the Venerable Bede, monks searched for a suitable coffin for St Etheldreda, the foundress of Ely Cathedral, and found a stone sarcophagus of Roman origin, at the foot of the Hill.[6]

As an example of its radicalism, and perhaps because of its relative proximity to reformers in Europe, Cambridge became what some consider the 'cradle of the English Reformation',[7] in the sixteenth century (chapter 16).

Two drivers of the Reformation were Thomas Bilney and Hugh Latimer, 'who might be seen in their daily walks about the Castle Hill, which led to it being nicknamed "Heretics' Hill". Together they also visited the criminal and the sick in the Castle gaol.'[8] Later, they were both burned at the stake for their reforming views.

Anti-monarchical

The area was also considered anti-monarchical in tendency, gravitating towards parliament or the barons rather than to the king. The best example of this was Oliver Cromwell, a local man from Huntingdon, and past student at Sidney Sussex College, later responsible for seizing the Castle (including the magazine of ammunition stored there) and fortifying it from 1643. This was at the beginning of the English Civil War that led to the overthrow of the monarchy.

Creative

The 'flat expanses' and 'rolling outlines' and 'wide skies' of East Anglia 'have had a curiously powerful hold on the English creative intellect and have been a striking stimulus to it'.[9] For example, Charles Tennyson, a grandson of the poet Alfred Lord Tennyson believed (for members of the University):

> [Cambridge's] generations have grown to a certain breadth, a certain austerity of temper foreign to her more worldly rival, a temper with more reserve, with a power of enthusiasm keener if less sustained. Less human perhaps and less responsive to the calls of practical life, but nearer in kinship to the winds and stars.[10]

In addition, the local Fens, despite the cold and damp conditions in winter, have stirred the likes of poets Lord Byron, Samuel Taylor Coleridge, Alfred Tennyson, Charles Kingsley and William Wordsworth. The latter wrote about his arrival by coach as a student in October 1787, including reference to 'the Castle' (Hill):

> Advancing, we espied upon the road
> A student clothed in gown and tasselled cap,
> Striding along as if o'ertasked by Time,
> Or covetous of exercise and air;
> He passed — nor was I master of my eyes
> Till he was left an arrow's flight behind
> As near and nearer to the spot we drew
> It seemed to suck us in with an eddy's force.
> Onward we drove beneath the Castle; caught,
> While crossing Magdalene Bridge, a glimpse of Cam;
> And at the Hoop alighted, famous inn.[11]

Interestingly Wordsworth reflects on whether this student he passes is in a hurry or 'covetous of exercise and air', as if this was an acceptable thing to do. This was an attitude that Wordsworth was later to explore, thereby contributing significantly towards exercise and sport becoming more widely acceptable (chapter 8).

Academic

Over many centuries the University, today recognised as the fourth oldest in the world, has established itself as one of the foremost centres of academic excellence, 'producing' many great scientists, philosophers, writers, poets, and politicians. Its 31 colleges have amassed enormous wealth, largely benefitting a select and privileged minority.

An example of such exclusivity is that whilst seven of the sixteen colleges in existence by the end of the sixteenth century were founded by women,[12] it took over 350 years before women were admitted to full membership of the University of Cambridge, occurring as late as 1947.

Also, the relationship between Town and Gown (a phrase used to distinguish the residents of the town from the students and staff at the University, who in the past wore academic gowns) has for centuries been an 'endemic border warfare with recurrent crises',[13] with the University being branded the 'cuckoo in the nest',[14] having arrived in 1209, many years after the Town. And nor did many in the University appreciate their new home; as one student described Cambridge in the nineteenth century as a 'college-studded marsh'.[15]

Cambridge's contribution to shaping sport

Perhaps because of the unique and wide-ranging characteristics described above, Cambridge was responsible, in the Victorian and Edwardian eras (1837 to 1910) for contributing towards an English leisure or sporting revolution,[16] which had 'extraordinary global consequences: political, cultural, economic, aesthetic, emotional and spiritual'.[17]

Its origins were both the public schools and their 'finishing schools', the universities of Oxford and Cambridge.[18] However, Cambridge University in particular, from 'the drawing up of rules to the development of sporting philosophies, played a major role in shaping sport as the world knows it today'.[19]

It would be easy to credit just the university, but local people, particularly Frank Fenner, played a part too, their contributions often going unheralded.

At the start of the nineteenth century, play and sport for many local people was restricted to animal sports and the opportunities afforded at the four local fairs, including Stourbridge Fair. As it was the largest fair in Europe, it was more famous than the university for many centuries, according to the historian G.M Trevelyan.[20] More on these local fairs is in chapter 7.

Sport and Castle Hill

It is possible Frank Fenner, despite being only a year old in 1812, might have attended the public hanging of Daniel Dawson, reported as a racecourse tout, as part of a crowd of 13,000. This was equivalent to the population of Cambridge at the time.[21]

Sadly, this execution was symptomatic of the depths that horse-racing and many other sports had plumbed in the early nineteenth century. Gambling was so prevalent that two villainous bookmakers persuaded Dawson to administer arsenic to drinking water used by horses which had been heavily backed for Newmarket's spring meeting. Three horses died as a result, and helped by a 500 Guineas reward (equivalent to nearly £40,000 today) offered by the Jockey Club, Dawson was duly hanged.[22]

He has been referred to as 'the most famous horse-poisoner in English history', and perhaps 'the most severely-punished sports cheat in all of modernity'.[23]

Whilst Castle Hill was the site of a gaol (or jail) from the fourteenth century at least, in 1929 it was replaced by Shire Hall, the headquarters of Cambridgeshire County Council until 2021.

From Castle Hill to the Museum of Cambridge

The view today walking down Castle Street towards the centre of Cambridge is shown below, together with the comparable view in 1830s, when Frank Fenner would have been in his late twenties. In the next chapter, we look around the Museum of Cambridge.

The Old Gatehouse

Wright, Thomas et al (1841) The universities. Le Keux's memorials of Cambridge published by Tilt and Bogue, Fleet Street page 249.

1   W. M. Palmer, (1976). Cambridge Castle. Oleander Press. Page 34.

2   Henry Bosanquet, (1976). Walks Around Vanished Cambridge: Bridge Street. Page. 3. Cambridge History Agency.

3   Alan Macfarlane (1978), The Origins of English Individualism, (Oxford: Blackwell) p 67.

4   Nicholas Chrimes (2017). Cambridge: Treasure Island of the Fens; The 800-year story of the university and town of Cambridge, 1209-2009. Hobsaerie Publications.

5   Charles G. Harper (1902). The Cambridge, Ely and King's Lynn Road. The Great Fenland Highway. Page 176.

6   Peter Bryan, (1999). Cambridge: The shaping of the city. Pg. 12.

7   David Berkley (2015). Cambridge. City of beauty, reformation and pioneering research. Day One Publications. Page 48.

8   Arthur Gray, (1912). Cambridge and its Story. Pg. 149.

9   T.S.R. Boase, English Art 1800 - 1870. Oxford History of English Art X (Oxford: Clarendon Press, 1959).

10   Charles Tennyson, (1913). Cambridge from Within. (Chatto & Windus) Page 26.

11   William Wordsworth (written by 1805, published 1850) The Prelude Book III. Residence at Cambridge. From page 156, A Book of Cambridge Verse by Kellett, E. E. (Ernest Edward) - published 1911.

12   Nicholas Chrimes (2017). Cambridge. Treasure Island of the Fens. Page 188.

13   'The city of Cambridge: Town and gown', in A History of the County of Cambridge and the Isle of Ely: Volume 3, the City and University of Cambridge, ed. J P C Roach (London, 1959), pp. 76-86.

14   Dr Horrox. Open Cambridge talk, 2012.

15   Leonee Ormond (1993). Arthur Hallam quoted in Alfred Tennyson: A Literary Life. Page 20.

16   'We (British) invented the majority of the world's great sports. And most of those we did not invent, we codified and helped to popularise throughout the world. It could be argued that nineteenth century Britain was the cradle of a leisure revolution every bit as significant as the agricultural and industrial revolutions we launched in the century before. (John Major (1995) Sport: Raising the Game.)

17   J. A. Mangan in 'Introduction - complicated matters' page 2 in J. A. Mangan - editor (2006). A Sport-Loving Society. Victorian and Edwardian Middle-Class England at Play. Routledge. Page 2.

18   'Oars and the man'. Pleasure and Purpose in Victorian and Edwardian Cambridge by J.A. Mangan. Pages 93 on.

19   Johnes, M. (2005). 'United Kingdom', in D. Levinsen and K. Christensen (eds.), Encyclopedia of World Sport. Great Barrington, USA: Berkshire Publishing.

20   G.M. Trevelyan (1946). English Social History: A survey of six centuries Chaucer to Queen Victoria. Page 186.

21   Cambridge City Historic Population from https://data.cambridgeshireinsight.org.uk/

22   Richard Evans writing in the Telegraph (online) on 21 April 2002.

23   www.executedtoday.com

CHAPTER 2

The Museum of Cambridge

The Museum is nearly 200 yards (180 metres) from Castle Hill, located at the bottom of Castle Street. Its collections today represent Cambridge and Cambridgeshire history and heritage over 300 years, including objects related to everyday life, customs and traditions of local people, places and events.

As a result, several displays (appreciating they often change) provide an insight into Frank's life as a tobacconist, and later inn landlord, and perhaps his early education. A range of sports are also exhibited, some of which relate directly to Frank Fenner.

INNS AND TOBACCO

The Museum of Cambridge was formerly known as the Cambridge & County Folk Museum, and before that, as the White Horse Inn, first licensed in 1646.

It is possible Frank drank at the White Horse Inn, easy to imagine next to the original open fire in the kitchen and the adjacent snug bar.

Image reproduced with permission from Museum of Cambridge.

The snug bar contains a display of clay pipes, common locally in the nineteenth century, when Frank was busy from the mid 1830s to 1862, running a tobacco shop, first in Sidney Street, then Parker's Piece (chapter 20), Regent Street (chapter 19) and finally the Market Square (chapter 16).

Image reproduced with permission from Museum of Cambridge.

SPORTS AT THE MUSEUM

Athletics

The snug bar also includes, along the top of the mantelpiece above the fireplace, an impressive silver belt belonging to Charles Rowell of nearby Chesterton, recognising him as the 'Long Distance Champion of the World'. This was won at Madison Square Garden, New York in 1879 and again in 1880.[1] These athletic competitions were sometimes referred to as 'go as you please events' where competitors could walk and/or run as they wished, and in 1882 he put up three records: covering 100 miles in 13hrs 26mins 30secs; 200 miles in 35hrs 9mins 28secs; and 300 miles in 58hrs 17mins 6secs.[2]

At about the same time, the 'walking lady of Chesterton', presumably spurred on by Charles Rowell, given they were both from the same local village, 'walked for a wager "a thousand miles in a thousand hours"' (nine hours short of six weeks) in a private garden in Church Street. She kept up her average of one mile per hour, walking day and night until she completed her task and won the wager'.[3]

However, it is believed the first person to achieve this feat was Captain Robert Barclay in 1809 at Newmarket Racecourse, reported as the 'greatest ever sporting event', winning him an estimated 16,000 Guineas (equivalent to £6million today). More on Captain Barclay, who was also a highly regarded bare-knuckle boxing trainer, at Trinity College (chapter 9), where he had been a student from 1798.

Cricket

Halfway up the cramped stairs at the back of the Museum there is a large, crude painting on display that was the pub sign for the Old Castle Hotel on St Andrew's Street, painted in about 1830 by Richard Hopkins Leach.

From the age of 16 Frank Fenner played cricket for the Castle, Hoop and Fountain inns intermittently from 1827 for about 10 years. During this time these pubs, plus the Union (at nearby Quayside, just over the river), were largely responsible for sustaining cricket in the town.

A summary of Frank's cricketing career (including a timeline) is found in chapter 20.

Rustic sports and a cricket match

In the largest room on the first floor of the museum there is a poster on display promoting the Rustic Sports celebrating Queen Victoria's Coronation that took place on Midsummer Green, Cambridge on 28th June 1838.

These sports involving sack races, orange bobbing and wheelbarrow races, following a dinner given to 15,000 of the 'deserving poor' on Parker's Piece watched by 25,000 spectators who bought tickets.

Source: Cambridge Coronation Festival. A complete account of the proceedings relating to the festival held at Cambridge in honour of the coronation of her most gracious Majesty Queen Victoria. Cambridge: Printed for J&J.J. Deighton, T. Stevenson, & E. Johnson: and C. Tilt, London 1838.

Cambridgeshire Collection, Cambridge Central Library.

Source: Cambridge Coronation Festival. A complete account of the proceedings relating to the festival held at Cambridge in honour of the coronation of her most gracious Majesty Queen Victoria. Cambridge: Printed for J&J.J. Deighton, T. Stevenson, & E. Johnson: and C. Tilt, London 1838.

Cambridgeshire Collection, Cambridge Central Library.

This view across Parker's Piece was taken from the tower of the town gaol, where the current Kelsey Kerridge Sports Hall is situated. King's College Chapel, and the University Arms hotel can also be seen in the background.

A couple of days before this dinner and the Rustic Sports, Frank Fenner, aged 27, played cricket in the Coronation Match at Lord's Cricket Ground, representing the South who beat the North. Although Frank scored only two runs, he bowled 16 balls for no run, and 'Heath was admirably caught off the point by Mr Fenner with his left hand.'[4]

Note the advertisement in the *Morning Advertiser* also promoted the forthcoming cricket Varsity match (the fourth one ever played), concluding there was 'good stabling on the ground'.

CRICKET.—A GRAND MATCH will be PLAYED in LORD'S GROUND, Marylebone, on MONDAY, June 25, 1838, and following Days. Grand Coronation Match, Nottinghamshire and Yorkshire, with Lillywhite and Wenman for the North, against the South of England.

PLAYERS.—NORTH :—Barker, Dearman, Garrat, Gibson, Guy, Heath, Jervis, Lillywhite, Marsden, Redgate, Wenman.—SOUTH :—The Hon. E. H. Grimston, the Hon. F. Ponsonby, A. Rich, jun., Esq., C. Taylor, Esq., Box, Broadridge, Clifford, Cobbett, Fenner, Millyard, Pilch.

Matches to come:—Monday, July 2d, at Lord's, the Marylebone Club against the undergraduates of Oxford; Thursday, July 5th, at Eton, the Marylebone Club agaist the Etonians; Friday, July 6th, at Lord's, the University of Oxford against the University of Cambridge. An Ordinary at Three o'clock. Good Stabling on the Ground.

Rowing

In this large room on the first floor there are a number of rowing oars on display, one relating to the Cambridge crew who beat Oxford at the Boat Race by 20 lengths in 1900. To date this is the largest margin of victory.

Boxing

A hat and boot of the Histon Giant are on display on the first floor. The Giant's real name was Moses Carter (born 1801 and died 1860), seven feet tall and 23 stone in weight. On one occasion, in addition to defeating all his boxing opponents at Sturbridge Fair, he 'threw out the Proprietor when he refused to pay him as promised'.[5]

Skates and skating

On the first floor is a cabinet-full of ice skates and medals, which is no surprise given the nearby Fens are considered the birthplace of skating in England.

Consequently, Cambridge was naturally the location of the newly formed National Skating Association in the late nineteenth Century, the headquarters being based on Mortimer Road (near Fenner's Cricket Ground). See chapter 21, where there is more on local skating and bandy (ice hockey).

FRANK'S EDUCATION

The museum, mostly through artifacts and themed interactive displays, is well-prepared to welcome groups of school children to explore how their forebears were educated.

It is not possible to link anything in the museum directly to Frank's education, because nothing is known about it. It is probable he was home-schooled, which was common for those in the middle classes, his father being a tailor. State-sponsored and legislated education only became available in the second half of the nineteenth century.

As far as Frank's ongoing education is concerned, comparisons might be made with the diarist Josiah Chater, who wrote about his local life experiences in his diary in the mid nineteenth century. His biographer, Enid Porter (also curator at the Museum for nearly 40 years) reported Chater 'sought consciously to improve [himself] by serious reading, by attending lectures and classes and by joining or even forming debating, literary and philosophical societies'.

For example, on 1 December 1847, Josiah was taken 'to hear a debate at the Philo-Union and a very interesting hour I spent there … I should very much like to join but I cannot afford it'.[6] It is known that Frank Fenner was a Vice President of the Cambridge Philo-Union in 1852, as well as being an excellent letter-writer, signifying he was well educated.

This was corroborated just before Frank died when Frederick Gale (a respected cricket writer) summarised his life as:

> F P Fenner of Cambridge, kept 'Fenner's Ground' there, now alive and well, and landlord of White Lion Hotel, Bath, first-rate all-round cricketer, one of the best Eleven of England, very superior and well-educated, and much respected by all classes, especially Cambridge men, hundreds of whom were his pupils.[7]

FROM THE MUSEUM OF CAMBRIDGE TO MAGDALENE COLLEGE

St Giles Church, across Castle Street from the museum, was rebuilt in 1875, to replace an earlier church founded in 1092.

St Giles Church today

St Giles Church demolished 1870
Capturing Cambridge website, Museum of Cambridge.

In 1847, the vicar was Harvey Goodwin, who in partnership with his curate, William Witts, were instrumental in establishing the Cambridge Industrial School for 'youthful offenders', their aim being to educate these boys rather than punish them for their misdemeanours:[8]

Those who knew Cambridge in those days, would remember what a large number of ne'er-do-wells were to be found in Barnwell and other parts, who, if left to themselves, must eventually swell the criminal class.[9]

The school was based just off nearby Victoria Road, on a street now called Harvey Goodwin Avenue, in recognition of his work.

In 1853, Harvey Goodwin also became the Principal of the Cambridge branch of the Working Men's College,[10] based on the market behind Frank Fenner's tobacco shop, where there was also a gymnasium (chapter 16).

Authentic street scene

Today, on the west side of Magdalene Street (the opposite side from Magdalene College), 'the only frontage of its age surviving in Cambridge of sufficient length to give any impression of the earlier street scene, from the sixteenth to eighteenth centuries'[11] can be seen.

Magdalene Street today

Magdalene Street looking towards the river before 1912

From the collection of David Gent.

On closer inspection of the buildings on this street, nearly opposite the main entrance of Magdalene College, there are wood carvings just above head height dating back to when the building was the Cross Keys Inn, reminding us of its colourful history,[12] including probably as a brothel.

Since at least 1459, the Proctors of the University had the right of 'arrest and expulsion of lewd women',[13] only ceded to the town in 1894.

From 1825, when the Cambridge University Constabulary was founded with full police powers, constables were able to operate within five miles of Great St Mary's Church[14] (more on Great St Mary's church in chapter 15).

Trial of these 'lewd women' was in the Vice-Chancellor's court, where there was no legal aid or defence witnesses, with punishment usually being a spell of imprisonment in the notorious Spinning House, or workhouse on St Andrew's Street.

This was often bitterly resented by many local people, resulting in pitched battles using 'bill-hooks, cudgels and flails'[15] in 1533 and 'ugly incidents' reported by Josiah Chater in the mid-nineteenth century in his diary.[16] At the very least Frank Fenner would have been aware of such incidents given he was a Town High constable from 1848, and later a Chief constable,[17] both voluntary roles.

1   Mike Petty (2018). Cambridge SPORT Chronicle. Chronology of Cambridge Sport 1888 to 1990 at https://archive.org/details/CambridgeSPORTSChronicle

2   Cambridge Daily News 29 December 1902.

3   The walking lady of Chesterton 21 March 1936. Mike Petty (2018). Cambridge SPORT Chronicle. Chronology of Cambridge Sport 1888 to 1990 at https://archive.org/details/CambridgeSPORTSChronicle

4   Brighton Gazette 28 June 1838.

5   'A Third Ramble About Our Village (Histon)' by Dellas Oates.

6   Enid Porter (1975). Victorian Cambridge. Josiah Chater's Diaries 1844 - 1884. Phillimore. Pages 11 and 12.

7   Frederick Gale (1887). The Game of Cricket. Page 259.

8   Malcolm Tozer (2015). The Ideal of Manliness. Sunnyrest Books. Page 110.

9   H.D. Rawnsley. (1896) Harvey Goodwin. London: John Murray, Albemarle Street. Pages 66 to 69.

10   Malcolm Tozer (2015). The Ideal of Manliness. Sunnyrest Books. Page 110.

11   The Royal Commission on Historical Monuments in Sara Payne (1983) Down your Street Vol 1 Central Cambridge. The Pevensey Press. Page 24.

12   A new look for Magdalene Street article at https://www.cam.ac.uk/news/a-new-look-for-magdalene-street

13   The way things were on Queens' College website: https://www.queens.cam.ac.uk

14   The Cambridge Student Newspaper 2 Nov 2009 https://www.tcs.cam.ac.uk/the-cambridge-bulldogs/

15   Rowland Parker (1983). Town and Gown. The 700 years' war in Cambridge. Patrick Stephens, Cambridge. Page 75.

16   Josiah Chater diary entry for 7 Jan 1847 in Enid Porter (1975) Victorian Cambridge. Josiah Chater's Diaries. Page 31.

17   Cambridge General Advertiser 18 Oct 1848; Cambridge Independent Press 16 Oct 1858 Cambridge General Advertiser 26 Sept 1849, and personal email communication from British Police History 4 July 2020.

CHAPTER 3

Magdalene College

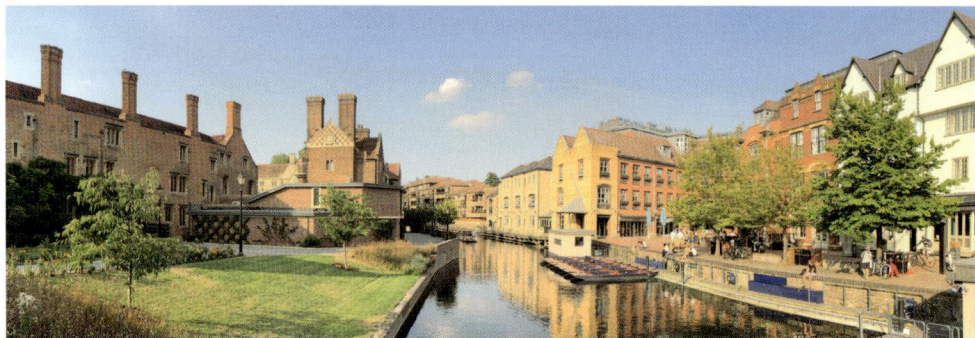

Magdalene College (left), River Cam, Quayside (right) from Magdalene Bridge

Magdalene College was established in 1428, making it the seventh oldest college of the University. Its name derives from Lord Audley who re-founded the College in 1542. Whilst it was dedicated to St Mary Magdalene, its name is pronounced 'Maudleyn', to accommodate Lord Audley's name.

The past Master of the College, Rowan Williams, who retired in 2020, was also Archbishop of Canterbury, a position also held by Thomas Cranmer, the leader of the English Reformation, and former student at the College.

SPORT BEFORE THE NINETEENTH CENTURY

Samuel Pepys

Pepys is probably the best known of all the graduates of Magdalene College, where he studied from 1651 to 1654, having been at the Grammar School at Hinchingbrooke, near Huntingdon (15 miles (25 km) northwest from Cambridge).

Pepys kept a diary over a period of nine years from age 27, sharing hundreds of scenes from his life, largely in London. Whilst this did not relate to his time in Cambridge,[a] it nevertheless provides an insight into sport in England in the seventeenth century.

---

[a] Throughout *Cambridge Sport: in Fenner's Hands* there are occasions, as with Samuel Pepys, where some or all of an individual's experience of sport occurred after they had left Cambridge. Where there is, or believed to be, a causal link back to their experience in Cambridge this is made clear, or speculated about, where there is not, it is hoped the account provides a general understanding of sport in England.

In addition to writing about the Plague and the Great Fire of London, Pepys recalls seeing 'a fine foot-race three times round (Hyde) Park[1]', and experiencing the social mix engaged in cock-fighting,

> Lord! to see the strange variety of people, from a Parliament man by name Wilder that was Deputy Governor of the Tower … to the poorest 'prentices, bakers, brewers, draymen and what not; and all these fellows one with another cursing and betting.[2]

Samuel Pepys: sport in the seventeenth century

Sammuel Pepys. Cropped close-up of colour process print. Wellcome Collection. Public domain.

Pepys realised people were hungry for pleasure at the start of the Restoration of the Monarchy in 1660, for example whenever Charles II played tennis, it drew admiring crowds.[3]

As far as Pepys's own participation in sport, he recalled playing bowls with his wife, and skating on the River Thames with Nell Gwynne,[4] praised by Pepys for her comic performances as one of the first actresses on the English stage, but best known for being a long-time mistress of King Charles II.[5]

Pepys also recorded in his diary on 14 April 1667:

> By and by away home, and there took out my wife, and the two Mercers, and two of our mayds, Barker and Jane, and over the water to the Jamaica House [Bermondsey], where I never was before, and there the girls did run for wagers over the bowling-green; and there, with much pleasure, spent little, and so home, and they home, and I to read …

According to the historian Joseph Strutt in *Sports and Pastimes of the People of England*,[b] (updated in 1903 by J. Charles Cox):

> Pepys and other well-known authorities give evidence of much football play in the latter half of the seventeenth century. It is alluded to in the *Spectator*, as a game played on village greens, but save in a few traditionary towns at certain dates usually Shrovetide football seems to have gradually died out during the eighteenth century, and to have remained quiescent during the first half of the nineteenth century. The revival began in our great public schools.[6]

---

[b] Strutt may be considered the first English social historian given his primary interest focused on the lives of the players, more than the rules of the game. (Reference: David Parlett's talk on Joseph Strutt's Sports and Pastimes of the People of England. 7 December 2016).

Strutt also comments that football seems to have been well established at Cambridge in the time of Charles II. In the second register book of Magdalene College the following entry of 1679 is given:

> That no schollers [students] give or receive at any time any treat or collation upon account of ye football play, on or about Michaelmas Day, further than Colledge beere or ale in ye open hall to quench their thirsts. And particularly that that most vile custom of drinking and spending money together upon ye account of making or not making a speech at that football time be utterly left off and extinguished.[7]

Whilst it is not known whether Pepys played football whilst a student, he nevertheless was admonished 'for having been scandalously overseen in drink' in 1653, according to the College Register.[8]

Field sports in Cambridge and public schools

The pervasiveness of field sports was experienced in 1602 when a foreign visitor to Cambridge noted that students 'perhaps keep more dogs and greyhounds that are so often seen in the streets, than they do books.'[9]

Later in the 1740s it was noted that wealthy students and noblemen at Magdalene College had:

> A preference for field sports … and were indulged in by tutors who hesitated to oppose the inclinations of gentlemen. The allure of preferments and benefices in the gift of titled families ensured that the dons [teaching staff] allowed students to substitute hunting parties for lectures much as they pleased. Privilege and patronage eroded the authority, power and control of the school beak [teacher] and the university don.[10]

Unfortunately, one impact for local people was highlighted in the following advertisement which appeared in the *Cambridge Chronicle* of August 1787:

> We poor farmers, who hire land in the parish of Grantchester, and fields of Coton, having some of our corn still standing, and some lying on the ground, do most humbly beg the favour of the Cambridge gunners, coursers, and poachers, (whether gentlemen, barbers, or gyps [male servants] of colleges), to let us get home our crops, even after the 1st of September, without riding or hunting their dogs over our property, that we may be able to pay the great expense of harvest, and servants' wages, rates, and rents, at Michaelmas: for we hope such gentlemen will remember what the frogs in the fable said to the idle boys who threw stones at them, 'Though 'tis sport to you, it is death to us'.[11]

It was largely because of these impacts that Thomas Arnold, the 'reforming Head Master of Rugby School'[12] wanted field sports abolished in the early nineteenth century.[13] Whilst this facilitated the substitution of readily acceptable alternatives, such as cricket and football, (subsequently copied by other public schools), field sports were not totally abandoned, 'particularly at Eton and Cambridge',[14] including at Magdalene College.

For example, Ralph Nevill, a student at the College from 1856, described it as:

> Easy-going to an extreme, besides being permeated by a sporting tone, [with] quite a number of undergraduates ... belonging to families which for generations had been identified with sport. Many of my contemporaries kept hunters and polo ponies, while one actually had a coach (which stood some little distance out of the town) and drove four in hand to Newmarket when racing was going on there.[15]

LINKS TO THE TOWN AND FRANK FENNER

Charles Kingsley, an avid tree climber and an enthusiastic walker, once walking the 52 miles from Cambridge to London in a day, had 'three pleasant and boisterous years at Magdalene College', being grateful for 'all the strength and hardihood I gained in snipe shooting and hunting and rowing and jack-fishing in those magnificent Fens.'[16]

He also hired a local professional black boxing prize-fighter, Sam Sutton, 'to give instruction in fisticuffs',[17] despite the vice chancellor issuing a draconian decree against members of the university from doing so.

Kingsley was also a celebrated pipe smoker,[18] so might have been a customer in Frank Fenner's tobacco shop on Sidney Street from 1838 to 1841, when Kingsley was a student at the college.

Sam Sutton

Sam Sutton, the prize fighter who instructed Charles Kingsley 'and others who were afterwards distinguished in Church and State'. Photo from Cyber Boxing Zone Encyclopaedia (online).

Thomas Wentworth Wills, a co-founder of Australian Rules football, played cricket in the 1856 Varsity match, and possibly the Rugby School version of football on Parker's Piece.

The Marquess of Queensberry only stayed at the College for two years from 1864, without taking a degree, being more adept at cricket, running, hunting, steeplechasing, and boxing,[19] including winning a lightweight boxing contest held at the University Gymnasium located on the Market in 1865, which had been managed by Frank Fenner.[20]

As a student, the Marquess was found guilty of 'bonneting' (to strike a man's cap or hat over his eyes) PC Berryman on the King's Parade, on a Saturday night, and was 'fined 10s and expenses'.[21]

ENGLAND'S SPORTING REVOLUTION

All three of these students went on to have an extraordinary and long-lasting impact on sport across the globe in the nineteenth century.

Muscular Christianity

After leaving the University as a student, Charles Kingsley was responsible in 1848 for founding Christian Socialism with Frederick Maurice (Trinity College – chapters 9, and 16) which, whilst it failed as a movement, helped to serve religion by associating the church with the alleviation of poverty. Kingsley's concern for social reform is best illustrated in his classic *The Water-Babies, A Fairy Tale for a Land Baby* published in 1863, which remained popular into the twentieth century.

Charles Kingsley
Photograph by Charles Watkins. Wellcome Collection. Public domain.

Another novel by Kingsley, *Alton Locke* (first published in 1850), also focused on social reform, relating to the injustices suffered by workers in the clothing and agricultural trades. In the same novel he also extolled the virtues of rowing.

The following is a lengthy quote from *Alton Locke*, but it best summarises how sport was being increasingly viewed in Cambridge and the public schools, and why later, it was 'exported' across the British Empire:

> And yet, after a few moments, I ceased to wonder either at the Cambridge passion for boat-racing, or at the excitement of the spectators. 'Honi soit qui mal y pense' [translated from Latin as 'shame on anyone who thinks evil of it']. It was a noble sport a sight such as could only be seen in England some hundreds of young men, who might, if they had chosen, have been lounging effeminately about the streets, subjecting themselves voluntarily to that intense exertion, for the mere pleasure of toil. The true English stuff came out there; I felt that, in spite of all my prejudices the stuff which has held Gibraltar and conquered at Waterloo which has created a Birmingham and a Manchester, and colonised every quarter of the globe that grim, earnest, stubborn energy, which, since the days of the old Romans, the English possess alone of all the nations of the earth. I was as proud of the gallant young fellows as if they had been my brothers of their courage and endurance (for one could see that it was no child's play, from the pale faces, and panting lips), their strength and activity, so fierce and yet so cultivated, smooth, harmonious, as oar kept time with oar, and every back rose and fell in concert and felt my soul stirred up to a sort of sweet madness, not merely by the shouts and cheers of the mob

around me, but by the loud fierce pulse of the rowlocks [a fitting to keep the oar in place], the swift whispering rush of the long snakelike eight oars, the swirl and gurgle of the water in their wake, the grim, breathless silence of the straining rowers. My blood boiled over, and fierce tears swelled into my eyes; for I, too, was a man, and an Englishman.[22]

As a result of these views, Kingsley is credited with paving the way for sport to be accepted as a legitimate and holistic lifestyle choice, through what generally became known as Muscular Christianity, a label first used in 1857.[23]

Darwin and 'survival of the strongest'

Kingsley was also a friend of Charles Darwin who published *On the Origin of Species* in 1859. Some believe Darwin's elaborate view of 'natural selection' was turned into a crude theory of the survival of the fittest which was widely misunderstood to mean 'the survival of the strongest'.[24] When this was combined with Kingsley's Muscular Christianity, it enabled a generation of 'great' headmasters, many from Cambridge to drive the development of sports in the English Public Schools.[25]

Whilst these developments increased the profile and legitimacy of sport, one unintended consequence was the creation of the 'gentleman amateur' – see towards the end of chapter 4.

Frank and Muscular Christianity

Frank Fenner had mixed feelings about Muscular Christianity. Writing later in life in 1893 in his Cricket Jottings,[26] he believed clergy:

> Acquire at their schools or colleges, before entering upon their real life, a proficiency in gymnastic practices, as well as in the pursuit of those hardier games, from which the future man is made. I have known many who have gone straight from their alma mater [school, college, or university that an individual formerly attended] to some poor and distant parish, who by their energy and tone of character – the growth of their antecedents – have become idolized by the people: for Muscular Christianity very often wins souls, that would be turned aside by the patent namby-pambyism [lacking energy, strength, or courage] of the day.

However, Frank also recalled 'the disappointment so frequently felt by the imperative abstentions of men just as their services in the game had won the acknowledgement and admiration of every genuine lover of it'.[27] For Frank the best example, because they played together in the same Cambridge Town Cricket Club team, was Thomas Anson, a student at Jesus College, considered 'one of the best wicket keepers in the country', and yet when aged only 24, gave up cricket entirely when ordained as a clergyman.

Australian Rules Football

Thomas (Tom) Wentworth Wills is credited along with three others of founding Australian Rules Football in 1857. This followed eighteen months in England described as 'the richest sporting experience on earth',[28] after Tom left Rugby School in June 1855. Whilst his father (living in Australia) wanted him to go on and study law at Cambridge, Tom 'roamed Britain in pursuit of cricketing pleasure', which included playing for Magdalene College and Cambridge University in the 1856 Varsity cricket match, despite not having matriculated [formally joining the University].[29] Apparently the Oxford captain agreed to the Rugbeian taking part, as his name was 'on the books'.[30]

Thomas Wentworth Wills: Australian Rules Football

Permission to use image by Sport Australia Hall of Fame.

When Tom returned to Australia he met with Thomas Smith (Melbourne headmaster and graduate from Trinity College, Dublin), and James Bogue Thompson and William Josiah Hammersley, both past students at Trinity College in the 1840s, to establish Australian Rules Football.

Given three of these individuals were present in Cambridge, across the middle of the nineteenth century when the 'Cambridge Rules' evolved as a compromise of the football rules from the different public schools, 'there seems every likelihood that Thompson and Hammersley would have been aware of that process',[31] and probably Tom Wills too.

It is therefore no surprise the first ten rules of Australian Rules, created in 1859,[32] are remarkably similar to the eleven Cambridge Rules formulated between 1837 and 1863 (see chapter 20).

The reason why Tom Wills is listed here under Magdalene College, despite a relatively tenuous connection with the college, is that from the middle of the nineteenth century before sport had gained recognition within the University, there are many examples of students who either failed to matriculate [formally join the University] or finish their degree because of their focus on sport. For example at Jesus College at this time, more than a third of their students left Cambridge without a degree, the role of the College being viewed in large part as a finishing school for young gentlemen.[33]

This applied not just to Tom Wills, James Thompson and William Hammersley, but to the Marquess of Queensberry too.

Rules of boxing and the Marquess of Queensbury

Soon after Frank Fenner left Cambridge, John Sholto Douglas, the ninth Marquess of Queensberry, started at Magdalene College in 1864 and stayed for two years, focussing on sports such as cricket, running, hunting, steeplechasing and boxing rather than academia.

Douglas is most famous for lending his title to 'The Marquess of Queensberry Rules' which were a code of generally accepted rules in the sport of boxing. They were published in 1867, having been written by John Graham Chambers (chapter 9).

In addition, in 1866 the Marquess was also one of the founders of the Amateur Athletic Club, later replaced by the Amateur Athletic Association of England.

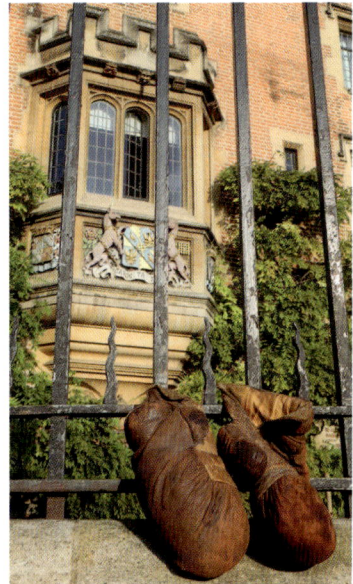

Pair of early 19th century straw-filled boxing gloves hung on railings outside Magdalene College - thanks to Leno, Il Barbiere.

Douglas was also famous for his role in the downfall of author and playwright Oscar Wilde, given his efforts to end the relationship between Wilde and his third son.

He was driven, not just by the embarrassment of the scandal, but by his belief, on which he based his court case, that homosexuality transgressed the natural norms of physical and moral masculinity, manifested in the boxing he had put his name to.[34]

'Pray God, no professional [cricketer] shall ever captain England'

Martin Bladen Hawke, generally known as Lord Hawke, attended Magdalene College from 1882 to 1885.

He was an English amateur cricketer active from 1881 to 1911 who played for Yorkshire and England. Between 1893 and 1908, as captain of Yorkshire, Hawke won the county championship eight times, making him the most successful captain in the history of county cricket. He also represented England on nine overseas tours.

After retiring from playing cricket he became an administrator including as President of the MCC,[35] famous for saying 'pray God, no professional shall ever captain England.' This outburst was in response to an article in the

Weekly Dispatch newspaper in 1925, arguing that the professional Jack Hobbs (originally from Cambridge Town – chapter 26) should captain England, instead of the Gentleman amateur Arthur Gilligan, educated at Pembroke College, Cambridge.

Chariots of Fire

David George Brownlow Cecil, also known as Lord Burghley, was an English athlete, sports official, peer, and Conservative Party politician who won the gold medal in the 400m hurdles at the 1928 Summer Olympics. Whilst at Magdalene College in 1927, his final year, he successfully completed the Great Court Run at Trinity College, inspiring the scene in *Chariots of Fire*. However, there was never a race in which Abrahams beat Burghley in this feat, as the film suggests.[36] (*Chariots of Fire* was a 1981 British historical sports drama film that won four Oscars including best picture, being based on the true story of two British athletes, Eric Liddell and Harold Abrahams, competing in the 1924 Olympics.)

1   Derek Birley (1993). Sport and the making of Britain. Manchester University Press. Pages 92 and 93.

2   Derek Birley (1993). Sport and the Making of Britain. Page 94.

3   Derek Birley (1993). Sport and the Making of Britain. Page 89.

4   http://www.iceskating.org.uk/index.cfm/about/history/

5   The diary of Samuel Pepys https://www.pepysdiary.com/encyclopedia/5037/

6   Joseph Strutt and J. Charles Cox (1903). The Sports and Pastimes of the People of England. Page 97.

7   Joseph Strutt and J. Charles Cox (1903). The Sports and Pastimes of the People of England. Page 97.

8   https://magdlibs.com/2019/12/12/the-quincentenary-of-magdalene-college-hall/

9   James Mangan (2006). A Sport-Loving Society. Ref 92 on page 53.

10 Francis Coventry in James Mangan (2006). A Sport-Loving Society. Page 53.

11 Cambridge Chronicle, 30 Aug 1787 in Henry Gunning (2012). Reminiscences of the University, Town, and County of Cambridge, from the year 1780. Vol 1 Page 18. Published by General Books, USA

12 Michael McCrum (1989). Thomas Arnold Head Master - a reassessment. Oxford University Press.

13 James Mangan (2006). A Sport-Loving Society. Ref 23 on page 47.

14 James Mangan (2006). A Sport-Loving Society. Page 50.

15 Ralph Nevill, in his 'Unconventional Memories', Page 23 Down your Street I. Central Cambridge. Cambridge Past and Present. Sara Payne (1983).

16 Charles Kingsley: his letters and memories of his life. https://core.ac.uk/download/pdf/86433764.pdf

17 Page 236. Famous Fights - past and present. Vol II. No 15. 1901-1904.

18 F.A. Reeve (1978). Victorian and Edwardian Cambridge from old photographs. Photo 72.

19 Davis, John (23 September 2004). "Douglas, John Sholto, ninth marquess of Queensberry". Oxford Dictionary of National Biography.

20 Bell's Life 1st April 1865.

21 Cambridge Independent Press. 1 April 1865.

22 Charles Kingsley (1862) Alton Locke.

23 Tozer, Malcolm (2015). The ideal of Manliness. Page 59.

24 Richard Holt (1993). Sport and the British. A Modern History. Page 94.

25 Malcolm Tozer. The Ideal of Manliness. The Legacy of Thring's Uppingham. Pages 7 and 8.

26 Cricket Jottings IV and V. Bath Chronicle. July and Sept 1893.

27 Cricket Jottings IV. Bath Chronicle July and September 1893.

28 Gregory Mark de Moore (2008) 'In from the Cold: Tom Wills – A Nineteenth Century Sporting Hero'. PhD thesis, Victoria University.

29 W. F. Mandle Australian Dictionary of Biography, Volume 6, 1976. Wills, Thomas Wentworth (1835–1880).

30 Chesterton, George and Doggart, Hubert (1989). Oxford and Cambridge Cricket.

31 Curry, Graham and Dunning, Eric (2016). Association Football. A study in figurational sociology. Page 83.

32 Ben Collins (May 17, 2019). When Australian Football was born, these were the first 10 rules. AFL website. https://www.afl.com.au/news/133990/when-australian-football-was-born-these-were-the-first-10-rules

33 Michael B. Morrison (2016). The worst golf course ever. Page 82.

34 Alex Stewart (2008) Title: The boxer's point of view: an ethnography of cultural production and athletic development among amateur and professional boxers in England. University of Bedfordshire.

35 MCC stands for the Marylebone Cricket Club, founded in 1787 and based since 1814 at Lord's Cricket Ground in St John's Wood, London. Until relatively recently it was the governing body of cricket, and when the England cricket team toured abroad it was referred to as the MCC.

36 Ryan, Mark (February 2012). "Flame & Fortune". Runner's World. (From Wikipedia).

CHAPTER 4

Magdalene Bridge and River Cam

HISTORY

It is generally accepted the name of the local Roman encampment in what became Cambridge was Durolipons, meaning 'a fortified site with a bridge'.[1] However, the first documented reference to a bridge was in 875, which is where Cambridge's name originates from, and because bridges were rare across England, the inclusion in the placename is significant. The current cast iron bridge was built in 1892.

The River Cam's source is close to Saffron Walden, Essex (20 miles (32km) south of Cambridge) and having flowed through Cambridge continues northeast into the Great Ouse, which in turn empties into The Wash at King's Lynn (45 miles (72 km) north).

Excellent road and river access, including the bridge, led to the area known as Bridgeland developing as a port, so much so that Cambridge was one of the top 20 wealthiest towns ranked by tax by 1300 AD.[2] This was largely independent from the impact of the University, which had not yet fully established itself, having been founded in 1209.

In 1672 a visitor referred to 'many pleasant walks in the environs of Cambridge, to which one may go on the river, the barks from the sea coming up to the great quay in the centre of the town'.[3]

Before the arrival of the railways in Cambridge in 1845, when horses were the primary mode of land-based transport, hay and straw were off-loaded at this port for the Haymarket held opposite St. Clement's Church on Bridge Street,[4] just over 100 yards (100 metres) into the town from the river.

RIVER SPORTS

There are four sports naturally associated with the river: fishing, punting, rowing, and swimming with these latter two sports covered in detail later in this chapter.

Fishing

The waters of the Cam belonged to the town, and because angling was popular with students, they often had to manage disputes with the University. This included the custom, up until the seventeenth century at least, for the mayor and senior members of the Town Corporation, to go on an annual fishing party to assert their claim on the river. The expenses for food, drink and the hire of boats were charged to the town accounts. In 1645 the town treasurers paid the sum of 12s for this trip (£70 today).[5]

Punting

The origins of the punt stretch back to their use in the shallow waters of the Fens in hunting wildfowl, fishing (including for eels), reed-cutting and transporting cargo.

Less pollution, and a reduction in commercial trade on the river, gave rowing and punting for pleasure their opportunity, exploited first by Maurice 'Jack' Scudamore in 1903. Scudamore's still provide punts for tours and hire at Magdalene Bridge.

Punting is an excellent and fun way to see 'the Backs' of the colleges, despite Jerome K Jerome's cautionary advice in *Three Men in a Boat*: 'Punting is not as easy as it looks. As in rowing, you soon learn how to get along and handle the craft, but it takes long practice before you can do this with dignity and without getting the water all up your sleeve.'[6]

Punting on the River Cam
Credited to Scudamore's Punting Ltd.

ROWING

The importance of rowing to Cambridge is demonstrated by there being 21 dedicated boathouses (belonging to the University / colleges, and town clubs) located today along the north bank of the River Cam, starting half a mile (750m) from Magdalene Bridge.

The Goldie Boathouse and Boat Race

The oldest surviving boathouse, built in 1882, is the Goldie Boathouse. Today it is the fitness and administrative base of Cambridge University Boat Club (CUBC), featured here because the annual Oxford versus Cambridge University Boat Race is probably Cambridge's most famous sporting event, having started in 1829 for men and 1927 for women.[7]

The 34th Boat Race in 1877, raced on the River Thames, ended in a dead heat. This is the only time this has occurred.

Goldie Boathouse - today

Source: Illustrated London News 31 March 1877.

Jesus College Boat House

Another iconic boat house belongs to Jesus College, which is easily identified because it has a weathervane and clock tower that sets it apart from its neighbours. This follows the convention that a weathervane can be installed on the boathouse after five consecutive years as head of the river at the end of the May Bumps,[a] and a clocktower after ten consecutive years. This occurred between 1875 and 1885.

Jesus College Boat House – after 1903
From the collection of David Gent.

One extraordinary family who rowed for the Jesus College 1st boat during this period was the Fairbairns. Steve Fairbairn rowed in six of those Head of the River crews, being one of five Fairbairn brothers and one of twelve members of the Fairbairn family to row in the College 1st boat.

This extraordinary success was largely thanks to the leadership of two unrelated Morgans, Henry and Edmund, who whilst only 'moderate academics' at Jesus College (both as students, and later as Fellows), were 'able, enthusiastic and committed athletes' acquired when they were both teachers at Lancing College, a public school. They used these skills to 'greatly influence the ethos of (Jesus) College and transform its standing', so much so that it led to a great rise in the number of undergraduates, following a 'disastrous drop' in admissions prior to the Morgans' arrival. Such growth was primarily driven by 'the fame of Jesus oarsmen'.[8]

It is understood Dr Corrie, the Master of the College from 1849, was asked to support the greater interest in sport: 'I will gladly support you … but you must not ask me for support to rowing, an occupation to which I can give no countenance, owing to the bedizened [to dress or decorate gaudily or tastelessly] women on the bank'.[9] Read about sport at Jesus College in chapter 6.

---

[a] **What are the Bumps?** With the River Cam not wide enough for two or more crews to race each other 'side by side', Cambridge University allegedly borrowed the bumps model from Oxford University in 1827 when the Cambridge University colleges Jesus, Trinity, St John's and Gonville and Caius competed against each other.

This bumps model, still used today by both Town and Gown, involves 17 boats (a crew of 8 and a cox to steer the boat) lining up one behind the other, which, once the starting gun has been fired, chase and attempt to bump the boat in front. Following the start, two boats involved in a bump then immediately pull into the bank, so the boats behind can continue with their chasing and bumping.

The starting positions in each division of 17 boats are defined by the finishing order of the previous year, and then by whatever happens during the subsequent four days' of racing.

Top boats can achieve 'Head of the River' if they manage to stay at the top of the first division throughout the four days of racing, and lower boat crews can be awarded their oars, if they bump up every day, or bump up at least four places. These can be painted up with the names and weights of the crew and the boats bumped.

Poor state of the River Cam

For most of the nineteenth century, when the population of Cambridge grew roughly fourfold and before the installation of the pumping station (now the Museum of Technology) in 1894, and a piped sewerage system, the river would silt up with sewage and dead animals, giving off an 'awesome stink'.

In 1859 the local press[10] reported under the headline 'University Boat Races':

> Cricketing and Boat Racing are the two great characteristics in the annals of Cambridge. On Fenner's picturesque and magnificent cricket field, is to be seen the former in its most exquisite science; on the Cam, boating is carried on periodically by the sons of Alma Mater [the University] with a vigour and interest quite refreshing to behold. Indeed, if old Cam could speak, we should fancy him, in the simplicity of his eloquence, exclaiming. "Gentlemen, I am glad to see you—proud to compliment you upon your prowess—but regret that I cannot find you better accommodation." The [University bump] races commenced yesterday week.

In addition to the smell, rowing techniques had degenerated into a shallow, stabbing paddle to avoid the massive blooms of entangling weed resulting from the high nutrient content of the water. Consequently, Oxford won nine Boat Races in a row by 1869, having trained on the broad, deep reaches of the Upper Thames, using long and strong strokes.

A fundraising drive in 1868 resulted in Queen Victoria and the Prince of Wales subscribing £100 and £50 respectively to increase the span of the railway bridge, straighten the banks and clean up the River Cam. This latter reason, many believed, was more to improve provision for rowing, than poor sanitation, providing 'fascinating if alarming evidence of Cambridge priorities.'[11]

This resulted in Cambridge rowing improving so dramatically that the University won the next five Boat Races beginning in 1870.

Town rowing

The 'City of Cambridge' is today the oldest town rowing club on the Cam, having originally been the 'Cambridge Boat Racing Club' founded in 1844, the largest contingent of which went on to become the 'Cambridge Town Rowing Club'. This was established in 1863 out of the Working Men's College, which Frank Fenner was closely associated with, given it was located on the same site as his tobacco shop and gymnasium at 6 Market Hill (chapter 16).

Members of the 1868 Town Rowing crew (see photo) included John Hodson (lying on the right), today more famous for building a folly on the riverbank, with links to swimming. Another crew member was John (Jack) Harvey (seated centrally on the lowest step) considered the founder, and later 'an authority on rowing matters (who) during the half century in which he has been connected with Cambridge rowing has coached more successful Light Blues [university rowers] than any of his contemporaries. At times when knotty points arose in connection with the University crew, Jack Harvey's opinion was always accepted as final.'[12]

It was this role as a professional rowing coach that would have ruled Jack Harvey out from any rowing competitions against gentlemen amateurs.

Cambridge Town Rowing Club 1868
Thanks to Capturing Cambridge www.capturingcambridge.org

GENTLEMEN AMATEURS

It was reasonable that when gentlemen made a sport of rowing towards the end of the eighteenth century that they should not compete against professional boatmen, or watermen. However, 'as class consciousness grew more acute (in the second half of the nineteenth century) … the amateurs went further and further into the indefensible to preserve their exclusivity … and extravagantly so',[13] in rowing. Their definition of 'professional' was extended to also exclude 'all who earned, or ever had earned a living from manual labour', which would not only have excluded Jack Harvey, as a professional rowing coach, but probably all the rest of his Town Rowing Club crew too.

Such exclusions were ostensibly introduced to make for equal competition, to avoid corruption (over gambling), and to take back control from those who had organised sports, such as the tavern keepers. However, what was also taking place was that the new 'middle classes [were standing] steady to defend the line of their own gentility with a judicious mixture of discrimination and neglect'.[14] The alternative, according to Walter Besant, writing in 1887 (having been a student at Christ's College, Cambridge from 1855) was that if 'the base mechanical sort' (i.e. the working classes) were to also enjoy 'middle class amusements', this would result in 'an effacement [elimination] of all classes'.[15]

Of course, these changes affected other sports but in different ways. Cricket, compared to rowing, lent itself more to a division of labour, between the more strenuous pursuit of bowling, performed by the servant, or professional, and batting, by the gentlemen.

The governing body of athletics followed a similar path to rowing, but 'association football was in the process of being abandoned to the working classes'.[16]

There are only a few known examples in Cambridge of the middle classes / gentlemen supporting the working classes participating in sport, some of them featured in this book, for example Frederick Furnivall in rowing on the Thames (chapter 10), Frederick Maurice at the Working Men's College (chapter 16), Frank Fenner in local cricket, sometimes supported by student cricketers at the University (chapter 20), and members of the local Temperance Movement who were instrumental in establishing a local rowing club.

Rob Roy Rowing Club

A few boathouses up from the Goldie boathouse (towards Cambridge) is that belonging to the Cambridgeshire Rowing Association, whose facilities today are also used by the Rob Roy Boat Club, founded in 1880:

> A new boat club has been started by the Church Temperance Society of Cambridge and Chesterton, under the name of 'Rob Roy', and it will be open to members of the various branches ... Strict temperance is to be enforced to liquors and language.[17]

Why a Temperance Society?

Increased prosperity and leisure time gave more opportunities to play sport, so that by the 1880s Britain was foremost in Europe in the amount of leisure the working class enjoyed. However, the moralists were greatly concerned by the connection between Saturday afternoon sport and drinking.[18] In Cambridge, the creation of the Rob Roy Boat Club appears to have been the local Temperance Society's attempts to manage this.

In addition to the moralists, there were Britain's empire-builders who viewed sport as much more than an agreeable recreation. So, whilst the amateur principle was 'a defence against social pollution by the 'untouchables' of the home country',[19] there was an understanding, reported in the *Cambridge University Magazine* in 1886 that:

> Politicians work out grand schemes with treaties and conventions to bind us and our colonies … but … we may also venture to say that a visit of a Canadian [rowing] crew to Henley … will bind us and our cousins of the tongue far more closely than any amount of diplomacy and trade conventions.[20]

There were however two major limitations of the middle classes in promoting sport. First, there was the 'self-serving amateurism', examples of which are described above, and second, 'the slow advance of women in the face of conventional gender obstinacy'.[21]

WOMEN'S ROWING

Whilst rowing and other sports played at Cambridge were taken around the world, rarely did this include women as participants. It was not until a hundred years after the men had first rowed their Oxford v Cambridge Boat Race that the women, competed in 1927, but under severe restrictions that prevented a real side-by-side race. It was more a competition of style and at a time of day when 'would-be spectators might be otherwise engaged, rather than cheering-on so unmaidenly a spectacle'.[22]

Women's rowing had officially started in Cambridge with the formation of the Newnham College Rowing Society in 1893, followed by the Girton College Club in 1906. Given women at Cambridge were only allowed to ride bicycles in 1894, 'boats were in use before bicycles' at Newnham College.

The first woman to cox a male crew

According to entries in A *Newnham Anthology* for 1876 and 1879 it records visits to the (Men's) May Bump Races, where a Newnhamite, Edith Sharpley, coxed a boat. This was clearly not widely reported because the world press of 1946 believed Connie Grayson from Oklahoma coxing the all-male Bull College[23] crew in the Bumps was a 'taboo breaking first'.[24]

SWIMMING

Whilst rowing was practised down river from Magdalene Bridge, swimming was up-river past the Backs (the generic label used to describe a number of the university's colleges that back onto the River Cam) towards Grantchester, to avoid the dangers of the town's sewage.

Public swimming

Until the public pool at Jesus Green (0.8 mile (1.3km)) north from the Mill Pond), was constructed in 1923, as one of the largest outdoor pools in Europe, people swam at Sheep's Green, just under half a mile (0.8km) upstream by river from the Mill Pond (crossed by Silver Street Bridge).

It is not known if Frank Fenner swam regularly in the Cam, but it was popular. For example, in the mid nineteenth century Josiah Chater wrote in his diary about early-morning swimming before work 'with his fellow apprentices',[25] and the boy choristers of King's College Chapel measured their prowess, by their progression from 'the Snobs' (a side-stream) to the deeper waters of the river.[26]

Hodson's garden and folly

For John Hodson to watch his daughter swim safely in the Snobs, he built a summerhouse on the riverbank in 1887. Hodson was a butler at Pembroke College, and according to Allan Brigham, the local historian, he also used the setting to grow food, relax and fish.[27]

In his younger days Hodson rowed for the Cambridge Town Rowing Club in 1868, founded by the Working Men's College and was a Lance Corporal in the 1st Cambridgeshire Volunteer Rifles, the same corps as Frank Fenner.

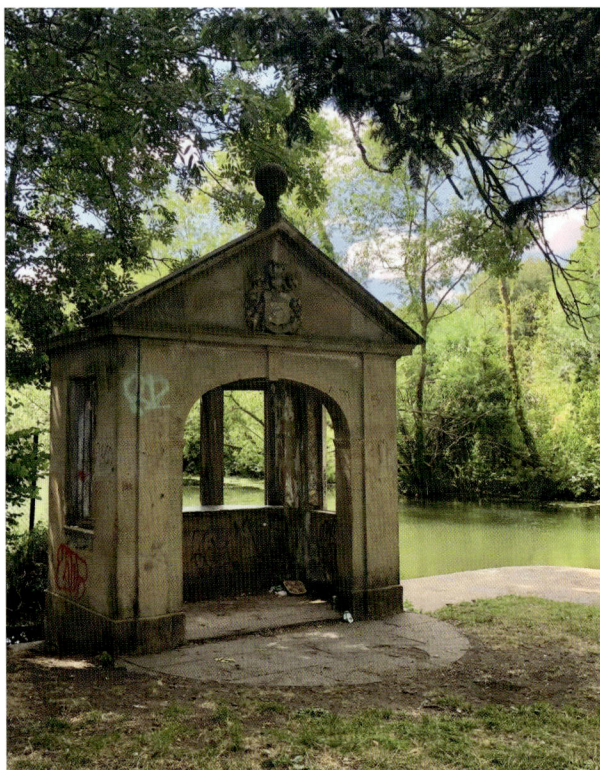

Hodson's folly on the River Cam at Newnham today

'Boys, as naked as God made them'

One of the challenges for those taking boating trips in the 1890s, according to Gwen Raverat (granddaughter of Charles Darwin), was:

> 'Boys, as naked as God made them' swimming in the river, for bathing drawers did not exist then; or, at least, not on Sheep's Green … Now to go up the River, the goal of all the best picnics, the boats had to go right by the bathing places, which lay on both sides of the narrow stream. These dangerous straits were taken in silence, and at full speed. The Gentlemen were set to the oars—in this context one obviously thinks of them as Gentlemen—and each Lady unfurled a parasol, and, like an ostrich, buried her head in it, and gazed earnestly into its silky depths, until the crisis was past, and the river was decent again.[28]

Courtesy of the Raverat Archive: www.raverat.com

Men and boys had long been able to swim on Sheep's Green, naked or otherwise, but in 1896 the town authorities provided bathing sheds for women in a more secluded spot opposite Hodson's Folly.

In addition to being a venue for swimming, Sheep's Green was also used for football. For example, Symonds D'Ewes (a student at St John's College from 1618) stated:

> [We] went out after supper to a spacious field at the back of Queens' College, called Sheep's Green,' having heard that there was to be 'some hot foot-ball playing.' Hurtful and unscholar-like though this game had been pronounced by the authorities, it was nevertheless still in vogue …[29]

University swimming

The earliest swimming records date back to 1567 when Walter Hadon (King's College) was drowned, resulting in swimming in the river being banned for students. Those caught, would be publicly whipped in their college, and again, on the following day in the Schools [teaching rooms close to the Senate House]. A second offence meant expulsion.

Attitudes presumably began to change with the publication in Latin of *The Art of Swimming* in 1587 written by Everard Digby, a Fellow of St John's College, translated by Christopher Middleton (also St John's College). This included advice on not swimming when rain is washing dung into the water, and how to cut one's toenails while floating.

First facilities, and Club

Christ's College and Emmanuel College had their own swimming pools 'on site' from the seventeenth century, no doubt prompting the creation of the first university pool facilities in 1705. These were built on the River Cam about a mile and a half (2.4 km) from the town, halfway to Grantchester, the location probably chosen because of the 100+ yards straight in the river, and being upstream from the town's sewage.

It was not until 1855 that the University established a swimming club at this same stretch of river, making it one of the oldest in the country.

Later, Girton College built their own pool in 1900 in the college grounds.

Close by to the University swimming club's base on the Cam is Skater's Meadow, with a lamppost in the middle, which is still visible today. People would pay 6d for an evening's skating when it flooded and froze.[30]

The river in literature

Geoffrey Chaucer refers to the river at the start of 'The Reeves Tale', written in the late fourteenth century, and legend has it he owned a mill in Cambridge.[31]

Later, the poet Rupert Brooke (student at King's College from 1906, then Fellow from 1913) wrote longingly about the river in 1912 in 'The Old Vicarage, Grantchester', with references to Byron, Chaucer and Tennyson:

> Still in the dawnlit waters cool
> His ghostly Lordship swims his pool,
> And tries the strokes, essays the tricks,
> Long learnt on Hellespont, or Styx.
> Dan Chaucer hears his river still
> Chatter beneath a phantom mill.
> Tennyson notes, with studious eye,
> How Cambridge waters hurry by ...

Rupert Brooke refers here to his vision of the ghostly Lord Byron, who studied at Cambridge from 1805, swimming in the pond near Grantchester (now called Byron's Pool), reportedly the favoured skinny-dipping haunt of Brooke, Virginia Woolf and others.

On dry land, Lord Byron was considered 'an ungainly mover as a result of his club foot, [but] in the water was a passionate and strong swimmer', including across the Hellespont (the four-mile (6.5km) stretch of water between Asia and Europe) on 3 May 1810. Following the swim, he wrote to his mother. 'I plume myself on this achievement more than I could possibly do on any kind of glory, poetical, political or rhetorical.'[32]

1   Peter Bryan (1999). Cambridge. The shaping of the City. Page 1.

2   http://www.oldvicarage.org/a-bit-of-history.html

3   Stephen Jorevin (1672). Translation in Grose, Antiquarian Repertory Vol. iv. P 518. On page 433. A book of Cambridge verse by Kellett, E. E. (Ernest Edward), 1864-1950 (published 1911).

4   http://www.oldvicarage.org/a-bit-of-history.html

5   Enid Porter (1969). Cambridgeshire Customs and Folklore. Routledge & Kegan Paul. Page 233.

6   Jerome K Jerome (1889) Three Men in a Boat. J.W. Arrowsmith. Chapter XV.

7   The Boat Race. Impact of a Single Day Major Event on a City. Arup & The Boat Race Company. October 2017.

8   J.A. Mangan (2006). 'Oars and the man'. Pleasure and purpose in Victorian and Edwardian Cambridge. Ch 3 in J.A. Mangan (2006). A sport-loving society. Victorian and Edwardian middle-class England at play. Page 102.

9   Robert Kenny (1990) Jesus College entry in This College-Studded Marsh. A humorous history of the Cambridge Colleges.

10 Cambridge Independent Press 28 May 1859.

11 Ged Martin. Magdalene College in mid Victorian times. https://www.gedmartin.net/martinalia-mainmenu-3/233-magdalene-college-cambridge-in-mid-victorian-times

12 Cambridge Independent Press 19 February 1904 from Mill Road Cemetery website.

13 Dennis Brailsford (1997). British Sport. A Social History. The Lutterworth Press. Page 98.

14 Peter Bailey (1978) in Eric Halliday. Chapter 10 'Of Pride and Prejudice' in J.A. Mangan (2006). A Sport-Loving Society. Page 239.

15 Eric Halladay. Of pride and prejudice. The amateur question in English nineteenth-century rowing, chapter 10, page 239. J.A. Mangan (2006) A sport-loving society.

16 Eric Halliday ref 'Of pride and prejudice' etc Page 239.

17 Cambridge Chronicle 5 June 1880 page 4.

18 Derek Birley (1993). Sport and the making of Britain. Manchester University Press. Page 265.

19 Harold Perkin. Teaching the nations how to play: sport and society in the British Empire and Commonwealth. Epilogue in J.A. Mangan (ed) (1992) The Cultural Bond: Sport, Empire, Society. From page 211.

20 Cambridge University Magazine, 20 June, 1886, 21 quoted on page 5 J.A. Mangan (ed) (1992). The Cultural Bond: Sport, Empire, Society. Frank Cass.

21 J.A. Mangan. Introduction. In 'A sport-loving society. Victorian and Edwardian Middle-Class England at play'. J.A. Mangan (Ed) (2006). Pages 2 and 3.

22 Jane Kingsbury and Carol Williams. (2015). CUWBC 1941 - 2014. Trireme.

23 Bull College was established during and after World War II for United States service personnel. It was located on the site of the Black Bull hotel now part of St Catharine's College.

24 Cam Issue 59 Lent 2010. Pages 32 and 33.

25 Enid Porter (1975). Victorian Cambridge. Josiah Chater's Diaries 1844-1884. Phillimore. Page 18

26 Enid Porter (1969). Cambridgeshire Customs and Folklore. London: Routledge & Kegan Paul. Pages 235 and 236.

27 Alan Brigham (2016). Hodsons Garden. A glimpse of nineteenth century Cambridge from a ditch on Coe Fen. Cambridge Local History Review.

28 Gwen Raverat (1952). Period Piece. A Cambridge childhood. Wood engravings by Gwen Raverat

29 Cambridge Chronicle and Journal 31 May 1851.

30 Skater's Meadow. The Inkling Magazine 25 July 2014.

31 Ref 14. https://poemsdisentangled.wordpress.com/2016/01/

32 Blog posted 2018 entitled '3 May 1810: Lord Byron and Lt. Ekenhead swim across the Hellespont' on http://figures-of-speech.com/2018/05/byron.htm

CHAPTER 5

Bridge Street

Location: starting from Magdalene Bridge, up to the junction with Jesus Lane / All Saints Passage, taking in seven stops on the way.

Stop 1. Pubs

The local area, Bridgeland, was served by 31 inns and pubs in the early nineteenth century. This includes the Pickerel Inn, licenced in 1608, opposite the pedestrian entrance to Magdalene College. The inn, now a popular pub, has 'in times past been a major brothel, gin palace, opium den and coaching inn',[1] with tales of a former landlady drowning in the river.

Just over the bridge at Quayside was the site of the Union Tavern, possibly the building on the far right in the old photograph below. A pub or tavern has been recorded as being on this site since 1623, serving the busy docks.

River from Magdalene Bridge showing Quayside and Union Tavern (right) before 1921
From the collection of David Gent.

The Union Tavern was home to one of the earliest pub cricket clubs, being founded around 1820. Its home ground was nearby Midsummer Common, which is why it was sometimes referred to as the 'Common Club' to distinguish it from its competitors who played on Parker's Piece. Frank Fenner played cricket as a teenager for the other three local pub teams (Hoops, Fountain and Castle), which together with the Union, were largely responsible for 'maintaining and rebuilding the town's cricketing culture'.[2] The Union's fixtures list included Islington and Biggleswade, demonstrating how high the standard of cricket was in Cambridge.

Stop 2. St Clement's Church

The current church was built in the first half of the thirteenth century, probably on the site of a Viking church, with St. Clement being the patron saint of Danish sailors. The tower including a spire was added in 1821, with the spire removed in 1928.

St Clement's Church c1900
From the collection of David Gent.

The Rev Arthur Robert Ward was vicar of St Clement's Church for 24 years from 1860 to 1884, having served his curacy at the nearby All Saints Church (opposite Trinity College), demolished in 1865. Ward spent all his adult life in Cambridge, coming to St John's College as an undergraduate in 1849. He died in 1884 when living at 45 Jesus Lane and was buried in Mill Road Cemetery. He never married.

Ward's father William was a famous cricketer (responsible also for saving Lord's Cricket Ground from being built on in 1825), so it was no surprise Arthur won his cricket Blue in 1853, also being captain in 1854 when he would have had contact with Frank Fenner, given the university cricket club played on 'Fenner's Ground'. This continued when Ward later became Treasurer and President of the University Cricket Club from 1873 to his death in 1884. One of his first tasks was to ask Fenner (who had left Cambridge to live in the West Country in the early 1860s, and yet still held the lease on Fenner's Ground):

> To remove part of his property which the University Cricket Club declined to take over, the said property consisting of a bell, some quoits, trap-bats, targets, and two casks! For these Fenner, who seems to have been a little grasping, had lodged a claim …[3]

In addition, in 1873 the Cricket Club stipulated that 'Fenner's' be referred to as 'The Cambridge University Cricket Ground', but 'the new name never caught on, notwithstanding Mr Ward's strenuous efforts to make it popular, and it is sad to be compelled to record that as lately as 1900 the captain of the [University Cricket Club] XI still alludes to the ground as "Fenner's"'.

Ward's role also included the University Cricket Club obtaining the lease on the cricket ground (after Fenner's lease had ended), and installing a new pavilion, which involved extensive letter-writing to raise the funds – see chapter 22.

Stop 3. Portugal Place and the Hawk's Club

Just beyond St Clement's Church is a lane called Portugal Place, lined with early nineteenth century townhouses, probably the best example in Cambridge of a residential street Frank Fenner would have been familiar with in his childhood and early adulthood.

Near the end of Portugal Place (as it bears right to the current Maypole Inn on Park Street) is the Hawks Club on the corner.

The club was founded in 1872 for the best sportsmen in the University, today also including the best sportswomen. The club has been located here since 1986, having had previous homes on Trinity Street, All Saints Passage, and the University Pitt Club on Jesus Lane.

Portugal Place - today with unchanged townhouses since early nineteenth century

One recent task for the Hawks Club was to research[4] the origins of the famous Cambridge Blue colour, and it is thanks to the Boat Race crew of 1836 for first choosing it.

Defined by the Cambridge University official colour style guide 8th edition (2019) as Pantone 557 C.

Stories abound as to why, including its similarity to 'Eton Blue', but the colour was simply in contrast to the much darker blue of Oxford, as well as not being a colour of any of the Cambridge college boat clubs. Since then, the colour has been adopted by every Cambridge team in all the sports played against Oxford.

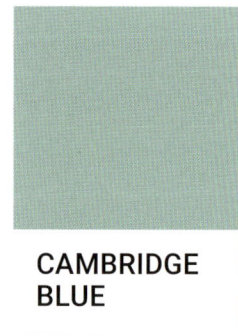

CAMBRIDGE BLUE

Stop 4. The Ram Inn

Just off Bridge Street, on Round Church Street, was the Ram Yard or Ram Inn, probably the location where Lord Byron kept his bear in the early 1800s.[5]

It was also where Nat Langham set up business as a boxing coach in 1852 as described by an anonymous Trinity College student:

> I remember well how eager we all were to cultivate the acquaintance of the celebrated Champion of the Middleweights, the most scientific fighter of his day. In those days the Varsity was sadly lacking in legitimate sport. Athletic sports were unknown, there was no such thing as football, and both rowing and cricket were very 'small pertaters' [potatoes] compared with what they are now.

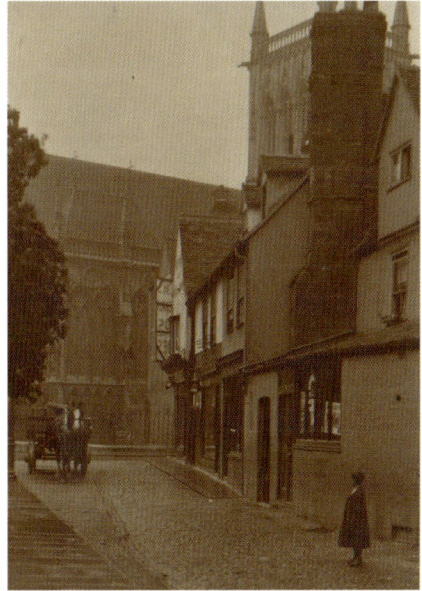

Ram Inn / Yard looking up today's Round Church Street towards St John's College chapel (before 1915)

From the collection of David Gent.

Before Langham's arrival, this same student reported he had to be content with:

> Cock-fighting, rat-killing, badger-drawing, dog-fighting; and for these pastimes we resorted either to the Spring at Chesterton, or to a ramshackle, tumbledown, disreputable old den in Ram Yard ... This haunt ... was bossed by a notorious character named Callaby, who supplied rats, pigeons, sparrows, to the noble sportsmen who enjoyed the exhilarating pastime of slaying 'such small deer'. A long, lean, wrinkled, shrewd, 'varminty' old cove was Callaby, and he had the queerest assortment of animals trained to 'fancy' work that I have ever seen ... But the sporting glories of Callaby's lost their lustre to our eyes when the Champion of the Middle-weights appeared among us. Nat [Langham] very soon had his hands full of pupils, many of them tip-top toffs, who looked upon him as a hero; indeed, I think they all regarded Nat as the greatest master of the noble art the world had ever seen.[6]

Later in 1857 the local press 'promoted' a match organised by Callaby at the Ram Inn, a rat-killing between a dog and a man due on 26th December, adding 'which is the favourite in the betting-world we have not heard'. The report also referred to the use of hawks and owls, with the press adding 'a pitiable sight it will be; and the intellect those who go to see the sight more pitiable still.'[7]

It appears Bridge Street already had a reputation for hosting animal baiting, as a bull ring was located there from the early seventeenth to the late eighteenth centuries.[8] There was also a bull ring on Peas Hill (just off the market).

Stop 5. Round Church to the Cambridge Union

The Round Church, or Church of the Holy Sepulchre, was built in 1130 by a 'fraternity' including crusaders returning from the first crusade to Jerusalem where they had seen The Church of the Holy Sepulchre. It is one of the four medieval round churches still in use in England today.

Frank Fenner's parents Jospeh Fenner and Elizabeth Welch were married in the Round Church on 1st September 1805, with Frank being born in March 1811.

The Cambridge Union Society is the oldest continuously running debating society in the world, today located immediately behind the Round Church.

The story goes it was founded in 1815 as the 'union' resulting out of a drunken brawl between three college debating societies. Its early location included the nearby Hoop Inn before finding its current permanent home in 1866.

It would appear the most attended debates in the nineteenth century were, according to the historian Ged Martin, 'on issues such as an attempt to ban boating through Grantchester Meadows … [Also] in 1885, an open meeting was convened with the aim of condemning the decision of the University soccer and rugby clubs for deciding to arrogate [claim without justification] to themselves the right of awarding "Blues", a mark of sporting distinction hitherto monopolised by cricketers, athletes and – of course – oarsmen. A motion demanding that the assorted footballers "bring themselves again into harmony with those unwritten laws by which the social relations of members of this University are governed" was rejected.'[9]

Ged Martin suggests the relative vitality of the two Unions (at Cambridge and Oxford universities) in their early years may be gauged from descriptions of the first joint debate. In November 1829, a delegation from Cambridge visited Oxford. This was the year of the first Oxford–Cambridge boat race and just two years after the start of an annual intervarsity cricket fixture, suggesting that the excursion was part of a developing 'Oxbridge' culture.

Stop 6. Hoop Inn

The Hoop Inn / Hotel at 3 Bridge Street, was built in 1729 and is still standing today, but functioning as a shop. Pubs have been on this site since at least 1588.

The inn is most famous for featuring in William Wordsworth's poem 'The Prelude', describing his experience of arriving by coach in Cambridge in 1787, already shared in chapter 1.

The Hoop Inn c1830 with Jesus Lane (mid right) **and Sidney Sussex College** (right)

By kind permission of Cambridge Antiquarian Society

Source: Proceedings of the Cambridge Antiquarian Society. Vol XXVI. 1923 - 1924. Page 17.

Cricket and politics links to Frank Fenner

In 1828, when Frank Fenner was 17 years old, he took 10 wickets in a match for the Hoop [Cricket] Club against Biggleswade, a year after it had formed. This match was managed by William Bird, landlord of the Hoop Inn and former local cricketer, later the first proprietor of the University Arms Hotel.

The Hoop was for many years the headquarters of the Whig party in the town, and because Frank was a candidate in the Town Council elections in 1857, must have meant he was a regular visitor.

FRANK FENNER AND THEATRE IN CAMBRIDGE

The Hoop possessed a large assembly room used by the Cambridge Union Society from 1831 to 1850, then as a billiard room, before being taken over by the University's Amateur Dramatic Club (A.D.C.)[10] when it was founded by Francis Burnand in 1855. In 1847 the inn also had a bowling green.

Footlights

William Redfern (later Mayor of Cambridge) founded the Bijou A.D.C. based at the Victoria Assembly Rooms on the Market in 1875. Having been out-bid (by the local Temperance Society) in buying the existing Theatre Royal Barnwell (in 1878), he used St Andrew's Hall in St Andrew's Street (near Emmanuel College), from 1878, the Hall having been used as a skating rink. It appears he gradually won over the University authorities by, for example running Greek Plays and 'overcoming the traditions of the undergraduates' and their 'rowdyism' by sitting amongst them at an opening night in 1882. He wrote:

> I was trying to establish a proper theatre ... and that any disturbance would fatally prejudice the University authorities against anything of the kind. These young fellows, being gentlemen, took the rebuke in good heart, and one of them very soon afterwards became the founder of the present flourishing Footlights Club.[11]

Footlights started, not with a theatrical performance, but with a cricket match in 1882 at Fulbourn Hospital (over 4 miles (6 km) east of Cambridge).

Footlights wanted to reach a wider and larger audience than the University A.D.C. resulting in them 'garnering huge public appeal ... [involving] the many different classes of which life in Cambridge is made up'.[12]

Frank Fenner and amateur dramatics

It is not known whether Frank was a keen theatre goer. When he was a young man, the University maintained a stranglehold over any activity that interfered with the education of their students, so that theatrical performances were, at best, restricted to a few weeks each summer at Stourbridge Fair, and a theatre on the edge of Town, rebuilt in 1816 as the Barnwell Theatre Royal.[13] However, 'Barnwell had become one of Cambridge's most notorious slums ... with thirty-seven drink shops within 200 yards of the theatre ... and rife with prostitution'.[14] (More on Barnwell and its poverty in chapter 20.)

The first known link to amateur dramatics for Frank occurred in 1842, when he played cricket for England against Kent in Canterbury.

Kent v England Grand Cricket Match 1842 advertising poster.
Permission to use granted by Knights Auctioneers.

The England team included 'Hon F Ponsonby' who, in addition to playing for Cambridge University and Cambridge Town, was also responsible that same year for establishing 'The Old Stagers', an amateur dramatic society which performed as part of the Kent Cricket Week. This continues to this day making it the oldest amateur dramatic society in the world.

This Match originated the Canterbury Week. [Written by Tom Taylor]

A Cricketer's Prologue.

Spoken in the Kentish Dialect, before the Play of " The Poor Gentleman,"
at the Theatre, Canterbury, during the Great Cricket Match,
August 1st, 1842.

(The speaker is carried on, struggling, by three men, who disappear,
leaving him in astonishment.)

Hearing they played to-night in the cause of cricket,
I thought I'd come and se 'em—that's the ticket !
          [Producing a ticket for the Play.
But scarcely had I reached the play-house door,
When three chaps rushed upon me, with a roar,
" We've found a prologue !" " Here, you sir," says one,
"Just clear your throat, shoulder your bat, and on !"
"On where ?" says I. " Why on the stage, at once !"
And here they've left me, looking like a dunce,
To speak a prologue—Heaven knows what upon.
          [After a pause.

Well, I suppose I must talk now I'm on.
Cricket's the only thing I know a bit about ;
Ten years my shins and knuckles have been hit about !
But, hollo ! who are those I see down there ?
          [Recognizing the Players in the Pit.
Pilch, Lillywhite, and Fenner—I declare !
How are ye all ? Where men like *you* assemble,
It's not a little that shall make me tremble.
While I stand here as champion of cricket,
You mind your fielding—*I'll* keep up my wicket.
You will stand by me ? Never mind my county :
Cricketers are all brothers : such I count ye.
Your cricketer no cogging practice knows,
No trick to favour friends or cripple foes ;
His motto still is " May the best man win,"
Let Sussex boast her *Taylor,* Kent her *Mynn.*
Your cricketer, right English to the core,
Still loves the man best he has licked before ;
Besides, in Kent, what should a cricketer fear ;
Wickets, you know, are *planted* and grow here ;
Bats come up ready made ; and *Balls,* (just try 'em),
It's quite a pleasure to be *ripped up* by 'em.
Yet, 'tis a nervous task—for *Umpires* rear
On every side official brows severe—
Enthroned, of course, beyond appeal or doubt,
Whose lightest word may *put* our best man *out.*
Still, tempering duty with good humour, say
To-night, at least, that you *admire our play* ;
We'll strive our hardest to keep up the ball,
Make a good *draw,* and with no *slips* at all ;
We promise you that no *long-stops* to-night
Shall tire your patience or your gall excite ;
And, *though our best man's arm be out of joint,**
Despite his splints, he'll try and make a *point.*
Then let one voice from boxes, gallery, pit,
Proclaim unanimous, " *A slashing hit* ;"
And, should we make to-night, the *hit* we seek,
Remember that our *run* will last a week.

* Alluding to C. G. Taylor, Esq., who, owing to a hurt received some weeks before,
whilst playing at cricket, acted with his arm in splints and a sling.

Given to me by F. P. Fenner, when calling
upon him at his hotel, the "White Lion",
Bath, Tues: 21 May, 1889.

A Cricketer's Prologue - featuring Frank Fenner (1842)

Frank Fenner was in the audience at the first performance at the Theatre Royal, Canterbury, even featuring by name in *A Cricketer's Prologue*, performed on the first evening of the first day of the Kent v England Cricket match.

This clearly made a significant impression on Frank because 50 years later, he had at least two copies of this script. One, he gave away to Walter Baily[15], as evidenced from hand-written notes on the original copy, recently sold at auction in 2020.

The second copy of this Prologue was spotted a few years later by a reporter from the *Sketch* in the White Lion Hotel, Bath in 1893[16], when interviewing Frank:

Among the many relics of Mr Fenner's cricketing days I found the prologue written for the 'Old Stagers' by Tom Taylor[17] when the Canterbury Week was inaugurated. Then and for many years after Mr Fenner assisted at the festival, and he is mentioned by name in this prologue …

> '*Cricket's* the only thing I know a bit about:
> Ten years my shins and knuckles have been hit about!
> But, hollo! who are those I see down there?
> *[Recognising the Players in the Pit]*
> Pilch, Lillywhite and Fenner I declare!
> How are ye all? Where men like *you* assemble,
> It's not a little that shall make me tremble.
> While I stand here as champion of cricket
> You mind your fielding - *I'll* keep up my wicket.
> You will stand by me? Never mind my county:
>
> Cricketers are all brothers: such I count ye.
> Your cricketer no cogging practice knows,
> No trick to favour friends or cripple foes;
> His motto still is "May the best man win,"
> Let Sussex boast her *Taylor*, Kent her *Mynn*,
> Your cricketer, right English to the core,
> Still loves the man best he has licked before'[18]

This reference to Frank was praise indeed, being associated with the cricketing greats of Pilch, Lillywhite, Mynn and Taylor, the same Charles Taylor who had been a student at Emmanuel College from 1835 to 1840 and a talented actor with the Old Stagers.

Cambridge Town actors

If Frank had taken an active interest in the local theatrical scene in Cambridge, he would probably have been aware of Jem Reynolds, who was also a talented sportsman. Jem was also for many years the driver of the Telegraph Coach from Cambridge to London, his best time being 4 hours 12 minutes.

Jem was 'remarkably swift of foot; and one evening, after an exhibition of his pedestrian powers on Parker's Piece, by which he was a considerable winner, over a convivial glass a witty and eccentric friend said – "Jem, I would write your epitaph, but your accomplishments are so numerous that I should hardly know where to begin and where to end."'. Reynolds was flattered when he received the following poem about him, later also included in his obituary.

> Reader, pause o'er this tomb, and 'ere thou departest,
> Know 'tis Jem Reynolds – nor Sir Joshua, the artist –
> The man so renowned for his "Telegraph" driving,
> That none could surpass him, dead or surviving.
> He was the beau of the road and the pride of the fair,
> Sat his box with a grace that was quite *debonair*.
> By nature created bold, active, and strong,
>
> In a foot-race or leap he was first in the throng.
> He could skate like a fenman, a somersault fling,
> And was a crack shot at a bird on the wing.
> He would ride like a Nimrod, like a Payton could drive,
> He could swim like Leander, like a pearl-hunter dive;
> Act *Iago* and *Shylock*, like Incledon sing;
> He could fence with old Angelo, or box with Tom Spring.
> He could dance the gavotte, too, with ariel grace,
> Like Proteus could change, but was always in place;
> Lords, Dons and Doctors, all the choice spirits,
> Acknowledg'd his worth and rewarded its merits;
> Integrity, candour, and truth stamp'd the *man*,
> And he honour'd the like, deny it who can.[19]

Jem died after a brief illness in 1868 aged 73 years and is buried in Mill Road Cemetery.

Stop 7. The Roman Bath Company on Jesus Lane

Just round the corner from the Hoop Inn on Jesus Lane is the recent location at street-level for Pizza Express.

In early 1861 the Roman Bath Company Limited was formed. It is not known why Cambridge was chosen for the company's first venture, probably just 'a feeling that an old-established university town had the type of population which would enthusiastically make use of the superbly designed facilities the board planned to provide'.[20] The company purchased the Hoop Inn's coaching yard and its entrance off Jesus Lane and built an elegant classical portico, swimming and plunge pools, and hot and cooling rooms, many features of which have been retained to this day.

This followed announcements in the local press, including 'Mr F.P. Fenner is to be the manager of the baths – a very proper appointment',[21] and public meetings to drum up support for the share issue.

The baths opened in February 1863 but were only in operation for eleven months before being mysteriously wound up early in 1864.[22]

TOWN AND COUNTY NEWS.
[See also Page 6.]

Roman Bath Company.—Of the £3,000 required to be raised in this locality, we hear that such a sum has already been subscribed for as has induced the Directors to proceed without more delay in making the necessary preliminary arrangements, and they have entered into an agreement for suitable premises, at such a price as the shareholders of the present Company will readily consent to give. Mr. F. P. Fenner is to be the manager of the baths—a very proper appointment.

Source: Cambridge Independent Press 13 April 1861.
Newspaper image © The British Library Board.
All rights reserved. With thanks to The British Newspaper Archive (www.britishnewspaperarchive.co.uk).

Understandably questions were asked as to what happened to the £4,000 raised, and if someone 'ran off with the money?'. Whilst there is no evidence that Frank Fenner was implicated, he did leave Cambridge in late 1862 / early 1863 to live in the West Country, without providing a reason for doing so (see chapter 23).

Today the property is owned by the University Pitt Club, a private members club established in honour of William Pitt the Younger in 1835. In 1864, after the demise of the Roman Bath Company, the club shared the premises with Orme's Billiards Rooms, eventually buying the whole building in 1907. More recently, for about 20 years, from 1966, it was also the home of the Hawks Club.

1   https://www.cam.ac.uk/news/a-new-look-for-magdalene-street

2   Willie Sugg (2009). Fenner's Men. Cambridgeshire Cricket 1822-1848. Part Three of a Tradition Unshared. Cambridge: Real Work Publishing. Page 18.

3   W.J. Ford (1902) The Cambridge University Cricket Club 1820 – 1901'. William Blackwood and Sons. Page 33.

4   https://www.hawksclub.co.uk/wp-content/uploads/2016/09/origins_of_the_cambridge_blue.pdf

5   Keith Walker (Trinity Review 1961) reported in Trinity College, Cambridge Annual Record (2011). Page 99.

6   Author unknown. Famous fights - past and present. Vol II. No 22. 1901. Page 338.

7   Cambridge Independent Press 26 Dec 1857.

8   Emma Griffin (2005). England's Revelry. A history of popular sports and pastimes 1660-1830. Oxford University Press. Page 225.

9   Ged Martin. The Cambridge Union: Sources and Rivals. https://www.gedmartin.net/the-cambridge-union-and-ireland-1815-1914-chapter-1, and Nicholas Chrimes (2017) Cambridge. Treasure Island of the Fens. Page 233.

10 https://innsofcambridge.com/

11 Robert Hewison (1984). Footlights! A hundred years of Cambridge comedy. Methuen. Pages 4 – 7.

12 https://www.cambridgefootlights.org/history

13 Theatres in 'The city of Cambridge: Town and gown'. Pages 76-86 from A History of the County of Cambridge and the Isle of Ely: Volume 3, the City and University of Cambridge. Originally published by Victoria County History, London, 1959. Internet: https://www.british-history.ac.uk/vch/cambs/vol3/pp76-86

14 Robert Hewison (1983) Footlights! A hundred years of Cambridge comedy. Methuen. Page 3.

15 It is not known what the relationship between Frank Fenner and Walter Baily Esq might have been, however he probably is the same Baily who matriculated in 1856 at St John's College, Cambridge, later called to the Bar in 1862, then becoming the Government Inspector of Schools from 1870-90, and serving on the Council of the University of London from 1893-1907 (A Cambridge Alumni Database at https://venn.lib.cam.ac.uk/)

16 Sketch. A veteran cricketer. 13 Sept 1893. Page 361.

17 Tom Taylor matriculated at Trinity College in 1837 https://enacademic.com/dic.nsf/enwiki/124371 and was later editor of Punch http://www.ricardophotoalbum.com/archive/old-stagers.php

18 The date of this was 1st August 1842, the performance at 7.45pm. The theatre was The Theatre Royal, Canterbury located in Orange Street. From the official history of the Old Stagers, "Canterbury, Cricket & Theatricals" by Richard Ritchie published by OS Publications in 2015.

19 Cambridge Independent Press 4 April 1868.

20 http://www.victorianturkishbath.org/_6DIRECTORY/AtoZEstab/England/CambJ/1PreludeEng.htm

21 Cambridge Independent Press 13 April 1861.

22 Cambridge Independent Press 30 Jan 1864.

CHAPTER 6
Jesus College

In 1133 the Cambridge Nunnery of St Mary and St Radegund was founded, which when it became derelict was converted into 'The College of the Blessed Virgin Mary, Saint John the Evangelist and the glorious Virgin Saint Radegund, near Cambridge'. Its common name used today comes from the name of its chapel, Jesus Chapel. John Alcock, Bishop of Ely, was the founder in 1496, which is why the symbol of the College is a cockerel, after the surname of its founder.

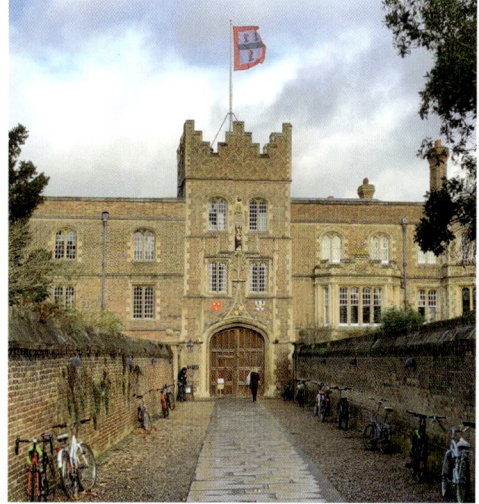
Jesus College looking down 'the chimney' from Jesus Lane

One twelfth century tradition the College inherited from the nuns was Garlic Fair, held in August in the extensive grounds of the nunnery, later moving to the junction of today's Park Street and Jesus Lane at a site then known as Garlic Lane.[1] Little is known of the Fair, other than the College accounts showing a sum of £1 being received annually as profits. The sporting contribution this fair and the other three made in Cambridge are explored further in chapter 7.

SPORT BEFORE THE NINETEENTH CENTURY

Henry Venn

Henry Venn is today credited with founding the Clapham Sect which played a significant role in the development of Victorian morality: 'the ethos of Clapham became the spirit of the age'.[2] A significant number of other past students from Cambridge were also involved, including William Wilberforce (past student of St John's College) and others influenced by Charles Simeon, the vicar of

Henry Venn: gave up cricket for the church
By kind permission of the President, Fellows and Scholars of Queens' College, Cambridge.

Holy Trinity Church, Cambridge for 54 years. Successes included the abolition of slavery and other initiatives designed to alleviate child abuse, poverty, illiteracy and other social problems. One of the indirect consequences was reversing the increasingly corrupt game of cricket where cheating and gambling were common.[3]

Henry Venn started as a student at Jesus College from 1742, later becoming a Fellow (senior teaching staff) at Queens' College for eight years from 1749. In addition to being a curate ('junior' church vicar) in Clapham, west London, Henry spent over 40 years in churches in both Barton and Yelling, villages close to Cambridge.

Venn was considered one of the best cricket players in the University. This included playing for England against Surrey in June 1747, which according to John Venn's *Annals of a Clerical Family*, 'excited considerable interest, being watched by a very numerous body of spectators'. Despite having won the game, he ended it by throwing down his bat, saying, 'Whoever wants a bat which has done me good service may take that, as I have no further occasion for it, because I am to be ordained on Sunday and I will never have it said of me, "Well struck, Parson!"'.

According to his great grandson he:

> Strictly adhered to this resolution, notwithstanding the remonstrances of his friends and even of the tutor and Fellows of his College … Nay though his health suffered by a sudden transition from a course of most violent exercise to a life of comparative inactivity he could never be persuaded to play any more.[4]

Sadly, this end to Henry Venn's cricket career at its peak was relatively common over the next 150 years for many talented sportsmen entering the church after university. Others from Jesus College who did so included Thomas Anson (cricket), and Herbert Luckock (football).

LINKS TO THE TOWN

Early golf in Cambridge

Whilst George Gosset is credited with introducing golf to Cambridge in 1869, including an attempt to create a golf course on Midsummer Common, he was followed soon after by William Linskill who played golf in 1873 on Coe Fen, opposite the Botanic Gardens, three years before he started as a student at Jesus College. 'There were three holes on this side of the Trumpington Road and four more on the narrow strip of grass over the other side of the road (probably on Empty Common)'.[5]

Later, as a student in 1876, he added:

> I had an awful job as a golf missionary there. They laughed at the idea. I taught a few chaps on Coe Fen and Sheep's Green, and then I discovered Coldham's Common. There was a rifle range there and they did coursing and pigeon shooting – all dead against me, and an unknown and idiotic Scotch game. I had to fight the commoners and explain the game to the unsympathetic town council. They all looked on it as a mad fad. At last I got it started with a few chaps, I cut the holes myself and the greens, marked the tees, mended the clubs, and made balls in an outhouse.[6]

Interaction with 'the Cambridge youth'

Whilst Town and Gown rows were considered a thing of the past, the college magazine, *Chanticleer* of 1889 reported this was:

> In spite of the enthusiasm of a few warlike spirits among the freshmen [new University students], who parade the streets at certain periods of the year, and of the rowdy impertinence of that most detestable creature the Cambridge youth which follows at a safe distance, usually very frightened but sometimes bold enough to knock a hat off here and there, for which brilliant feat it very properly gets imprisoned for a week, as was the case only the other day.[7]

Local cricket

There are three examples of cricket bridging the gap between the College and the town.

First, Thomas Anchitel Anson, a student at Jesus College from 1838 to 1842 not only won his cricket Blue but played a number of times for the Cambridge Town Club including in 1841 against the MCC.[8] Despite being rated one of the best wicket keepers in the country, aged only 24, he gave up cricket entirely when ordained as a clergyman, later reflected on as 'a disappointment' by Frank Fenner (chapter 20).

Before Thomas Hayward from the Town established himself as an England cricketer he played as a professional for Jesus College in 1856, including in an early-season inter-college fixture versus King's College.[9]

John, father of Jack Hobbs, changed his career in 1889 from a slaters labourer to become the cricket groundsman and umpire at Jesus College. This gave Jack his earliest opportunities including playing for the Choir XI aged only 11 years.

Later when his father died, Jack took over as college groundsman aged 20, but it was F.C. Hutt, a college servant who encouraged Jack to play cricket professionally (chapter 20).

ENGLAND'S SPORTING REVOLUTION

Samuel Taylor Coleridge

Whilst as a child Coleridge 'took no pleasure in boyish sports',[10] his later work had a significant indirect impact on exercise and sport establishing itself as a legitimate lifestyle choice in the nineteenth century.

He arrived at Jesus College in February 1791, staying for less than two years. Whilst in Cambridge he may well have taken solitary walks, probably 'with his hat off … jumping over gates, hedges and streams',[11] but:

Samuel Taylor Coleridge in 1795: indirect impact on sport gaining wider acceptance

Permission granted by kind permission of the Master and Fellows of Jesus College, Cambridge.

> Cambridge [was not] a kind nurse, and writers as diverse as George Herbert and Samuel Taylor Coleridge have suffered from the damp and the mist which rise from the circumambient fens; for many centuries various forms of rheumatism, consumption, and feverish ague afflicted the undergraduates toiling in their cold rooms …[12]

A few years after Cambridge in 1796, he retreated to central Somerset being joined by like-minded poets including William Wordsworth and his sister Dorothy. Together they resolved to turn their back on the material world conceiving of a way to transform humanity through the power of the poetic imagination, beginning with the exploration of their own minds: 'From revolution to revelation, but for this they needed another kind of liberty, the freedom for their bodies to roam along with their minds across the moors and coastal paths of the Somerset coast.'[13]

The impact of Coleridge and Wordsworth on individuals central to the development of the manliness / Muscular Christianity agendas across the nineteenth century, such as Thomas Arnold, Frederick Maurice, Charles Kingsley and Thomas Hughes, is expertly described in Malcolm Tozer's 2015 book, *The ideal of manliness: The legacy of Thring's Uppingham.*

Winning over the hostile University to sport

As mentioned in chapter 4, Jesus College's success on the river was largely down to the leadership of Henry and Edmund Morgan. However, credit must also be given to the Master, George Corrie, so that together they formed a powerful triumvirate. Their motives have been variously described starting with rescuing an ailing college, to using sport to keep men both out of mischief, and as character formation.[14]

Their influence grew so that in partnership with Leslie Stephen (Trinity Hall) and others, they were able to win over the hostile university authorities to the idea of 'fresh inter-University competitions of a non-intellectual nature', making it possible for Percy Thornton (a student at Jesus College), and Charles Lawes (student at Trinity College), to visit Oxford University early in 1864 to make arrangements for the first inter-university athletics meeting which took place later in the same year.[15]

Edmund Morgan: responsible for sport becoming more acceptable in the university

Permission granted 19 Aug 2022 by kind permission of the Master and Fellows of Jesus College, Cambridge.

One outcome was that such activities 'characteristic of the rivers and playing fields of late nineteenth-century Oxford and Cambridge [became the] load-bearing supports underpinning the moral structure of British and imperial society. Attitudes, relationships and administration owed much to the ethical imperatives of the playing fields.'[16]

Taking sport beyond Cambridge

There are three examples of Jesus College graduates, who later as a teacher, colonial administrator and missionary used their sporting experiences 'to train the child at home in Britain and the 'child-like' native in the colonies'.[17] A fourth example, focusing on Association Football, demonstrates that sadly this did not include local Cambridge people.

The first example was James Robertson, a student from 1854, later to become the headteacher at Haileybury from 1884 to 1890. He was typical of 'Victorian sporting pedagogues ... possessed of a persistent youthfulness, a firm commitment to athletics as a moral instrument and a determination to ensure they had a central role in educational theory and practice.'[18]

The second example was the colonial administrator Charles Hose who had left Jesus College prematurely in 1884, later taking up the post as the government resident in Sarawak, Borneo. One of his achievements was to introduce an annual rowing race between the war canoes of all the villages 'where no spears or other weapons were to be carried'.[19]

The missionary was Cecil Earle Tyndale-Biscoe, a student at Jesus College from 1882 who, after winning a rowing Blue and coaching both the University and college crews, worked in London's East End organising gymnastics and boxing, and starting both swimming and rowing clubs for the Band of Hope Boys Club in the parish of St Mary's, Whitechapel.[20] His only known contribution to Cambridge Town when a student was helping in the local Sunday School.

Cecil Earle Tyndale-Biscoe: taking sport to Kashmir

Author's image. Source: Tyndale-Biscoe Of Kashmir an autobiography published in 1951 by London: Seeley, Service and Co. Ltd. Page 48.

Later Tyndale-Biscoe became a missionary in Kashmir, the northernmost geographical region of the Indian subcontinent, for a period of 46 years from 1890. This work included establishing a missionary school where he introduced rowing and other sports. The school expanded to six schools, including one for girls. Unfortunately, this came at a price. An example of an early approach to introducing and persisting with the use of a leather football, considered unholy by the local young men, illustrates the 'imperial self-confidence ... ethnocentricity [lack of respect for other ways of living], arrogance and determination'[21] that largely characterised Britain's efforts taking sport across the world – see also chapter 25.

The fourth example was Herbert Luckock (standing back left in photo) who spent nearly forty years in or near Cambridge from 1854, beginning as a student at Jesus College, later becoming a Fellow, and then priest at All Saints Church, directly opposite the entrance to the college on Jesus Lane. Despite being one of the ten signatories responsible for formulating the 1856 version of the Cambridge Rules of Association Football whilst a student, there

An 1854 portrait, featuring both Herbert Luckock (top left) **and Edward Horne** (top right - Clare College), **two of the creators of the 1856 'Cambridge rules' of football**
Used with permission from Shrewsbury School.

is no evidence he subsequently used his skills as a footballer or rule-maker for the benefit of the people in his parish.

Herbert Luckock was buried in Mill Road Cemetery.[22]

According to the Jesus College magazine of 1889, it reported 'there is little other evidence the University worked with Cambridge Town to promote its more codified and non-violent version of the game of football', despite adding 'the greatest promoters of football and sports were graduates who entered teaching or the church'.[23]

Without this magazine article giving any reasons as to why, the probable explanation is that students at Cambridge, as gentleman amateurs pursuing their sport for its own sake, 'did not welcome the involvement of the working class, seeing that the nature of their work, being essentially very physical, would give them a distinct advantage' at playing football. In fact, the sports historian Richard Holt believed that 'most middle-class sportsmen seem to have wanted to keep as far away from the working classes as possible'.[24]

1. Alison Taylor (2017). Cambridge. The hidden history. The History Press. Page 113.

2. Stephen Tomkins, (2010). The Clapham Sect: How Wilberforce's circle transformed Britain. Lion Books.

3. Derek Birley (1999). A social history of English cricket. Aurum. Page 63.

4. John Venn (1904) Annals of a Clerical Family. London:Macmillan. Pages 70 - 71.

5. Cambridge Review 27 Feb 1896.

6. D. Cameron, Social Links, pp 166-167, 2010 in Michael Morrison (2016) The worst golf course ever. Coldham Common. A history of the Cambridge University Golf Club. 1869 – 1919. Pages 34 - 35.

7. In cap and gown. Article in The Chanticleer. No 13 Michaelmas Term 1889 page 5.

8. Willie Sugg (2009). Fenner's Men. Cambridgeshire Cricket 1822 - 1848. Part 3 of A Tradition Unshared. Page 41.

9. Keith and Jennifer Booth (2018). The Haywards. The biography of a cricket dynasty. Chequered Flag Publishing. Page 52.

10. https://englishhistory.net/poets/samuel-taylor-coleridge/

11. H.M. Margoliouth (1966). Wordsworth and Coleridge 1795 – 1834. Archon Books. Page 14.

12. Foreword written by Peter Ackroyd in Graham Chainey (1995) A literary history of Cambridge. The Pevensey Press. Page xi.

13. Simon Shama. The Romantics and Us. BBC documentary – Sept 2020.

14. J.A. Mangan (2006). 'Oars and the man'. Pleasure and purpose in Victorian and Edwardian Cambridge. Ch 3 in J.A. Mangan (2006). A sport-loving society. Victorian and Edwardian middle-class England at play. Routledge.

15. J.A. Mangan (2006). 'Oars and the man'. Pleasure and purpose in Victorian and Edwardian Cambridge. Ch 3 in J.A. Mangan (2006). A sport-loving society. Victorian and Edwardian middle-class England at play. Routledge.

16. J.A. Mangan (2006). A sport-loving society. Victorian and Edwardian Middle-class England at play. Pages 93 and 94.

17. J.A. Mangan (2006). A sport-loving society. Victorian and Edwardian Middle-class England at play. Page 111.

18. J.A. Mangan (2006). A sport-loving society. Victorian and Edwardian Middle-class England at play. Page 111.

19. J.A. Mangan (2006). A sport-loving society. Victorian and Edwardian Middle-class England at play. Page 111.

20. Cecil Earle Tyndale-Biscoe (1951). Tyndale-Biscoe of Kashmir. An Autobiography. London: Seeley, Service and Co. Ltd. Page 43.

21. J.A. Mangan (1986). The games ethic and imperialism. Page 184.

22. Mill Road Cemetery website http://millroadcemetery.org.uk

23. The Chanticleer (Jesus College magazine) No 13 Michaelmas Term 1889.

24. Amateurism and its interpretation: The social origins of British Sport. Richard Holt Pages 19-31 | Published online: 24 Jan 2012 in Hayes, Win. The Victorian Paradox. Sport for the Wealthy to Sport for the Masses: a Conflict of Class and Ideals In: Paradoxe(s) victorien(s) – Victorian Paradox(es) [online]. Tours: Presses universitaires François-Rabelais, 2005. Pages 141 – 156.

CHAPTER 7
The Cambridge Fairs

People have always had 'an instinctive urge to run, to race, to throw, to dance, and to compete', but for many centuries 'opportunities for leisure were limited by the unremitting demands of survival in a hard world'. Where there were 'communal games these were dependent on set points in the ecclesiastical or agricultural year', some of which invariably coincided with the holding of fairs. Unfortunately most of the written evidence for such play before the sixteenth century comes from 'miscellaneous sources as sermons, court proceedings, ecclesiastical records, a few moral tales, and edicts to control or limit games'[1] which limits any understanding of early play, including in Cambridge.

HISTORY OF THE CAMBRIDGE FAIRS

There were four main medieval fairs associated with Cambridge: Reach (May), Midsummer (June), Garlic (August), and Stourbridge, formerly known as Sturbridge (September), the first two still taking place today. They each had different locations. Reach is a small village 9 miles (14 km) northeast from Cambridge, Midsummer Fair was located on Midsummer Common, Garlic Fair at the Cambridge end of Jesus Close (see map on page 6), and Stourbridge Fair, 1.5 miles (2.5km) east along the River Cam from the centre of Cambridge.

Midsummer Fair was granted by King John in 1211 on the site of a spring:

> Called by the English Bernewelle [Barnwell], the children's springs, because that once a year, on the Eve of St. John the Baptist, boys and lads met there, and amused themselves in the English fashion by wrestling matches and other games, and applauded each other in singing and playing on instruments of music. Hence, by reason of the crowd of boys and girls who met and played there, a custom grew up that on the same day a crowd of buyers and sellers should meet in the same place to do business.[2]

This is the earliest known mention of a sport being played in Cambridge.

'Biggest fair in the world'

Of the four fairs, Stourbridge 'was not only the greatest in the whole nation, but in the world',[3] which is why the historian G.M. Trevelyan claimed the fair, for many centuries, was more famous than the university.[4]

In addition to business taking place at Cambridge's fairs there is evidence that:

> Cock-fighting, bull and bear-baiting were extremely popular displays for a social cross-section of spectators, nowhere better exemplified than in Cambridge where at the animal fairs there would be gathered graduates, undergraduates, college servants and townsfolk.[5]

For example, in 1581 a warrant was issued 'to cease that disordered pastime', of bear-baiting watched by a great congregation of both town and gown. 'A university beadle attempted to disperse the crowd but was deliberately pressed against the bears and beat a hasty retreat, only to learn later that the bearward [bear keeper] had in fact been lawfully licensed by the constable'.[6]

In addition to animal baiting, local fairs and festivals offered a wide range of activities, drinking, eating and much more, expertly portrayed in a painting by Pieter Brueghel the younger, available to view at the Fitzwilliam Museum, Cambridge. Dating from 1632, it is considered 'a panorama of contemporary northern European village life'.[7]

A typical seventeenth century festival

Source: Pieter Brueghel, the younger (1564-1638) 'A village festival.... 1632'.
© The Fitzwilliam Museum, Cambridge.

Vanity Fair and John Bunyan

It is no surprise such behaviour, including probably at Cambridge's Stourbridge Fair, attracted the attention of John Bunyan from nearby Bedford, who referred to Stourbridge Fair as *Vanity Fair* in Pilgrims Progress, first published in 1678. For Bunyan, who 'saw the light whilst playing a game'[8] as a Puritan preacher, Vanity Fair comprised all the worldly activities which distracted from Christian salvation.

Play and sport in England was going through significant changes during this time. Whilst the Restoration of the monarchy in 1660 provided a release from Puritan constraints, which presumably was a great disappointment to Bunyan, 'there were some elements in the controlled life-style of the Commonwealth years (1649 to 1660) which made a continued appeal to law-makers and administrators'.[9] So, whilst 'popular festivals and games had their place again, they were likely to be more hedged in than in the past', such as by the authorities in Cambridge.

CONTROL BY THE TOWN AND UNIVERSITY

In addition to inspecting 'products for sale', both the town and university authorities in the second half of the seventeenth century were briefed 'to be careful to observe whether any unlawful cards or bowls are played, any flesh dressed on a fasting day, or any quarrel or fights takes place'.[10]

It would appear that because of these interventions, the playful elements of Stourbridge Fair, observed by Daniel Defoe in 1722 were restricted to:

> The latter end of the fair … when the great hurry of wholesale business begins to be over (and) the gentry come in from all parts of the county round; and though they come for their diversion, yet it is not a little money they lay out, which generally falls to the share of the retailers, such as toy-shops, goldsmiths, braziers, ironmongers, turners, milliners, mercers, etc., and some loose coins they reserve for the puppet shows, drolls [jesters and entertainers], rope-dancers, and such like, of which there is no want, though not considerable like the rest. The last day of the fair is the horse-fair, where the whole is closed with both horse and foot races, to divert the meaner sort of people only, for nothing considerable is offered of that kind'.[11]

Later, in the nineteenth century travelling fairground booths for prize fighting would also visit Cambridge.[12]

Vanity Fair and William Makepeace Thackeray

William Makepeace Thackeray was born in 1811, coincidently the same year as Frank Fenner. He was admitted to Trinity College in 1826, officially becoming a student there in 1829, leaving a year later. Whilst an energetic walker, horse-rider and fencer, he also enjoyed 'a daily tide of temptations – such as wine parties',[13] and the college ale. He was also addicted to gambling, so much so he lost £1,500 (equivalent to £100,000 today) to professional card-sharpers. One of these sharpers was to be used as the model for his character Deucease, who features in his novel *Vanity Fair*.

Because Thackeray had relatives in Cambridge, with his first cousin Frederick referred to as a 'townsman' in the local press (see chapter 12), it is probable William also visited Stourbridge Fair and used the experience to write *Vanity Fair*, summarised in the book's first paragraph:

> As the manager of the Performance [puppet show] sits before the curtain on the boards and looks into the Fair, a feeling of profound melancholy comes over him in his survey of the bustling place. There is a great quantity of eating and drinking, making love and jilting, laughing and the contrary, smoking, cheating, fighting, dancing and fiddling; there are bullies pushing about, bucks ogling the women, knaves picking pockets, policemen on the look-out, quacks bawling in front of their booths, and yokels looking up at the tinselled dancers and poor old rouged tumblers, while the light-fingered folk are operating upon their pockets behind. Yes, this is VANITY FAIR not a moral place certainly; nor a merry one, though very noisy.[14]

Set in the early nineteenth century, Thackeray's *Vanity Fair* is broadly critical of the new commodity culture, as well as the vain attempts by the rising middle classes to fit into the society of the nobility. Neither does he have a good word to say about the established gentry and aristocracy, who he considered 'idle, game-preserving dilettantes'.[15]

THE COMMODITY CULTURE, NEW MIDDLE CLASSES AND FRANK FENNER

It is not known whether Frank Fenner visited any of the fairs, nor what he thought of them. However, there is no doubt he was a member of the new middle classes, which involved him mixing with 'the higher classes', especially through cricket. In addition, in opening both a cricket ground and a gymnasium where admission was charged (making sport a commodity to be bought), Frank was in danger of facing criticism, given the impact of the *Vanity Fair* novel.

It is likely these factors had an impact on his relationship with Frederick Maurice, who founded the Christian Socialism movement, including the Working Men's College, which Frank was responsible for siting behind his tobacco shop on the Market. Frank was also responsible for opening a gymnasium behind this same shop, where he probably also had contact with Thomas Hughes (chapter 16).

Thomas Hughes and defeating materialism

In addiion to being a great advocate for sport, Thomas Hughes (author of *Tom Brown's Schooldays*) contributed much to the development of the co-operative movement, and trade unionism, driven by a desperate urgency to defeat materialism. He observed 'in the intoxication of this great materialist movement we English have somewhat lost our heads',[16] which would have been at odds with Frank's commitment to making sport in Cambridge a business. It is not known whether they discussed this.

ALL SAINTS PASSAGE

At the end of Bridge Street, at the junction with Jesus Lane, on the opposite side of the road, there is a small 'cut through' called All Saints Passage.

Halfway down All Saint's Passage on the right was the location of Clapham's Coffee House, a destination for wealthier students, and referred to in 'the Lounger', a poem from 1751:[17]

> I rise about nine, get to breakfast by ten
> Blow a tune on my Flute, or perhaps make a Bow;
> Read a play till eleven, or cock my lac'd hat,
> Then step to my Neighb'rs till Dinner to chat.
> Dinner over, to Tom's or to Clapham's I go
> The news of the town so impatient to know;
> …
> From the coffee-house then to Tennis away,
> And at six I post back to my college, to pray:
> I sup before eight, and secure from all duns,
> Undauntedly march to the Mitre or Tuns …

From 1782 Clapham's became the Union Coffee House and was frequented by Robert Barclay (Trinity College), later the long-distance walker, and prize-fighting promoter (chapter 9).

The Dolphin and Thomas Cranmer

Thomas Cranmer was a leader of the English Reformation and Archbishop of Canterbury during the reigns of Henry VIII, Edward VI and, for a short time, Mary I, given the credit for the editorship and overall structure of the 1549 Book of Common Prayer.

Cranmer entered Jesus College aged 14 in 1503, lodging with, and perhaps working for, relatives of his mother who kept the Dolphin Inn, located on All Saints Passage, 'stretching from All Saints churchyard to Bridge Street'.[18]

Subsequently he became of Fellow of Jesus College in 1511, but his appointment was suspended in 1515, when he married Joan, daughter of the proprietor of the Dolphin Inn. Unfortunately, she died within a year of their marriage, which is why he resumed his fellowship.[19][20]

As a child, though Cranmer's father was minded to have his son educated in learning, he still permitted him to 'hunt and hawk, and to ride rough horse'. This is why, when Cranmer later became a Bishop, 'he feared not to ride the roughest horses that came into his stables, which he would do very comely'.

Denounced by the Catholic Queen Mary I for promoting Protestantism, Cranmer was convicted of heresy and in 1556 burned at the stake in Oxford.

[1]   Dennis Brailsford (1997). British Sport: a social history. Cambridge: The Lutterworth Press. Pages 1 and 2.

[2]   Conybeare J W E, A history of Cambridgeshire, London: 1906, p.291 in Dr R.S. Baxter (2019) History of Midsummer Fair.

[3]   Daniel Defoe (1724) Tour Throughout the Whole Island of Great Britain.

[4]   G.M. Trevelyan (1946). English Social History. A survey of six centuries Chaucer to Queen Victoria. Longmans, Green and Co Ltd. Page 186.

[5]   Neil Wigglesworth (1996). The Evolution of English Sport. Frank Cass. Page 15.

[6]   Ref 2: Report in the Cambridge Record Office ms. PB. Vol. 31 in Neil Wigglesworth (1996). The Evolution of English Sport. Frank Cass. Page 15.

[7]   https://fitzmuseum.cam.ac.uk/objects-and-artworks/highlights/1192

[8]   Derek Birley (1993). Sport and the making of Britain. Manchester University Press. Page 91.

[9]   Dennis Brailsford (1997). British Sport. A social history. The Lutterworth Press. Page 43.

[10] Evelyn Lord (2014) The Great Plague: A People's History. Yale University Press.

[11] Daniel Defoe (1722). Tour through the Eastern counties of England.

[12] Cambridge Sports Chronicle 11 Feb 1910 collated online at https://archive.org/stream/CambridgeSPORTSChronicle by www.mikepetty.org.uk

[13] Graham Chainey (1985). A literary history of Cambridge. Cambridge: The Pevensey Press. Page 128.

[14] William Makepeace Thackeray (1985). Vanity Fair. Penguin Classics. Page 33.

[15] Altick, Richard D. (1973). Victorian People and Ideas. London: W. W. Norton & Company.

[16] Edward Norman (1987). The Victorian Christian Socialists. Cambridge University Press. Page 81.

[17] Tripos, Tennis and Tatler: The Pastimes of an Eighteenth-Century Undergraduate. Guest post by the Trinity Hall Library summer intern Kate Foxton on 15 August 2019 at https://www.trinhall.cam.ac.uk/library.

[18] 'The city of Cambridge: Inns', in A History of the County of Cambridge and the Isle of Ely: Volume 3, the City and University of Cambridge, ed. J P C Roach (London, 1959), pp. 115-116. British History Online http://www.british-history.ac.uk/vch/cambs/vol3/pp115-116 [accessed 4 August 2022].

[19] https://www.british-history.ac.uk/vch/cambs/vol3/pp115-116

[20] http://www.cranmerlhg.org.uk/thomascranmer/index.php

[21] James Williams. Hunting, Hawking and the Early Tudor Gentleman. History Today. Volume 53 Issue 8 August 2003.

CHAPTER 8
St John's College

St John's College was founded in 1511 (making it the thirteenth oldest college) following the death of Lady Margaret Beaufort in 1509, mother of King Henry VII. She had begun the process of transforming the ancient hospital of St John the Evangelist (founded circa 1200) into a college for students in the liberal arts and theology. Unique to Cambridge is that seven of the first 16 Colleges were founded by women, compared to none at Oxford.

The Great Gate, or Front Gate was completed in 1516 displaying Lady Margaret Beaufort's coat of arms, and above it a statue of St. John the Evangelist. One of the main tourist attractions in Cambridge is the Bridge of Sighs within St John's College, named after the Bridge of Sighs in Venice.

Great Gate
Painting by Phil Couch.

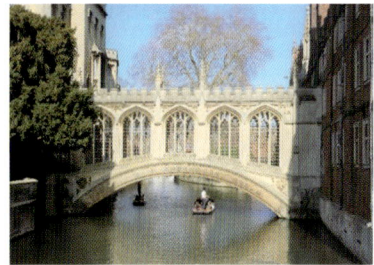

Bridge of Sighs

SPORT BEFORE THE NINETEENTH CENTURY

Olympic Games

During the Plague in the sixteenth century, the Gog Magog Hills were used for the Olympic Games from at least 1574,[1] also complying with restrictions on 'pernicious and unhonest games'[2] being played within five miles of the University. We only know the Games took place until about the 1640s, because they were repeatedly banned, such as in 1580 when the University Vice-Chancellor, Lord North, did so 'on the evidently lawless Gogs'.[3]

St John's College students were involved, such as John Adamson, who attempted to stage an 'Olympic Games' on the Gog Magog Hills in 1619 with 'horseraces, bull bayting, beare bayting, Loggattes, ninehoales, ryflings, dicinge'[4] but were warned off by the town authorities, unnerved by large crowds.

Another student, Symonds d'Ewes, wrote of the planned 'bull bayting' at the Gog Magogs, because a prized bull had arrived in Cambridge[5] (see also the 'two bull rings' in Cambridge, in chapters 5 and 16).

A Queen's College student, Robert Dover, was probably inspired by these Olympics to establish an annual Whitsun sporting competition called the Cotswold Games in Gloucestershire in 1612, featuring horse racing, wrestling, jumping, tumbling, shin-kicking, rural dancing and much feasting and merriment, that continues to this day.[6]

Just over two hundred years later, in 1817, William Mason, having been a student at St John's College, created the Necton Guild in Norfolk. Today the Guild is credited with influencing William Penny Brookes, the creator of the Much Wenlock Olympic Games, in Shropshire (seen as the official birthplace of the British Olympics[7]), which in turn inspired Pierre de Courbertin (founder of the modern Olympics), who visited in 1890.

The Necton Guild was considered the first English athletic club,[8] a claim also made later by the Athletic Clubs at both Oxford and Cambridge universities (chapter 22).

The importance of such sports was identified by Lord John Manners (student at Trinity College from 1838, later MP for Cambridgeshire for over 20 years). Having lamented the 'souring of the national character from the loss of the old 'manly' sports, he proposed to revive the former holy days'[9], calling for rest days for the working classes. The Wenlock Olympic Games was therefore 'perfect to his taste', and because he was considered a 'member of the Young England movement (born on the playing fields of Eton and Cambridge)'[10] that his attendance at the Games was viewed so positively by its organisers.

Early football injury

Many years before the Cambridge Rules of football were created students at Cambridge University celebrated the publication of the *Book of Sports* by James I in 1618, which listed the sports and recreations permitted on Sundays and other holy days. Symonds d'Ewes (student at St John's from 1618), noted in his diary how the publication had been celebrated, as a goad to Puritan Fellows [teaching staff], through indulging in 'floppish recreations', and invading the Fellows' bowling green[11].

To celebrate the first anniversary, they played football, where d'Ewes broke his shin.

Early reference to cricket

Randle Cotgrave (student at St John's from 1586) compiled and published *A Dictionarie of the French and English Tongues* in 1611. It contains the first printed references and definition of the French verb *crosser*, meaning 'to play at cricket', while the entry for the feminine noun 'crosse' refers to 'a Crosier or Bishops staffe; also, a Cricket-staffe; or, the crooked staffe wherewith boyes play at cricket.'[12]

Cheating and gambling in cricket

William Wilberforce, a student at St John's College from 1776, was largely responsible through the Clapham Sect for driving through the abolition of slavery[13] and addressing a wide range of other social problems. Whilst Wilberforce believed 'the people could only innocently recreate themselves on the Sabbath by attending to their religious duties' and that recreation was best 'played' in the privacy of the home,[14] he and other members of the Sect are also credited with changing the increasingly corrupt game of cricket where cheating and gambling were common.[15] As a student at St John's College however, Wilberforce enjoyed cards, gambling and late-night drinking sessions – although he found the excesses of some of his fellow students distasteful. He made many friends, including the more studious future Prime Minister William Pitt the Younger (Pembroke College).[16]

Stag takes refuge in a college doorway

> If we walk along the south side of the Court we may notice on the underside of the lintel of G staircase the words, "Stag, Nov. 15, 1777." It seems that on that date a stag, pursued by the hunt, took refuge in the College, and on this staircase; the members of the College had just finished dinner when the stag and his pursuers entered.[17]

It is not known whether the stag survived.

At this time 'deer hunting had almost disappeared with the destruction of forests, enclosure of wastes, and the encroachment of arable farming',[18] but obviously not yet outside the back of St John's College.

LINKS TO THE TOWN AND FRANK FENNER

It would appear St John's College had a relatively good relationship with the Town over the nineteenth century not just in terms of sports, but attitude too, if Arthur John Story's advice, published in 1893 in the 'The Fresher's Don't',[19] was taken up by his fellow students:

> Don't let your residence in Cambridge cause you to assume superiority over others less fortunate. The object of a University career is to improve the mind by study and social intercourse, so that the former School-boy may be fitted for an honourable and useful career, for the good of his country and the benefit of those with whom he may come in contact in after life......Don't walk the streets as if you were the proprietor of the Town....

Cricket

Cambridge Town and County Cricket Club was one of the most successful cricket teams in the country in the mid nineteenth century, when Frank Fenner was largely responsible for bringing Town and Gown together to play in the same team. Arthur Malortie Hoare, both a student and Fellow at St John's, was a player and committee member of the Town club from 1845 to 1847. Other students were John Morky Lee and Arthur Robert Ward – later the local vicar of St Clement's Church. However, as we saw in chapter 5, Arthur Ward, when Treasurer and President of the University Cricket Club from 1873 to 1884, clearly had a strained relationship with Fenner.

Israel Haggis – manager of the St John's Cricket Club tent

Israel Haggis was a talented town cricketer who played with Frank Fenner, including for England in 1841, and in a single wicket competition at Lord's Cricket Ground in 1838.

However, as with most professional cricketers living in Cambridge in the middle of the nineteenth century, they were unable to make a living from playing cricket alone, which is why Israel Haggis found employment as manager of St John's College Cricket Club tent.

Unfortunately, in 1845, six cricket bats, stumps and a ball were stolen from the St John's Cricket Club tent on Parker's Piece, of which Haggis had supervision. The defendant, George Johnson, though seen offering the stolen bats for sale, was acquitted on the grounds of his tender age of eight.[20]

St John's College servants

It became increasingly commonplace in the second half of the nineteenth century for men who worked in domestic service at the Cambridge colleges to enjoy a variety of sports, including rowing and cricket. Whilst partly subsidised by the colleges they were primarily self-organised.

The local press of September 1857[21] reported on the cricket match between St John's College Gentlemen versus Servants considered 'the first that ever was played … on Fenner's beautiful ground … and there was a goodly attendance of spectators, among whom were several Fellows of the College, who seemed highly pleased with the sport'. The press report added:

> It was an excellent display of cricket on both sides, but the more frequent practice of the gentlemen with the bat gave them a decided advantage. In the course of the day, a good substantial dinner was served in the Pavilion, to which all sat down and partook of with a zest that cricket only can give.

Racquets

Whilst Real Tennis had been played in Cambridge since at least 1574, it was not until 1858 that both an indoor and outdoor racquets court[a] and a dressing room were erected on the Backs of St John's College.

Indoor and outdoor racquets courts at St John's College 1858
Archive reference: SJCA/D33/1/27/15 by permission of the Master and Fellows of St John's College, Cambridge.

Harry Gray was a talented racquets player and later world champion, which is why he was appointed 'court keeper' in 1858, a position he held until 1883. This was on the back of having recently launched his racquet coaching and equipment business, HJ Gray & Sons in 1855. In addition, Harry had also been the professional coach using facilities first at the University Arms from 1847, and at Wellington Court (near the current Fire Station on Parker's Piece) from 1857.

Harry paid St John's College annual court expenses of £95, initially making 15 shillings a week, by charging 2/6 an hour, and 18/- for a gross (144) of balls. The racquets court annual income reached its peak of £427 in 1864[22] (worth nearly £57,000 today). Read more on Harry Gray and his sporting business in chapter 20.

---

[a] Racquets is similar to modern-day squash.

Boxing / fisticuffs

There is a legend from the first half of the nineteenth century that:

> A Dean of the College [a senior staff role with administrative and managerial responsibilities] once invited the well-known pugilist, Peter Crawley (heavyweight boxing champion of England in 1827), to breakfast at his rooms under the impression that he was a member of the University. Peter, who had been invited to Cambridge by some sporting undergraduates, had on the previous evening, arrayed in cap and gown, rescued the Dean from a nasty melee in the 'Town and Gown' row, and the grateful Dean, struck with admiration at the young man's fistic prowess asked him his name and college. Peter had been duly coached, and promptly replied 'Smith, of Magdalen.' 'You are a very fine, powerful young man,' said the Dean; 'and your skill in boxing is extraordinary. I shall like to know how you acquired such proficiency, and shall feel gratified if you will give me the pleasure of your company at breakfast tomorrow.' But when the morning came Peter was safely back in his own crib, 'The Queen's Head and French Horn' in Smithfield, and the Dean was left to ponder on the deplorable fact that such efficiency in pugilism should be accompanied by such deficiency in manners.[23]

Joseph McCormick, a student at St John's from 1853, was at the time considered such a good boxer he 'could hold his own with the scientific Langham and other leading professionals'.[24] Nat Langham was based at the nearby Ram Inn (chapter 5) where he had established himself as a boxing coach in 1852.

McCormick was also a rowing and cricket Blue, claiming that while playing cricket on Parker's Piece, to have hit a fast bowler to leg and run nine runs for it. This was in the days before boundaries were introduced.

ENGLAND'S SPORTING REVOLUTION

William Wordsworth and manliness

Although William Wordsworth appears to have been a sceptical participant in sporting activities when at St John's College from 1787,

> We sauntered, played, or rioted; we talked
> Unprofitable talk at morning hours;
> Drifted about along the streets and walks,

> Read lazily in trivial books, went forth
> To gallop through the country in blind zeal
> Of senseless horsemanship, or on the breast
> Of Cam sailed boisterously ...[25]

he perhaps started to value them differently when a year before he graduated, he walked 2,000 miles as a 'great adventurer' on a tour through France, northern Italy, Switzerland and Germany,[26] and about ten years later when walking the countryside in north Somerset and the Lake District with his sister Dorothy, and Samuel Taylor Coleridge.

This coincided with them jointly publishing their poems, inspiring the English Romantic movement. The second edition of *Lyrical Ballads*, published in 1800, begins with Wordsworth discussing what he sees as the elements of a new type of poetry, one based on the 'real language of men'.[27]

William Wordsworth: indirect impact on sport gaining wider acceptance

Thanks to Division of Rare and Manuscript Collections, Cornell University Library.

This had a major impact on raising the profile of manliness in society, picked up especially by Frederick Maurice (chapters 9 and 16) and Charles Kingsley, who established the link with sport through their development of Muscular Christianity (chapter 3).

Wordsworth believed in his autobiographical poem *The Prelude*, that some experiences in his childhood, he called 'spots of time ... took an extraordinary turn, leading unexpectedly to powerful feelings of fear and joy', that had a continuing influence on him, resulting in his mind being 'nourished and invisibly repaired'. One such experience he wrote about (see chapter 21) was skating on Windermere (a lake in the Lake District, close to where he was born and spent his childhood).[28]

Derwent Coleridge and the value of exercise

Whilst his father Samuel Taylor Coleridge had been a student at Jesus College, Derwent Coleridge attended St John's College starting in 1820. Soon after being ordained in 1826, he was appointed master of the grammar school at Helston, Cornwall where one of his pupils was Charles Kingsley.

Later Derwent became the first Principal of a teacher college in Chelsea from 1841 to 1864, which included him promoting the value of active sport, 'with advantage both to the mental and bodily health of the pupils. It is important not merely to keep up the elasticity of youthful feeling, but to encourage a certain spirit and animation.'[29]

Origin of the Oxford v Cambridge Boat Race

The Oxford v Cambridge Boat Race is the result of two friends, Charles Wordsworth (a student at Oxford and the nephew of the poet William Wordsworth) meeting with Charles Merivale of St John's College during the holidays in Cambridge, to set up a rowing challenge between the two universities. The first Boat Race took place on 10 June 1829 at Henley on Thames, with Oxford winning this race easily.

Rules of football

Over the 25 years that Cambridge University students grappled with writing an agreed set of football rules from 1837 to 1863, John Charles Thring, a student at St John's College from 1843 to 1848, may be considered the most important. In addition to being one of the 34 students credited with producing these 'Cambridge Rules' (see chapter 20), Thring went on to modify them again in 1862, when a teacher at Uppingham School, by publishing *The Winter Game: Rules of Football*. Two versions (dated 1862 and 1863) are currently held in the Cambridge University Library.

John Charles Thring: rules of Association Football

Thanks to Uppingham School Archives

In the Preface, Thring writes 'I can only hope that whichever set of rules becomes most popular, football may become the Englishman's National Winter Game, and if so, I shall be proud of giving a helping hand to this good end.'[30] He is also credited with coining the phrase 'football is a simple game', still used by many club managers, players and commentators today.

Football and Frank Fenner

It is not known whether Frank Fenner had any interaction with the students creating these rules of football, but as football and cricket were both played on Parker's Piece, and Fenner created Fenner's Cricket Ground in 1848, Thring's last year in Cambridge as a student, then it is possible.

University athletics

According to the Cambridge University Athletics Club[31] the driving force for creating the club was probably John Russell Jackson of St. John's (student from 1853 to 1857) given he 'induced athletes from the various Colleges to gather on Fenner's ground, to try their speed at various competitions'. These were initially within-college affairs, but Jackson soon realised that inter-college competitions would draw better competition. He was then responsible for initiating the first 'University foot races' (as they were called), held on 16, 17 and 18 March 1857 at Fenner's Ground.

Anthony Wilkinson (St. John's 1854–59) was also involved in the planning, as was Robert Barclay (Trinity 1855–59).

Protecting the amateur rugby game against professionalism

Rev Francis Marshall (student at St John's College from 1864) was a British schoolmaster, cleric and rugby administrator who was so fierce an advocate of amateurism in the early years of rugby football that it contributed to the schism in the game, and the birth of the breakaway Rugby League. He was opposed to the introduction of 'broken-time payments', made by clubs in northern England to compensate working men for wages lost while playing matches, even banning his own club Huddersfield in 1893, for breaching the amateur code.

An 1895 cartoon, entitled 'The Rugby Rumpus', shows Marshall (in a clerical collar) speaking to James Miller (a long time opponent of Marshall):

> *'Oh, fie, go away naughty boy, I don't play with boys who can't afford to take a holiday for football any day they like!'*
>
> Miller: *'Yes, that's just you to a T; you'd make it so that no lad whose father wasn't a millionaire could play at all in a really good team. For my part I see no reason why the men who make the money shouldn't have a share in the spending of it.'*[32]

[1] Heywood, James; Wright, Thomas (1854). Cambridge University transactions during the Puritan controversies of the 16th and 17th centuries, Volume 1. H. G. Bohn. p. 160.

[2] Joseph Tanner (ed) (1917). The historical register of the University of Cambridge, being a supplement to the Calendar with a record of University offices, honours and distinctions to the year 1910. Cambridge University Press. Page 200.

[3] Peter Linehan (ed) (2011). St John's College Cambridge: A history. The Boydell Press. Pages 133 - 134.

[4] Peter Linehan (ed) (2011). St John's College Cambridge: A history. The Boydell Press. Pages 133 - 134.

[5] From page 356 in Annals of Cambridge by Cooper, Charles Henry, 1808-1866; Cooper, John William, 1845-1906. (Publication date 1908) under 'Additions and Corrections' Vol. III. p. 135, insert after 1. 35 in addition to a reference from D'Ewes's College Life, 109, 110.

[6] Birley, Derek (1993). Sport and the making of Britain. Manchester University Press. Page 81.

[7] Beale, Catherine (2011). Born out of Wenlock. William Penny Brookes and the British origins of the modern Olympics. DB Publishing.

8   Montague Shearman (2005). Athletics and Football. The History Of Athletic Sports In England. Part 7 online at https://chestofbooks.com/sports/athletics/Football/The-History-Of-Athletic-Sports-In-England-Part-7.html

9   Brailsford, Dennis (1991). Sport, Time and Society. The British at play. Routledge. Page 12.

10   Beale, Catherine Beale. Born out of Wenlock. William Penny Brookes and the British origins of the modern Olympics. DB Publishing. Page 27.

11   Birley, Derek (1993). Sport and the making of Britain. Pages 80-81.

12   The Yorker. Journal of the Melbourne Cricket Club Library Issue 43, Summer 2010 / 2011.

13   Cambridge University are embarking on an inquiry, reporting in 2021, to 'uncover how the institution might have gained from slavery and the exploitation of labour' and recommend how the University might acknowledge any involvement. Times 30/4/19.

14   Robert W. Malcolmson (1973). Popular recreations in English society. Page 105 and 156.

15   Derek Birley (1999). A social history of English cricket. Aurum. Page 63.

16   Therlee Gipson (2019). Anglo-Saxon Liberated Blacks. Page 39.

17   Robert Forsyth Scott (1907) St John's College, Cambridge.

18   Derek Birley (1993). Sport and the making of Britain. Manchester University Press. Page 130.

19   Exhilaration and anxiety: The Dos and don'ts of fresher life – Victorian style. St John's College website https://www.joh.cam.ac.uk/exhilaration-and-anxiety-dos-and-don%E2%80%99ts-fresher-life-%E2%80%93-victorian-style

20   Willie Sugg (2009). Fenner's Men. Cambridgeshire Cricket 1822 - 1848. Part Three of A Tradition Unshared. Real Work Publishing. Page 36.

21   Cambridge Independent Press 05 September 1857.

22   Richard Gray (2019). Grays of Cambridge – a short history. Email communication 27 Dec 2019.

23   Famous Fights past and present. 1901 Vol I. No 2. Page 15.

24   Sport, ancient and modern: Boxing. Pages 292-295. A History of the County of Middlesex: Volume 2, General; Ashford, East Bedfont With Hatton, Feltham, Hampton With Hampton Wick, Hanworth, Laleham, Littleton. Originally published by Victoria County History, London, 1911.

25   https://rhollick.wordpress.com/2020/04/08/wordsworths-in-cambridge/

26   William Wordsworth (1790). Excerpt from Wordsworth's earliest surviving letter - to his sister Dorothy (6 and 16 September). Wordsworth Grasmere Museum (Aug 2022).

27   Malcolm Tozer (2015). The ideal of manliness. The legacy of Thring's Uppingham. Sunnyrest Books. Pages 7, 8, 47 and 48.

28   William Wordsworth (1850) The Prelude - Growth of a Poet's Mind. Poster display headed 'There are in our existence spots of time' at Wordsworth Grasmere Museum (Aug 2022).

29   J.A. Mangan and Colm Hickey (2015). Soccer's Missing Men. Schoolteachers and the spread of Association Football. Routledge. Page 14.

30   J.C. Thring (1863 – 2nd edition). The winter game: rules of football, by J.C.T. to which are added the rules of the Cambridge University Committee and London Association. London: Hamilton, Adams and Co.

31   C.J.R. Thorne (February 2018). Cambridge University Athletic Club. 160th Anniversary Games. https://www.cuac.org.uk/history

32   Collins, Tony (2006). Rugby's Great Split: Class, Culture and the Origins of Rugby League Football. Routledge.

CHAPTER 9

Trinity College

Trinity College was founded in 1546 by Henry VIII who, persuaded by his sixth wife Catherine Parr, ordered two existing Cambridge colleges (Michaelhouse and King's Hall) and seven hostels to amalgamate under a new name, Trinity College. It is the fourteenth oldest college in the University.

King's Hall had been established by Edward II in 1317 and re-founded by Edward III in 1337. This is why Trinity's flag has as its design the royal standard of Edward III, and beneath the statue of Henry VIII on the Great Gate (pictured) are Edward III's coat of arms, and those of his five sons including William of Hatfield, whose shield is blank, as he died as an infant.

Great Gate
Painting by Phil Couch.

Above all the other colleges, Trinity has probably contributed more great sporting rule-makers, administrators, players and 'thinkers', than any other. It is believed a number had direct contact with Frank Fenner.

SPORT BEFORE THE NINETEENTH CENTURY

Football

When Henry VIII founded Trinity College in 1546, he was already the owner of a pair of football boots made for him in 1525, costing 4 shillings.[1] Although there is no evidence Henry VIII's love of football and sport had any direct impact on the life of the college, it is well known that the 'forceful assertion of his own preferences was a major factor in the emergence of a peculiarly English, as distinct from European, idea of sport'.[2]

Soon after Trinity College was founded, in 1593, Henry Peacham was a student there. In 1612 he wrote and illustrated a poem on 'footeball' in *Minerva Brittana* which combined pictures and verse on matters of morality and manners. Peacham's theme was that life was like football, that our worldly wealth 'is tossed too and fro', and in the game of life there are winners and losers.

For whatever reason Peacham modified his attitudes ten years later.

In 1622, he published *The Compleat Gentleman* in which he referred to football and other sports played by the 'common people', including poor

81   *Divitiæ*.

T HE country Swaines, at footeball heere are seene,
      Which each gapes after, for to get a blow,
The while some one, away runnes with it cleane,
It meetes another, at the goale below
      Who never stirrd, one catcheth heere a fall,
      And there one's maimd, who never saw the ball.

This worldly wealth, * is tossed too and fro,
At which like Brutes, each striues with might and maine,
To get a kick, by others overthrow,
Heere one's fetch't vp, and there another slaine,
      With eager haft, and then it doth affront
      Some stander by, who never thought vpon't.

* Caduca hæc fragilia, puerili- busque consenta- nea crepundiis, quæ vires atque opes humanæ vo- cantur: Valerius lib 6. cap vltimo.

Arbiter

Henry Peacham's 1612 poem on 'footeball'
By permission of the Warden and Scholars of Winchester College.

scholars, to be the object of derision. Conversely noble sports such as hunting and tennis were considered only suitable for noble people and 'that such gentlemanly amusements were not suited to the lower orders and might indeed be damaging to their moral fibre'.[3]

Football games between the Cambridge colleges

It is possible that Peacham was made aware of two games of football that took place between 1618 and 1620 between Trinity, his old college, and their neighbours, St John's, as recorded in Symonds D'Ewes diary.[4]

On the first occasion, played on Trinity Green (very close to the existing Wren Library), Trinity did not show up, so St John's played their own game resulting in D'Ewes 'returning to his chamber with a broken shin'. A few days later St John's returned for another game, and again, 'the Trinitician faction showed the white feather. Upon this the Johnians grew insolent; and as they returned to their College, some of the lustiest of them … showed their anger on being thus continually deluded, set upon the back gates of Trinity, and brake them open, and with long poles drove into the college all they found in the walks, offering some violence.'

Early rules of football

Francis Willughby (student from 1652) was an ornithologist as well as a student of linguistics and games. His *Book of Games*, written in about 1660, 'is a unique and outstandingly rich source of information on an important domain of human activity, with very little in the way of close parallels elsewhere in the medieval or early modern tradition'.[5]

He describes football (including diagrams) as taking place in a cleared field, 'a close that has a gate at either end. The gates are called goals'. The ball is well described: 'They blow a strong bladder and tie the neck of it as fast as they can, and then put it into the skin of a bull's cod [bull's scrotal sack] and sew it fast in'. He adds: 'The harder the ball is blown, the better it flies. They used to put quicksilver [mercury] into it sometimes to keep it from lying still.'

There are some important rules too. It was not lawful to simply kick another player in the shins: 'they must not strike higher than the ball'. Another rule, still in use in Australian Rules, Gaelic Football and Rugby Union today, relates to the calling of a 'mark' when a player catches the ball 'on the full', that is, without it bouncing first. After calling a mark he may not be tackled, and he marks the ground with his heel and may take a free kick from that point.[6]

Leaving dinner early to play football

From 1700 to 1738 the Master of Trinity College was Richard Bentley, who had been a student at St John's College. Unfortunately, Bentley was in constant disagreement with the Fellows of Trinity College, one of their many grievances relating to Bentley allowing the undergraduates to leave dinner before Grace 'to run home to their studies, others to try a fair fall upon the grass, and others a match at Football or Cricket'.[7]

Cricket

Early players and rules

The financial accounts for 1299–1300 for Prince Edward, afterwards Edward II, disclosed that £6 was paid out for the fifteen-year-old prince to play at *creag*[8] which may be an early version of cricket. It is more certain that cricket's ancestor is probably *pila baculorea*, translated as 'club-ball', which Edward III banned in 1369 as detrimental to the war efforts during the Hundred Years War.[9]

The first recorded rules of the game were created by two Cambridge graduates (Mr Alan Brodrick (Clare College) and Charles Lennox (College unknown)) in 1727 as much to pre-empt any gambling disagreements as anything. Improvements to these rules were made in 1774 when the Rev Charles Powlett (finishing at Trinity College in 1755), one of the early patrons of the Hambledon (Cricket) Club in Hampshire was a member of the select committee of noblemen and gentlemen that formulated the revised laws of cricket at the Star and Garter Club, London.[10] These included a special section relating to bets. The responsibility for formulating the laws was later taken up by the MCC, created in 1787.

Powlett had been curate of a parish near the Hambledon Club for nearly 30 years when it grew into the foremost club in England. He was not above gambling on the outcome of matches or of betting against his own team. He was joined at the Club by Philip Delany (another Trinity College graduate), who was also on the select committee revising the rules in 1774.

Cricket and gambling

Gambling exploded in eighteenth century England, according to Mike Atherton (Downing College – and later England cricket captain in the 1990s) 'when the casual disposal of wealth almost became a badge of virility in the aristocracy, (sometimes) reaching levels of absurdity'.[11]

Perhaps the best example was Lord Frederick Beauclerk, a descendant of Charles II and Nell Gwynn, who, having left Trinity College in 1790 to join the Church of England, proceeded to dominate the game of cricket. He was not only considered to be the first gentleman player to be as good as the leading professionals, but augmented his curate's salary of £60 / year by making 600 Guineas (or £630) per year from cricket, including betting, 'in a period when gambling on matches was rife and match fixing not unknown'. Later he was to become the second President of the MCC and a leading advocate for changes to the laws of the game.[12]

Beauclerk attracted a lot of criticism, which coincided with the changes occurring across society, brought about by the Clapham Sect and the Methodists, who in addition to being largely responsible for the abolition of slavery, addressed child abuse, poverty, illiteracy, and other social challenges such as blood sports, duelling and gambling.[13]

Wrestling and boxing

Isaac Newton started as a student at Trinity College in 1661, remaining mostly in Cambridge for the next 35 years. Throughout his life, he was not a great advocate of play and sports, including not being able to abide hunting. Whilst he purchased 'a chess board and Chesse Men' and played backgammon with Flamsteed, the astronomer, his secretary said

> 'I never knew him to take any recreation or pastime, either in riding out to take the air, walking, bowling, or any other exercise whatever, thinking all hours lost that were not spent in his studies.'[14]

However, he is curiously referred to by Sir Thomas Parkyns (student at Trinity College from 1680) who wrote *The Inn-Play or Cornish-Hugg Wrestler*, where he acknowledges his tutor, and:

> The Use and Application of the Mathematicks here in Wrestling, I owe to Sir Isaac Newton, Mathematicks Proffessor of Trinity College in Cambridge, who seeing my Inclination that Way, invited me to his public Lectures, for which I thank him.[15]

The wrestling Parkyns was being so scientific about in this book involved headbutting, punching, eye-gouging, chokes, and hard throws, that later evolved into prize-fighting, then boxing.

Four of the greatest advocates for boxing

Over many centuries, the University restricted any activity that might cause a distraction to studying, which is why there is very little official evidence of the boxing experiences of the following four students from Trinity College. It is likely they did box as undergraduates, given they then went on to have a significant impact on the sport.

Despite the efforts of the University, boxing, horse racing and cricket shared the distinction in the late eighteenth and early nineteenth centuries of being the first three sports to 'entice mass popularity in Britain'. In addition, because these sports were characterised by an 'amalgamation of nobility and peasantry', something that Frank Fenner later achieved with the Cambridge Town cricket club, there is a possibility he might have been aware, when a young man, of the boxing exploits of Robert Barclay, Lord Althorp and Lord Byron.

The fourth advocate was John Graham Chambers responsible for creating much safer rules for boxing – see under 'England's sporting revolution' later in the chapter.

Robert Barclay

Robert Barclay packed in a lot of sport for the year and a half he was a student at Trinity College from 1798. With his friends he went fishing, shooting, hunting with staghounds and kept fighting cocks. With Newmarket nearby, horse-racing, and the betting associated with it, had a considerable hold over students even though the university authorities strongly disapproved. Barclay also played cricket, 'battledore and shuttlecock' [forerunner to badminton], swum, and participated in a range of what today we would consider children's games such as tag, leapfrog and swinging on ropes.[17]

Whist in Cambridge he also learned to spar with boxing gloves.[18]

After leaving Cambridge, he became the most famous athlete of his age, through making a fortune walking 1,000 miles, in 1,000 hours, then becoming one of boxing's most famous trainers where he used his 'system of manly corporeal exercises' to make the next generation 'robust', 'hardy' with a 'martial spirit'.[19] Whilst not new, Barclay brought this system of training to prominence, with its focus on 'regular sweating, daily exercise, minimal sleep and a simple, nutritious diet',[20] considered 'the first ever text to resemble sports science'.[21]

John Charles Spencer

John Charles Spencer, later Lord Althorp, was a student at Trinity College from 1800, where a great deal of his time and even more money was spent in hunting and racing. He did however figure more than creditably in his college examinations.

He had a career as a British statesman including as Chancellor of the Exchequer, but his real passion was for country life, and sport including prizefighting. G. M. Trevelyan, the historian, wrote:

> The prize-ring in its 'most high and palmy state' was thus described by that soul of chivalry and honour, Lord Althorp, speaking in his old age to a friend: 'He said his conviction of the advantages of boxing was so strong that he had been seriously considering whether it was not a duty he owed to the public to go and attend every prize-fight which took place. In his opinion, cases of stabbing arose from the manly habits of boxing having been discouraged.[22]

Lord Althorp also described having dinner together with Lord Byron the night before a big fight, referring to 'the men stripping, the intense excitement, the sparring: then the first round, the attitude of the men - it was really worthy of Homer'.[23]

Lord Byron

George Gordon, later Lord Byron, was a student for three years from 1805 to 1807 at Trinity College where he engaged in cricket, horse riding, gambling and keeping a pet bear in college, probably obtained from Stourbridge Fair.[24] He was also a very keen swimmer, having a part of the River Cam named after him (chapter 4).

In addition, whilst noblemen were unfit for bare knuckle prize-fighting, sparring was highly regarded, with Lord Byron keeping a diary of his sparring exploits and opponents, mostly supervised by Gentleman Jackson. Jackson had won the English boxing championship in 1795, on the back of which he opened a boxing academy for gentlemen on Bond Street, London.[25]

Entries in Byron's diary included, on 17 March 1814:

> I have been sparring with Jackson for exercise this morning … At any rate, exercise is good, and this is the severest of all; fencing and the broad-sword never fatigued me half so much…

A few weeks later, on 10 April 1814 he wrote:

> The more violent the fatigue, the better my spirits for the rest of the day; and then, my evenings have that calm nothingness of languor, which I most delight in. Today I have boxed an hour – written an ode to Napoleon – copied it – eaten six biscuits – drunk four bottles of soda water – redde away the rest of my time.

His enthusiasm for boxing at this time included finishing off a three-year project decorating a 6-foot-high folding screen with pictures and cuttings of boxers.[26]

Several years after his death, Pierce Egan, the foremost sportswriter of the period, believed Byron had consistently:

> Mixed with society in all its different shades' … and 'his Lordship, like his poetry, always entered into the spirit of the thing; – he viewed boxing as a national propensity – a stimulus to true courage.[27]

Whilst Robert Barclay, Lord Spencer and Lord Byron all contributed towards boxing becoming more widely acceptable, it was still banned by the University authorities, so that by the middle of the nineteenth century, one anonymous Trinity College student was limited to visiting the Ram Inn (chapter 5) to be coached by Nat Langham, the celebrated Champion of the Middleweights.

LINKS TO THE TOWN, AND FRANK FENNER

Town's welcome to two non-British sportsmen

Deerfoot was a Seneca Native American runner, who in December 1861 ran at Fenner's Ground in front of between five and eight thousand spectators, including the Prince of Wales – then a student at Trinity College. The two were introduced by Frank Fenner who reported they 'affably chatted' and shook hands (chapter 22).[28]

Frank had visited America to invite Deerfoot to England, which on his arrival 'excited much comment' including 'philosophic dissertations as to whether the savage man is not physically superior to the man in the civilised state'.[29] His attendance at dinner at Trinity College, in the presence of the Prince of Wales, was considered a 'monstrous and absurd offence against all the laws of decency and good taste'.[30]

The furore prompted the Rev William Beaumont, a Fellow at Trinity College, to write a letter to the press to explain why he had invited Deerfoot to dinner.[31] First, Deerfoot was 'a religious man ... who [had recently attended] church ... at King's College'; second, 'he [was] a stranger in a foreign land'; third, he had 'attained considerable distinction ... worthy of commendation'; and fourth, 'we should often do better if we associated more with a person of a different rank in life whose character is good, and less with those of the same rank, whose character is notoriously bad'.

The contrast between the college and Frank Fenner's welcome to Deerfoot could not be starker.

***

Kumar Shri Ranjitsinhji, or 'Ranji', as he was popularly known, was a student at Trinity College from 1889. He was considered 'the first non-white sportsman ever to win international renown'[32]. It was not just that he played cricket for England, but that he did so with a batting

Ranjitsinhji: first non-white sportsman ever to win international renown

Source: K.S. Ranjitsinhji (1897 - 4th ed). The Jubilee Book of Cricket. William Blackwood and Sons. Page 207.

style that was so unorthodox that it revolutionised the game; he was called the 'the *Midsummer Night's Dream* of cricket'.³³ Some credit for this is due to Daniel Martin Hayward, a member of the famous Hayward dynasty of local cricketers (chapter 20), also the professional coach at Corpus Christi College. Early on in his playing career Ranji had a fault, where he moved out of the line of a fast ball, which was corrected by Daniel nailing his boot to the ground during practice. This stratagem was probably the reason why Ranji was able to develop his most iconic shot, the leg glance, 'a stroke of his own invention [that] was to cause a revolution in the way [cricket] was played'.³⁴

It was not just his unorthodox batting that made it difficult for Ranji to be selected to play for Cambridge University, but almost certainly, his race.

While he was waiting, through playing local cricket on Parker's Piece, Ranji gained a huge following around Cambridge. It was only later, in the winter of 1892–1893 when Francis Stanley Jackson (Trinity College student from 1889) was touring India with Lord Hawke's party of amateur cricketers, that gave him a new-found respect for the cricketers of the Indian subcontinent. This led to Jackson picking Ranji for the first match of the new University season.³⁵

Quickly Ranji made his mark, gaining recognition by the national cricketing press, and a local farmer:

> For the match between the Cantabs [Cambridge University] and the Australians at Fenner's in 1893 … his play was something of a revelation. He scored 58 and 37 not out, by batting, which for ease and grace I had seldom seen approached on Fenner's. Even then, that beautiful leg-stroke of his was fully developed, and he employed it with great effect. An old farmer from the Fens, out Ely way, sat next to me open-mouthed for a time; but one of Ranji's 'glances' at last elicited from him this remark: 'Whoy, he only tooch it and it go to th' boundary!'³⁶

In addition to impressing local spectators, Ranji also had a very close relationship with Mary Holmes, whose parents owned a grocery store on Sidney Street. This is evident from 37 letters he wrote to Mary, now in the Wren Library, Trinity College.

Ranjitsinhji with Mary Holmes and her family - circa 1890s
Used with permission and thanks to the granddaughter of Mary Holmes.

Whilst not linked to Ranji's relationship with the town, he nevertheless also played a part in creating one of England's best sporting schools.

Ranji and the founding of Millfield School

Having been a student at Pembroke College from 1923, including winning his Blue for cricket, Jack Meyer – later the founder of Britain's best known specialist sports school - then went to India as a cotton broker; this included playing for All India against the MCC in 1926, when he was thanked by Ranji for his services to Indian cricket.[37]

On returning to England in 1929, Jack again met Ranji, who became Jack's mentor and encouraged him to go into education, rather than remain in the cotton industry. This resulted, on 6 June 1935 with Millfield School being established, based in Street, Somerset. It had a mix of pupils including a range of Indian princes, one of whom later wrote:

> It is an intriguing reflection that Millfield initiated, under royal auspices, as a school for Indians later opened its doors to (British) natives and come-who-may to become the first cosmopolitan school in the West[38]

'Boss' (as Jack Meyer was known) ran Millfield School with a 'Robin Hood philosophy', where 'global plutocrats' subsidised the less privileged[39]. This included children talented at sport, which is why the school developed into one of the best sports schools in the country, and still is today.

The first two secretaries of the MCC – and Frank Fenner

Robert Allan Fitzgerald was a student at Trinity College from 1853, later appointed in 1863 at the age of 29 as the MCC's first Secretary, a post he held for 13 years. Fitzgerald had won his University Cricket Blue in 1854 and 1856 so would have played on Fenner's Ground, where invariably he must have met Frank Fenner. Presumably Fitzgerald would also have known of Frank's efforts to establish both a Cambridgeshire County Cricket Club in 1858, and one in Gloucestershire in 1863 (chapter 23) when Fitzgerald was managing cricket across the country in his new role as MCC's Secretary.

Fitzgerald was succeeded by Henry Perkins, another past student from Trinity College, who served as MCC Secretary from 1876 to 1898.

Henry Perkins, founder of Cambridgeshire County Cricket Club with Frank Fenner in 1858

Image from The Cricket Field 6 May 1893, used with permission from Willie Sugg.

Perkins, born in Sawston (7 miles (11 km) south of Cambridge), played cricket for Cambridge Town, and the University (from 1850 to 1854), and together with Frank Fenner endeavoured to establish a Cambridgeshire County Cricket Club in 1858.[40]

John Walker and cricket as social unifier

There were seven Walker brothers who had been students at Trinity College, with at least two of them largely responsible for later launching Middlesex County Cricket Club in 1864.

John Walker developed a reputation as a well-known benefactor of cricketers fallen on hard times. As Captain of Cambridge University in 1848 he may well have benefited from being coached by William Buttress. Buttress was a local professional cricketer known as 'the father of break (spin) bowling' which is why, when he was in dire poverty and distress and near the end of his life, John came to his aid in 1866.[41]

Additionally, there were at least three Trinity College students who played for Cambridge Town cricket club in the middle of the nineteenth century – Henry Perkins (later MCC Secretary), Frederick Ponsonby (who also founded 'The Old Stagers', amateur dramatic society – see chapter 5) and Oliver Claude Pell. This mix of Town and Gown was not only recognised in Felix's unique painting (see chapter 20), but more generally, by the historian, G.M. Trevelyan (student, fellow and Master of Trinity College for a combined total of 30 years from the late nineteenth Century) who wrote 'if the French noblesse had been capable of playing cricket with their peasants, their chateaux would never have been burnt'.[42]

ENGLAND'S SPORTING REVOLUTION

This section is split into those students from Trinity College who had impacts as rule makers and organisers, players and 'thinkers'.

Rule makers and organisers

The governing body of world football, FIFA, report that Cambridge is 'the birthplace of the laws of football',[43] with Trinity College taking most of the credit, given 22 of the 34 framers of the laws, drafted and re-drafted from 1837 to 1863, were students there. These include Henry de Winton (student at Trinity from 1842), who with John Charles Thring (St John's College), created a version of the rules in 1846, forged on Parker's Piece. Unfortunately, no written versions of these rules exist, but bringing students from different public schools (and their own versions of the rules) together, to establish a compromise set called the 'Cambridge Rules', was a success soon built on by others.

For example, in 1848, Henry James Malden wrote about a further set of rules being drafted by 14 Trinity College students in room F7 New Court:

> We met in my rooms … at 4pm, anticipating a long meeting. I cleared the tables and provided pens, ink and paper. Several asked me on coming in whether an exam was on! … Our progress in framing new rules was slow … We broke up five minutes before midnight. The new rules were printed as the 'Cambridge Rules', copies were distributed and pasted up on the Parker's Piece, and very satisfactorily they worked.[44]

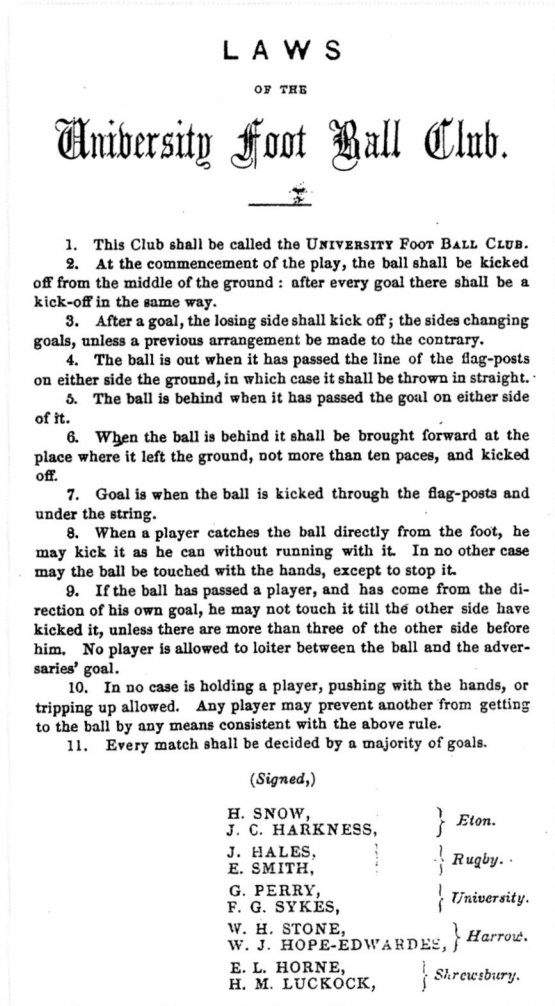

LAWS

OF THE

University Foot Ball Club.

1. This Club shall be called the UNIVERSITY FOOT BALL CLUB.
2. At the commencement of the play, the ball shall be kicked off from the middle of the ground : after every goal there shall be a kick-off in the same way.
3. After a goal, the losing side shall kick off; the sides changing goals, unless a previous arrangement be made to the contrary.
4. The ball is out when it has passed the line of the flag-posts on either side the ground, in which case it shall be thrown in straight.
5. The ball is behind when it has passed the goal on either side of it.
6. When the ball is behind it shall be brought forward at the place where it left the ground, not more than ten paces, and kicked off.
7. Goal is when the ball is kicked through the flag-posts and under the string.
8. When a player catches the ball directly from the foot, he may kick it as he can without running with it. In no other case may the ball be touched with the hands, except to stop it.
9. If the ball has passed a player, and has come from the direction of his own goal, he may not touch it till the other side have kicked it, unless there are more than three of the other side before him. No player is allowed to loiter between the ball and the adversaries' goal.
10. In no case is holding a player, pushing with the hands, or tripping up allowed. Any player may prevent another from getting to the ball by any means consistent with the above rule.
11. Every match shall be decided by a majority of goals.

(*Signed,*)

H. SNOW,
J. C. HARKNESS, } *Eton.*

J. HALES,
E. SMITH, } *Rugby.*

G. PERRY,
F. G. SYKES, } *University.*

W. H. STONE,
W. J. HOPE-EDWARDES, } *Harrow.*

E. L. HORNE,
H. M. LUCKOCK, } *Shrewsbury.*

Cambridge Rules of football (1856)
Used with permission from Shrewsbury School.

A sculpture celebrating Cambridge's contribution, on which is etched the 1856 version of the rules (- see image above), was installed on Parker's Piece in 2018.

Although Albert Pell is credited with being the first to attempt to introduce the Rugby School version of football to Cambridge in 1839,[45] it was not the preferred version of the game at Trinity College or Cambridge University. The reason for this was that the more academic students from Eton College were more likely to play the 'Wall Game' (a cross between football and rugby) before entry to King's College, Cambridge. However, the less gifted at Eton, called 'oppidans', or 'townboys', played the 'Field Game' (more like football), before going on to Trinity College. With Eton having the highest status of all the public schools, and Trinity College 'controlling' Cambridge football, it is no surprise the 'anti-Rugby (school), mainly kicking and minimal handling game', became more established.[46]

There is also some evidence that suggests Oxford undergraduate students favoured the Rugby form of football anyway.[47]

Popularising Association Football

Arthur Kinnaird (student at Trinity College from 1864) may be considered football's first superstar who played in nine FA Cup Finals.[48] He was also on the FA Committee at the age of 21 in 1868, followed by its treasurer, then President, a post he held for 33 years. In his time and under his leadership, football rose from obscurity to become Britain's national sport, so it is no surprise he has been credited as doing 'more to popularise soccer than any man who ever lived'.

Creation of Australian Rules football

Both James Bogue Thompson and William Josiah Hammersley were students at Trinity College, from 1845 at the same time as the laws of football were being created by their fellow students.

After leaving Cambridge these two met together with Thomas Wentworth Wills (Magdalene College – chapter 3) and Thomas Henry Smith (Trinity College, Dublin) in 1859 in Melbourne, Australia to 'decide upon a set of regulations for football as played in Melbourne'.[49] They felt there was a need for cricketers to play a winter game, which is why most of the early football clubs sprang from cricket clubs and played on cricket fields.[50] These four men are considered the founders of Australian Rules Football.

Given the involvement of Trinity College students in establishing 'the Cambridge Rules' (later the rules for Association Football), 'Australian Rules', and perhaps other codes too, the College has been credited with being 'a centre of innovation and diffusion'.[51]

Boxing rules / sports management

John Graham Chambers, a student at Trinity College from 1861 to 1865, was a double rowing Blue and president of Cambridge University Boat Club. Later he was involved in revising the rules of rowing and contributing towards devising a management structure for Henley Royal (Rowing) Regatta, later adopted by de Coubertin for the International Olympic Committee.[52]

He was also one of the instigators of the first inter-varsity athletics match in 1864 being a gifted athlete himself, 'reputed to be the best walker in the University'.[53]

After Cambridge he also co-founded the Amateur Athletic Club (AAC) including the first national championships in athletics. A primary objective for the AAC was securing a dedicated sports ground with Frank Fenner's private sports ground in Cambridge (where both University cricket and athletics were played) probably an inspiration to Chambers.[54]

Chambers also staged some of the earliest track cycling races, during the time of penny farthings, and hosted the second FA Cup Final. He also rowed beside Matthew Webb as he swam the English Channel, as well as edited a national newspaper.[55]

Perhaps his most famous and enduring achievement was in creating the rules of boxing in 1865, later publicly endorsed by his friend from Cambridge, the Marquess of Queensberry, and staging the first boxing tournaments under these rules. These included the use of boxing gloves, the 10-second knockdown count and 3-minute rounds, rules which became a byword for fair play and sportsmanship in the twentieth century.[56] It is probably one reason why there are so many boxing phrases used today in everyday life, such as 'below the belt', 'throw in the towel', 'having [someone] in my corner', 'sucker punch', 'saved by the bell', and so on.

What is also remarkable is that these rules regularised prize fighting, that the law refused to accept as a sport, and refashioned it to closely resemble an activity, whose sporting credentials were clear.[57] Whilst this benefitted all classes, Chambers was much more driven to serve the sporting needs of 'gentlemen amateurs', across all the sports he was involved in – see chapter 4.

Players

In any revolution there will be individuals who act as role models for others to follow, with Trinity College providing some of the best sporting examples.

John Graham Chambers (1860): creator of boxing's Queensberry Rules
Reproduced by permission of the Provost and Fellows of Eton College.

In addition to Arthur Kinnaird, the first football superstar, Alfred Lyttelton was the first person to represent England at both cricket and football. Ivo Bligh successfully captained the England cricket team by winning the first ever Ashes series against Australia in 1882/1883. His name is inscribed on the original Ashes urn alongside other Cambridge University players Allan Steel (Trinity Hall), George Studd and his brother Charles.

The first non-white sportsman ever to win international renown was Ranjitsinhji who played cricket for England. Perhaps the greatest ever sporting allrounder was Maxwell 'Max' Woosnam, a student at Trinity College from 1912 to 1919, who won a Grand Slam, Olympic gold and silver medals for tennis, compiled a maximum 147 break in Snooker, scored a century at Lord's Cricket Ground, captained both Manchester City F.C, (runners-up for the Football League Championship in 1920–21), and the England national football team in 1922.

'Thinkers'

Just as notable as the formation of the laws of football, and boxing, Trinity College, through its students can also lay claim to contributing significantly towards the creation of Muscular Christianity.

Frederick Maurice was a student at Trinity College from 1823[58] which included membership of the Apostles, a literary society. An early member was Alfred Tennyson (also a student at Trinity College from 1827), in whose biography it was claimed:

F.D. Maurice: origins of Muscular Christianity

Source: J.F.C. Harrison (1954). A history of the Working Men's College. 1854 – 1954. Routledge & Kegan Paul.

> The effect which [Maurice] has produced on the minds of many at Cambridge by the single creation of the Society of the 'Apostles' (for which the spirit though not the form was created by him) is far greater than I can dare to calculate, and will be felt, both directly and indirectly, in the age that is upon us.[59]

Tennyson was right, as Maurice was later jointly responsible for establishing Christian Socialism, which whilst it did not survive as a Movement, nevertheless spawned some key initiatives,[60] such as:

- the foundation of Queen's College, London for the education of women
- friendly societies (protecting members against debts incurred through illness, death, or old age)
- sanitary reform, with Charles Kingsley
- housing for the poor, with Octavia Hill
- the Co-op Movement, with Thomas Hughes (author of Tom Brown's Schooldays), who was also very keenly involved in both the
    - o Working Men's College (chapter 16), and
    - o the concept of manliness or Muscular Christianity, in close partnership also with Charles Kingsley (chapter 3).

The link to Muscular Christianity may be considered strange given the Apostles at Trinity College was 'a refuge for the outsider – the scholar and intellectual who had been rejected by the bloods [aristocrats] and athletes'.[61]

1   Sean Coughlan (2004). Henry VIII wore football boots. BBC News online.

2   Derek Birley (1993). Sport and the making of Britain. Manchester University Press. Page 59.

3   Derek Birley (1993). Sport and the making of Britain. Manchester University Press. Pages 80 – 81.

4   Cambridge Chronicle 31 May 1851, p 6.

5   Cram et al (2003) Francis Willughby's Book of Games. Ashgate, Aldershot. Page 43.

6   Christopher Rowley (2015). The shared origins of football, rugby and soccer. Rowman and Littlefield. Page 86 and 87.

7   Willie Sugg (2002). A tradition unshared. A history of Cambridge Town & County cricket 1700 - 1890. Part 1. Page 50.

8   Derek Birley (1999). A social history of English cricket. Aurum. Pages 3 and 4.

9   Derek Birley (1999). A social history of English cricket. Aurum. Page 3.

10   Mike Thompson (2017). The Lord of Lord's. Christopher Saunders. Page 54.

11   Mike Atherton (2006). Gambling. A story of triumph and disaster. Hodder & Stoughton.

12   Mike Thompson (2017). The Lord of Lord's. Christopher Saunders.

13   Derek Birley (1999). A social history of English cricket. Aurum. Page 63.

14   Glimpses of the Human Side of Sir Isaac Newton Author(s): Henry P. Macomber Source: The Scientific Monthly, Vol. 80, No. 5 (May, 1955), pp. 304-309.

15   Thomas Parkyns (1727 - 3rd edition). The Inn-Play: or Cornish-Hugg Wrestler. Page 12.

16   Dennis Brailsford (1988) Bareknuckles: a social history of prize fighting. Cambridge: Lutterworth Press. Page 2.

17   Peter Radford (2001). The celebrated Captain Barclay. Sport, money and fame in Regency Britain. Pages 48 to 51.

18   Gareth A Davies (8 March 2007) 'Oxford and Cambridge prepare for centenary boxing match' in The Telegraph.

19   Peter Radford (2001). The celebrated Captain Barclay. Sport, money and fame in Regency Britain. Page 218.

20   Peter Radford ibid Page 218.

21   Dissertation by Alex Stewart (2008) Title: The boxer's point of view: an ethnography of cultural production and athletic development among amateur and professional boxers in England. University of Bedfordshire.

22   G.M. Trevelyan (1946). English Social History. Longmans, Green and Co Ltd. Page 504.

23   G.M. Trevelyan (1946). English Social History. Longmans, Green and Co Ltd. Footnote on page 504.

24   Dr Michael Hrebeniak (2015). Stirbitch: mapping the unmappable. https://www.cam.ac.uk/research/features/stirbitch-mapping-the-unmappable

25   Pastnow. History, Arts and Stuff - website https://pastnow.wordpress.com/2014/03/17/march-17-1814-byron-boxing-with-gentleman-john-jackson/

26   Peter Radford (2001). The celebrated Captain Barclay. Pages 220 - 222.

27   Dove Cottage and the Wordsworth Museum. Boxing with Byron: https://wordsworth.org.uk/blog/2016/01/22/boxing-with-byron/

28   A Veteran Cricketer. Article (on Frank Fenner) in the Sketch 13 September 1893. Pages 361 and 362.

29   Sporting Life 18 December 1861.

30   Cambridge Chronicle and Journal 28 December 1861.

31   Cambridge Chronicle and Journal 14 Dec 1861.

32   Simon Wilde (1999). Ranji. A genius, rich and strange. Aurum. Page xi.

33   This quote on Ranjitsinhji is widely credited to Neville Cardus, but the original source is unknown.

34   Simon Wilde (1999). Ranji. A genius, rich and strange. Aurum. Page 2.

[35] Giles Phillips (2005). On Fenner's Sward. A history of Cambridge University Cricket Club. Tempus Publishing Ltd. Pages 70, 72 and 73.

[36] Between the Innings. Cricket: a weekly record of the game. Aug 6 1896. Page 331.

[37] RJO Meyer. 'Jack's own account of his correspondence with Ranji' provided by Millfield School archivist in email 15 Sept 2020.

[38] Barry Hobson. The History of Millfield 1935-1970. https://resources.finalsite.net/images/v1600168102/millfieldschoolcom/mozmfsrmqczlpi9o4rnh/BarryHobsonAHistoryofMillfield.pdf

[39] Rollo Meyer: Visionary and Founder of Millfield School article on 'Last Words on Sports' website by PJ Lennon 15 August 2016 quoting David Foot (Guardian reporter).

[40] Willie Sugg personal communication Oct 2017.

[41] G Derek West (1989). Twelve days of Grace. Darf Publishers Ltd. Page 16.

[42] G.M. Trevelyan (1946). English Social History. A survey of six centuries Chaucer to Queen Victoria. Longmans, Green and Co. Page 408.

[43] Cambridge, the birthplace of the laws (2010). FIFA website.

[44] H. C. Malden (Trinity 1847). Contents of letter written in 1897 reported in The Fountain. Trinity College Newsletter. Issue 7. Autumn 2008.

[45] Albert Pell (1908) The reminiscences of Albert Pell. London: John Murray.

[46] Graham Curry and Eric Dunning (2015). Association Football. A study in figurational sociology. Routledge. Pages 81 - 83.

[47] Graham Curry and Eric Dunning (2015). Association Football. A study in figurational sociology. Routledge. Page 77.

[48] https://www.scottishsporthistory.com/arthur-kinnaird-first-lord-of-football.html

[49] Graham Curry and Eric Dunning (2015). Association Football. A study in figurational sociology. Routledge. Page 83.

[50] http://www.emelbourne.net.au/biogs/EM00593b.htm

[51] Graham Curry and Eric Dunning (2015). Association Football. A study in figurational sociology. Routledge. Page 83.

[52] Ian Volans (2016). In search of John Graham Chambers: sport's serial law maker. Sporting Landmarks website https://sportinglandmarks.co.uk/in-search-of-john-graham-chambers/

[53] Venn Cambridge Alumni Database. https://venn.lib.cam.ac.uk

[54] Ian Volans. Personal email communication. 16 Nov 2021.

[55] Ian Volans (2016) In search of John Graham Chambers: sport's serial law maker. Sporting Landmarks website. https://sportinglandmarks.co.uk/in-search-of-john-graham-chambers/

[56] CUABC website: http://www.cuabc.org/cambridge-boxing

[57] https://www.researchgate.net/publication/241744752_'Under_Queensberry_Rules_So_to_Speak'_Some_Versions_of_a_Metaphor

[58] Frederick Maurice spent a total of nine years in Cambridge across his life.

[59] Ref 4: Willey, 1956, p 63; Lubenow, 1998, p 141 in Malcolm Tozer (2015) The Ideal of Manliness. Sunnyrest Books. Page 44 and 45.

[60] Malcolm Tozer (2015). The Ideal of Manliness. The legacy of Thring's Uppingham. Sunnyrest Books. Page 44.

[61] Victoria Rosner (ed - 2014) The Cambridge Companion to the Bloomsbury Group. Cambridge University Press. Ref 88 on page 44.

CHAPTER 10
Trinity Hall

Trinity Hall was founded by Bishop Bateman of Norwich in 1350, probably due to the shortage of clergyman and lawyers following the Black Death of 1349. It is the fifth oldest college of the University of Cambridge.[1]

CRICKET

First Varsity match in any sport

Herbert Jenner (student at Trinity Hall from 1824) was jointly responsible, with Charles Wordsworth (nephew of the poet) for instigating the first Varsity Cricket match in 1827 played at Lord's Cricket Ground. Jenner was also captain, later playing for England and becoming President of the MCC in 1833 at the age of 27.

Cricket was the first Varsity sport to be played between Oxford and Cambridge Universities, with rowing ('the Boat Race') following two years later.

When Jenner first arrived in Cambridge, he would have played his university cricket on their newly established home ground on the current Mill Road Cemetery site where Frank Fenner (as a child from the age of 6) probably saw him play. Later, Frank credited Herbert Jenner as being:

> The most notable all-round player of his time ... It was as a wicket keeper that Mr Jenner first became distinguished, for he was especially classed as one of the best, if not the very best, of that day; but as a bowler and batsman he was also conspicuous for his skill, indeed for his general mastery in every department of the game ... for which there was a finished pre-eminence.[a]

---

[a] For the colleges which follow, starting here at Trinity Hall, the majority did not have the same level of impact on sport as those visited up to now (Trinity, St John's, Jesus and Magdalene Colleges), which is why the structure in these chapters are more flexible - to cover their sporting history, links with the town, and any impact on England's sporting revolution.

First overseas cricket tour

William Percival 'Bull' Pickering started at Pembroke College but within a year moved to Trinity Hall in 1840, winning his cricket Blues in 1840 and 1842.

In 1852 he emigrated to Canada, playing cricket in Toronto, Montreal and Vancouver, and for the Canadian national team against the United States on four occasions between 1853 and 1857. These were the first international cricket matches, and the first in any sport.

Pickering was also instrumental in arranging the first major tour by an international team when George Parr (Nottingham) led a side of 12 English professionals to North America in 1859. This included three cricketers from the Cambridge Town Club: Robert Carpenter, Tom Hayward and Alfred Diver – see chapter 13.

Frank Fenner and Bull Pickering

Fenner, for Cambridge Town, and Pickering for the University, played against each other at least once. For example, on the 13 and 14 May 1841 on Parker's Piece, the University scored 122 in their first innings, thanks to Pickering's innings of 42 (not out), with Fenner taking 6 of the University wickets, but only 49 runs in their second innings, Fenner taking 5 of their wickets. In response the Town Club scored 222, with Fenner making 80 runs, so winning by an innings and 51 runs.

WALKING

Leslie Stephen was probably more responsible, above any of his peers in the second half of the nineteenth century, for winning over the university to the importance not just of competitive sport (see later in the chapter), but the value of everyday exercise such as walking.

This was probably not the outcome Leslie's father had expected, given he had chosen Trinity Hall for his son to attend in 1850 because it was a small college and would not overtax the strength of his delicate boy.[2] This is probably why Leslie started walking, which he continued to do throughout his time in Cambridge, including as a Fellow at the college until 1867, gaining the reputation as 'a Cambridge theoretician of walking'.

Local walks, and benefits

Leslie Stephen certainly walked the 'Grantchester Grind' (a circular walk of nearly 6 miles (9km) from Cambridge to Trumpington, then Grantchester, returning along the river), popular with many students, but he needed more demanding walks.

Later he boasted that every term he devised a new route for walking the sixteen miles from the university to Ely:

Leslie Stephen in 1862: winning over the university to sport

Permission granted by Smith College Special Collections as the holder of the original material.

> In a steady march along one of the great dykes by the monotonous canal with the exuberant vegetation dozing in its stagnant waters, we were imbibing the spirit of the scenery ... we felt the curious charm of the great flats.

At this time not everyone was keen on the state of the local waterways, especially the rowers, who found the 'exuberant vegetation' affecting their stroke. Also, the 'stagnant waters', especially for those who lived in Cambridge, gave off a dreadful smell, because of poor sanitation (chapter 4).[3]

On one occasion Leslie Stephen walked with three other clergymen from Bedford to Cambridge, passing a post marked 'Cambridge 30 miles' at 11.30am and reaching the back gates of St John's College at 6pm. The experience of passing through Eaton Socon, a village on their route, prompted the local Vicar to declare his parish had been invaded by 'four lunatics', who he was told were clergymen from Cambridge.[4]

It was reported to Stephen's biographer he 'was always guarding his men [students] against idleness and effeminacy, and that these weekly tramps were organised for the better prevention of loafing. That the long walk is a moral agent of great power was an article of faith based upon personal experience.'

Eventually undergraduates bought him a walking stick 'in honour of his having outwalked them all,' one of them also describing him as having 'a tall, almost gaunt body, devoid of all superfluous flesh and with muscles like steel.'[5]

Stephen praised the 'very predictability and lack of excitement' of walking, adding 'the true walker ... finds that the muscular efforts of the legs is subsidiary to the "celebration" stimulated by the effort, as well as the intellectual harmony which is the natural accompaniment to the monotonous tramp of his feet'.[6]

Walking for the working classes

At the Working Men's College (WMC), founded in London in 1854 and established a year later in Cambridge, walking 'took pride of place in the College summer social activities ... (for example as) Sunday tramping'. With walking becoming 'one of the new sports of the professional classes in mid-Victorian England', it was natural that some of the more athletic founders and teachers of the WMC 'should seek to extend its benefits to their working men friends in the College'. These walkers included Leslie Stephen and Frederick James Furnivall (both Trinity Hall), Richard Litchfield, Llewelyn Davies (both Trinity College) and Thomas Hughes.

On two occasions Furnivall walked with a party of students from London to St Albans, a round trip of forty-four miles in the day, observing 'when you've had ... a forty mile walk with men who put their backs and legs into their work [regular employment], you get to respect them'.[7]

In becoming 'one of the most energetic men in the University',[8] Leslie Stephen turned to various athletic activities beyond walking.

ATHLETICS AND BOXING

Cambridge University Athletic Club (CUAC) was established in 1857, making it one of the oldest athletic clubs in the world.[9] This coincided with the Cambridge University Foot Races and Athletic Sports taking place at Fenner's Ground in the same year, with Frank Fenner as host, promoter, organiser (via his tobacco shop on Market Hill) and judge at the sports. Leslie Stephen competed, and won the two-mile races in both 1860 and 1861, where he posted his best time of 10mins 55 secs, watched by the Prince of Wales as a spectator.

Varsity athletics

It did not take long before the first Varsity match between Oxford and Cambridge took place in 1864 in Oxford under the leadership from Cambridge of students Henry Kennedy (Trinity Hall), Percy Thornton (Jesus College), Richard Webster, John Graham Chambers, and Charles Lawes (all Trinity College) supported by Henry Arthur Morgan (Jesus College) and 'the eccentric don' Leslie Stephen (Trinity Hall).[10]

In addition to winning the 120-yard race in 19 secs against Oxford in the second Varsity athletics match in 1865 at Fenner's,[11] Tom Milvain (Trinity Hall student) was a keen and talented boxer, later becoming the heavyweight boxing champion of All-England in 1868-69.

Milvain's contact with the Town

According to a local press report:

> Harry Cox of King Street was an old pugilist who learnt in a hard school where gloves were regarded as unnecessary. He started in a travelling fairground booth but when he visited Midsummer Fair decided to settle in Cambridge. He took part in many open-air fights without the sanction of the law which were witnessed by large numbers. Pupils from the University attended his rooms at the Green Lion in Short Street [between Midsummer Common and Christ's Pieces] and later at the Royston Arms, Jesus Lane. 'Professor Cox' also gave lessons at St John's and other colleges and several University champions passed through his hands including Thomas Milvain of Trinity Hall.[12]

During a Town versus Gown disturbance, however:

> Tom Milvain met with a remarkable misadventure. He and another man of his college, Trinity Hall, were leading a party of gownsmen down Green Street, the townsmen were retreating before them, for there was none among them bold enough to tackle the redoubtable Tom of 'The Hall'. Suddenly, however the 'town' rallied and faced the 'gown'. 'We've got a chap as'll fight the best of ye!' they yelled. Milvain strode forward quickly to meet this unknown champion. Suddenly the opposing ranks opened, and six lusty roughs, with a large pole, or battering-ram, charged straight at Tom who was utterly unprepared for this manoeuvre. Before he could move hand or foot, the barge pole took him full in the pit of the stomach, doubled him up, and he fell gasping for breath and half dead. With a whoop of triumph, the 'town' fled, leaving the barge-pole behind them, whilst the 'gown' gathered round their fallen leader.[13]

'WINNING OVER THE UNIVERSITY' AND MUSCULAR CHRISTIANITY

The illicit use of boxing coaches by students such as Milvain probably did not help the cause of Henry Arthur Morgan (Jesus College) and Leslie Stephen to win over the often hostile University authorities in their endeavours to establish Varsity athletics and sports as 'fresh inter-University competitions of a non-intellectual nature'.[14]

These two believed sport was able to inculcate esprit de corps, with success being dependent on the individual acting in concert with his fellows, especially true in rowing, another sport Leslie Stephen was passionate about. Their case had grown out of the 'manliness' or 'Muscular Christianity' agenda initiated by Frederick Maurice (chapter 9) and Charles Kingsley (chapter 3), which believed a feeble body could not support a powerful brain. Leslie Stephen must have considered himself a walking example of this, given his own physical frailty as a child.[15]

FRANK FENNER AND LESLIE STEPHEN

Athletics

As already mentioned, not only were annual inter-college athletic sports events held at Fenner's Ground, but so too did many of the individual college games, which is why Leslie Stephen, in his role as a Fellow, and competing athlete, must surely have had direct contact with Frank Fenner in helping to organise the Trinity Hall athletic sports.

In addition, in 1861 Leslie Stephen was on the organising committee for the visit of Deerfoot (the Seneca Native American) to run in a six-mile race at Fenner's, with Frank as starter, watched by up to 8,000 spectators including the Prince of Wales (see chapter 9 for the scandal that ensued and chapter 22 for details of Deerfoot's race).

Smoker

It is also highly likely that Leslie Stephen was a customer in Frank's tobacco shop on Market Square given he was a famous smoker. Stephen, who was a very keen mountaineer, believed that an Alpine experience was improved if tobacco was imbibed, attracting criticism from some, including John Ruskin.

Working Men's College

Leslie Stephen was also a founder of the local Working Men's College (chapter 16), located behind Fenner's tobacco shop on the Market Square, giving occasional lectures there, as did his brother, James Fitzjames Stephen (Trinity College).[16]

It is through the Working Men's College that Stephen had contact with Frederick Maurice (Trinity College), its founder, learning from him the importance of offering working men an education, including sport. Whilst Leslie Stephen loathed Maurice,[17] he nevertheless admitted he was 'the greatest Anglican of the century'.[18]

Leslie Stephen's family

Leslie was married to Harriet (Minny) Thackeray, the daughter of the author William Makepeace Thackeray. Sadly, she died in childbirth aged only 35 years. Leslie married again to Julia Duckworth, having four children including Virginia Woolf, considered one of the most important modernist twentieth century authors.

ROWING

Working Men's College

Frederick James Furnivall was a student briefly at University College London before starting at Trinity Hall in 1842. Whilst he later became one of the co-creators of the New English Dictionary, he also had a significant impact on rowing, especially opening up the sport to the working classes.

Frederick Furnivall: rowing for the working classes

Thanks to Peter Gilliver (author of The Making of the OED) and Charlotte Brewer.

It started in the 1850s when Furnivall became involved in various Christian socialist schemes when his circle of friends included Charles Kingsley and John Ruskin. It was through this group that he became one of the founders of, and teachers at the Working Men's College in London.

Furnivall conceived of the college as a classless, democratic community of learning which he gave over 50 years to, including as rowing coach and president of successive rowing clubs. However, there were problems with using 'Working Men' in the name of the club, which was a misleading title, only because of its association with manual labour and professionalism, in the eyes of the gentlemen amateurs.[19]

The challenge for 'Working Men' to participate in rowing led Frederick Furnivall to co-found The National Amateur Rowing Association (NARA) in 1890, inspired by the ideals of Muscular Christianity whilst 'dismissing the social exclusivity of the Amateur Rowing Association (ARA)', co-founded by John Graham Chambers (Trinity College).

> 'We feel' he wrote 'that for a University to send its earnest intellectual men into an East End or other settlement to live with and help working-men in their studies and their sports, while it sends its rowing-men into the ARA to say to those working-men, 'You're labourers; your work renders you unfit to associate and row with us' is a facing-both-ways, an inconsistency and contradiction which loyal sons of the University ought to avoid.[20]

In 1896 Furnivall founded the Hammersmith Sculling Club (now called Furnivall Sculling Club), initially for working-class girls, with George Bernard Shaw as a Vice President and one of its donors.

It has been suggested that 'Ratty' in the *Wind in the Willows* was modelled on Furnivall, who was a friend of the author Kenneth Grahame.

Being sight impaired: no barrier to rowing

Another rower was Henry Fawcett, briefly a student at Peterhouse in 1852 before moving to Trinity Hall where he later became a professor, as well as a keen sportsman.

However, in 1858 aged 25, he had a tragic accident with a shotgun which left him visually impaired, but this did not stop him regularly rowing, swimming, diving and skating. For example, when the River Cam froze over, he skated to Ely, a distance of 16 miles (26 km), heedless of the dangers of a plunge into the icy waters.

Henry Fawcett: a disability, no barrier to playing sport
Photograph by Lock & Whitfield. Public domain image from Wellcome Collection.

TENNIS GRAND SLAM WINNERS

Both Reginald (or R.F.) Doherty and his younger brother Laurie were students at Trinity Hall in the late nineteenth century.

They accumulated 10 Singles Grand Slam titles between them, nine at Wimbledon, and the other at the US Championships in 1903 when Laurie became the first non-American to take the title. Together they also won 10 Doubles Grand Slam titles, which included two at the US Championships. The brothers also won a total of four Olympic Gold medals and one Bronze in the 1900 and 1908 Games, in singles, doubles and mixed doubles. See chapter 22 for more on tennis.

The Doherty brothers: multiple Tennis Grand Slam winners
Source: A.W. Myers, 1903. Lawn Tennis at home and abroad. New York: Charles Scribner's Sons. Page 24. Hathi Trust Digital Library.

What is very sad is that both brothers died young having suffered from respiratory problems throughout their lives. Reggie died aged 38, after a life in which he said he had never felt really well for a whole day, and Laurie at 43. It is believed both brothers had been urged to take up lawn tennis by their father because of their poor health.[21]

Rugby Union in Japan

Whilst rugby had first been introduced by British troops, the first recorded game played by Japanese students at Keio University was in 1899, coached by Edward Bramwell Clarke (Corpus Christi College) and Ginnosuke Tanaka who in addition to having been a student at Trinity Hall, also attended the Leys School, Cambridge.[22]

1   Frank Fenner (1893) Cricket Jottings. V. Bath Chronicle. July and Sept 1893.

2   Peter Searby (1997). A History of the University of Cambridge Vol III 1750-1870. Cambridge University Press. Pages 642 to 644.

3   Ged Martin. Magdalene College in mid Victorian times. https://www.gedmartin.net/martinalia-mainmenu-3/233-magdalene-college-cambridge-in-mid-victorian-times

4   Peter Searby (1997). A History of the University of Cambridge Vol III 1750-1870. Cambridge University Press. Ref 12 Page 643.

5   Peter Searby (1997). A History of the University of Cambridge Vol III 1750-1870. Cambridge University Press. Page 643.

6   Peter Searby (1997). A History of the University of Cambridge Vol III 1750-1870. Cambridge University Press. Page 643 and 643.

7   J.F.C. Harrison (1954). A history of the Working Men's College. 1854 – 1954. Routledge & Kegan Paul. Page 75.

8   Peter Searby (1997). A History of the University of Cambridge Vol III 1750-1870. Cambridge University Press. Page 642.

9   Cambridge University Athletics Club website https://www.cuac.org.uk/history

10 Cambridge University Athletics Club website https://www.cuac.org.uk/history.html

11 Chris Thorne (2020). History of athletics in Cambridge - Chronological worksheet. Document emailed to Nigel Fenner.

12 Mike Petty, Cambridge SPORT Chronicle. Chronology of Cambridge Sport 1888 to 1990 followed by sections on range of sports. Entry 1910 02 11. Report emailed to Nigel Fenner.

13 Famous Fights - past and present. Vol II. No 18 (1901?-1904?) Page 285.

14 J A Mangan 'Oars and the man'. Pleasure and purpose in Victorian and Edwardian Cambridge. Page 106. Chapter in J A Mangan (2006) A sport-loving society. Routledge.

15 Ref 17: N.G. Annan. Leslie Stephen: His thoughts and character in relation to his time (London, 1951) p 29. In Keith A.P. Sandiford (1982) Cricket and the Victorians: A historiographical essay in Historical Reflections. Vol 9. No 3 pp 421-436.

16 J.F.C. Harrison (1954). A history of the Working Men's College. 1854 – 1954. Routledge & Kegan Paul. Page 46.

17 Malcolm Tozer (2015) The ideal of manliness. Sunnyrest Books. Page 225.

18 Malcolm Tozer (2015) The ideal of manliness. Sunnyrest Books. Ref 8 on page 46.

19 Dennis Brailsford (1997). British Sport. A Social History. The Lutterworth Press. Page 98.

20 Richard Holt (1993) Sport and the British. A modern history. Clarendon Press, Oxford. Page 109.

21 https://olympics.com/en/athletes/reginald-frank-doherty

22 The Roots of Rugby in Japan: A Brief History of the Keio Rugby Football Club. https://www.keio.ac.jp/en/keio-times/features/2019/6/

CHAPTER 11

Clare College

Clare College was founded in 1326, and endowed by Lady Elizabeth de Clare, a granddaughter of King Edward I. In 1336 King Edward III granted it a licence providing for a maximum of fifteen 'Scholars' (subsequently to be called 'Fellows'), of whom no more than six were bound strictly by priestly orders. Provision was also made for ten 'poor scholars' (*pauperes*, or 'students'), who were to be maintained by the college up to the age of twenty.[1] It is the second oldest college in the University.

Clare College including King's College chapel (to the left)

ARCHERY PRACTICE

There are two known locations in Cambridge, called Butts Green, where the men of Cambridge would have been obliged to hone their archery skills shooting at the butts. One is located on Midsummer Common near Maids Causeway and the other within Clare College's gardens.[2]

Across the country football was banned by a succession of kings: Edward III in 1365, Richard II in 1388 and Henry V in 1414 because it interfered with archery practice, thus affecting English soldiers in battles, in particular against the French.[3]

CRICKET

Early rules

Alan Brodrick, a student at Clare College from 1717 / 1718 was jointly responsible for creating cricket's earliest known written rules in the 1727 season. Both Brodrick and Charles Lennox (Cambridge University graduate, college unknown) drew up Articles of Agreement to determine the rules that must apply in their contests, itemised in sixteen points. The first nationally agreed codification of the Laws of Cricket followed in 1744.

The bravest cricketer of them all

Siegfried Loraine Sassoon read history at Clare College from 1905 to 1907. Sassoon has been referred to as 'the bravest cricketer of them all'[4] not just for his physical bravery at the Battle of the Somme where he won the Military Cross, but for writing a statement about the horrors of the trenches read out by an MP in the House of Commons, for which Sassoon could have been court martialed for treason. This resulted in Sassoon being sent to Craiglockhart hospital, where he protested even more eloquently in his war poems, inspired by the company of Wilfred Owen. For example, in 'Dreamers', Sassoon wrote:

> Soldiers are dreamers; when the guns begin
> They think of firelit homes, clean beds and wives.
> I see them in foul dug-outs, gnawed by rats,
> And in the ruined trenches lashed with rain,
> Dreaming of things they did with balls and bats.

Sassoon also wrote in his diary on 16 July 1916 about his passion for the game:

> And I'm thinking of England, and summer evenings after cricket matches, and sunset above tall trees, and village-streets in the dusk … Perhaps I've made a blob [scored no runs], but we've won the match, and there's another match tomorrow … So things went three years ago; and it's all dead and done with. I'll never be there again. If I'm lucky and get out alive, there's another sort of life waiting for me.

He did get out alive which is why he also featured himself as a young lad playing cricket for his village in *The Flower-Show Match* published in 1941.[5]

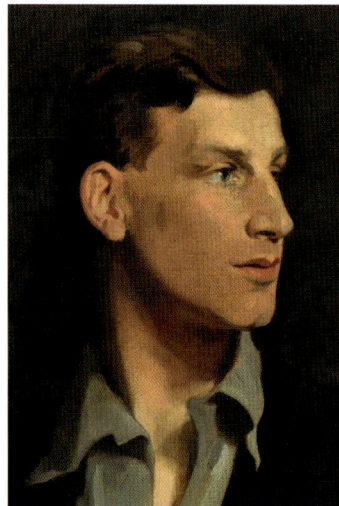

Siegfried Sassoon
Detail of original painting by Glyn Warren Philpot used with permission © The Fitzwilliam Museum.

Team of cricketing poets

'In idle speculation I wish that Siegfried Sassoon could have led into the field a team consisting of other English poets versed in the game', so wrote Edmund Blunden, in *Cricket Country*.[6] Also selected were Lord Byron, 'if he was not busy otherwise, taking boxing lessons or swimming the Hellespont [the world's oldest swim], should be on the bowling strength. Perhaps it would be winked at if the Hon L.H. Tennyson represented his tuneful grandfather, and Christopher Wordsworth did the same for his uncle.'

[1] https://www.clare.cam.ac.uk/College-History/

[2] Nicholas Chrimes (2017). Cambridge. Treasure Island of the Fens. Hobsaerie Publications. Page 170.

[3] Graham Curry and Eric Dunning (2015). Association Football. A study in figurational sociology. Routledge. Pages 14 and 15.

[4] Daily Telegraph 25 Apr 2011.

[5] Siegfried Sassoon (1941). The flower-show match and other pieces. Faber and Faber Ltd.

[6] Edmund Blunden (1944). Cricket Country. Collins. Pages 44 – 45.

CHAPTER 12

Gonville & Caius College

Gonville & Caius College is the fourth oldest college of the University of Cambridge. It was founded as Gonville Hall by Edmund Gonville, Rector of Terrington St Clement in Norfolk, in 1348, and refounded in 1557 by John Caius as Gonville & Caius College.

First set of compromise football rules

Whilst there are 34 known Cambridge University students responsible for framing the rules of football from 1838 to 1863, it was Edgar William Montagu, a student at Gonville & Caius from 1837 / 1838, who is recognised as the first rule-maker. He wrote that:

> I and six other representatives of the School [Shrewsbury] made a Club, and drew up rules that should equalise the different games. I had it in my hands just now when looking for the plan I spoke of. It was then we had two matches on Parker's Piece. I fancy I was our best man, having the speed. But, in the second match, just as I gave the return off kick, a Rugbeian bore down on me after the kick off and kicked my knee cap off so that I had to wait in goal all the contest.[1]

It was at this time that because students from the different public schools arrived in Cambridge with their own variations of football, it was necessary to 'equalise the different games'. As to how this was achieved, see chapters 9 and 20.

'Camp ball' in East Anglia

Robert Forby had been a student at Gonville & Caius College from 1777, later writing *The Vocabulary of East Anglia*,'[2] when Rector of St Martin's Church, Fincham (10 miles south of King's Lynn, Norfolk) for over 25 years. The book attempted 'to record the Vulgar Tongue of the twin sister counties, Norfolk and Suffolk, as it existed in the last twenty years of the Eighteenth Century'.

There is a lengthy entry for 'CAMP, an ancient athletic game at ball, now almost superseded by cricket, a less hardy and dangerous sport'. Forby continues that the game 'combined all athletic excellence; that to excel in it, a man must be a good boxer, runner, and wrestler', as well as being endorsed by William Windham, a Norfolk MP, Lord Rochford, who owned estates in Suffolk and Essex, and others from the titled classes.

'Of the sport itself, however, two varieties are at present expressly recognized; rough-play, and civil-play. In the latter, there is no boxing'.

Rules

'Two goals are pitched at the distance of 120 yards from each other. In a line with each are ranged the combatants; for such they truly are. The number on each side is equal; not always the same, but very commonly twelve. They ought to be uniformly dressed in light flannel jackets, distinguished by colours. The ball is deposited exactly in the mid-way. The sign or word is given by an umpire. The two sides, as they are called, rush forward … The sturdiest and most active of each, encounter those of the other. The contest for the ball begins, and never ends without black eyes and bloody noses, broken heads or shins, and some serious mischiefs … The ball can be carried, kicked, or thrown to one of the goals.'

The game has 'been known to last two or three hours', but sometimes 'the game is placed against time, as the phrase is. It is common to limit it to half an hour; and most campers, now-a-days, have in that time got enough of so hardy a contest'.

'The prizes are commonly hats, gloves, shoes, or small sums of money. And the rustic [winner] who bears off the first, is not less conspicuous in the little circle in which he is known, than the Grecian victor decorated with his chaplet of olive or of pine'.

Forby describes Camping as an 'ancient game [which] deserves the more attention from us, because, if it was not peculiar to the East Angles and East Saxons … it is now degenerated, and some meaner exercises unworthily usurp its name'.

For more on the local history of Camp Ball and football go to chapter 20.

CRICKET AND FRANK FENNER

There were several talented cricketers such as Fred Thackeray (first cousin of William Makepeace Thackeray) who on attending Gonville & Caius College from 1836 played for the University, the Town, and joint Town and Gown teams. This reflected the high standing of Cambridge town cricket that talented university cricket players wanted to be part of.[3]

His close relationship with Town cricket resulted in Thackeray being referred to as a 'townsman' in the local press in 1840,[4] plus the fact he had also been born in Cambridge as the son of Frederick Thackeray, physician at Addenbrookes Hospital.

When the Town Club was re-launched in 1843 as the Town and County Club, the Club Secretary was Fred Thackeray, assisted by Frank Fenner.[5]

Fenner's Cricket Ground on Gonville & Caius College land

During the winter of 1847 Frank Fenner had been approached by Cambridge University members to provide a private ricket ground, resulting in him leasing two fields from the college.[6] Whilst the relationship with Fenner at this time was excellent, there was later considerable friction over money matters and the poor state of the pavilion, so that in 1873 Arthur Ward, representing the University Cricket Club, took over the lease from Frank when it expired.

It was Edmund Henry Morgan (Jesus College) who for many years was treasurer of the leading university athletic clubs (who also used Fenner's), who played a major part in organising the subscription fund for the purchase of Fenner's Cricket Ground in March 1892 when it became available from the Master and Fellows of Gonville & Caius College.

Supporting the education of local youthful offenders - and Frank Fenner

Harvey Goodwin had been a student at Gonville & Caius College from 1835, later the vicar of St Giles (chapter 2) when, in 1847 he co-founded the Cambridge Industrial School for 'youthful offenders', to reform rather than punish them. [The school site was just off Victoria Avenue on what is today called Harvey Goodwin Avenue.] Later this grew into a Cambridge branch of the Working Men's College, located behind Frank Fenner's tobacco shop on Market Hill (chapter 16), with Goodwin becoming its first principal.[7]

Harvey Goodwin: first principal of Cambridge's Working Men's College

Source: H.D. Rawnsley (1896). Harvey Goodwin. Bishop of Carlisle. London, John Murray.

Venn's bowling machine

John Venn, best known for inventing the Venn Diagram, was descended from a long line of church evangelicals. This includes Henry Venn, founder of the Clapham Sect, and excellent cricket player.

For John Venn, whilst a student at Gonville & Caius College from 1853:

> Walking, not cycling, was the norm, and long afternoon walks were the commonest form of exercise. Some rowed on the river, and there was some cricket. But lawn tennis and croquet were unborn. Real tennis and hunting were of course confined to the wealthy few. Hockey and football were left to boys. As a student, [John Venn] never saw rugby played; but he relates his younger brother's account of a new game from Rugby school, where they all made a circle round a ball and butted each other.[8]

Following four years away from Cambridge as an Anglican priest, he returned to the college as a lecturer in moral science, where he remained until his death in 1923.

It is not known whether John Venn was a keen cricket player or spectator. However, as reported in the local press of 1909:[9]

> A mild sensation has been caused in the cricketing world by a bowling machine which has been invented and patented by Dr Venn, the President of Caius College, and his son, Mr J. A. Venn. The capabilities of the machine were put to the test by the Australians [playing the University at Fenner's] on Thursday, and Victor Trumper [known as the most stylish and versatile batsman in the world at the time] has expressed an opinion that the new machine will be of special value for schools and for practice generally.

According to Venn's obituary written for the Royal Society they added that 'the redoubtable Victor Trumper was clean bowled by it four times!'.[10]

Knighthood for services to sport

Francis Eden Lacey, having started at Gonville & Caius College in 1878, won his football and cricket Blues in 1881. Later he was to become the third secretary of the MCC, a post which he held from 1898 to 1926, after Fitzgerald and Perkins (both Trinity College) – a total span of 63 years of this illustrious post being held continuously by past students from Cambridge University. Lacey was not only the first man to be knighted for services to cricket, but also in any sport.

Chariots of Fire

The *Chariots of Fire* film tells the fact-based story of two athletes running at the 1924 Olympic Games in Paris. These are Eric Liddell, a devout Scottish Christian who runs for the glory of God, and Harold Abrahams (a student at Gonville & Caius College from 1919), an English Jew who runs to overcome prejudice.

Abrahams won the 100m in a time of 10.6 seconds, beating all the American favourites following six months of intensive training led by Sam Mussabini, a professional coach.

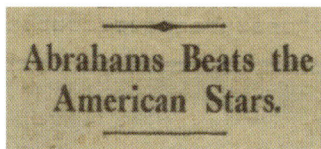

Abrahams Beats the American Stars.

Harold Abrahams: immortalised in the Chariots of Fire film.

Source: Leeds Mercury 8 July 1924.

Reflecting in 1948 on Abrahams' athleticism, Philip Noel-Baker (King's College – chapter 14), Britain's 1912 Olympic captain and a Nobel Prize winner, wrote:

> I have always believed that Harold Abrahams was the only European sprinter who could have run with Jesse Owens, Ralph Metcalfe, and the other great sprinters from the U.S. He was in their class, not only because of natural gifts – his magnificent physique, his splendid racing temperament, his flair for the big occasion – but because he understood athletics and had given more brainpower and more will power to the subject than any other runner of his day.[11]

[1]   Graham Curry and Eric Dunning (2015). Association Football. A study in figurational sociology. Routledge. Page 64.

[2]   The Vocabulary of East Anglia ('an attempt to record the Vulgar Tongue of the twin sister counties, Norfolk and Suffolk, as it existed in the last twenty years of the Eighteenth Century') - Volume 1 - by the late Reverend Robert Forby, Rector of Fincham. Published in 1830 by J.B. Nichols & Son of Parliament Street, London. In Bill Atkins. References to the East Anglian Sport of Camping (updated 7 March 2013). http://www.oldshuck.info/pdf/camping.pdf

[3]   Willie Sugg (2009). Fenner's Men. Cambridgeshire Cricket 1822 - 1848. Part 3 of A Tradition Unshared. Real Work Publishing. Page 41.

[4]   Cambridge Independent Press 11 July 1840. Page 3.

[5]   Cambridge Chronicle and Journal 30 Sept 1843. Page 2.

[6]   Percy Piggott. Fenner's. Reminiscences of Cambridge University Cricket. F&P Piggott, Cambridge. Page 7.

[7]   Malcolm Tozer (2015). The ideal of manliness. The legacy of Thring's Uppingham. Sunnyrest Books. Page 110.

[8]   Professor A.D.D. Craik (2008). Mr Hopkins' Men: Cambridge Reform and British Mathematics in the nineteenth Century. https://epdf.pub/mr-hopkins-men-cambridge-reform-and-british-mathematics-in-the-nineteenth-century.html

[9]   Cambridge Independent Press 11 June 1909.

[10] John Venn's Obituary notice by the Royal Society. https://royalsocietypublishing.org/doi/pdf/10.1098/rspa.1926.0036

[11] Jews in Sport website. https://www.jewsinsports.org/olympics_profile_ID_511.html

CHAPTER 13

Senate House

Built in 1722 by James Gibbs, one of Britain's most influential architects, and opened in 1730, the Senate House of Cambridge is the Parliament building of Cambridge University (in the centre of the photo, with Gonville & Caius College behind it to the right).

Formerly used to host the meetings of the University's Council of the Senate, this historic building is now the location for the graduation ceremonies of the University.

CHANCELLORS OF THE UNIVERSITY – AND SPORT

Whilst the role of the Chancellor of the University today is largely symbolic, in the past the postholder took a leadership role in the management of the university. Here are two examples of Chancellors who also had an association with sport.

George Villiers

Whilst the Cambridge University Golf Club was founded in 1869, the same year two University students created a golf course at Royston (12 miles (20km) southwest from Cambridge), this was not the first golf played there. George Villiers, Duke of Buckingham is credited with playing the first recorded game in England, at Royston, and because of this, the first known Englishman to play golf. His accounts list the purchase of clubs and balls and a lost golf wager from 1624.[1]

George Villiers was Chancellor of the University of Cambridge from 1628 to 1629[2] but was stabbed to death before he completed his term, given his unpopularity in having 'unbounded influence at Court', and the failure of two foreign expeditions.

Prince Albert

From 1847 until his death in 1861, Prince Albert was Chancellor of the University, successfully campaigning for a reformed and more modern university curricula, expanding the subjects taught beyond mathematics and classics to include modern history and the natural sciences.

As a child he excelled at sport, especially fencing and riding, and when married to Queen Victoria was considered 'a beautiful and graceful skater'[3] who kept goal in a game of Bandy (or hockey on ice) at Windsor Castle in 1853, watched by the Queen (more on this in chapter 21).

Whilst it is extremely unlikely Frank Fenner met Prince Albert, he did welcome his son the Prince of Wales to an athletics meeting at Fenner's (chapter 22), a few days before Albert died.

THE WOODEN SPOON

In 1748, not long after the Senate House was opened, a tradition was started whereby the final exam results of all students were displayed outside the front door. Students had to wait until 2018 before they could choose not to have their results so publicly revealed.

Wooden spoon winner 1909
By permission of the Master and Fellows of St John's College, Cambridge.

The use of the wooden spoon as an award for the team or individual who comes last, such as in the modern-day Six Nations Rugby Union Championship, originated at the Senate House.

Starting in at least 1795,[4] the wooden spoon was awarded to the student who came last in the final exams for the maths honours degree, called the Maths Tripos.

On the day of the graduation ceremony, the spoon was suspended on strings held by two 'friends' in the Gallery of the Senate House, so that it hung above the 'winner' as the degree was awarded. The spoon was then lowered to the ground and two other 'friends' cut the string and presented the spoon to the individual concerned. The proceedings were carried out with the utmost ceremony and decorum with the tolerant consent of the Vice-Chancellor.[5]

In the early days, the spoon was a manageable size but by 1909 it had grown appreciably.

The 'winner' in the photograph was Cuthbert Lempriere Holthouse (a student at St John's College) carried through the streets of Cambridge in 1909, the last year for this tradition.[6]

What makes the award particularly unfair is that roughly 300 students out of the 400 taking the Maths Tripos exams in the 1860s were not eligible to 'win' the wooden spoon because they were only awarded an Ordinary Degree or failed altogether.[7]

THE DIFFERENT EXPERIENCES OF BEING FIRST

First black student to graduate

The Rev Alexander Crummell from America who studied at Queens' College achieved his degree in 1853. Despite becoming the first black student to graduate, at the degree ceremony in the Senate House:

> A boisterous individual in the gallery called out, 'Three groans for the Queens' [racial slur]', prompting the response from another who shouted in a voice which re-echoed through the building, 'Shame, shame! Three groans for you, Sir!' and immediately afterwards, 'Three cheers for Crummell!'. This was taken up in all directions … and the original offender had to stoop down to hide himself from the storm of groans and hisses that broke out all around him.[8]

Crummell's supporters and sponsors included William Wilberforce and Edward Benson, later Archbishop of Canterbury.

The senior wrangler

From at least 1748, the student obtaining the best marks in their final maths exams was referred to as the senior wrangler, which was a great honour, regarded at the time as the greatest intellectual achievement attainable in Britain.

Walking was considered an activity prospective winners might take part in, because a short walk off Brooklands Avenue (close to the existing Botanic Gardens) alongside Hobson's Brook, became known as Senior Wranglers Walk, or Finch's Walk, probably after Gerard Finch who was senior wrangler in 1857.[9] The route was shorter than other walks, such as the Grantchester Grind, undertaken by undergraduates whose academic aspirations were lower.

A woman with top marks

One individual who scored top marks was Philippa Fawcett in 1890. However, because women were not yet official members of the university, she did not become the official senior wrangler. This went to Geoffrey Bennett who scored 13 per cent fewer marks.

Intelligent women who also cycle – an object of derision

With Philippa Fawcett's success, plus the growing reputation of the two women-only Colleges in Cambridge, Newnham and Girton, a proposal was put before Cambridge University's Senate in 1897 to grant full degrees to female graduates.

This photograph, taken from the first floor of Gonville & Caius College looking towards the existing Cambridge University Press bookshop, with Great St Mary's Church behind, shows the scene on the day of the debate in the Senate House (out of photo on the right). An effigy of a woman on a bicycle was suspended out of the window next to banners reading 'No Gowns for Girtonites' and 'Varsity for Men'.

At the time of the protest, women were permitted to study at Cambridge, but were not granted full degrees. The resolution did not pass, resulting in the triumphant crowd tearing down the effigy, with the shredded remains later stuffed through the gates of Newnham College.

Effigy of a woman on a bicycle close to the Senate House 1897

Thanks to Capturing Cambridge website www.capturingcambridge.org

Women studying at Cambridge University were not to receive the titles of full degrees until 1921, and even then it was without associated privileges. Finally in 1947 Cambridge degrees were granted on equal terms for both men and women.[10]

Despite the hanging and trashing of the woman cyclist, many argue that cycling for women in general 'made the greatest contribution to the physical liberation of women',[11] with participation in other sports, having to take place 'behind closed doors'.

Given the two women's colleges at the time were on the outskirts of Cambridge (and therefore not on the walking route chosen for each chapter of this book) it is important to include a section here on women and sport.

WOMEN'S EDUCATION AND SPORT IN CAMBRIDGE

The story of women's collegiate sport began modestly in 1869 when Emily Davies' plan to make university education accessible to women resulted in the opening of Hitchin College in Hertfordshire to five young women, soon relocating to Girton, on the outskirts of Cambridge, in 1873.

Early in her campaign for educational reform Emily Davies noted the 'importance of physical health to the life of the nation' and lamented that 'women are not healthy…..[and show] a want of stamina'.[12] Her concern was for both physical as well as mental development which is why she encouraged her students to take long country walks, and to play croquet, fives and a crude form of cricket in the seclusion of the college garden, which they apparently did 'with great laughter and fun, but small skill'.[13]

Since none of the students could swim, Miss Davies urged them to patronize the local open-air swimming bath on the one day a week it was open to them, and even provided an aquatic role model by taking to the water herself. When they began to play a very mild form of football however, she quickly forbade it on the grounds that outside knowledge of such an overtly masculine activity would be taken as incontrovertible proof of the 'unsexing consequences of higher education'. Despite a lack of facilities in its early days, the authorities of the new Girton College considered students' health of such importance that free time for physical recreation was provided each afternoon.[14]

Girton College Cricket Team – 1898
Permission granted with thanks to The Mistress and Fellows, Girton College, Cambridge.

Impact of Muscular Christianity

It is not known what Frank Fenner's views were on women playing sport, however when he was a child and young adult, 'Georgian women played an active role in cricket' compared with 'Victorian women, on the whole, who did not'.[15]

An analysis of the impact of Muscular Christianity indicates that whilst responsible for the growth of sports in the public schools and Oxford and Cambridge universities (and the English sporting revolution), the 'movement strengthened the tendency towards male chauvinism and led Victorians to disparage female participation in outdoor sports'.[16]

Sport for local women

Outside of the developments of women's sport in both Girton and Newnham Colleges, the opportunities for local women during the Victorian period were practically non-existent. In Eglantyne Jebb's research of poverty and inequality between town and gown published in 1906, there were some limited opportunities for men, but for local women:

> The unceasing round of domestic duties leaves little or no time for leisure and recreation ... The girls find no better happiness than that of parading the streets in their best clothes growing up into women who spend the day gossiping on their doorsteps or in reading penny novelties.[17]

THE GROWING STATUS OF LOCAL CRICKET

'Degree Day' was painted by Robert Farren in 1863 portraying a lonely student accompanied by a small dog, in the foreground, who has failed his final exams, presumably having just seen his results posted outside the Senate House, the building just behind him on the right of the painting. To the left of this student, close by, is the wooden spoon winner. Note the relatively small size of the spoon, compared to what it grew into.

Degree Day - 1863
Permission granted by Museum of Cambridge.

Surrounding the 'failed' student, and wooden spoon 'winner' (thanks to a detailed key of all individuals featured in the painting) are the most important academics including Charles Kingsley, Henry Sedgwick, Henry Fawcett and Leslie Stephen, accompanied by their families, as well as two bowler-hatted figures standing on the corner of Great St Mary's Church, behind the white and black dog, next to the women in a grey dress on the left of the painting. These are two of the four England cricketers from the town, Thomas Hayward and Robert Carpenter, at a time when Cambridgeshire cricket was as strong as any other side in the country.

Their inclusion in the painting indicates their social importance, thanks to the increasing status of cricket, and perhaps sport more generally in the University, with Hayward (see photo - back row – last right - standing), Carpenter (back row – left), and Alfred Diver, another local cricketer (front row – left) all representing England on the first cricket tour to North America in 1859, having an impact.

England cricket tour to North America (1859)
The Roger Mann Collection.

Thomas Hayward

Thomas Hayward was born in Chatteris, Cambridgeshire, in 1835, to Daniel ('the elder') Hayward, a gardener.

Thomas's cricketing career started in Cambridge, including as the professional for Jesus College in 1856. To make a decent living from cricket he travelled far and wide, including to the Richmondshire Club in North Yorkshire and to Stockton-on-Tees. When he was an established player he represented the All-England Eleven on numerous occasions at various venues. This included being a member of England's first overseas tour to North America in 1859, where he joined his two fellow Cambridge cricketers Robert Carpenter and Ducky Diver. William Percival 'Bull' Pickering (chapter 10) was instrumental in arranging this tour, having emigrated to Canada in 1852.

Thomas was the youngest player on the tour, topping the batting average. The tourists shared £1,700 between them, enough to demonstrate cricket gave entrepreneurs and players the chance to make some money.[18] On their return to Cambridge they were welcomed back at a reception hosted at the Old Castle Inn (chapter 19).

Thomas married Lizzie Dell and they had eight children. Whilst Thomas made a lot of money, through betting and gaming he was subject to liquidation and bankruptcy orders, so ending his life penniless. He died of consumption (tuberculosis) in 1876 at the age of 41, and was buried in Mill Road Cemetery. The location of his grave is unknown.

Robert Carpenter

Robert Carpenter was born in 1830 on Mill Road where he lived the 70 years of his life, close to Mill Road Cemetery where he was buried. His father was a butcher, with Robert starting as a bootmaker before becoming a professional cricketer.

The pinnacle of Robert's career, with Thomas Hayward and Ducky Diver, was going on the first overseas tour by an England team to the US and Canada in 1859, and touring Australia and New Zealand in 1862-63.

His playing career also included cricket on ice, for example in 1867 and 1870 playing against Swavesey (a village 8 miles (13km) northwest from Cambridge), when Robert captained an All-England and University team, watched by a very large number of people, many arriving by train.[19] In 1878 Robert also captained a side against the University playing over three days on the ice of Granchester Meadows.

At his death in 1901, he left a widow, Eliza, having had nine children including Herbert Arthur Carpenter who played cricket for the Anchor team (chapter 20).

As with Thomas Hayward, the whereabouts of Robert's grave in Mill Road Cemetery is unknown.

It is possible, given Frank Fenner's contribution to local and university cricket, that he too might have been featured in Farren's 1863 painting, but whilst he still held the lease on Fenner's Cricket Ground, he had already left Cambridge to live in the West Country.

MARBLES ON THE SENATE HOUSE STEPS

In June 1920 the local press reported:[20]

> An unusual scene was witnessed outside the Senate House, Cambridge when a number of young graduates attired in evening dress and wearing bachelors' hoods over their gowns settled down to a game of marbles on the steps of the building.

> An old statute [law] of the University permits its graduates to indulge in this enthralling pursuit on the Senate House steps but for many years no graduate has availed himself of the privilege. Saturday's players attended the Senate House to be admitted to their degrees and as soon as the ceremony was concluded they produced chalk and bottles and marbles and entered into a lively game on the top step of the southern exit from the building.

> Marbles were a popular game at one time. The marbles themselves could be carried about so easily that at the 'elevens' past generations of

Cambridge tradesman, having broken from business for refreshment, challenged neighbours and friends to try conclusions on the street pavements. The gutters ran with marbles and it appears that the University statute was framed in order that graduates might enjoy their contests in comparative privacy. A doctor in his scarlet robe could not with dignity flop

New graduates playing marbles on Senate House steps - 1920

Source: Cambridge Chronicle and Journal 23 June 1920. Page 7. Cambridgeshire Collection, Cambridge Central Library.

down in Petty Cury and carry on a marble competition with any don who he chanced to meet. The cunning of the men of learning with the nimble glass alleys could not be revealed to the vulgar crowds of loafers and errand boys. So the sedate old Fellows went inside the Senate House railings and without interference or interruption.

1   Scottish Golf History – earliest golf sites and golfers. https://www.scottishgolfhistory.org/oldest-golf-sites/

2   Venn's Cambridge Alumni Database. https://venn.lib.cam.ac.uk/

3   Neville Tebbutt (1896). A handbook of Bandy; or Hockey on Ice. London: Horace Cox. Page 2.

4   Ambiguous Expressions at Cambridge elucidated, by "a Cantab" published in The Gentleman's Magazine: and Historical Chronicle (London) of January 1795. From wordhistories website.

5   Stephen J. Cowley, DAMTP, University of Cambridge. http://www.damtp.cam.ac.uk/user/sjc1/selwyn/mathematics/spoon.html

6   Hear the Boat sing website: https://heartheboatsing.com/2020/09/24/cuthbert-lempriere-holthouse-the-man-with-the-last-wooden-spoon/.

7   Galton, Francis (1869). Hereditary Genius-An Enquiry into its Laws and Consequences.

8   The Life of Edward White Benson, by A.C. Benson, 1899, Vol. 1 p. 109.

9   Capturing Cambridge website: https://capturingcambridge.org/newtown/brooklands-avenue/finchs-walk/

10   https://www.sheilahanlon.com/?p=292

11   Kathleen McCrone. Page 156 and 161 in The 'lady blue'. Sport at the Oxbridge women's colleges from their foundation to 1914. Chapter 6 in J.A. Mangan - ed (2006). A sport-loving society.

12   Kathleen McCrone. Page 156 in The 'lady blue'. Sport at the Oxbridge women's colleges from their foundation to 1914. Chapter 6 in J.A. Mangan - ed (2006). A sport-loving society.

13   Kathleen McCrone. Page 156 in The 'lady blue'. Sport at the Oxbridge women's colleges from their foundation to 1914. Chapter 6 in J.A. Mangan - ed (2006). A sport-loving society.

14   Kathleen McCrone in the 'lady blue'. Sport at the Oxbridge women's colleges from their foundation to 1914. Chapter 6 in J.A. Mangan - ed (2006). A sport-loving society. Page 156.

15   Keith A.P. Sandiford (1982). Cricket and the Victorians: A historiographical essay in Historical Reflections. Vol 9. No 3 pp 421-436. https://www.jstor.org/stable/41298796. Page 428.

16   Keith A.P. Sandiford (1982) Cricket and the Victorians: A historiographical essay in Historical Reflections. Vol 9. No 3 pp 421-436. https://www.jstor.org/stable/41298796. Page 428.

17   Eglantyne Jebb (1906) Cambridge: a brief study in Social Questions. Page 139.

18   Keith and Jennifer Booth (2018). The Haywards. The biography of a cricket dynasty. Chequered Flag Publishing. Page 76.

19   Norwich Mercury 19 Feb 1870.

20   Cambridge Chronicle and Journal 23 June 1920 page 7.

CHAPTER 14

King's College

The King's College of Our Lady and St Nicholas in Cambridge was founded in 1441 by King Henry VI, making it the eighth oldest in the University. The college was to be filled by students from Eton College, founded by the King a year earlier.

Henry VI's plans for the college were disrupted by the Wars of the Roses, so little progress was made until 1508 when Henry VII took an interest. The building of the college's chapel, begun in 1446, was finally finished in 1544 during the reign of Henry VIII.

SPORT BEFORE THE NINETEENTH CENTURY

Children's education in the Elizabethan Age

Richard Mulcaster published two books analysing the education of his time, setting out some basic principles organised around the needs of the state, and that education be open to all, rich and poor, male and female (though he did not approve of women continuing in school). His *Positions Concerning the Training up of Children* (published in English in 1581) argued in favour of physical education.[1]

For example, Mulcaster was one of the first advocates of referees, or 'neutral arbiters':[2]

> For if one stand by, which can judge of the play, and is judge over
> the parties, & hath authoritie to commande in the place, all those
> inconveniences have bene, I know, & wilbe I am sure very lightly
> redressed, nay they will never entermedle in the matter, neither
> shall there be complaint, where there is no cause.

He also proposed positions on the pitch for players ('standings'), a coach
('trayning maister'), smaller teams and less violence:

> Some smaller number with such overlooking, sorted into sides and
> standings, not meeting with their bodies so boisterously to trie their
> strength: nor shouldring or shuffing one another so barbarously ... may
> use footeball for as much good to the body, by the chiefe use of the legges.

Mulcaster was a sixteen-year-old student at King's College in 1548,
transferring to Peterhouse, and after five years in Cambridge[3], moving to
Oxford to finish his degree and escape from his master Dr John Caius (later
founder of Gonville & Caius College Caius) who Mulcaster probably stole
from.[4] Later he was to become the headteacher of Merchant Taylor's School
and St. Paul's School, both in London.[5]

Inventor of 'the weekend'?

Sir Robert Walpole was the first prime minister in British political history,
who served uninterrupted for 20 years from 1721. He shared an interest with
King George I in hunting, which Walpole wrote publicly about being addicted
to. This resulted in letters from his huntsmen being opened before official
correspondence. In the season, he hunted on one weekday and also on Saturdays,
which influenced Parliamentary timetables and inspired the notion of the
weekend, reputedly an English invention.[6]

His work as Prime Minister involved close collaboration with Charles or
'Turnip' Townshend, in the 'Walpole–Townshend ministry' lasting from 1721
to 1730. 'Turnip' Townshend is often mentioned, alongside Jethro Tull, Robert
Bakewell and others, as a major figure in England's 'Agricultural Revolution',
contributing to the adoption of agricultural practices that supported the
increase in Britain's population between 1700 and 1850.

However, Townsend's early life was not without controversy. For example,
prior to serving in Walpole's government, a broadsheet in 1712 condemned
him and the deposed Duke of Marlborough for corrupting the 'innocent sports
of those inferior in age and grandeur' by playing cricket with two boys in
Windsor Forest on the Sabbath and betting twenty guineas on the result
(worth about £4,500 today).[7]

Charles Townshend started as a student at King's College in 1691, Robert
Walpole in 1696.

Cricket

The first description of the game of cricket in literature was written by William Goldwin in 1706 when a Fellow at King's College. He lived in or near Cambridge. On seeing 'a chosen company, with curving bats armed gallantly … with shouts into the field they go', he wrote the following in Latin verse:

> They pitch two sets of wickets, each with a milk-white bail perched on two stumps, toss a coin for first knock, the umpire calls 'play' and the 'leathern orb' is bowled.[8]

It is likely he was referring to cricket being played within the confines of a college's own grounds, or possibly on Midsummer Common or Jesus Green, given their relative flatness compared with Parker's Piece (which up until the early nineteenth century 'lay in ridges and furrows, with ditches and hawthorn trees about; on the west side was a small brook'.)[9]

Introduction of the LBW law

William Draper, student at King's College from 1740, was later a British military officer who fought at Manila, Menorca, Culloden and Flanders. Between times he chaired the committee that formulated some of the earliest laws of cricket, including, for the first time, the 'leg before wicket' (LBW) rule, in London in 1774.

LINKS TO THE TOWN

First Cambridge golfers – on Midsummer Common

A letter written to The Field dated 4 November 1869 signed off under the pseudonym 'Light Iron' is believed to be by George Gosset, a student at King's College from 1866 to 1870 who describes the early efforts of playing golf on Midsummer Common:

> Sir, having had my croquet mallet recognised by a Cambridge rustic as 'something for tapping beer', I was surprised at a whispered 'Look at they hockies!' as K [believed to be Cecil George Kellner, also a student at King's College] and myself proceeded for the first time down Trinity Street with a few golf clubs and a hole-cutter under our arms. Arrived at Midsummer Common [the area today known as Jesus Green], a hole is cut near the end of Park Street; then, having teed our balls, we drive

for the Lock House [about 280 yards], near which another hole is cut. At this point the small boys who had followed us retire, I fancy disappointed at our not having laid our cleeks [club like a driving iron] on each other's shins. Thence we skirt the river for about half a mile, and returning inland to our starting point we find that we have cut a course of eight holes, over ground which is equal to the Manchester links in the uncertainty of getting a good lie, or rather in the certainty of getting a bad lie.[10]

Not long after, Andrew Graham Murray (student at Trinity College from 1868) started practicing golf on Midsummer Common, so becoming friends with Gosset. Both agreed that Midsummer Common was unsatisfactory 'in the first place … you really could not have links; secondly, you would get into frightful trouble for hitting people'.[11]

Cricket shaping Keynesian economics?

John Maynard Keynes (JMK) was perhaps the most important economist of the twentieth century. His life was intimately connected with King's College; he came as an undergraduate in 1902 and was a Fellow from 1909 until his death in 1946. It is known that JMK had a love of cricket throughout his life, born out of watching the sport with his father at Fenner's, which was very near to the family home.

The book *Golden Age at the Fenner's Margin*, written by Adrian Wykes,[12] speculates that this is where JMK as a child may well have also developed his love and understanding of economics:

> The (cricket) captain he feels acts like the entrepreneur in some great financial enterprise, dispensing his resources in a variety of purposeful directions, trying to maintain the cohesion of the disparate parts in the pursuit of an attainable aim, and grasping any opportunities lent by the opposition to further the cause of the team. Crucial to this are the visible signs that JMK sees as a spectator: the decisions about who should bowl and who should field where, which lend themselves very well to the concept of productive efficiency and least-cost operation.

Wykes also believes that JMK and Jack Hobbs (chapter 20) would have watched the same cricket matches at Fenner's as children, given they were both the same age, and frequent visitors.

ENGLAND'S SPORTING REVOLUTION

A sporting ethos

Edward Thring (student at King's College from 1841, then a Fellow from 1844 to 1853) was a celebrated British educator who from 1853 to 1887, turned a poor provisional grammar school in Uppingham with '25 boys and 2 masters, in mean premises' to 'a foremost position amongst the public schools, with 30 masters … and 320 boys'. In addition, 'Uppingham was the first great public school to make special provision … for a varied culture outside the traditional range of Classical study … who set great value on music, art, and the study of modern languages'.[13]

**Edward Thring (1889):
celebrated British educator**
Thanks to Uppingham School Archives.

This also included Thring 'exulting in the rush of life in the tree and grass, so that late into his career he demonstrated his enthusiasm by taking part in the boys' football and cricket matches. Apparently, 'Thring had a Wordsworthian passion for nature, [and] a Kingsleian delight in bodily exercise including the wisdom that "life is one piece … health of body, health of intellect, health of heart all uniting to form the true man."' This is why Uppingham became the first school to open a gymnasium in 1860, complete with a full-time German instructor. If Charles 'Kingsley was the prophet of this revolution in educational ideals', Thring was perhaps its priest.[14]

Edward was brother to John Charles Thring, author of The Simplist Game, endeavouring to create a common code for football (chapter 8).

A further student at King's College who later promoted the link between sport and education was James Welldon, a student from 1873 and Fellow from 1878 to 1889, later headteacher of Harrow for 15 years. He was also a fervent imperialist believing:

> Englishmen are not superior to Frenchmen or German in brains or industry, or the science or apparatus of war.' In what then, did their superiority reside? It was 'the health and temper which games impart' that set the British apart. 'The pluck, the energy, the perseverance, the good temper, the self-control, the discipline, the co-operation, the esprit de corps, which merit success in cricket or football, are the very qualities which win the day in peace or war.

'In the history of the British Empire,' he concluded, 'it is written that England has owed her sovereignty to her sports.'[15]

Rugby introduction to Wales

The first competitive rugby match ever played in Wales was in 1850 between St David's College, Lampeter and nearby Llandovery College. Credit is given to the Rev. Professor Rowland Williams, who became Vice Principal of St David's College in 1850[16] having probably played the Rugby School version of football when a student at King's College. Williams had started as a student at King's in 1836, becoming a Fellow in 1839 until 1850.[17]

Rowland Williams: introduction of Rugby Union to Wales

Thanks to University of Wales Trinity Saint David: Special Collections and Archives.

Whilst the experience of King's College for Thring, Welldon and Williams may well have positively informed their attitudes to sport, this was not shared by everyone.

Sport (and hot water bottles) frowned upon

For example E. M. Forster, a student from 1897, believed the college to be 'civilised and proud of its civilisation. It was not sufficient glory to be a Blue there, nor an additional glory to get drunk'.[18] But nor was it acceptable to use a hot water bottle either, with Shane Leslie recalling in the early twentieth century that a third-year student was actually discovered using one:

This was considered a disgrace to the college and Hope-Jones challenged its owner to run the quarter mile round the front court on a windy dawn. It was agreed that the challenger should run stark [naked] while the challenged wore as much clothing as he wished. The race was won by the less encumbered party and the offending hot-water bottle was duly confiscated and sent to Doctor Barnardo [charity for poor children] with the compliments of the Provost, the Fellows and Scholars of the college.[19]

Other students went beyond sport to achieve much more.

Philip John Noel-Baker

Philip John Noel-Baker (student at King's College from 1908) is the only person to win an Olympic medal, Silver in 1500m (athletics) in 1920, and a Nobel Prize for peace in 1959 for his work on global disarmament.

Philip Noel-Baker: first Olympic medalist and Nobel Prize winner

The Papers of Baron Noel-Baker, Churchill Archives Centre, Cambridge. Document reference NBKR 6/22.

When the First World War began, he co-founded the (Quaker) Friends Ambulance Unit for which Noel-Baker was decorated for his service in France.

1   Oxford Dictionary of National Biography. Entry on Richard Mulcaster 23 Sept 2004.

    https://www.oxforddnb.com/

2   Derek Birley (1993). Sport and the making of Britain. Manchester University Press. Page 69.

3   Venn. A Cambridge Alumni Database. https://venn.lib.cam.ac.uk

4   Oxford Dictionary of National Biography. Entry on Richard Mulcaster 23 Sept 2004. https://www.

    oxforddnb.com/

5   Venn. A Cambridge Alumni Database. https://venn.lib.cam.ac.uk

6   Derek Birley (1993). Sport and the making of Britain. Manchester University Press. Page 107.

7   Derek Birley (1993). Sport and the making of Britain. Manchester University Press. Page 106.

8   Willie Sugg (2002). A Tradition unshared. A history of Cambridge Town and County Cricket 1700

    - 1890. Part 1. Real Work Publishing. Page 36.

9   Henry Payne Stokes (1915). Outside the Barnwell Gate. Pages 44 and 45.

10   Michael Morrison (2016). The worst golf course ever. Coldham Common. A history of the Cambridge

    University Golf Club. 1869 – 1919. Page 15.

11   Michael Morrison (2016). The worst golf course ever. Coldham Common. A history of the Cambridge

    University Golf Club. 1869 – 1919. Page 17.

12   A.P.A. Wykes (2005). Golden Age at the Fenner's Margin – an investigation into cricket, economics,

    Cambridge and Keynes. Serendipity.

13   Entry for Edward Thring on Venn Cambridge Alumni Database: https://venn.lib.cam.ac.uk/

14   Dominic Erdozain (2010) The problem of pleasure: sport, recreation and the crisis of Victorian

    religion. Studies in Modern British Religious History. Vol 22. Page 108.

15   Richard Holt (1993) Sport and the British. A Modern History. Clarendon Press. Page 205.

16   https://students.uwtsd.ac.uk/event/150th-anniversary-celebrations-lampeter-the-birthplace-of-

    welsh-rugby/

17   Entry for Rowland Williams on Venn Cambridge Alumni Database. https://venn.lib.cam.ac.uk

18   J.A. Mangan (2006). A sport-loving society. Victorian and Edwardian Middle-Class England at play.

    Routledge . Page 98.

19   J.A. Mangan (2006). 'Oars and the man'. Pleasure and purpose in Victorian and Edwardian

    Cambridge' in J.A. Mangan (ed) 'A sport-loving society'. Page 98.

CHAPTER 15

Great St Mary's Church

HISTORY

A church on Cambridge Market Square was first mentioned in 1205, known as St Mary-by-the-market, before the foundation of the University in 1209. It is called Great St Mary's to distinguish it from Little St Mary's Church, just under half a mile away, next to Peterhouse. It is a parish church, as well as being known as the University Church.

The use of the church for university functions was established from an early date. It was this connection, during the Peasants' Revolt of 1381 backed by the local mayor, which led to Great St Mary's being ransacked, including the burning of the University's archives which were stored there.[1] Margaret Starre led the mob in a dance to the rallying cry 'Away with the learning of clerks, away with it!' while the documents burned.[2]

The church has had many famous preachers and members of royalty visit, and before the Senate House was built was used by the University for meetings and examinations.

In 1607 students were banned from taking tobacco into St Mary's Church, the penalty being a fine of 6s 8d [equivalent to about £40 today].[3]

Great St Mary's is the official centre of Cambridge and has been since 1725, when William Warren began measuring the roads out of Cambridge choosing the door of the church as his milestone starting point. This is why today there is a datum disc set up in the wall.

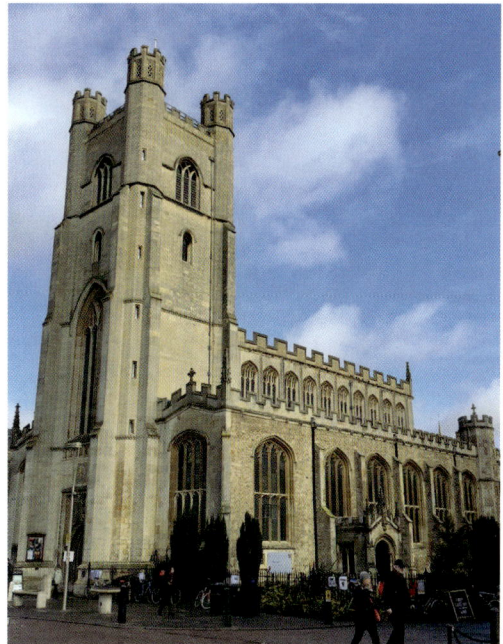

The tune of the chimes at Great St Mary's, the 'Cambridge Quarters', was composed in 1793, made famous after 1859 when it was copied for the 'Westminster Chimes' of Big Ben at the Houses of Parliament, still used today.

Great St Mary's is unusual in having two organs, which is a hangover from the rivalry between Town and Gown. With Great St Mary's being in the middle of the town, it is an interesting and powerful image for Cambridge, having at its heart two organs.

SPORTING LINKS

James I

During his reign, James I of England made four known visits to Cambridge to take a break from hunting at nearby Newmarket. His first visit in 1615 involved a lively debate in Great St Mary's Church as to whether dogs could use logic – with James believing that by 'yelling arguments', his hunting dog could persuade other dogs to follow a scent.[4]

Frank Fenner – senior churchwarden

Frank was the senior churchwarden at Great St Mary's Church in 1858. As the lay guardian of the church his formal responsibilities included not only maintaining the edifice and goods of the church, with the financial obligations involved, but also demonstrating a strong Christian faith. Evidence of this work, and the quality of Frank's writing is seen in a letter of thanks dated 20 August 1858, and published in the local press:

> To the Rev. Francis Gerald Vesey. Dear Sir – your connection with the parish of St Mary the Great having terminated, I am called upon, as Senior Churchwarden, to perform a duty as pleasing to myself, as it is felt to be deserved by you. For nearly three years you have assisted to discharge the ministerial duties of our parish; and by the exercise of constant and untiring zeal, by a series of benevolent acts, by continuous kindness, and especially indefatigable attention to the welfare – temporal as well as spiritual – of your poorer neighbours, have inspired in all a sentiment of genuine esteem. Your removal from us to a more enlarged sphere of duties is a matter for congratulation, as well as regret; and a few of those who have benefitted by the examples of your calling have thought fit to show their appreciation of your worth by the enclosed small memento [inscribed silver inkstand] of your connection with their parish. We do not ask you, Sir, to look upon this small gift as bearing intrinsically any proportion to the respect we feel, but simply to prize it as a souvenir of a brief but we hope happy epoch in your life. If the recollection of your sojourn amongst us should ever fail, we trust to this as a pleasurable reminder; and animated with an ardent desire for your future welfare, believe me when I subscribe myself, on behalf of the contributors, with sincere admiration and respect, Your very truly F.P. Fenner. 6, Market Hill, Cambridge.

The newspaper also then added 'He [Vesey] was a sincere friend to the cause of education in Cambridge, as his labours in connection with the Working Men's College testify'.[5]

The loss of Vesey in 1858 coincided with Harvey Goodwin, the Principal of the Working Men's College also leaving, which understandably unsettled the college as a relatively new initiative. This is explored further in Chapter 16, including Frank Fenner's contribution to the Working Men's College.

[1]   The city of Cambridge: Churches Pages 123-132. A History of the County of Cambridge and the Isle of Ely: Volume 3, the City and University of Cambridge. Originally published by Victoria County History, London, 1959.

[2]   Edgar Powell (1896). The rising in East Anglia in 1381. Cambridge University Press. Page 52.

[3]   Queens' College website: https://www.queens.cam.ac.uk/visiting-the-college/history/university-facts/the-way-things-were

[4]   Great St Mary's website: http://www.gsm.cam.ac.uk/heritage/history/royal-cambridge/

[5]   Cambridge Chronicle and Journal 28 August 1858 page 4.

CHAPTER 16

The Market

From left to right: **Frank's tobacco shop and gym (1855), the Guildhall and Gt St Mary's Church**

HISTORY OF THE MARKET

Today the market is on the Market Square, with the road that surrounds it called Market Hill, with the word 'hill' also meaning firm ground.

The first recorded mention of a market is from 973,[1] over 200 years before the University was founded, serving as a 'reminder that the town is older than the University and has an independent raison d'être'.[2]

The medieval marketplace was much larger than it is now, providing a range of goods and services, for example at Butter Row, Cheese Market, Cordwainers' [shoemakers] Row, Cutlers' [cutlery] Lane, Goldsmiths' Row, Malt Market, Saddlers' Row, Shraggery [timber] Market and a Spicery. It also had a Peasmarket at Peas Hill and bull ring and butchery.

In 1614 the branch of Hobson's Conduit, bringing freshwater to the market, was completed. A major fire in 1849 resulted in the structure housing the fountain being moved to the corner of Lensfield Road and Trumpington Road, where it stands to this day. A replacement, a Gothic Revival gabled fountain, was erected in 1855, with only the base remaining.

The southern part of the old medieval marketplace gradually became occupied by municipal buildings in the nineteenth Century including the Town Hall or Guildhall.

SPORT ON THE MARKET

In the early seventeenth century students were banned from 'walking on Market Hill, sitting on stalls, going to pubs on Fridays', and wearing or sporting 'curled locks, great ruffs, velvet pantables, velvet breeches, and coloured nether stocks', when caps, gowns and hoods were the regulation uniform. The University also banned football, dogs, bull-baiting, bear-baiting, bowling, nine holes, 'Dagges, Gunnes, Crossbowes and Stonbows', plays, and public shows'.[3]

Later, in 1727, students were also forbidden 'to join the disorderly assemblies upon Market Hill, drawn thither on Shrove Tuesday by the prospect of cock-fighting.'[4]

Jumping forward to 1923, the local paper reported:

> One hundred years ago the Royal and ancient game of rugby football was initiated, and today an alleged representation of the first game was given in Cambridge Market Square. Sometime before noon the square was roped off and surrounded by police. The fountain was converted into a Royal box and the telephone kiosk into a press box. At noon the teams marched on to the ground. At their head was carried a large and considerably elongated football on a butcher's tray.'[5]

It was perhaps this celebration that resulted in the formation of Cambridge Rugby Club in the same year, the first local club, following the creation of Cambridge University Rugby Union Football Club in 1872, 51 years previously.

This chapter is now sub-divided into six sections that follows a clockwise route round the market, starting at Rose Crescent, and then leaving it along Peas Hill, and Bene't Street.

Stop 1: Rose Crescent – H J Gray & Sons first sports shop

Just off the market is Rose Crescent (today a pedestrianised street off the northern end of the market) where H J Gray & Sons opened their first sport shop in 1892 at number 8. For more on Harry Gray go to St John's College (chapter 8), and University Arms, Parker's Piece (chapter 20).

Today Grays International, famous for its Gray-Nicholls cricket bats, Gilbert rugby balls and Hazells hockey sticks has an annual turnover of £25 million.

Stop 2:
6 Market Hill - Fenner's Cigar Stores

This stop takes in three important facilities at the same address: Fenner's cigar stores, a gymnasium and the Working Men's College.

Frank Fenner opened his cigar stores here in 1855, believed to be on the same site as the shop using an awning in the postcard above (where the current Marks & Spencer store is located). The replacement for Hobson's fountain is in the foreground, the base of which is still visible in the centre of the Market.

It is possible to imagine what would have been displayed in Frank's stores, thanks to the variety of artefacts at today's Museum of Cambridge (chapter 2), such as a large range of pipes, some with novelty heads, and a wooden sign, sadly portraying the contribution African slaves made in harvesting tobacco.[6]

Site of Frank Fenner's Cigar Stores - postcard image before 1904
From the collection of David Gent.

Tobacco, snuff and cigar advertising sign
Image reproduced with permission from Museum of Cambridge.

Celebrated pipe smokers, and Frank's shops in Cambridge

For the 25 years Frank was a local tobacconist, celebrated pipe smokers included Charles Darwin and Charles Kingsley, which coincided with Frank having his first shop on Sidney Street from 1836, aged 25.

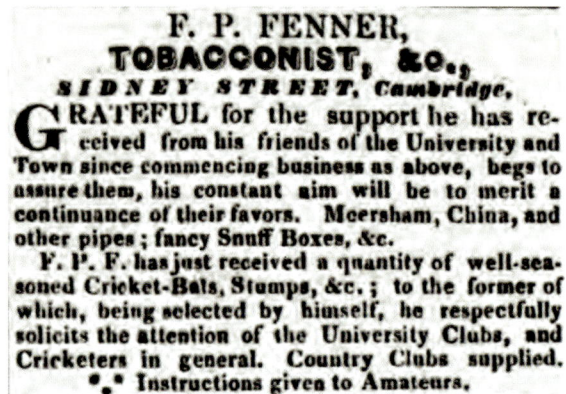

F. P. FENNER, TOBACCONIST, &c.,
SIDNEY STREET, Cambridge.

GRATEFUL for the support he has received from his friends of the University and Town since commencing business as above, begs to assure them, his constant aim will be to merit a continuance of their favors. Meersham, China, and other pipes; fancy Snuff Boxes, &c.

F. P. F. has just received a quantity of well-seasoned Cricket-Bats, Stumps, &c.; to the former of which, being selected by himself, he respectfully solicits the attention of the University Clubs, and Cricketers in general. Country Clubs supplied.

** Instructions given to Amateurs.

Source: Huntingdon, Bedford & Peterborough Gazette 12 March 1836.
Newspaper image © The British Library Board. All rights reserved. With thanks to The British Newspaper Archive (www.britishnewspaperarchive.co.uk).

Later he had a shop just off Parker's Piece (chapter 20), followed by Regent Street (chapter 19) and lastly one here on Market Hill, where Leslie Stephen, as a keen smoker and sports enthusiast, was probably a frequent visitor.

Anti-smoking campaign

Charles Bristed (student at Trinity College from 1840) writing from the perspective of an average undergraduate, reported 'he often starts himself for his morning's work with the stimulus of a cigar.'[7] Certainly, the number of tobacconists in Cambridge were steadily increasing at this time, which led to some opposition. For example, in November 1854 a Thomas Reynolds of London (who founded the Anti-Tobacco Society) came to deliver a lecture against tobacco. Large crowds of undergraduates went to the Guildhall to hear him, but as soon as the lecture began they all lit up pipes and cigars and shouted abusive remarks which so enraged the lecturer that he became equally abusive. The police had finally to clear the hall and next day two Johnians (St John's College students) were fined £5 each for assaulting a constable.[8]

CAMBRIDGE'S SPORTING HUB?

Frank's investment

We know from an advertisement auctioning the freehold on which Fenner's shop stood, dated 1858, that 6, Market Hill comprised:

> A very roomy dwelling house, with attractive Front Shop, and Rooms behind, very superior and extensive cellarage, principal and back staircases, leading to numerous excellent rooms on three floors, together with private entrance from the Market Hill. The back premises comprise a large newly-erected brick building with iron roof, having two floors, and now used as the Working Men's College, an extensive plot of ground behind, on which has been lately erected the University Gymnasium, the whole well supplied with water, and now let on a Lease to Mr F.P. Fenner, for a term of 11 years, from the 25th March 1855, at the very low rent of £100 per annum, in consideration of the great outlay (several hundred pounds) by the Leasee.[9]

When Frank made these alterations (as the leasee), completed in September 1855, the local press reported 'the spirit Mr Fenner has shown in fitting-up this building [the University Gymnasium], and also the Working Men's College, deserves great praise.'[10]

Consequently, Frank's window display would not only have promoted his tobacco products, but also Fenner's Ground and the cricket matches, University athletics and other community events hosted there, as well as his on-site gymnasium and the Working Men's College, both located behind his shop. He could not have had a better location in the centre of town to do so.

Athletics

In the first year of the University Foot Races and Athletic Sports, held in 1857, they were both at Frank's ground and advertised at his shop, where entry subscriptions were also taken.

For example the entry in the Cambridge Chronicle and Journal of 7 March 1857 reads

> University Foot Races - These races will commence on Monday 16th March, on Fenner's cricket ground. Gentlemen desirous of entering, or of subscribing to them, are requested to enter their names at Mr Fenner's, Market-place, on or before Thursday 12th March. A programme of the sports may be seen, and further information obtained at Mr Fenner's, Subscriptions, 2s. 6d. : entrance to each race, etc, 1s.

This was the same year the Cambridge University Athletics Club was formed.[11]

The annual University Foot Races and Athletic Sports continued to be held at Fenner's Ground, with Frank having an increasing involvement in their organisation. For example, in 1859, notice was posted in the press that 'there will be a meeting of the gentlemen interested in these races at Mr. Fenner's [at 6, Market Hill], on Monday evening next, for the purpose of choosing a committee and making other arrangements.'[12]

Cricket meetings

Frank's efforts to raise the standard of local cricket (not just at the University) included, in 1858, working with Henry Perkins (later MCC Secretary) to found Cambridgeshire County Cricket Club, which included holding its General Meetings at Fenner's premises at 6 Market Hill in 1860 and 1861.[13]

Towards the end of Frank's life, he recalled that 'as secretary of the University Cricket Club for a quarter of a century I saw what an impetus it gave to the game,'[14] which from the club's minute books included meetings held at 6 Market Hill in 1855, 1856 (twice), 1857 (twice), 1860, 1861 (twice), and the Pavilion on Fenner's Ground in 1862.[15]

Cambridge (University) sport: in Fenner's hands?

At the time Frank contributed significantly towards the management of local and University cricket and athletics, including opening his own ground, and a gymnasium, he was leading a new approach to promoting sport.

Up until the early nineteenth century, sport across England was mostly organised by a chaotic mix of publicans, fair vendors, the betting and gambling fraternity, aristocrats, the military and peasants (following their oral traditions).

As far as the public schools were concerned, 'sport and games were of very little interest to the headmasters',[16] instead being run by the students themselves.

However, when these same students arrived in Cambridge in the mid nineteenth century, staying only for the duration of their university studies (usually three years), a significant number were probably impressed enough with Frank's experience as a leading sports player, coach and administrator, and his provision of dedicated facilities, to follow his leadership. In addition, Frank apparently had the support of individual staff within the University, who it was reported were 'eager to hear his manly and generous deductions'[17] up until the 1860s.

These University staff may well have included Leslie Stephen and a number of Jesus College fellows, including Henry Arthur Morgan and Edmund Henry Morgan, who are credited as winning over the often hostile University authorities in their endeavours to establish Varsity athletics as 'fresh inter-University competitions of a non-intellectual nature'.[18]

Leslie Stephen's interest in sport has already been described (chapter 10), followed by Jesus College's rise to 'athletic prominence, during the decade of the 1870s'[19] led by the Morgans (chapter 6).

Other influential University staff include Arthur Ward (student at St John's College from 1849 and later Treasurer of the University Cricket Club from 1873 – chapter 5).

Gymnasium

The local press of 29 September 1855 reported:

> There is nothing better for the health or spirits, especially of reading men, than moderate exercise. In this country, this cannot always be out of doors in the winter. We are therefore grateful to state, that a Gymnasium has been nearly completed, by Mr Fenner at the back of his premises, No 6 Market Hill. The building is a very capacious one and will be fitted up in the most approved manner, with every sort of apparatus designed for developing muscular strength and expanding the chest. We believe that the Gymnasium is intended for the exclusive use of University men during Term time: and we understand that several Tutors and others have visited the building, and expressed themselves pleased with the arrangements, to make which perfect no expense is being spared. Everything will be in readiness for our youthful athletes by the time next Term begins.[20]

Frank followed this
up with regular adverts
in the press.

F. P. FENNER'S CIGAR WAREHOUSE.
No. 6. MARKET-HILL,—The UNIVERSITY GYM-
NASIUM is admirably situated at the back of the above.

To understand how
pioneering this venture
was, the Oxford Gymnasium
was opened later in 1858, with the first in any public school at Uppingham in
1860 thanks to Edward Thring's leadership, and at Rugby School in 1868.[21]

Soon after the opening of the gym in 1855 the local press also reported on a
display of 'passages at arms, wielding the Indian club, feats of dexterity with
the sword, and gymnastic exercises', supported by a band playing music during
the intervals, promoted and hosted by Fenner.

Highlights included two performers having:

> A match at quarterstaff, administering to each other sundry rattling
> whacks, which it would have delighted the heart of Robin Hood or Little
> John to witness; and next came 'Professor' Harrison, one of the strongest
> men in the world, who astonished the spectators by the ease and grace
> with which he handled enormous Indian clubs and dumb-bells ... But
> now came the most astonishing part of the performance. Mr Jackson
> who is perhaps unrivalled as a swordsman, cut a bar of lead suspended
> by a piece of cord from the end of a pole in two - not at one blow, as he
> generally does, but very nearly so, and subsequently first a leg of mutton
> and secondly a whole sheep in two, at one stroke. The sword used was a
> common naval one.[22]

> 'Professor' Harrison then ... cut a lemon on a man's hand held out at
> arm's length, in two pieces by a down stroke without touching the hand
> of the holder; also an egg and a small apple in a similar manner ...
> These extraordinary exploits elicited thunders of applause ...
> The whole performance gave great satisfaction.

The gymnasium and the Working Men's College

One of the earliest individual users of the gym was probably James Clerk
Maxwell (later recognised as the link between Isaac Newton and Albert
Einstein), a student at Trinity College from 1850 to 1856 who, given his
enthusiasm for exercise, took 'strenuous sessions in the new gymnasium'.
This tallies, because Maxwell also helped 'to set up a Working Men's College
in Cambridge, giving some of the first lectures 'at least one evening a week'.[23]

It would appear Maxwell had to use the gymnasium because whenever he exercised in his college he would jog in the middle of the night upstairs and along corridors 'until the inhabitants of the rooms had shots at him with boots, hairbrushes, etc as he passed'.[24]

Maxwell also joined in efforts to persuade local businesses to shut early on lecture nights (at the Working Men's College) so that 'workers could attend'.[25]

Naturally the students at the Working Men's College used Fenner's gymnasium for gymnastics and boxing.[26] These included Josiah Chater, a prolific diary writer who had a drapery shop nearby at 1 Market Hill, who joined the gymnastics club in 1858, and in 1859 went with 10 members of his class:

> To our boxing master's (Mr J.S. Hughes') rooms at Trinity Hall for tea and a very pleasant party it was. After tea we adjourned to his brother's rooms where there was a piano and a big bowl of punch, and several of Mr Hughes' friends coming in we set to some singing; Mr Gray played, and one chap, a Mr Ainger, amused us till nearly 12 o'clock with some comic pieces, and kept us roaring with laughter.[27]

Enid Porter, the distinguished local social historian, believed these boxing, fencing and gymnastic classes taught by members of the University 'did more, probably than all the other (classes), to promote friendly intercourse between University men and townspeople'.[28]

Rowing and tea meetings

The City of Cambridge club is the oldest town rowing club, reported as being founded in 1863 as 'Cambridge Town Rowing Club' by John (Jack) Harvey in the Working Men's College.[29] Census records list Harvey as a gas fitter and bell fitter, but he was also a professional rowing coach credited with coaching 'more successful Light Blues than any of his contemporaries. At times when knotty points arose in connection with the University crew Harvey's opinion was always accepted as final'.[30]

Fenner's Gymnasium was also used for tea meetings, for example in 1856 when Harvey Goodwin (the first Principle of the Working Men's College) and F.D. or Frederick Maurice (the founder) joined 300 people, 80 of whom were from the University.[31] The gym continued to be used by 'the Teachers and Students [having] their customary social gathering'[32] at the end of each term.

THE WORKING MEN'S COLLEGE

If the long and distinguished list of founders, supporters and teachers responsible for establishing and running the Working Men's College is anything to go by, Frank would invariably have rubbed shoulders with a significant number of the 'great and the good' committed to opening up education beyond the University.

The driving force was Frederick Maurice (Trinity College student from 1823) who was one of the earliest and probably most influential members of 'the Apostles', a secret literary society at Cambridge University that included Alfred Tennyson as a member. Their 'political application of education' agenda was 'to extend a Cambridge education beyond Cambridge',[33] a practical outcome of which was the creation of Working Men's Colleges, first in London in 1854, then one behind Fenner's tobacco shop in Cambridge, the following year.

In an address given to students in 1858, Maurice said it 'was a great source of delight' to establish a Working Men's College 'in Cambridge more than in any other town in England', adding:

> In looking upon the noble buildings of the University, founded by men who had the civilization and education of the people at heart, they (the working men) meant to say, "We claim a right to have a share in the blessings which those buildings were designed to effect: we claim to be members of the British nation, members of the same society as you, and therefore like to have the same name [college] which you have gloried in" (loud cheers).[34]

Maurice believed that 'teachers and learners are equally members',[35] and that later, once the college was established, existing students would induct new ones, as a means of accessing the poorer working classes.

Maurice's plans attracted a rich mix of supporters and co-founders who were 'related by blood and united by common interests, experiences, and upbringing … forming a distinguished circle of men and women who provided the intellectual and moral leadership of Victorian society'.[36]

Five of the eight founders were Cambridge University men, four of them (FD Maurice, John Westlake, Llewelyn Davies (brother to Emily Davies), and Richard Litchfield) being from Trinity College, with the fifth, Frederick Furnivall from Trinity Hall. The only Oxford man among the founders was Thomas Hughes, who published *Tom Brown's Schooldays* a couple of years later in 1857.

Others from Cambridge included Leslie Stephen (Trinity Hall), William Cory (King's College), Francis Gerald Vesey (Trinity College), James Clerk Maxwell (Trinity College), Henry Montagu Butler (later Master of Trinity College), and

Rev Harvey Goodwin (Gonville & Caius) who was also appointed the first principal of the Working Men's College in Cambridge.

Other family links to the Working Men's College extended to the Trevelyans, Macaulays, Huxleys, Darwins and the Venns. Charles Kingsley was possibly involved, and the local booksellers and publishers Daniel and Alexander Macmillan most certainly were. Daniel had already drawn attention to the social conditions of the poor in Cambridge as early as 1842.[37]

Subjects taught, including gymnastics

At the end of the college's third year the principal, The Rev Harvey Goodwin, reported:[38]

> During the October term [Harvey Goodwin himself] had given a course on Astronomy … During the Lent Term Mr. Liveing, fellow of St John's College, had given a most effective and popular course in Chemistry … Mr. Churchill Babington, fellow of St. John's, had lectured on coins, chiefly such as illustrated Bible history; Mr. Farrar, fellow of Trinity, had delivered one 'Englishmen,' Mr. Liveing, again, on Minerals, and Prof. Henslow on Coprolite, a subject of local interest, most interestingly handled; Mr. Cooper, the Town Clerk, one on 'Old Cambridge', which, both from its treatment and its subject, of course was much valued; Mr. Macmillan gave a reading of Tennyson's 'Maud'. To all these gentlemen their hearty thanks were due. [Cheers].

The principal also recognised the importance and popularity of the gymnastics classes:

> Last term they had also introduced for the first-time classes in gymnastics, conducted by their good friend Mr Hughes, and as it was a very popular class he had no doubt they would not fail in thanks to their teacher. [Cheers]. And surely they would be much wanting in gratitude too, if they failed to acknowledge the great kindness of Mr. Fenner in granting them the use of the gymnasium, both for the purposes of this class and also for the social meetings. [Cheers].

The Mr Hughes reported here is almost certainly Thomas Hughes, author of *Tom Brown's Schooldays*, and very active supporter and teacher of sports at the Working Men's College. The inclusion of gymnastics classes had two months earlier been sanctioned by Maurice who also appreciated the 'social effects of boxing'[39] and yet was astonished when Hughes first organised such classes.[40]

Over the three years the College had been in existence in Cambridge, the principal reported the average number of students on the roll each term had been 145, then 72, and 117 in its third year (1857 / 1858).

Demise of the Working Men's College

At the end of 1858 the principal, Harvey Goodwin, and the secretary, Francis Vesey, both left for church appointments away from Cambridge, which is one reason why 'the College began to languish'.[41] This was also linked to the collapse of Maurice's Christian Socialism in 1854,[42] which whilst it spawned a number of important social initiatives, the college was not one of them.

It can also not have helped that Frank Fenner left Cambridge in 1861 / 1862. The college was finally wound up in 1871.[43]

As far as the University gymnasium was concerned, after Frank Fenner left Cambridge, a Mr Jackson took over as its proprietor. This included using it for boxing, for example at an exhibition after the second Varsity Athletics match at Fenner's Ground in 1865, where the Marquess of Queensberry won the lightweight prize.[44]

Mr Jackson also advertised 'opening a juvenile class for the practice of Calisthenics, Gymnastics, Drilling etc exercises in the morning'.[45]

FENNER'S OTHER BUSINESS INTERESTS

In addition to running a tobacco shop, gymnasium, and Fenner's Ground, Frank also had other business interests.

In the local newspaper of 1 October 1859[46] under an advertisement headed 'Guardian Fire and Life Assurance' (11 Lombard Street, London EC) regarding the availability of life insurance, FP Fenner is listed (alongside one other) as the Cambridge agent. It is not known how long he sold life insurance.

In 1859 Frank also went into partnership at 6, Market Hill as Fenner & Bowles, Grocers, Tea Dealers, Tobacconists etc.

However, this only lasted just under a year and a half when the partnership was dissolved, with John Bowles using Fenner's tobacco shop solely as his grocer's store.

A week after the announcement of the dissolution of the Fenner &

NOTICE.—NOW OPEN.
FENNER & BOWLES,
GROCERS, TEA DEALERS, TOBACCONISTS, &c.

MESSRS. F. & B. beg to invite attention to their Enlarged Establishment, and most respectfully to solicit the kind patronage of their Friends and the Public generally. Quality commensurate with Price in every

Cambridge Independent Press Saturday 10 December 1859.

DISSOLUTION OF PARTNERSHIP.

NOTICE is hereby given, that the Partnership lately subsisting between us, the undersigned, FRANCIS PHILLIPS FENNER and JOHN BOWLES, of the Town of Cambridge, Grocers, Tea Dealers, and Provision Merchants, was this day DISSOLVED by mutual consent, and that the business will be, in future, carried on by the said JOHN BOWLES alone, by whom only all Debts due to and from the said Firm will be Received and Paid.
Witness our hands this Twenty-fifth day of March, One Thousand Eight Hundred and Sixty-one.
F. P. FENNER.
J. BOWLES.
Witness: JOSEPH GARRATT,
Solicitor, Cambridge.

JOHN BOWLES,
Grocer, Tea Dealer, and Provision Merchant,
MARKET-HILL, CAMBRIDGE,
In continuing the above Business, begs to thank the Inhabitants of this University, Town, and County, for the very liberal patronage conferred upon him and his late partner, and to assure them that it will be his study to deserve a continuance of their kind favours.
12, MARKET-HILL, CAMBRIDGE.

Cambridge Chronicle and Journal - Saturday 06 April 1861.

Bowles partnership, an advertisement dated 13 April 1861[47] in the local press promoted a share issue to finance a Roman Bath venture, adding that 'Mr F.P. Fenner is to be the manager of the baths – a very proper appointment'.

It is not known how involved he became in this project because he left Cambridge at the same time as the baths were opened in February 1863, only lasting a further eleven months before it too was wound up (chapter 5).[48]

Chapter 22 details Frank's use of Fenner's Ground, not just for cricket and athletics, but also for a range of commercial and community uses.

Although Frank left Cambridge in the early 1860s he still held the lease on Fenner's Ground, which is why he continued to manage the cricket, athletics and community events held there. This was from the West Country, in his new role as a hotel proprietor (chapter 23).

Stop 3: Guildhall

This site (at the southern end of today's market) has been used for a variety of purposes, such as a private house owned by a Jew named Benjamin, which King Henry III later granted to the town for use as a prison in 1224.

Later it was used as a toll booth, where tolls for entry to the town and trading at the market were paid, and a venue for troupes of actors to perform, in the second half of the sixteenth century. It was then used as a location for the courts, and more recently, from the late 1840s, as the Guildhall, the seat of local government.[49]

As in other larger towns and cities, the Victorian middle class (of which Fenner might be considered a member) would have believed it was their civic duty to 'build Jerusalem' (*on England's green and pleasant land*) 'motivated by aesthetic and cultural aspirations above and beyond the desire for making money. This would have included establishing literary and Philosophical societies, the administration of local government and justice, a concern for the poorer members of society, and the provision of public spaces to play'.[50]

Cambridge Guildhall c1900
From the collection of David Gent.

Frank's civic duty, profile and 'Town and Gown'

The Guildhall therefore represents an important focus for listing Frank Fenner's contribution to enriching Cambridge town, across a range of civic, church and community roles, such as:

- a petitioner aiming to prevent the railway companies avoiding tolls, key to paying for Cambridge paving, cleaning, and lighting (1846),[51]
- a high constable in Great St Mary's parish (1848), later chief constable of the borough (in the volunteer police force), appointed in 1854[52] and re-appointed in 1858,
- vice president of the Philo Society, or Cambridge Literary Society (1852),
- a burgess or freeman – appointed in 1853 enabling the postholder 'to practise a trade without paying a toll'. Twenty years before Frank's appointment, there were '118 resident freeman in Cambridge',[53]
- supporter of the Working Men's College (from 1855),
- prospective Liberal candidate in the Town Council elections (1857),
- senior church warden at Great St Mary's (1858), and
- colour sergeant in the 1st Cambridgeshire Rifles Volunteer Corps (1860), including being enrolled under oath at the Guildhall.

Frank Fenner also had a high profile through his business interests. These included his tobacco shop, gymnasium, the selling of cricket equipment, being a professional cricket bowler/coach, and operating Fenner's Ground for cricket and athletic matches and other community events for profit, but also free of charge for other events.

When these civic and community roles are combined with his range of business activities, and his success both on and off the cricket pitch, Frank was clearly 'a man about town', an outcome of which was the 'building of good relationships, especially between the town and university'.[54] For someone from the town this was an extraordinary achievement.

As a young man aged 25, it was cricket that revealed to Frank the potential for bringing 'Town and Gown' together, as evidenced in a letter he wrote to the press in 1836. Whilst he was complaining about the injury caused to the Parker's Piece cricket square by horses being ridden over it, his letter was also a spirited defence of 'this truly English game that produces that happy concord of social enjoyment,' that could 'strengthen the links of society'.[55]

For more on 'Town and Gown' relationships and the role of sport, go to chapter 20.

Guildhall events

PC Robinson

William Robinson PC 17 of the Cambridge Borough Police Force was described as 'the most popular policeman' and 'hero' of the Tom Thumb riots.[56]

General Tom Thumb was an adult of short stature, advertised as a dwarf who achieved great fame as a performer under circus pioneer P.T. Barnum, who appeared in 1846 at the Cambridge Guildhall resulting in student riots, and Robinson being bludgeoned to the ground.[57]

Robinson was a cricket enthusiast who would manage the crowds on Parker's Piece. In the same year as the Tom Thumb riots, the crowd at the Gentlemen of England match was said to have stayed in an orderly circle 'having adopted the civil suggestions of PC Robinson'.[58]

In recognition of his importance to local cricket he appeared in Felix's painting of town and University cricketers in 1847 (chapter 20).

Following his retirement from the police force as a Chief Inspector, Robinson became an enthusiastic promoter of cricket through writing letters to the press, arranging public meetings and in particular, setting up testimonials and relief funds for local cricketers fallen on hard times.

His importance to cricket was also recognised by Robert Allen Fitzgerald (Trinity College), the MCC Secretary who featured a photograph of Robinson in a scrap book currently held at Lord's Cricket Ground.

Fenner's enrolment to the Cambridge Town Rifle Corps

On the 6 February 1860 Frank Fenner was enrolled, under oath at the Guildhall, into the Cambridge Town Rifle Corps, known as 'the Pensioners'. The 67 new recruits, including Frank Fenner were listed in the programme.

After joining, Frank very soon had the rank of Colour Sergeant and offered his gymnasium and Fenner's Ground for parades, inspections, training and

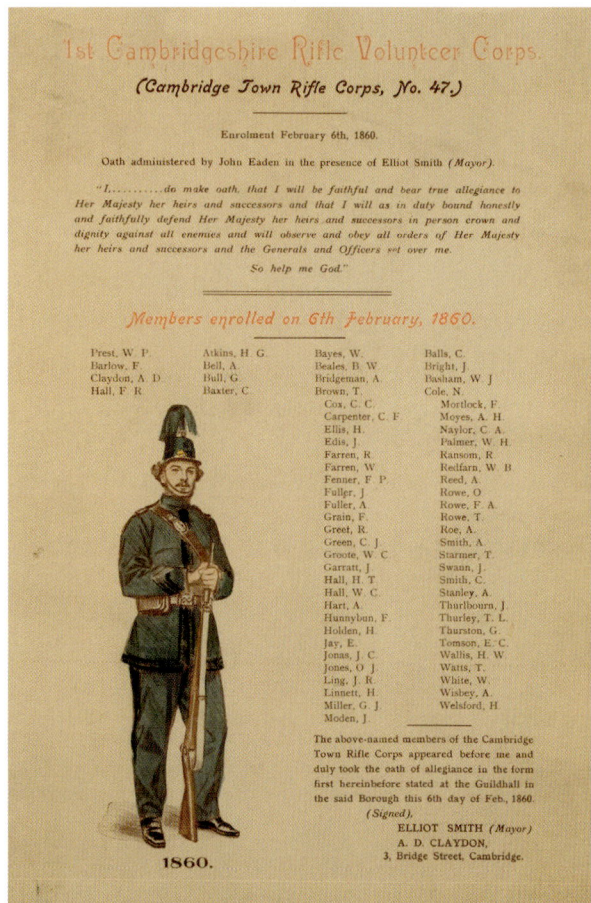

List of the 67 recruits to Cambridge Town Rifles including Frank Fenner

Thanks to The Suffolk and Cambridgeshire Regiments Museum.

drills, recognised in the local press who reported 'over 50 members ... assembled at Mr Fenner's Gym' three evenings a week.[59]

However, in June 1861, just over a year after he enrolled, the two local papers wrote lengthy pieces on 'a very stormy discussion ... and the greatest excitement' at a meeting called to discuss Sergeant Fenner's resignation.[60]

Frank Fenner had been censured alongside a number of officers for poor attendance at drills, despite Frank apparently being given leave of absence by the captain because of illness and other important engagements.

It was hoped Frank might reconsider, because 'he has spent much time and money in advancing its [the Volunteer Rifle Corps'] objects, and has frequently shown great kindness in lending his ground and his gymnasium for the purposes of drill'. However, at a general meeting held later in the Town Hall, Frank's letter, standing by his decision to resign, was shared with the Committee.[61]

This would have been an easy decision for Frank because he had probably decided he was leaving Cambridge.

Jack Hobbs dinner

When Jack Hobbs beat WG Grace's record of number of first-class cricket centuries scored in 1925, a celebratory dinner was held at the Cambridge Guildhall organised by the Cambridge Cricket Association. In Jack's speech he expressed deep affection for his birthplace. 'If this old town of Cambridge takes pride in her sons, her sons are no less proud of her', adding, to loud applause, that out of the three cricketers in the world who had scored one hundred centuries, 'two of them were born on the banks of the Cam',[62] the second being Tom Hayward (chapter 20).

Formation of the National Skating Association

A local journalist, James Drake Digby felt skating needed a national organisation to promote, control and protect it, for example from cheating and betting. As a result, the National Skating Association (NSA) was formed in Cambridge in 1879 at the Guildhall.

Apart from the promotion of amateur and professional speed skating championships, the aims of the association were to establish standards for figure skating, provide rules for 'the game of hockey on ice' (called Bandy), and establish international contests.

The headquarters of the NSA remained in Cambridge until 1894 at Mortimer Villas, Parker's Piece (chapter 21).

Stop 4: Peas Hill - Town v Gown battles, and boxing

The area or road to the right of the Guildhall (viewed from the market stalls) is called Peas Hill, after the 'pesemarket' held there in medieval times. 'Pese', or peas, were a staple item for poorer people, being an essential ingredient in pottage, along with oats, beans, onions and carrots.[63]

Battle of Peas Hill

The dust jacket of Rowland Parker's book *Town and Gown - The 700 Years' War in Cambridge* features an image of 'The Battle of Peas Hill' circa 1820, when Frank Fenner was nine years old.

Gown! Gown! - Town! Town! or the Battle of Peas Hill.

The Battle of Peas Hill c1820

Cambridgeshire Collection, Cambridge Central Library.

The battle was the subject of many a contemporary ballad including the following poem written by a 'Brace of Cantabs' and published in *Gradus ad Cantabrigiam* (or 'a university guide to the academical customs').

> (Verse 3) Round Hobson's conduit quick array'd
> Each GOWNSMEN rush'd the cause to aid,
> And fast about him each one laid,
> With blows that told most terribly.

> (V9) No sound was heard of martial drum,
> No bugle blast, but one wild hum
> Floated o'er all: "the SNOBS![a] they come,
> On! On! and meet them cheerily."

---

[a] Snobs were people not from the University.

(V10) And then was shout, and noise, and din,
As rallying forwards poured in
Hundreds and hundreds, to begin
The work of fame so gloriously.

(V11) Then rush'd undaunted, to the fight,
The tall - the low - the strong - the light;
And, Oh! it was a glorious sight,
That strife of TOWN and GOWN to see.

(V18 of 20) No thoughts were there, but such as grace
The memory of that crowded place
The memory of that gallant race
Who took and gave so heartily.

The battle took place when the Reform movement, striving for many more people to have the vote, and therefore supported by the town, lost the backing of Queen Caroline (married to King George IV), much to the pleasure of 'the University'. Whilst the poem in one of its many other verses refers to 'Caroline's base treachery' on the one hand, references to 'that gallant race', 'the work of fame so gloriously', and 'meeting [the SNOBS] so cheerily', suggest this was probably more about 'fisticuffs as sport', than politics.

Because prize fighting in general, in the early nineteenth century were 'festivals of the common people', often presided over by the aristocracy,[64] it begs the question how and where did the students acquire their fighting skills for use in the Battle of Peas Hill?

Boxing in the University

One of the first students to be considered a good boxer was Richard Bancroft, a future Archbishop of Canterbury, who despite his athletic prowess had to be saved from a lynching by a Cambridge mob by Laurence Chaderton, later the first Master of Emmanuel College (chapter 18).[65] This would have taken place in the early 1560s when both were students at Christ's College.

At this time boxing was being increasingly viewed as an alternative to the futility of the duel that often resulted in the death of one or more of the participants, according to Fynes Moryson, educated at Peterhouse from 1580, where he was also a Fellow.[66]

At the same time as the Battle of Peas Hill, Lord Byron (having been a student at Trinity College from 1805) was an advocate of boxing, viewing it 'as a national propensity … and a stimulus to true courage'.[67] Other Trinity College students around the same time (late eighteenth/early nineteenth centuries) were John

Charles Spencer, later Lord Althorp, who was convinced of the benefits to society of boxing, and Captain Robert Barclay who 'became the central figure in the world of Regency pugilism'.[68]

Later Charles Kingsley, a student in Cambridge from 1838 to 1841, hired a local professional black prize-fighter 'to give instruction in fisticuffs', despite the Vice Chancellor in 1842 making it an offence for any student "to be found resorting to or having any communication whatever with any professed teacher of the art of boxing, or be found attending any prize fight".

Nevertheless, as an example of how popular boxing training was, Nat Langham offered this service from 1852 at the Ram Inn, opposite the Round Church (chapter 5.4), as did Peter Crawley (chapter 8) and Harry Cox (chapter 10).

A significant shift away from fisticuffs and prize-fighting was the creation of the Queensberry Rules by John Graham Chambers (student at Trinity College from 1861 to 1865), sponsored by the 9th Marquess of Queensberry. Perhaps the regular fights between Town and Gown were the spur to these two creating these Rules in 1867?

Town fighting opportunities

Whilst university students had opportunity to develop their boxing, so too did the local population through prize fighting, financed by betting and gambling.

A further sport the participants at the Battle of Peas Hill might have engaged in was camp ball, the version of folk football prevalent across East Anglia. According to Robert Forby (writing in 1830), there were two varieties: 'rough-play, and civil-play. In the latter, there is no boxing'.[69] In addition, in 1899, William Dutt wrote 'The last Camping match', associating its history with 'the old-fashioned wrestling matches and ring-fights'.[70]

It would appear such wrestling for local people had a long history, given Midsummer Fair, formally established in 1211 by King John, was established where boys met to wrestle and play other games (chapter 7), which presumably continued.

At the time of the Battle of Peas Hill, Moses Carter, also called the Histon Giant, would have been nearly 20 years of age and at 7 feet tall and 23 stone would have been a great asset to the town (his hat and boot are on display at the Museum of Cambridge). However, it is not known whether Moses Carter was at the Battle, nor who 'won'.

The Battle of Peas Hill was not an isolated incident, as tensions between 'Town and Gown' often escalated into street fights, until relatively recently.[71]

Frank Fenner and boxing

In his role as a local constable Frank Fenner would probably have had to manage the results of Town versus Gown fights. Maybe as a direct result, Frank opened a gymnasium in the centre of town, where boxing classes took place for local young men, taught by members of the University.

It is not known whether Frank boxed, however his son also called Frank, certainly did, with the local newspaper in Cheltenham reporting:[72]

> Like every young man with a wholesome and manly heart in his bosom, he gloried in a bout with the gloves, for which he had a 'very useful' turn, as might be supposed by those who knew him at eighty, still stocky and straight, and looking very likely to be able to deal a good, sturdy straight one should it be demanded by any good cause.

Read more on the two Frank Fenners in chapter 23.

Stop 5: St Edward King and Martyr Church

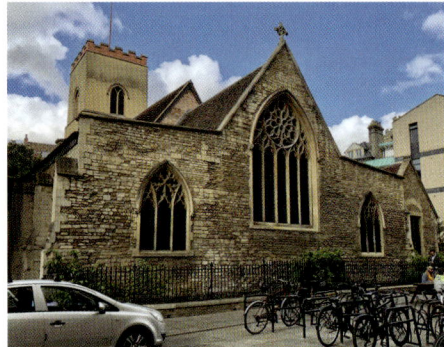

The church (opposite the side of the Guildhall on Peas Hill) is one of the oldest in Cambridge, dating back to the beginning of the eleventh century, with the current building dating from the fourteenth century.

The cradle of the English Reformation

In 1446 the Church was used by Trinity Hall and Clare College as the church they both shared had been demolished to make way for King's College. Because St Edward King and Martyr Church was under the patronage of the King, rather than the Bishop of Ely, as other churches in the town would have been, this gave opportunity for preachers to question, explore, develop and present the key characteristics of the English Reformation, without being reproached.

This is why Thomas Bilney, Robert Barnes, Thomas Cranmer, Nicholas Ridley and Hugh Latimer are just some of those closely associated with the church, making it, some believe 'the cradle of the Reformation' in England.[73]

Desiderius Erasmus (the Dutch Christian humanist) was the Lady Margaret Professor of Divinity at the University from 1511 to 1514, staying at Queens' College because of his close friendship with its president, Bishop John Fisher.[74] He is credited with contributing significantly towards the Reformation.

The Reformation is believed to have had an indirect impact on the playing of sport and leisure. For example, 'the reformers in Europe found themselves either holding the political power or being persecuted. In neither case could sport and leisure figure very highly in their priorities. Their English counterparts, by contrast, were left free to deliberate, to preach and to convert. It was from these deliberations that many of the values ultimately associated with modern sport derive'.[75]

Erasmus himself wrote about sport and exercise,[76] even allowing students to practice their Latin because 'practically nothing is learned better than what is learned in a game'. He believed honour, not money, was what should be at stake, also warning about the perils of sweating, after several notable cases of royal persons, after a bout of tennis, catching chills that led to serious illness, or worse.

Churchmen known to Frank Fenner

Harvey Goodwin was vicar of St Edward King and Martyr Church between 1848 and 1858, overlapping with being principal of the Working Men's College located behind Frank's tobacco shop on Market Hill. In addition, Frederick Maurice was the church's chaplain from 1870 to 1872. Inside the church a memorial recognises his educational work with working men and women.

Maurice has been credited as 'the pre-eminent Anglican divine of the nineteenth century', likened to Erasmus, in that they both 'articulated how and why the life of faith is perennially relevant to public life'.[77]

Stop 6: Two bull rings – and Bull College

Nearby to St Edward King and Martyr Church was a bull ring on Peas Hill near the Market Cross, from at least the first half of the seventeenth century, to which a bull would have been chained.

However, from at least 1604 through to the 1790s, this bull ring (and another located on Bridge Street) were used for bull baiting. Whilst banned for students as a sport in 1763,[78] it was obligatory, given the regulation that 'no butcher must kill a bull till baited', in the erroneous belief that 'baited beef' made for 'flesh softer in digestion'.[79]

The bull ring was also the venue for dog-tossing, with a Cambridge Fellow, Thomas Crosfield, concluding:

> In the throwing or tossing of the dogs often they are kill'd or maimed, but to save them men run & catch them in the fall … otherwise they should be quite quasht, maimed or slaine by the Bull.[80]

Sometimes the bull ring was unable to accommodate the large crowds, which is why Symonds D'Ewes (St John's College from 1618) reported that in early

July (around 1620) 'a famous Bull arrived in Cambridge, and it was intended that it should be baited at Gog Magog Hills, where bowling, running, jumping, shooting, and wrestling were to be practised for a month or six weeks, under the designation of the Olympic games'. It is however understood that the Vice-Chancellor prevented the expected pastime.[81]

The Black Bull (Inn), opposite Corpus Christi College, mentioned in Edward IV's reign, was bequeathed to St. Catharine's College in 1626 and rebuilt in 1828 as a hotel. It preserved its character until 1941 when it became 'Bull College', a centre for United States soldiers in Cambridge, until just after the end of World War II.

[1]   Cambridgeshire. Gazetteer of Markets and Fairs in England and Wales To 1516. Originally published by List and Index Society, Kew, 2005.

[2]   The city of Cambridge: Economic history. Pages 86-101. A History of the County of Cambridge and the Isle of Ely: Volume 3, the City and University of Cambridge. Originally published by Victoria County History, London, 1959.

[3]   Rowland Parker (1983). Town and Gown. The 700 years'war in Cambridge. Patrick Stephens, Cambridge. Pages 119 and 120.

[4]   https://www.queens.cam.ac.uk/visiting-the-college/history/university-facts/the-way-things-were

[5]   Mike Petty (2018). Cambridge SPORT Chronicle. Chronology of Cambridge Sport 1888 to 1990 at https://archive.org/details/CambridgeSPORTSChronicle

[6]   The Museum of Cambridge (at 2022) have an online exhibition "ReStorying Our Museum" which includes exploring the history of the representation of Africans in tobacco advertising. Go to https://www.museumofcambridge.org.uk/resources/restorying-our-museum/online-display/

[7]   Charles Astor Bristed (1873) Five years in an English University (Trinity College, Cambridge).

[8]   Enid Porter (1969). Cambridgeshire Customs and Folklore. Routledge & Kegan Paul. Page 322.

[9]   Cambridge Independent Press 10 April 1858.

[10]   Cambridge Chronicle and Journal 29 Sept 1855.

[11]   Cambridge University Athletics Club website: https://www.cuac.org.uk/history

[12]   Cambridge Independent Press 19 February 1859.

[13]   Cambridge Independent Press 3 Mar 1860.

[14]   A Veteran Cricketer article (13 Sept 1893). Sketch. Page 361.

[15]   WS email (1 Jan 2021): I have seen the minutes of the CUCC from 1853 onwards. The venues during the time Frank Fenner was in Cambridge were The University Arms in 1853 and 1855, Fenner's building on Market Hill in 1855, 56x2, 57x2, 60 and 61x2 and the Pavillion in 1862.

[16]   Mark Burley (18 May 2020). The History of Sport in Public Schools. https://www.winchestercollege.org/stories/the-history-of-sport-in-public-schools

[17]   James Lillywhite Yearbook 1897 on page 54 Willie Sugg (2009). Fenner's Men. Cambs Cricket 1822-1848. Part 3 of A Tradition Unshared.

[18]   J. A. Mangan (2006). 'Oars and the man'. Pleasure and purpose in Victorian and Edwardian Cambridge. In A Sport-loving society. Routledge. Page 106.

[19]   J.A. Mangan - ed (2006). A sport-loving society. Victorian and Edwardian middle-class England at play Routledge. Ref 68 on page 102.

[20]   Cambridge Chronicle and Journal 29 Sept 1855.

21 Charles Darwin (1989). The Correspondence of Charles Darwin: Volume 5, 1851-1855. Footnote 8 on page 322.

22 Cambridge Chronicle and Journal 15 Dec 1855. Page 5.

23 Basil Mahon (2003). The Man who changed everything. The life of James Clerk Maxwell. Wiley. Page 45.

24 Basil Mahon (2003). The Man who changed everything. The life of James Clerk Maxwell. Wiley. Page 38.

25 Basil Mahon (2003). The Man who changed everything. The life of James Clerk Maxwell. Wiley. Page 66.

26 Enid Porter (1975). Victorian Cambridge. Josiah Chater's diaries. Phillimore. Pages 75 – 76.

27 Enid Porter (1975). Victorian Cambridge. Josiah Chater's diaries. Phillimore. Page 90.

28 Enid Porter (1975). Victorian Cambridge. Josiah Chater's diaries. Phillimore. Page 90.

29 City of Cambridge Rowing Club website: http://www.cityrc.co.uk/history/

30 Mill Road Cemetery website: https://millroadcemetery.org.uk/harvey-annie-l/

31 Enid Porter (1975). Victorian Cambridge. Josiah Chater's diaries. Phillimore. Page 88.

32 Cambridge Independent Press 05 June 1858.

33 Philip Aherne (2018) The Coleridge Legacy: ST Coleridge's Intellectual Legacy in Britain and America 1834 – 1934. Palgrave Macmillan. Page 258.

34 Cambridge Chronicle and Journal 03 April 1858. Page 7.

35 Philip Aherne (2018) The Coleridge Legacy: ST Coleridge's Intellectual Legacy in Britain and America 1834 – 1934. Palgrave Macmillan. Page 258.

36 J.F.C. Harrison (1954). A History of the Working Men's College: 1854-1954. London: Routledge & Kagan Paul. Page 45.

37 Malcolm Tozer (2015). The ideal of manliness. The legacy of Thring's Uppingham. Sunnyrest Books. Page 47.

38 Cambridge Independent Press 05 June 1858.

39 Cambridge Chronicle and Journal 3 April 1858. Page 7.

40 Edward Norman (1987). The Victorian Christian Socialists. Cambridge University Press. Ref 59 on pages 88 and 89.

41 Enid Porter (1975). Victorian Cambridge. Josiah Chater's diaries. Phillimore. Pages 132 - 133.

42 Edward Norman (1987). The Victorian Christian Socialists. Cambridge University Press. Page 2.

43 Enid Porter (1975). Victorian Cambridge. Josiah Chater's diaries. Phillimore. Page 133.

44 Bell's Life 1 April 1865.

45 Cambridge Chronicle and Journal 23 April 1864.

46 Cambridge Independent Press 1 October 1859.

47 Cambridge Independent Press 13 April 1861.

48 Cambridge Independent Press 30 Jan 1864.

49 Capturing Cambridge website: https://capturingcambridge.org/museum-of-cambridge/museum-exhibit-stories/guildhall/

50 Morgan, SJ (2018) John Deakin Heaton and the 'elusive civic pride of the Victorian middle class'. Urban History, 45 (4). pp. 595-615. ISSN 0963-9268 DOI:

51 Cambridge Chronicle and Journal 25 April 1846.

52 Cambridge Independent Press 14 October 1854.

53 'The city of Cambridge: Constitutional history', in A History of the County of Cambridge and the Isle of Ely: Volume 3, the City and University of Cambridge, ed. J P C Roach (London, 1959), pp. 29-68. British History Online http://www.british-history.ac.uk/vch/cambs/vol3/pp29-68 [accessed 30 April 2021].

54 Willie Sugg (2009). Fenner's men. Cambs Cricket 1822 - 1848. Part 3 of A Tradition Unshared. Real Work Publishing. Page 45.

55 Willie Sugg (2009). Fenner's men. Cambs Cricket 1822 - 1848. Part 3 of A Tradition Unshared. Real Work Publishing. Page 47.

56 Willie Sugg (2009). Fenner's men. Cambs Cricket 1822 - 1848. Part 3 of A Tradition Unshared. Real Work Publishing. Page 38.

57 Enid Porter (1975) Victorian Cambridge. Josiah Chater's Diaries. Phillimore. Pages 30-31.

58 Willie Sugg (2009). Fenner's men. Cambs Cricket 1822 - 1848. Part 3 of A Tradition Unshared. Real Work Publishing. Page 38.

59 Cambridge Independent Press 24 Dec 1859.

60 Cambridge Independent Press 8 June 1861.

61 Cambridge Chronicle and Journal 15 June 1861.

62 Leo McKinstry. Jack Hobbs. England's Greatest Cricketer. London: Yellow Jersey Press. Page 264.

63 Peter Bryan and Nick Wise. (2002) A reconstruction of the Medieval Cambridge Market Place. XCI pp 73-87.

64 GM Trevelyan (1946). English Social History. Longmans, Green and Co. Page Page 503.

65 David Berkeley (2015). Travel through Cambridge. Day One. Page 67.

66 Derek Birley (1993). Sport and the making of Britain. Manchester University Press. Page 68.

67 Boxing with Byron. 22nd January 2016 at https://wordsworth.org.uk/blog/2016/01/22/boxing-with-byron/

68 Gareth A Davies (8 March 2007) Oxford and Cambridge prepare for centenary boxing match in The Telegraph.

69 The Vocabulary of East Anglia ("an attempt to record the Vulgar Tongue of the twin sister counties, Norfolk and Suffolk, as it existed in the last twenty years of the Eighteenth Century") - Volume 1 - by the late Reverend Robert Forby, Rector of Fincham. Published in 1830 by J.B. Nichols & Son of Parliament Street, London. IN Bill Atkins. References to the East Anglian Sport of Camping (updated 7 March 2013). http://www.oldshuck.info/pdf/camping.pdf

70 The Last Camping Match By William A. Dutt From: The Badminton Magazine of Sports and Pastimes edited by Alfred E.T. Watson. Volume IX (July to December 1899) published 1899 by Longmans, Green and Co.

71 Rowland Parker (1983). Town and Gown. The 700 years' war in Cambridge. Patrick Stephens, Cambridge. Dust jacket.

72 Cheltenham Chronicle 5 Jan 1929.

73 St Edward King and Martyr website http://stedwardscambridge.co.uk/about#history

74 Lindsey Askin (2013). Erasmus and Queens' College, as Queens' Old Library blog - Rare Books and Manuscripts at Queens' College https://queenslib.wordpress.com/2013/07/12/erasmus-and-queens-college/

75 Denis Brailsford (1991). Sport, time and society. The British at play. Routledge. Page 17.

76 Derek Birley (1993) Sport and the making of Britain. Manchester University Press. Pages 50 to 51.

77 Ron Dart (no date). Erasmus, The English Reformation and the Church Fathers: A man for all seasons.

78 Robert Forsyth Scott (1907). St John's College, Cambridge. J. M. Dent & Co.

79 Hedley Peek (1898) The Encyclopaedia of Sport (Vol 2). London: Lawrence and Bullen Ltd. Page 390.

80 Crosfield Diary. 1 Feb 1636. Page 85.

81 Annals of Cambridge by Cooper, Charles Henry, 1808-1866; Cooper, John William, 1845-1906. (Publication date 1908). Page 356 under 'Additions and Corrections'.

CHAPTER 17

Corpus Christi College

FOUNDED BY THE TOWN

Corpus Christi was founded in 1352 'born out of a disaster beyond imagining'.

The bubonic plague pandemic, known as the Black Death, was sweeping across Europe, resulting in three town businessmen founding a new town guild, supported by its earliest known benefactor, Margaret Andrew. Unfortunately, she was one of its victims in 1349, alongside one third of the Cambridge population who also died from it.

In general, guilds were established for economic and educational purposes including charitable work, which is why the purpose of the new Guild of Corpus Christi was to establish a new college, the sixth in Cambridge, for 'priests to say masses for the repose of the souls of the departed', and for students studying academic subjects.

'This was a unique achievement. Other colleges were founded by royal, rich, or great individuals; Corpus Christi College is the only one in Cambridge or Oxford to have been founded by the townspeople'.[1]

Life in a poor college could be austere, with rooms not being heated, apart from the fire in the hall.

The normal diet was mutton, varied by the occasional pigeon and dried cod on Fridays, and because the college did not generally trust commercial suppliers of food and drink, it had its own brewhouse and bakehouse for nearly 500 years.

Feasts included one-third of the budget spent on actors and plays, as well as the college putting on its own entertainment.

In 1381 the Peasants' Revolt resulted in the college being ransacked not by peasants but probably by members of some of the rival town guilds. To avoid a repeat in 1460, during the Wars of the Roses, the college purchased gunpowder, protective clothing, artillery, 12 arrows and 'defended' some of its windows.[2]

SMOKING TOBACCO – OVER THE CENTURIES

Richard Fletcher became a Fellow of the college in 1569, later being quickly promoted to Bishop of London, but he fell out of favour with Elizabeth I, and so 'fell into disgrace, banishment, debt, and addiction to a new drug, and seeking to lose his sorrows in a mist of smoak, died of the immoderate taking thereof'.[3]

Following the publication of 'Counterblaste to Tobacco' in 1604 by James I, the Vice Chancellor of the University forbade students from smoking in 1607.[4]

However, the use of tobacco became increasingly popular with students. John Cowper, a student and Fellow at Corpus Christi from 1755, later recalled 'Haistwell and I are two bright suns that sit in clouds of fumigation every night'. It is not known whether this smoking hastened his early death, but he died in college aged only 33.[5]

Fresh air for the patient!

Frank Fenner's day-to-day business was selling tobacco, and as the following quote demonstrates, there were clearly plenty of smokers across the middle of the nineteenth century:

> When I [William Heitland] was a student [at St John's College from 1867] I heard one evening that an [old school friend] at Corpus had just broken his leg at football. I went off to see him. He lay in bed in his keeping-room, which it was not easy to enter. His friends were in such force that there was hardly standing room for one more. All were smoking hard, and a thick cloud from twenty or more pipes and cigars made the atmosphere choking and obscure. A sly hint that this air might not be quite the best thing for the patient, who could not leave his bed, evidently opened a consideration that had not occurred to the company. This is a good instance of the general blindness of young men to the claims of others. For the most part they mean no harm by this indifference, and only the coarser minority carry this social defect into later life.[6]

COLLEGE SPORT

Fives and tennis

As far back as the fifteenth century, the students could play hand-tennis (similar to modern-day fives) in an un-finished bakehouse. In the mid sixteenth century, a larger and covered 'Tennis Court' was erected to the east of St. Botolph's Church, marked on Hammond's map of 1592. It again would have been used for fives, given its dimensions were too small for real tennis.[7]

The court was a timber construction with the floor being paved with red terracotta tiles about 9 inches or 21cm square, given the results of recent excavation. This court was demolished in 1766, ending 300 years of a tennis/fives court being available on the college site.

Donation of land - for football

In 1474 Dr John Botwright, who had just finished over 30 years as the college's Master, gave some land close to the church in Swaffham, Norfolk for the benefit of the local parishioners. It was referred to as the Camping Land, used for Camp Ball, the variation of folk football played across East Anglia. In addition to being Master of the college, Botwright was also the Rector of Swaffham.

Horse-racing

James de Lancey was a student at Corpus Christi from 1750, later being credited as the father of New York horse-racing.[8] His stables were on First Street, a paddock on Second Street, and a private track nearby to train his horses, and from which most of the great racehorses of America, prior to the Civil War, were related.

Gunshot holes in a student's room

John D'Oyly was noted as a sportsman playing chess, bowls, billiards and shooting in the Fens. He was also responsible for filling his room in the college with soot by firing his gun up the chimney, as recorded in his diary from 1792 to 1800 when he was a student and Fellow at the college.[9] There is still evidence of these gunshot-holes in the ancient panelling of room Q1.

Establishing Rugby Union in Japan

Whilst rugby had first been introduced by British troops, the first recorded game played by Japanese students at Keio University was in 1899, coached by Edward Bramwell Clarke (student at Corpus Christi from 1893) and Ginnosuke Tanaka (Leys School, and Trinity Hall, Cambridge).

TENNIS COURT ROAD

Between Corpus Christi College and Emmanuel College, where Pembroke Street becomes Downing Street, there is a joining road called Tennis Court Road, so called because it was the location of a tennis court from at least 1564.

The first (real) tennis courts built in Cambridge were located in a number of the colleges during the latter part of the sixteenth century, such as St John's, Trinity College, Corpus Christi, Queens', Christ's and Peterhouse.

A rebuilt court was demolished in 1880 to make way for new Pembroke College buildings.[10]

1   Patrick Bury, revised 3rd edition by Oliver Rackham (2013). A short history of The College of
    Corpus Christi and the Blessed Virgin Mary in Cambridge. Falcon Printing.

2   Patrick Bury, revised 3rd edition by Oliver Rackham (2013). A short history of The College of
    Corpus Christi and the Blessed Virgin Mary in Cambridge. Falcon Printing.

3   Patrick Bury, revised 3rd edition by Oliver Rackham (2013). A short history of The College of
    Corpus Christi and the Blessed Virgin Mary in Cambridge. Falcon Printing.

4   https://www.queens.cam.ac.uk/visiting-the-college/history/university-facts/the-way-things-were

5   Venn's Cambridge Alumni Database: https://venn.lib.cam.ac.uk/

6   William Heitland (1926). After Many Years. Cambridge University Press. Pages 117 to 118.

7   Roger Morgan (2001). Real tennis in Cambridge: the first six hundred years.
    University Press, Cambridge.

8   Patrick Bury, revised 3rd edition by Oliver Rackham (2013). A short history of The College of
    Corpus Christi and the Blessed Virgin Mary in Cambridge. Falcon Printing.

9   Patrick Bury, revised 3rd edition by Oliver Rackham (2013). A short history of The College of
    Corpus Christi and the Blessed Virgin Mary in Cambridge. Falcon Printing.

10 Roger Morgan (2001). Real tennis in Cambridge: the first six hundred years.
    University Press, Cambridge.

CHAPTER 18
Emmanual College

Emmanuel College was founded in 1584 on the site of a Dominican priory by Sir Walter Mildmay, Chancellor of the Exchequer to Elizabeth I. It was intended the college should train Protestant preachers. By the 1620s it was the largest college in Cambridge.

In the 1630s, many Puritan[a] clergy went into exile to avoid persecution. Of the first 100 graduates who migrated to New England, in America, fully one-third were Emmanuel College men, which is why Cambridge in Massachusetts was so named. Perhaps Emmanuel's most famous graduate is John Harvard who emigrated in 1637. He died the following year and left his books and half his estate to the new college that was to bear his name and become the first American University.

THE PURITANS AND SPORT

Laurence Chaderton and Richard Bancroft both started as students at Christ's College in the early 1560s. Together they were later involved in the translation of the King James Version of the Bible, with Chaderton becoming the first Master of Emmanuel College in Cambridge and Bancroft appointed Archbishop of Canterbury.

When students, both were known specifically for their athletic prowess. Bancroft was known for 'boxing, wrestling and quarterstaff', and Chaderton once saved Bancroft from a lynching by a Cambridge mob.[1]

Perhaps because of Chaderton's interest in sport, when he was Master of Emmanuel College, his Fellows would relax by playing bowls on Sundays in the late 1580s.

[a] Puritans were English Protestants in the sixteenth and seventeenth centuries who sought to purify the Church of England (CoE) of Roman Catholic practices, maintaining that the CoE had not been fully reformed and should become more Protestant.

As Cambridge was considered distinctly Puritan, where Sunday was devoted entirely to God, this outraged Lancelot Andrewes, student, Fellow and future Master of Pembroke College,[2] who wrote:

> Yet these Hypocrites did bowle in a private green at their colledge every Sunday after Sermon; and one of the Colledge (a loving friend to Mr. L. Andrewes) to satisfie him, one time lent him the Key of a Private back dore to the bowling green, on a Sunday evening, which he opening, discovered these zealous Preachers with their Gownes off, earnest at play.[3]

Whilst considered 'anti-sport', the Puritans and the many heirs to their tradition made much more of a positive contribution to sport than this portrayal.

In fact, they reduced the crudity in sport, improved its honesty, and set it within firm limits of time. According to the historian Dennis Brailsford:[4]

> The old sports that the original Puritans saw around them on their village greens, with their drunkenness, their license, and their irregularity of timing, could never have survived into an industrialized and urbanized world. They and their successors inculcated standards into British life which at length proved strong enough to displace the amorality of both a fading aristocracy and a rising working class. They were standards and expectations which came in the end to dominate all aspects of Victorian behaviour - including, and inevitably if it was to prosper, its sport. The 'gentling' of the masses was never a Puritan aim, but it was a process which their influence made all the more feasible.

COLLEGE CRICKETERS AND FRANK FENNER

Whilst a student at Emmanuel College from 1835 to 1840 Charles George Taylor

> Could play any game, and indulged in all manner of pursuits with versatile whimsicality ... where he might be found playing tennis with a ginger-beer bottle for a racket or involving himself in various wagers, once undertaking – successfully – to learn to play the piano and sing in six weeks, and on another occasion to appear on the King's Parade in a pair of trousers of his own make.[5]

Taylor was the first cricket captain of Sussex, appointed when the club was founded in 1839 and holding the post until 1846.

Charles George Taylor was known to Frank Fenner because they both played in the same England cricket team against Kent in 1842 and featured in the epilogue at the first performance of the Old Stagers amateur theatre group (chapter 5). Frank was also a professional for the University when Taylor played there.

Robert Turner King started as a student at Emmanuel College in 1845 being a 'fine forcing batsman', a fairly fast bowler and one of the best fielders of his day,[6] 'far-famed for his wonderful catches as a fielder at "point"'.[7]

In addition to being a University cricket Blue from 1846 to 1849, including as captain in his last year, he also played eight matches for the Cambridge Town and County Club in 1846–1847[8] and is featured alongside Frank Fenner in Felix's painting of the Town and Gown cricket teams (chapter 20).

King later became a clergyman, mostly in the Fens between March and Wisbech from 1871 to 1884.[9]

Charles George Taylor: with King's College chapel in the background
Permission to use image from Knights Auctioneers.

Robert Turner King: university and town cricket player, later vicar in the Fens
Thanks to the parish of Friday Bridge for providing this image.

TOWN VERSUS GOWN TENSIONS

Whilst Frank Fenner was effective in bringing Town and Gown together in the same cricket team, the relationship was a lot more problematic on the river.

William Heitland, a student at St John's College from 1867 wrote about his student years including a section on 'Riots and Discipline'. He comments:

> The traditional Town-and-Gown rows belonged to an earlier social condition … The dying out of barge-traffic on the river gradually put an end to another source of conflicts. Bargees [people who worked on barges] were not in a hurry to clear the way for College [rowing] boats. Boat captains were not always conciliatory. Hence there was friction, and now and then a fight. Tales of prowess floated in the air. A famous strong man, [George Philip] Haydon of Emmanuel [student from 1864] was said to have picked up a bargee and thrown him into the river. For this I cannot vouch, but anyone who saw him row in the Emmanuel Four would not doubt his ability to do so.[10]

[1] David Berkeley (2015). Travel through Cambridge. Day One. Page 67.

[2] Emmanuel College website: https://www.emma.cam.ac.uk/about/history/college/?

[3] Orville Michael Cawthon (1983). Lancelot Andrewes' life and ministry. A foundation for traditional Anglican Priests. Ref 34.

[4] Dennis Brailsford (1991). Sport, Time, and Society. Routledge. Page 28.

[5] G.D. Martineau (1956). They made cricket. Museum Press. Page 113.

[6] Willie Sugg (2009). Fenner's Men. Cambs Cricket 1822 - 1848. Part 3 of A Tradition Unshared. Real Work Publishing. Page 42.

[7] Venn Cambridge Alumni Database. https://venn.lib.cam.ac.uk/

[8] Willie Sugg (2009). Fenner's Men. Cambs Cricket 1822 - 1848. Part 3 of A Tradition Unshared. Real Work Publishing. Page 42.

[9] Venn Cambridge Alumni Database. https://venn.lib.cam.ac.uk/

[10] William E. Heitland (1926). After Many Years. A tale of experiences and impressions gathered in the course of an obscure life. Cambridge University Press. Page 196.

CHAPTER 19

St Andrew's Street

The road on which Emmanuel College is located is St Andrew's Street, which continues in a south easterly direction, becoming Regent Street after about 150 yards (140m), just before the University Arms hotel.

There are seven buildings / locations with sporting links along this route including 5 Regent Street, where Frank Fenner lived at the time of the 1851 census aged 40, providing opportunity to explore the people, professions and families who shared this neighbourhood with him and his family.

Bird Bolt Inn (1870)
Used with permission from the Cambridgeshire Collection, Cambridge Central Library.

Stop 1: Bird Bolt Inn

Opposite the entrance to Emmanuel College on the other side of St Andrew's Street, on the corner with Downing Street, is the site of The Bird Bolt Inn or Hotel, which was in use from at least the 1630s. There is no explanation as to why the name was chosen, but a bird bolt is a short blunt missile used for killing birds without piercing them.

In the eighteenth century the Inn appears to have had close ties to cricket. For example, on 11 August 1792, the following advertisement was featured:

> The Public are humbly informed. That there will be a match of cricket played on Cambridge Cricket Ground on Tuesday 14th between the Gentlemen of Cambridge and Saffron Walden. The wickets to be pitched by 10 o'clock. A Good Ordinary [fixed-price meal] will be provided, where all Gentlemen cricketers and others will meet with a hearty welcome from their most obedient servant, R. Rayment. Bird Bolt Inn.[1]

Castle Hotel, 38 St Andrew's Street
Capturing Cambridge website: https://capturingcambridge.org

Stop 2: Castle Hotel

The original hotel sign, just visible in the sketch above the ground floor bay window, is today displayed in the Museum of Cambridge (chapter 2).

In 1817 a dinner was held at the Castle Inn after the Cambridge v Biggleswade cricket match on Parker's Piece. Before the match the local press reported:

> We observe, by Bills that have been distributed and placarded, that the Match is for 100 Guineas [£9,000], and that the Cambridge, with their usual philanthropy and politeness, will permit the Biggleswade to choose one Player not a Member of their Club, to play on their side in the Match … The Royston Club have challenged the Conquerors.

Cambridge won the match by five wickets watched by 'a circle composed of upwards of 1,000 persons', adding that 'the Cambridge undoubtedly are equal and perhaps superior in play, to any Club in this part of England.[2]

As a youngster Frank Fenner played for the Fountain Inn and Hoop Clubs, but mostly for the Castle, which was effectively his home base for 10 years, alongside his half-brother James. In 1829, aged 18, Frank scored 20 runs and took seven wickets for the Castle against Potton.[3]

Later, Frank was unanimously elected as Secretary of the Cambridge Town Cricket Club at its meeting held at the Castle Inn, reported in the Cambridge General Advertiser on 12 Feb 1840. Frank would have been 28 years old.

Other members of the Committee include Frederick Thackeray (first cousin to the famous author, and student at Gonville and Caius College).

The creation of the Cricket and Boating Club for College Servants was formally established on the 9 August 1856 at a meeting held at the Castle Inn. Mr Wise (a College Servant at Gonville and Caius College) took the chair, which included:

Dwelling upon the value of unanimity and cordial union, which he said would, he doubted not, enable them to beat any club of similar resources, who might be presumptuous enough to take the field against them.[4]

Thomas Hayward and Robert Carpenter (two Cambridge cricketers) were honoured with a dinner at the Castle Inn, on their return to Cambridge. This was after touring North America with the England cricket team in 1859, which because of the money the tour made indicated, according to the biographers of the Hayward family:

That overseas tours to places where the enthusiasm for the game was growing provided not only evangelical and missionary opportunities to develop and spread the game, but more significantly for entrepreneurs and players, the chance to make some money … Recognised for some times as being the country's leading players and now established as 'internationals', they saw the occasion as a catalyst to launch a decade of Cambridgeshire as a 'first-class' county.[5]

The local press of 19 November 1859 reported 'The admirers and supporters of cricket at Cambridge met the 'heroes of the American matches' at the Castle Inn on Wednesday evening at dinner. The party was large and included many of the old cricketers of the town'.[6]

There is no doubting Frank Fenner would have been invited to this event, but at about this time (precise dates unknown) Frank visited America himself, which included booking Deerfoot (the Native American) to run at Fenner's Ground (chapter 22).

In 1913 the Castle Hotel was the Headquarters of the Vincent Ramblers Cycling Club, Cambridge Town Football Club, Cambridgeshire Cricket Association, 99 Rowing Club, and Cambridge Horse Club.[7]

Stop 3: St Andrew's Street Baptist Chapel

Next to the Castle Hotel was St Andrew's Street Baptist chapel, where Josiah Chater records in his diary in 1855 that Charles Spurgeon came twice to preach. Aged only 23, Spurgeon was soon Victorian England's best-known Baptist minister.

Earlier in 1846, Josiah recorded that during the Irish famine a collection was made at the church totalling £500, worth around £60,000 today.

The chapel had a church hall, across the street, used as a skating rink from 1876. Perhaps because another skating rink opened nearby on New Corn Exchange (off Downing Street), in the same year,[8] the church hall/skating rink was rebuilt as 'The New Theatre Royal'.

Stop 4: Spinning House and police station

Next to the chapel was The Spinning House, built in the early seventeenth century as a workhouse and house of correction, following a donation of land by Thomas Hobson. The main use of The Spinning House was 'the confinement of such lewd women as the proctors [University 'police'] apprehend in houses of ill fame; though sometimes the [town] Corporation send small offenders thither, and the crier of the town is often there to discipline the ladies of pleasure with his whip.' It was demolished in 1901.[9]

It is highly probable Frank Fenner, in his capacity as a High Constable in 1848, and later as Chief Constable of the Borough would have had dealings with The Spinning House, as well as the Borough Police Station next door.

Next door to the police station was the Fountain Inn.

Stop 5: The Fountain Inn

Little appears to be known about the history of the Fountain Inn, but Frank Fenner played for their cricket club probably because of the support the Inn gave to Frank's father and other local tailors. On 1 April 1825, when Frank was 14 years old, a thankyou was printed in the Cambridge Chronicle:

> THE SOCIETY OF JOURNEYMEN TAILORS respectfully return their thanks for the kind offer of the compositors, pressmen, masons, and joiners, and also feel grateful for the contributions of the Fountain Cricket Club, and other private individuals, and beg at the same time to state that the late differences between them and their employers is amicably adjusted.

A couple of years later Frank, aged 16, scored 34 runs against the much-heralded Hoop Club on 22 August 1827, being an effort of considerable promise.[10]

It used to be said that the range of buildings just described, starting with the Fountain Inn, represented 'Pleasure', then 'Law and order', 'Morality' (the Spinning House being considered a place of correction) and 'Religion'[11] at St Andrew's Street Baptist Church.

A few doors up from the Fountain Inn was Llandaff House (opposite the start of Park Terrace).

Stop 6: Llandaff House

The older part of the house, which dated from 1710, had at one time been a tavern bearing the sign 'Bishop Blaize'. It was acquired in 1784 by Dr Watson, Bishop of Llandaff, and Regius Professor of Divinity at Cambridge University, who converted it into his private residence.

Later in 1817 Llandaff House became a boarding school preparing children for university, including using the outdoor opportunities on Parker's Piece, and the fields and a rented garden behind, belonging to Downing College. Alice Johnson, the granddaughter of the head teacher described the house in the second half of the nineteenth century.

> It was a large, rambling old house, - the earliest part, with a beautiful wide staircase and gallery and panelled rooms, dating back probably to Queen Anne, originally the last house on the south-east exit from the town. The pillared porch extending over the pavement once bore great extinguishers … on the porch [used] to put out the torches of link-boys [who carried a flaming torch to light the way for pedestrians at night].

> The garden at the back led into the semi-private grounds of Downing College, now mostly built over, but in our childhood an open space about a third of a mile long with fields and trees haunted by rooks and many other birds. Our garden opened on to one part, the much-loved "Grove," to which only we and our next-door neighbours had access.[12]

Early venue for sport in Cambridge

Prior to Downing College being founded in 1800 the land on which it was built was called the Marsh, with an adjacent smaller portion known as St Thomas's Leys or Layes. In 1655 this venue was described as the 'Campus Martius of the scholars here exercising themselves sometimes too violently; lately disused, either because young scholars now have less valour, or more civility'.[13]

The original Campus Martius, which translates as the 'Field of Mars', was used as the military exercise ground in ancient Rome, implying this was also an important location in Cambridge.

However, efforts to keep the colleges of the University apart when playing sport had been made in 1632, when an order was issued stating 'that C.C.C. [presumably Christ's College Cambridge] should be upon St Thomas Layes, and Pembroke upon the [Marsh] to ensure they were "not within 5 or 6 layes neere one to the other"'.[14]

People, professions and families living nearby

In 1851 the neighbours to Llandaff House who might also have used the Grove would probably have included Frank Fenner, his wife Mary and four children, Emma (aged 10), Frances (aged 6), Ellen (aged 3) and a son, Frank (aged 1). In addition, Eliza (Frank's sister, a milliner, aged 41) and Sarah (aged 19) and Eliza (aged 16), both general servants, all lived at 5 Regent Street, above the ground floor tobacco shop. This was located opposite the current pedestrian and cycle crossing from Parker's Piece.[15]

Other neighbours nearby included Henry Bond and his nine children (ages ranging from 3 to 13 years), who lived next door to Llandaff House. This was in the same year Henry was appointed as the Regius Professor of Physic [medicine], a post he held until 1872, with 'his tenure of office contemporary with a great rise in the reputation of the Cambridge Medical School'.[16]

Up Regent Street towards today's Hill's Road lived a piano maker, civil engineer, governess, teacher, magistrate, and John Howes, aged 22, a coachmaker living at 9 Regent Street, with his mother, three sisters and a lodger.

Later in 1869, John Howes started making bicycles, including opening a shop on Regent Street reputed to be the oldest bicycle shop in the country when it closed in 2013 after 173 years. (More on cycling in chapter 20.)

Stop 7: 5 Regent Street and Frank's family and homes

The life of Frank Fenner was a very busy mix of sporting, business, civic and church responsibilities, but he also had a family at 5 Regent Street where he both lived and ran his business around 1851, aged 40 years old.

It is not known where Frank was born in 1811, other than in Cambridge. His father, Joseph, a tailor had married Mary Welch in the Round Church, Bridge Street in 1805, subsequently living close to Frank, just off Parker's Piece for the rest of their lives. Both Joseph and Mary had long lives, 91 and 83/84 years respectively, inherited by Frank who lived until he was 85 years of age.

The earliest reference to Frank returning to Cambridge, after his three years in Chatteris, is from an 1836 advertisement promoting his tobacco shop on Sidney Street, also selling cricket equipment, and instruction. It is not known where he lived, but it was probably above the shop. He was 25 years old.

In 1841 Frank, his wife Mary, and their baby daughter Emma lived at the Red House, Parker's Piece (chapter 20), and in 1851 at 5 Regent Street (the current location). Later in 1861 they lived at 12 Emmanuel Road (facing Christ's Pieces) which was separate to his business address on the Market (chapter 16). Living with him in 1861 were his wife Mary, five daughters, one son and two servants.

Nothing more is known of Frank's role as husband or father. However, because of his other commitments, and the traditions of the day, he would probably have left most of the family responsibilities to his wife Mary.

It is not known for certain how Frank met Mary, but it is probable that cricket was involved. When he was 19 years old in 1830, Frank left Cambridge and lived in Chatteris, which is where Mary was from.

Frank had been invited to strengthen the local cricket team alongside Daniel Hayward 'the elder' (later father and grandfather to two of England's greatest cricketers of their time, Tom and Thomas Hayward). This invitation had originated from Thomas Skeels Fryer, president of the Chatteris club as well as local brewer, magistrate, and High Sheriff, sometimes referred to as the 'King of Chatteris'.

According to Willie Sugg the club now had new players, fixtures against top local clubs as well as the MCC, annual meetings and dinners, suggesting a well-run club going places.[17]

By 1833 however, Frank had returned to his hometown to play cricket for the Cambridge Town team, open his tobacco shop on Sidney Street and on 19 May 1836 at Trinity Church (close to the Market) marry 'Miss Mary Williams, eldest daughter of Mr. John Smith, late of Chatteris, auctioneer'.[18]

Frank Fenner and his family left Cambridge in 1861/1862 to live in the West Country (see chapter 23).

[1] Willie Sugg (2002). A tradition unshared. A history of Cambridge Town & County Cricket 1700 – 1890. Part One. Real Work Publishing. Page 58.

[2] Huntingdon, Bedford, Peterborough & Cambridge Gazette 19th July 26th July & 2nd Aug 1817. p 3. at https://www.cambscrickethistory.co.uk/1800-21/

[3] Willie Sugg (2009). Fenner's Men. Cambs Cricket 1822-1848. Part 3 of A Tradition Unshared. Real Work Publishing. Page 45.

[4] Cambridge Independent Press 09 August 1856.

[5] Keith and Jennifer Booth (2018). The Haywards. The biography of a cricket dynasty. Chequered Flag Publishing. Page 76.

[6] Cambridge Independent Press 19 Nov 1859.

[7] Capturing Cambridge website: https://capturingcambridge.org

[8] Capturing Cambridge website: https://capturingcambridge.org

[9] http://www.workhouses.org.uk/Cambridge/

[10] Willie Sugg (unpublished) Seminar Sixteen on F P Fenner. Page 1.

[11] Michael J. Murphy (1978). Poverty in Cambridgeshire. Oleander Press. Page 16.

[12] Kenneth Parsons (1984). A Nonconformist School - The Story of Llandaff House and its Academy. Cambridge Local History Society Bulletin No. 39.

[13] H.P. Stokes (1915). Outside Barnwell Gate quoted in the Cambridge Review, 4 March, 1909.

[14] H.P. Stokes (1915). Outside Barnwell Gate quoted in the Cambridge Review, 4 March, 1909.

[15] Thanks to Roger Lilley (Museum of Cambridge) confirming this on 29 Nov 2020.

[16] Venn Cambridge Alumni Database. https://venn.lib.cam.ac.uk/

[17] Willie Sugg's history of Cambridgeshire cricket - new writing at https://www.cambscrickethistory.co.uk

[18] Cambridge Chronicle and Journal 20 May 1836.

CHAPTER 20

Parker's Piece

HISTORY

Edward Parker, a local cook, leased the land from Trinity College in 1587. Twenty-five years later ownership was transferred to the town in exchange for land they owned behind the College, close to the river. The Town Corporation agreed that Parker's Piece was 'to be converted to grass and used as common pasture for ever'.[1] This agreement has been honoured to this day, being only briefly threatened when it was considered as the location for Downing College in the eighteenth century.[2]

Parker's Piece is one of a number of large open places that surround the university's medieval heartland. The others are Midsummer Common, Christ's Pieces, Coldham's Common, Sheep's Green, Lammas Land, Jesus Green and Coe Fen.[3]

It is unlikely Parker's Piece was used for many years for sport because 'the land lay in ridges and furrows, with ditches and hawthorn trees about … divided by a hedge and ditch'.[4]

The first known cricket match on Parker's Piece was in 1792 against Newmarket, about the same time as it also became 'the resort in the spring for the youth of the town who went their maying. At length three college cricket clubs levelled and re-laid part of it to play upon, and afterwards it was all levelled and fenced round, chiefly by the exertions of Mr Humfrey, who was mayor at the time' in 1837.[5]

In addition, Parker's Piece was also the location of the town gaol from 1827 to 1879 when it was demolished.

Town Gaol

In the 1851 census there were 36 men and 8 women as prisoners. Their crimes were mostly stealing, and their profession mostly labourers, with three of the women recorded as prostitutes. One prisoner was a Chelsea Pensioner who having set fire to a stack of wheat straw, was sentenced to seven years transportation.[6]

Cambridge Town Gaol - 1870s
Cambridgeshire Collection, Cambridge Central Library.

SPORT ON PARKER'S PIECE

The importance of Parker's Piece for the playing and watching of sport in Cambridge, certainly over the nineteenth century by both Town and Gown, sometimes together, cannot be overstated.

Chapter 1 provided opportunity to explore what was unique about Cambridge, including its association with sport. In this chapter there are eight locations on or around Parker's Piece providing further impressive evidence, given this is considered the home of the modern-day laws of association football, as well as being largely responsible for launching the sporting careers of four Cambridge Town 'greats'. These are Harry Gray, Sir Jack Hobbs, Frank Fenner and the Haywards, all of whom lived, worked and / or played here. We will look at each of these later in the chapter.

In addition, there is opportunity to explore the role sport played in bringing Town and Gown together on the sports field, at the 'Reality Checkpoint' in the middle of Parker's Piece, as well as the contributions, more generally, made by cycling, and the YMCA. Again, we will look at these contributions in this chapter.

All these sections to this chapter follow a criss-cross route round / across Parker's Piece, displayed below on the map of Cambridge, the grey circles indicating buildings or landmarks 'not yet built' in about 1836 when the map was produced.

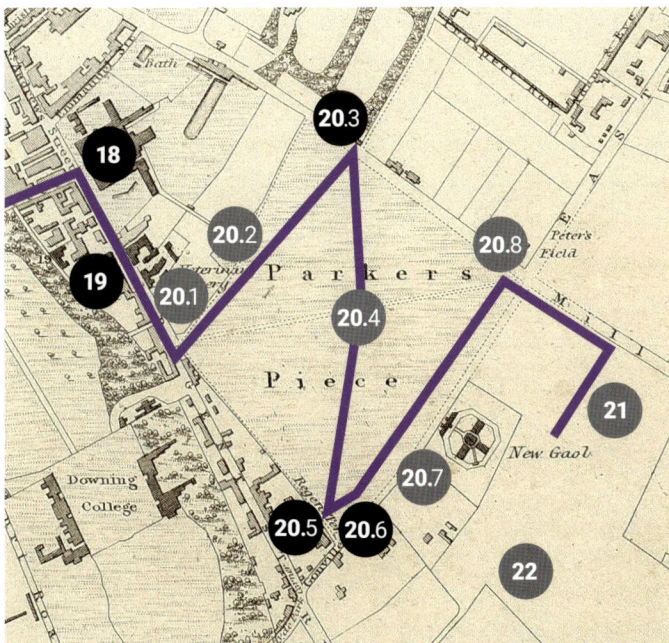

18	Emmanuel College
19	St Andrew's Street
20.1	University Arms
20.2	Hobbs Pavilion
20.3	Red House
20.4	Reality Checkpoint
20.5	Prince Regent Pub
20.6	Gonville Place
20.7	Cambridge YMCA
20.8	Cambridge Rules 1848 Sculpture
21	Mortimer Road
22	Fenner's Cricket Ground

Original map by kind permission of Cambridge Antiquarian Society.

Stop 1: University Arms – Harry Gray

First opened in 1834, the University Arms is the oldest hotel in Cambridge, replacing a veterinary surgery that previously occupied part of the site.

University Arms as the backdrop to preparations for the Street Child United Cricket World Cup 2019

The importance of cricket

One of the earliest images (below) of the hotel, appeared at the top of their billhead from the 1840s. This includes cricket being played nearby on Parker's Piece; note the tents erected for players to use.

Cambridgeshire Collection, Cambridge Central Library.

Even early advertising stated, 'the situation of the Hotel' was 'on the verge of the extensive Cricket-field', before referring to the proximity of Emmanuel and Downing Colleges.[7] This relationship had been forged by the hotel's first proprietor, William Bird, a former Cambridge cricketer and Hoop landlord (chapter 5).

In providing for the needs of the best Town and Gown cricketers, it was no surprise that the re-vamped Cambridge Town Club's first meeting took place at the University Arms in 1837. Frank Fenner (aged 25) was appointed assistant honorary secretary alongside Frederick Thackery[8] (first cousin of William Makepeace Thackery), who had started at Gonville & Caius College the year before. This was at a time when Town and Gown players would turn out for the same side, testament to 'the high standing of Cambridge Town cricket'.[9]

Important cricket meetings continued to be held at the University Arms, including for the Cambridge University Cricket Club (formed in 1820) who met there at least in 1853 and 1855, thereafter moving to Frank's tobacco shop and gymnasium on the Market.

Racquets and fives - Harry Gray

Henry John Gray, known as 'Harry', was born in 1836 on Pound Hill, close to Castle Hill, largely into poverty, with his father being a labourer.

As an 11-year-old, Harry started his career at the University Arms, on their racquets and fives courts. This is where he learned the trade of making racquets and balls, and coaching over a period of 11 years, prompting him to start his own business in 1855. Later, when his sons Willie and Horace were old enough, it became HJ Gray & Sons.

Not long after 1855, Harry also took on running racquets and fives courts at Wellington Court (opposite the existing Zion Baptist Church at the start of East Road, just across Parker's Piece) in 1857 and at St John's College from 1858 to 1883 (chapter 8). His reputation was further enhanced by Harry becoming world racquets champion in 1863, an achievement he shared with two of his brothers.

Harry was also an accomplished cricketer, for example playing in a three-day match in August 1859 on Parker's Piece between Cambridge Amateurs against an All-England XI, so was certainly known to Frank Fenner. He continued to play for Cambridge Town, and Cambridge College Servants Cricket Club until 1874. He was also keen on golf, inaugurating a course on Grantchester Meadows.

HJ Gray & Sons opened its first sports shop at 8 Rose Crescent in 1887 (chapter 16), when Harry's sons, Willie and Horace were aged 27 and 21 respectively. This was followed by shops on Searle Street, Sidney Street and in London.

H.J. Gray: founder of one of the most successful sports equipment firms

Permission to use image granted by Richard Gray, Director of Grays of Cambridge (International) Ltd.

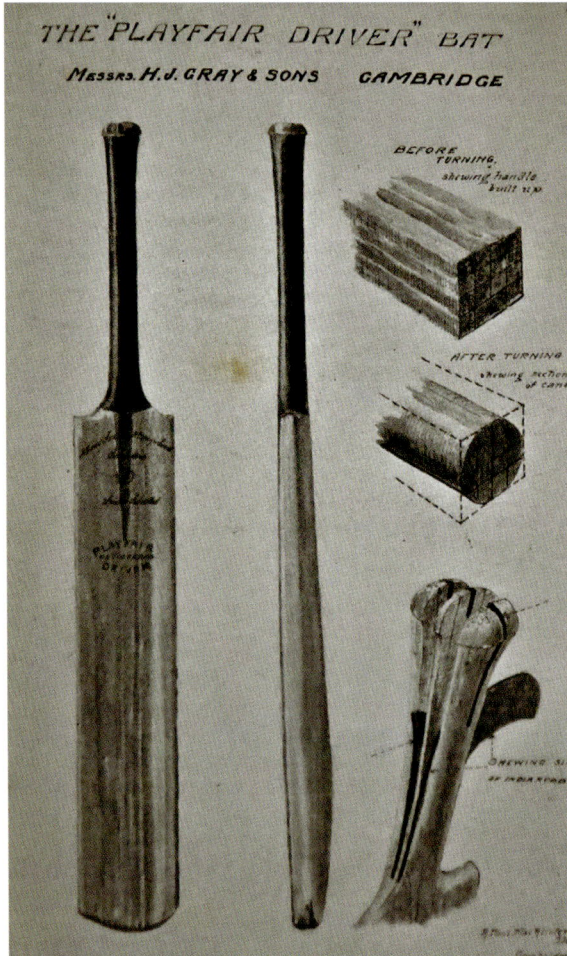

H.J. Gray & Sons cricket bat advert (1897)
Source: K.S. Ranjitsinhji (1897 - 4th ed). The Jubilee Book of Cricket. William
Blackwood and Sons, Page 147.

Customers for his cricket bats included WG Grace and Ranjitsinhji, and much
later in the 1960s, the captains of all five Test playing countries at the same
time (Ted Dexter, Richie Benaud, Frank Worrell, John Reid and Trevor Goddard)
who all used the iconic Gray-Nicholls cricket bat.

Harry died in 1915 and is buried alongside his wife and daughters at the
Ascension Road Cemetery, Huntingdon Road.

The Gray family continued to grow the company including operating a factory
on Benson Street (off Huntingdon Road) which opened in 1912, at its height
employing 150 staff up until 1986.[10]

From making racquets and cricket bats, Grays diversified into selling rugby balls,
hockey sticks, netballs and more across the world as Grays International, with
headquarters currently in Sussex. In 2018 the company had an annual turnover
of £25 million.

Hobbs Pavilion with University Arms hotel (behind)

Stop 2: Hobbs Pavilion – Sir Jack Hobbs

The pavilion was opened by Jack Hobbs in 1930 and celebrated with a cricket match featuring seven England captains, and including himself and Jack O'Connor, both born in Cambridge from cricketing families – featured in the photo on the next page. 'By two o'clock there were at least 5,000 spectators massed three and four deep round the entire field. Others stood on the running boards of cars drawn up in Park Terrace to see the game'.[11]

John Hobbs and the Anchor cricket team

Sir Jack Hobbs' father, John Cooper Hobbs, was also a keen cricketer, which is why alongside some fellow labourers he created the Anchor Cricket Club, based at the pub they frequented on Silver Street, next to the bridge and overlooking the Mill Pond. Established in the 1880s, the club soon became 'the talk of the Town' because of its achievements on the cricket pitch.

Whilst a roofing slater, John had wanted to make his living from cricket, and because of the Anchor Cricket Club's success he was offered a position as a professional at Fenner's to bowl at university students, umpire matches, as well as become the groundsman at Jesus College. 'He was now, effectively, one of Cambridge's large regiment of underpaid [university] college servants, but at least he was involved in the game that he loved'.[12]

The 1892 Anchor team contained a significant number of players from Cambridge's local cricketing family dynasties.

Thanks to Mike Petty MBE.

- (Front left) Herbert Arthur Carpenter later played for Essex County Cricket Club from 1893 to 1920, was the son of Robert Carpenter, the famous England cricketer (chapter 13).

- (Front second left) John Cooper Hobbs, father of Sir Jack Hobbs.

- (Front right) John O'Connor later played for Cambridgeshire and Derbyshire. His son Jack O'Connor was born in Cambridge in 1897 and played cricket for England and Essex. John O'Connor's brother-in-law was Herbert Carpenter.

- (Second row seated first left – all in white) Tom Hayward, later to play for Surrey and England, becoming one of the best batsmen in the world, playing alongside Jack.

- (Back row - elderly gentleman wearing the tall bowler hat towards the centre) Walter Watts was groundsman of Fenner's Cricket Ground from 1861 to 1908, a period of 47 years. Walter would have been engaged by Frank Fenner.

- (Back row second from right, with moustache and beard, next to Walter Watts) FC or Francis Hutt was the Jesus College scorer who became a father figure to Jack Hobbs, after Jack's father died. Hutt encouraged Jack to become a professional cricketer.

- Dan Martin Hayward (in black jacket, arms crossed, seated back left behind the team), brother to Tom, was cricket coach at Corpus Christi College, famous for coaching Ranjitsinhji. Later in 1908 Dan Martin became Walter Watt's successor as groundsman at Fenner's, a post he held for 27 years until 1935.

The Cambridge that Jack was born into

Jack Hobbs was born on 16 December 1882 at 8 Brewhouse Lane (off East Road, just beyond Norfolk Street), the oldest of 12 children. Soon after, the family moved to 4 Rivar Place, off Sleaford Street (over half a mile (1 km) from Parker's Piece), where Jack spent most of his childhood. These homes were in the area of Cambridge called Barnwell, characterised by overcrowding and poverty, which had a long-term effect on Jack, despite having a happy childhood.

> 'Certainly I had an inferiority complex, growing out of the conflict between town and gown, between poverty and privilege … later to find its echo in the cricket world through the dichotomy between professional and amateur, between the paid servants and the aristocratic establishment. In late Victorian Cambridge, not only was there serious poverty in the working class but the hostility between undergraduates and the townspeople could be ferocious.'[13]

Early sight of Ranjitsinhji

With Parker's Piece being so close, Jack would take any opportunity as a child to play and watch cricket there. Given Ranjitsinhji, later to become the first non-white sportsman ever to win international renown, was not picked in 1892 to play for the University, probably because of prejudice against his ethnicity and certainly his unorthodox playing style, it gave Ranji opportunity instead to score 2,000 runs playing local cricket. This included scoring three centuries in three separate matches on the same day on Parker's Piece,[14] perhaps seen by the 10-year-old Jack.

At the age of 12, Jack worked in domestic service each day, before attending the nearby St Matthew's school (on East Road). On leaving school he worked as an errand boy, a college servant, and when aged 16 he became an apprentice gas fitter. This coincided with Jack's father John changing his career in 1889 to professional cricketer, umpire and groundsman.[15]

Death of Jack's father

Aged 20, and a week after he had played his first match as a professional for Royston in which he scored a century, his father died of pneumonia, 'the darkest spot in Jack's career', according to his mother. What helped to sustain him was the astonishing outpouring of affection from the people of his hometown and the cricket world. For example, a charity cricket match was held on Parker's Piece where Tom Hayward agreed to bring up a strong side from Surrey County Cricket Club. The Cambridge Chronicle reported:

> In the annals of Parker's Piece, this game must surely take a unique place. Never before has a team of cricketers of the first rank played in the town's best play-ground and the crowd of spectators was certainly the greatest ever assembled to witness a local match.[16]

The final sum raised was over £200 (£25,000 today), providing Jack's mum with a small pension.

One of the three best batsmen in the world

Jack Hobbs joined Surrey County Cricket Club in 1905 where he achieved extraordinary cricketing success, as listed on his Blue Plaque today located on Hobb's Pavilion: 61,237 runs, 197 centuries in first class cricket and 61 Test matches for England. In 1923 Jack Hobbs became the third player in the world to score a hundred first-class centuries after WG Grace and Tom Hayward,[17] who also had a very close association with Parker's Piece, having been born at the Prince Regent Pub (see Stop 5 later in this chapter) in 1861.

Jack Hobbs's cricket links with Fenner's

On reflecting on his whole first-class career, it appears batting in front of his own Town crowd at Fenner's adversely affected his performance; he played five First Class matches there with a highest score of 93 and an average of only 21.75, when his overall first-class average was over 50. Of the 24 grounds across England, he played five or more matches at, he only had a worse batting average at Hove Cricket Ground, Sussex. By complete contrast his bowling average at 6.66 (runs for each wicket taken) was significantly better than any other ground where he bowled 10 or more overs in his career. His best figures of 5 for 22 at Fenner's are exceptional.

Why not 200 centuries?

The local press in 1935 reported on Jack's views on his retirement, and his achievement of 197 first-class centuries.

'Mrs Hobbs thinks I ought to go on to get my 200 centuries', he said, but 'after many years in the field (my legs) get very tired nowadays about four o'clock'. He will continue to play in club cricket and all in Cambridge hope to see that flashing bat in action again on Parker's Piece, the scene of his early triumphs'.[18]

He did continue playing, for example for the Old Cantabs Cricket Club.

Old Cantabs Cricket Club on Parker's Piece – early 1930s

Thanks to Andrew Stephen whose Great Uncle Les Hunt kept wicket – seated front right next to Jack Hobbs.

Hobbs sports shops

Given Jack's success he opened a sports shop at 59 Fleet Street, London in 1919 run by his younger brother, Sydney. Jack sometimes served in the shop, maintaining he earned more from the shop than playing cricket.

The commute from Cambridge into London was too much for Sydney, so in 1931 he opened Hobbs Sports at 38 Trinity Street. The shop continued at this location until 2006 when Hobbs Sports moved to replace Gray's Sports shop on Sidney Street, until 2017 when it closed altogether.

Jack Hobbs's legacy

In 1953, Hobbs was knighted, the first professional cricketer to be so honoured. He was reluctant to accept the award, only doing so when convinced it was an honour to all professional cricketers, not just himself:

> Hobbs's own journey was symbolic of the change, from the dire poverty of late-Victorian Cambridge to the affluent respectability in mid-1930s suburbia … But even in stratified England, Hobbs could never be defined by a single class. Perhaps more than any other celebrity of his age, he was symbolic of England and its values. In his famous wartime essay 'The Lion and the Unicorn', George Orwell wrote that 'the gentleness of English civilisation is perhaps its most marked characteristic. You notice it the instant you set foot on English soil. It is a land where bus conductors are good-tempered and policemen carry no revolvers'. This was the spirit that Jack Hobbs so perfectly encapsulated. He managed to be a star and an Everyman, another reason he was beloved by a public that recognised one of their own.[19]

John Arlott (cricket commentator on BBC Test Match Special, and friend of Jack's) said that Hobbs was 'the best man I ever knew in my life. I would say this even if he had never made a run. There was something almost Christ-like about him…'.[20]

The location of the pavilion was no surprise as Jack, later writing in his memoirs, believed Parker's Piece to be 'probably the finest and most famous cricket ground in the world; it is certainly one of the best.'[21]

Stop 3: The Red House and Barnwell

The 1841 census records the 'Red House, Parker's Piece' as the home of Frank Fenner, aged 30, with his wife Mary, daughter Emma aged 8 months, a lodger, and female servant, Jane Watts, aged 15.

Whilst the Red House does not exist anymore, it was most recently the home of the live-in caretaker of Parkside Secondary School. According to a current teacher, he recalls it as 'a rather handsome, substantial building'.

The Red House (on the far left-hand-side), **on Parkside, Parker's Piece (before 1909)**
From the collection of David Gent.

Before outlining the cricketing career of Frank Fenner and some of his peers, given the proximity of the Red House to Parker's Piece, where he played most of his cricket, it is important first to describe this area of Cambridge, called Barnwell.

Barnwell

In the early nineteenth century Cambridge Town was split into 14 parishes, one of which was St Andrew the Less covering the east side of Cambridge, corresponding to the area of town called Barnwell. Its boundary with the rest of the town included the river in the north, Jesus Green and Parker's Piece.

When Frank Fenner was living in the Red House, Barnwell had a very poor reputation, 'so wretched as to be a disgrace on civilisation; it is next to impossible for the inhabitants to be healthy, moral, decent or honest' according to a Public Health Report presented to the Town Council in 1849.[22]

Charles Bristed (student at Trinity College from 1840), writing about his experiences in Cambridge, described Barnwell as synonymous with prostitution.[23] It also contained many public houses, with 22 in under half a mile on Newmarket Road.[24]

Another observer wrote 'those who knew Cambridge in those days, would remember what a large number of ne'er-do-wells were to be found in Barnwell and other parts, who, if left to themselves, must eventually swell the criminal class'.[25]

Population growth

A significant reason for this reputation was that Barnwell expanded rapidly, by 15% in 10 years between 1841 and 1851, 'by which time it accounted for 44% of Cambridge's population, probably exceeding even the most rapid growth of any industrial town in the north or midlands'.[26]

Unfortunately, 'there was an absence of any civic or philanthropic concern over the social conditions as the town grew in a very haphazard way that could not fail to have a deleterious result'.[27] There were some positive initiatives later in the nineteenth century, but long after Daniel Macmillan (the local publisher) first drawing attention in 1842 to the social conditions of the poor. Macmillan had approached Frederick Maurice for help, but without success.[28]

Impact of the University

A visitor to Cambridge (clearly only the centre of the town) in 1844 appreciated 'the quiet of the place, the non-permission of theatres and the non-existence of manufactories and trade are all favourable to the undisturbed pursuit of knowledge'.[29]

Where there was trade, significant parts of it were regulated by the University, such as the licensing of wineshops and alehouses, the inspection of weights and measures including at markets and fairs, and the 'discommoning', or banning of local traders. One innkeeper was banned for allowing students to play billiards.[30]

Such management of Cambridge by the University had been evident for a long time. Daniel Defoe, writing about his tour through the Eastern Counties in 1724 concluded:

> To any man that is a lover of learning, or of learned men, here is the most agreeable under heaven … but it is to the honour of the University to say that the governors so well understand their office and the governed their duty, that here is very little encouragement given to … dancing, gaming, intriguing … It is to the honour of the whole body of the University that no encouragement is given to them here.[31]

The University had the power to arrest and punish women suspected of being prostitutes.[32] Clearly the 'privileged University had a crippling hold over civic and commercial affairs'.[33]

Town versus Gown tensions

It is no surprise therefore that there was resentment sometimes spilling over onto the streets, particularly in the middle of the nineteenth century.

Josiah Chater records in his diary 'after 1845 … there was much fighting between the Town and University', including riots nearly every night for two weeks in early 1848.

A single newspaper report from 9 November 1850[34] referred to the violence between Town and Gown on the 5 November when:

> The weapons used were not confined to fists … the violence of both parties … This mob (of 300 townsmen) had the complete control of the streets all the evening … the assailant of (a townsman) was most severely beaten … the gownsmen linked arm-in-arm, soon cleared the street of the mob, who set about parading the town … (The next night) the townspeople again attempted a riot, as did a body of gownsmen … A man of Christ's College had his front teeth knocked out; another gownsman had his spectacles broken on his face, which was severely cut by the pieces of glass … (The next night) one poor solitary gownsman was set upon by a low mob outside the Town Hall; his cap and gown were destroyed; he was trampled on by the mob.

According to J W Clark, an undergraduate at Corpus Christi College in the 1850s 'It was dull work to meet merely for the sake of a boxing match, but a street disturbance offered an enjoyable diversion, much blood was shed….and many heads were broken'.[35]

This love of the fight was also experienced by those students who wrote about the Battle of Peas Hill between Town and Gown in 1820 (chapter 16).

Positive initiatives

There were initiatives to support the poor in Cambridge, such as the Industrial School just off Victoria Road (chapter 2) established by Harvey Goodwin, who later was the first principal of the Working Men's College (chapter 16).

Ion Keith-Falconer (considered one of the fastest cyclists in the world while at Cambridge), opened a mission in 1875, a year after he arrived as a student at Trinity College, and in 1878, with others, bought the failing Theatre Royal on Newmarket Road to serve as a permanent mission hall.[36]

Frank Fenner

By offering Frank's gymnasium to students at the Working Men's College, Enid Porter believed the boxing, fencing and gymnastic classes taught by members of the University 'did more, probably than all the other [classes], to promote friendly intercourse between University men and townspeople.'[37]

Cricket also made a significant contribution too. Despite the significant tensions between Town and Gown, 'the annual early season fixture, Cambridge Town Cricket Club v Undergraduates of Cambridge - or 'Town versus Gown', as it was popularly known – dating from 1817, did much to bring the two communities together',[38] explored further in this chapter.

Frank's tobacco and cricket equipment businesses

Having had a tobacco shop on Sidney Street from 1836, Frank then advertised cricket bats, balls and stumps for sale at the Red House in 1844.

The claim in the advert he sells exclusively to the University demonstrated Fenner's 'business acumen and his ability to network ... his confidence, opportunism and pragmatism ... In the context of a town divided, often angrily, between University and Town such opportunism is particularly noticeable'.[39]

> **F. P. FENNER,**
> **CIGAR MERCHANT,**
> RED HOUSE, PARKER'S PIECE, Cambridge.
>
> BEGS respectfully to call attention of Cricketing Connoiseurs to his unequalled Stock of BATS which have been selected by himself with great care from the Repositories of the first makers. All that great experience could accomplish has been, in the adaptation of his Bats to the present improved style of playing; the wood being so scientifically placed, as to give an ease and elegance to the finished player, while to the mere tyro they afford a facility in vain looked for in any other.
> BALLS, STUMPS, &c. Wholesale & Retail.
> N.B.—None but Fenner's are used in the practice and great Matches of the University Club.[14 m

Source: Cambridge Chronicle and Journal 20 April 1844.

Selling cricket equipment was founded on an outstanding cricket career including many feats achieved on Parker's Piece, just across the road from the Red House, as well as elsewhere across the country, including as an All-England cricketer.

Frank's likely early exposure to cricket

Whilst it is not known where Frank lived in Cambridge in his early life, it is highly probable Parker's Piece was not far away. Therefore Frank, aged 6, probably saw the first recorded Town v Gown cricket match there in 1817. That same year Cambridge Cricket Club played a match against Biggleswade for a 100 Guineas prize, watched by 'a circle composed of upwards of 1,000 persons'.[40] Late in his life, Frank recalled 'an extraordinary match played at Cambridge [in 1827 when Frank was 16 years old] in which Fuller Pilch [played for] Bury St Edmunds against the University of Cambridge'. Frank believed it to be the lowest scoring match of the nineteenth century – see chapter 22.

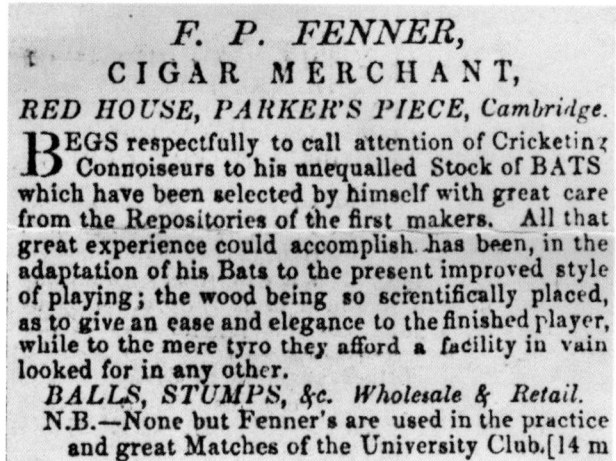

Frank's playing and coaching career

Frank played 'cricket in the reign of William IV and was an old hand when he took part in the Coronation Match arranged in honour of the accession of Queen Victoria [in 1838] '.[41]

A right-handed top order batsman, standing five foot ten inches tall, Fenner was said to begin his innings 'in his usual quiet way' but once set, to play 'with great spirit' in a 'neat, skilful and scientific' manner.[42]

Another perspective saw Fenner as holding 'a prominent position in the cricket world, being very scientific and steady – so steady, in fact, as once to distinguish himself by remaining at the wickets upwards of five hours for 34 runs.'[43]

Up until the start of his cricketing career underarm bowling was the norm, but Frank (who bowled fast) and others were using the new but controversial round-arm style, which relied more on sympathetic umpires than rule changes by the MCC, who took until 1835 to formally permit such bowling. As Denison, the noted cricket chronicler put it, the new style's early proponents 'became the objects of copy for every man or lad having any pretension to bowl', and Fenner was clearly one of those.[44] It was not until 1864, after Frank retired, that the over-arm action we are familiar with today, became permissible.

As a fielder he was capable of handling the ball 'like lightening', generally fielding somewhere between cover point and first slip from where he marshalled his team to great effect when captain.[45]

Career statistics and coaching

By 1848, when Frank was aged 37, he had scored 2,000 runs and taken 450 wickets in 95 matches,[46] including 39 occasions when he had taken at least 5 wickets in an innings,[47] including 17 in one match.

In addition to coaching the local town players, Frank also 'trained the best of the university cricketers'.[48] He would also travel too, including Frank being 'invited to visit the Black Country to assist in coaching a local team; his presence became known to the opposing team, whose friends and supporters became so exasperated on the day of the match that (although he attended merely as a spectator) he had to fly for his life, and only escaped with a whole skin in consequence of his fleetness of foot – the story was almost worthy of some latter-day football scrimmages'.[49]

Timeline of Frank's cricketing career

1827 to 1837 – played for three of the local pub sides, the Hoop Club, based on Bridge Street, the Fountain on Regent Street and the Castle on St Andrew's Street, who he played consistently for, for 10 years.

In 1828, when Frank Fenner was 17 years old, he took 10 wickets in a match for the Hoop against Biggleswade prompting him to send a single wicket challenge to *Bell's Life* (the national sporting paper).

1830 to 1833 – moved to and plays for Chatteris (about 20 miles (30km) north of Cambridge), including a game against the MCC. After three years he returned to Cambridge.

1834 – As examples of the standard of cricket Frank Fenner was playing, and the distances travelled, he played for Cambridge against Nottingham, first on Parker's Piece over two days in July, and then five weeks later, the return match on the Forest Ground in Nottingham.

Nottingham were far too strong for Cambridge, winning both matches easily thanks to Barker and Redgate's bowling, which 'had entirely destroyed [Cambridge's] confidence in their own play,' watched by 'several thousand spectators each day'.[50]

Also turning out for Nottingham was William Clarke who had effectively taken control of Nottingham cricket in 1831, including establishing Nottingham's first pay-to-enter cricket stadium, in the latter 1830s.

It is not known whether they ever met to discuss this, but it is interesting that Frank's cricketing career, regarding the provision of a dedicated cricket facility, followed William Clarke's. They were also the new breed of entrepreneur – see also chapter 22.

1835 – Frank played a single wicket competition[a], on Parker's Piece, teaming up with

- Thomas Sanders (Eton, student, then Fellow at King's College from 1831), and
- Fuller Pilch ('the best batsman that has ever yet appeared'), to play against
- Charles Parnther (Eton, Trinity College),
- William Caldecourt (later coach and umpire at Harrow and Cambridge) and
- Samuel Redgate, ('the most feared fast bowler in England' from Nottingham).

---

[a] Single wicket cricket is normally played between two individuals, who take turns to bat and bowl against each other. The one bowling is assisted by a team of fielders, who remain as fielders at the change of innings. The winner is the one who scores more runs. Presumably these standard rules were extended to accommodate the three-aside format referred to here, played in 1835.

According to *Bell's Life*, 'this was truly the finest display of cricketing skill ever witnessed on Parker's Piece' also commenting specifically on the 'formidable bowling of Fenner' and his admirable batting.

This prompted Frank to challenge 'any cricketer, within fifty miles of Cambridge, to a single wicket match, home and away … for a moderate stake'.[51]

1836 – Frank represented the North of England versus the South.

1838 – represented South of England against the North, in the coronation match played at Lord's Cricket Ground. (Frank playing for the South in 1836, and two years later, for the North, reflects the confusion as to where Cambridge was in England.)

A few days later Frank would no doubt have been back in Cambridge to participate in the dinner celebrating Queen Victoria's Coronation given to 15,000 of the 'deserving poor' on Parker's Piece, watched by 25,000 spectators who bought tickets (see image on page 27).

1838 – won the single-wicket championship of England. Frank made this claim in 1883, nearly 50 years later.[52] If true it probably would have been the two matches he played against Alfred Adams of Saffron Walden, one away, followed by one a week later on Parker's Piece.[53]

1839 – Played for Cambridge University as the club professional, having been engaged in this role in 1836.

1841 - Played for the Players against the Gentlemen at Lord's Cricket Ground (see poster) which also lists, under 'matches to come' that a week later, the town of Cambridge will also soon play at Lord's, a match Frank also played in.

CRICKET.

A GRAND MATCH

WILL BE PLAYED IN

LORD'S GROUND,

MARYLEBONE,

On MONDAY, JULY 12th, 1841,

And following Day,

Eleven Gentlemen of all England against Eleven Players.

PLAYERS.

Gentlemen	Players.
The Hon. F. PONSONBY	COBBETT,
Sir F. H. BATHURST	FENNER,
Capt. READY	GOOD,
T. A. ANSON, Esq.	GUY.
W. BARTON, Esq.	HAWKINS.
G. L. LANGDON, Esq.	LILLYWHITE,
A. MYNN, Esq.	PILCH,
R. C. NICHOLSON, Esq.	REDGATE,
W. PICKERING, Esq.	SAMPSON,
C. G. TAYLOR, Esq.	SEWELL.
C. G. WHITTAKER, Esq	WENMAN,

MATCHES TO COME

Wednesday, *July 14th, the University of Cambridge against the University of Oxford.* Friday, *July 16th, the Marylebone Club against the Undergraduates of Oxford.* Monday, *July 19th, at Lord's, the Marylebone Club and Ground against the Town of Cambridge*

Cricket Bats, Balls, Stumps, Score Papers, and the Laws of Cricket, as revised by the Marylebone Club in 1840, to be had of Mr. J. H. DARK, at the Pavilion, and at the Manufactory on the Ground.

An Ordinary at Three o'clock.

Admittance, 6d.   Good Stabling on the Ground.   No Dogs admitted.

MORGAN, Printer, 39, New Church Street, Portman Market.

The Roger Mann Collection.

1841 – Frank was placed eighth in national batting averages, reported in *Bell's Life*.

1840 to 1842 - played for All-England on eight occasions.

Frank later reminisced about one of these England appearances, in 1842, as:

> An instance of the remarkable changes of fortune to which the game is subject. England was playing Kent, and the latter had secured the very creditable score of 274. Everyone was in high fettle, and Kent was backed to the tune of 50 to 1 [as betting odds]. When their opponents compiled a score of 268 the enthusiasm became intense. Then [in preparation for Kent's 2nd innings] Lillywhite called his team out [Frank and the other players for an England 'team talk'] and dismissed them with the remark, 'Englishmen can do anything – we must win.' 'Lilly' bowled magnificently and all fielded well, so that man after man went out for a small score. When Kent was all out for 44 in little more than an hour the scene was indescribable. For the remaining twenty minutes I [Frank] was sent in to bat with a partner I soon lost, but next morning we quickly got enough runs to win without further loss.[54]

The Kent locals were not best pleased, according to Frank 'had the heavens opened and hurled its thunder over the scene the changed countenances of these sturdy men could not have been more complete'.[55]

It was no surprise this match subsequently caused quite a stir in the press with accusations that Kent had 'sold the game'. This prompted Frank to write a letter to *Bell's Life* defending Kent and the integrity of cricket, a theme he would often return to, and champion.[56]

In reflecting also on the reasons for the win, Frank identified:

> 'the attributes of our countrymen when placed under their mettle', such as muscular power, physical endurance, and a thorough command and mastery over self. These qualifications (which to the honour of our race, I am proud to say, are national characteristics) become much strengthened by the constant demand for their exercise, and the invariable necessity for their application ... I have never yet seen an open condemnation of the game or its consequences; and so long as it is governed by the manliness and fine spirit of honour that have distinguished it in the past, so long will it retain its rank in the growing records of our national athleticism.[57]

1842 - played for Players v Gentlemen at Lord's Cricket Ground, using his 'cleanly habits'. When bowling, Frank dismissed Captain P Mundy who:

> Assures [the press] that had he not been suddenly dazzled by a bright glare of sun falling upon the snow whiteness of Fenner's linen shirt, he

might have been successful! (in his plan to go in first, and score more than the rest of his side altogether.) As it was, this hero of artillery, fell a victim to the cleanly habits of the Cambridge bowler.[58]

1840s – player protection, and Frank's hands. In 1893 Frank reminisced about this period:

> 'When we played in tail-coats and top-hats, and without pads and that kind of thing … [resulting in getting] a good deal knocked about. There' – holding up his left hand – 'is a finger of which the top was completely knocked off when I was batting one day. I had the piece sewn on again, and, except for the marks of the stitching, it is none the worse.'[59]

His hands had quite a reputation, because in the same year (1893), three years before he died, a Mr Jesse described the old hands of Frank:

> As worthy of preservation in a glass case in the pavilion at Lord's, like Galileo's at Florence, as 'trophies of his suffering and glory. Broken, distorted, mutilated, half-nailless, they resemble the hoof of a rhinoceros, almost as much as a human hand.'[60]

1843 – played for Hampshire and Midland Counties.

1844 – took 17 wickets in one match for Town v Gown on Parker's Piece, one of only 22 players to do so in the history of the First Class game.[61]

1850 – Fenner played a single wicket competition on Fenner's Cricket Ground, winning easily having scored 176 runs.

1854 – scored 62 runs for the Town versus the University on Parker's Piece.

1856 - Frank's last first-class match was on 5 and 6 May at Fenner's for the Town versus the University. Frank made 5 and 4 runs in the 1st and 2nd innings respectively, took one catch and does not appear to have bowled.

Other Town cricketer players

The Cambridge Town Cricket Club (which, over the nineteenth century had a variety of other names and structures including sometimes being combined with the county) was one of the best three cricket teams in the country across the middle of the nineteenth century. Whilst largely due to Frank's captaincy, and skill as a coach, player and administrator, he also relied on some very talented local players.

The stories of four of them: Israel Haggis, Charles Arnold, George Tarrant and Billy Buttress, are shared next, after Robert Carpenter, and Thomas Hayward were featured at the Senate House (chapter 13). Later in the current chapter (Stop 5: Prince Regent Pub) there is also a focus on the Hayward cricketing family dynasty.

Israel Haggis

Whilst Israel Haggis was considered a stalwart for the Cambridge Town Cricket Club, playing many times on Parker's Piece, he had to earn a living beyond playing the game professionally.

Over his short life of 41 years (he was born in 1811, the same year as Frank Fenner) he had a range of jobs, from manager of St John's College Tent on Parker's Piece, to running a dance band and booth at local fairs, for which he was fined in 1836 for selling spirits without a licence, at Cambridge's Stourbridge Fair.[62]

Haggis was also the landlord of five local pubs starting at the Flower Pot, before moving to the Six Bells, then onto the New Inn on Parker's Piece, the Tiger on East Road and the Salmon in Fair Street.[63]

Direct competition with Frank Fenner

In 1844 Haggis promoted the New Inn as the local 'Cricketing Hotel & Tavern', where he 'hope[d] to merit a continuance of those favours which have been so liberally bestowed on him for these last twelve years, by the University and Town, and likewise various Clubs in the County'. He offered a range of different goods and services:

- cricket equipment, having 'just returned from London with a most splendid assortment of BATS...and BALLS; newly-invented light cork Leg Pads, and Finger Guards ... Scoring Papers and the Laws of the Game,
- LILLYWHITE, the great Sussex Bowler, is stopping at the above-named Inn, and is always ready at the shortest notice to wait on Gentlemen, lovers of the noble game of Cricket'. [Lillywhite was helping the local Cambridge Town Cricket Club.][64]
- MARQUEES, large and commodious BOOTHS of all sizes fitted up on all occasions on the most reasonable terms, and
- A CATAPULTA [cricket bowling machine] on the ground daily.'[65]

This was in direct competition to Frank Fenner's business nearby at the Red House, with their respective advertisements in the local paper being located next to each other. This reflected the significant interest in cricket locally. Interestingly Frank boasted being the exclusive supplier of cricket equipment to the University Club, whereas Israel's claim is more general.

Sports promoter?

In raising his profile in the local press Haggis also vouched for the pedestrian Alabaster, in his record walk in 1845 of 1,000 miles and 1,000 furlongs in 1,000 continuous hours, on Parker's Piece.[66]

However, not everything associated with Parker's Piece was positive for Haggis. In June 1840, while watching a cricket match on Parker's Piece, Haggis challenged some students teasing his horse, and was threatened twice at gunpoint. This resulted in one student being bound over by the university authorities to keep the peace, but being allowed to leave town without facing any further action.[67]

In 1845 six cricket bats, stumps and a ball were stolen from the St John's Cricket Club tent on Parker's Piece, of which Haggis had supervision. The defendant, George Johnson, though seen offering the stolen bats for sale, was acquitted on the grounds of his tender age of eight.[68]

Finally, Israel met a sad and lonely end, bringing a salmon from London in contaminated water and contracting cholera as a result of eating it. Fearing contamination, no one ventured to go near him, and he died after two days, alone in a tent, with his wife and relatives engaging in an unseemly struggle over his possessions.[69] It is understood he was buried in Mill Road Cemetery, but the exact whereabouts is unknown.

Charles Arnold

Charles's birth year is variously given between 1820 and 1826. Nothing is so far known of his childhood or schooling, however it is believed he started a bakery apprenticeship, given this was his profession listed in the 1841 census when he was living with a baker, John Garner, his wife, four children, and three other servants.

Charles made his first-class cricketing debut with the Cambridge Town Club in 1843, where he started as a professional. He also played for other clubs around the country including South Hants, Audley End, Bury St Edmunds, and Beverley in Yorkshire. He was ranked third in *Bell's Life* bowling averages for 1846 with 105 wickets, later playing regularly for the All-England XI in 1853, and taking 11 wickets in a match against the Gentlemen of England including those of Alfred Mynn, C G Taylor and Fuller Pilch (twice).

As a bowler Charles Arnold had 'great pace but ... was not very straight' which was the perfect complement to the accuracy of Fenner and Diver (when they played together for Cambridge Town). 'The steam of Arnold' on the rough pitches of the day was famous for 'producing lethal shooters' [which were balls, when bowled, kept very low after pitching]:

> And Arnold with his useful shoot
> Look out! He'll have your legs to boot[70]

Charles Arnold is featured in Felix's 1847 painting of Town and University players earlier in the chapter, standing on the extreme left (see page 208).

Charles married Penelope in Linton in 1847 and by 1851 the couple were living at 24 Melbourne Place, Cambridge (off Parker's Piece). They did not have any children, but nor did they appear to live together, as shown in the 1871 census. When he died in 1873, aged 49, he was living in a separate address again, but he did leave his 'effects of less than £100 to Penelope'.[71]

Three years after Charles's death, Penelope married Thomas Cave in Reading, Berkshire, in 1876. It is not known how long they lived together because when Penelope died almost 20 years after this second marriage, she was recorded as living in the Fulbourn Lunatic Asylum, near Cambridge. She died in 1895, aged 64 and was buried with her first husband Charles Arnold in Mill Road Cemetery.

Charles Arnold's headstone in Mill Road Cemetery.

Of all the cricketers buried there, known to have played with Frank, Charles's grave is the only one that today can be identified.

George Frederick Tarrant (or George Wood)

In his boyhood days, 'Tarrant was known as "Pepper", and among his youthful escapades was the riding of horses bare back round the Common standing circus-like-fashion on their backs.[72]

Whilst he played most of his cricket for George Parr's All-England XI and Cambridgeshire, he did travel as a professional to Bottesdale, Suffolk, and later to Manchester.

His best batting performance was probably scoring 108 runs playing for Cambridgeshire against the University, on Fenner's Ground, in 1866. However, he was much better known as a bowler, and because of his speed, was known as 'Tear-em'. His best bowling was 10 wickets for 40 runs for All-England against a XIII of Kent at Lord's in 1863.[73] 'For his size his bowling was terrifically fast, and it was a marvel to me how he kept it up as long as he did.[74]

All-England XI in 1865. George Tarrant standing fourth from right in the back row (of the cricket players), with Thomas Hayward back left
Used with permission and thanks to MCC archive and library.

Tarrant was also a very good boxer which was why George Parr always had him near at hand whenever there was a disturbance.[75]

> 'On long-distance (cricket) tours among outlandish people, he would act as his captain's bodyguard. When anyone attempted to pick a quarrel with George Parr, he [Parr] would murmur 'Go at him Tear'em!' Then, but not till then, Tarrant would oblige, which was a sign, I think, of a pretty equable temperament'.

George was only 5 feet 7 inches tall, weighing a little over 9 stone, which given the amount of bowling he did, was believed at the time to have contributed to his early death aged only 31, from 'a strained heart', or pleurisy.

He died in 1870 at his home on Newmarket Road survived by Martha, his wife, and three children, having lost one twin, born a few weeks before George died. George is also buried in Mill Road Cemetery, but the whereabouts of his grave is unknown.

Billy Buttress

Billy Buttress, born in 1827, was considered 'the father of break [spin] bowling'. In 1861 he lived on Eden Street, a two-minute walk from Parker's Piece.

In addition to having to travel across the country to secure work, Billy would coach and play cricket on Parker's Piece. 'The difficulty was to keep Buttress sober', not helped by the Cricketers Inn at 18 Melbourne Place, just a short distance from the Red House, being on his route home. Some therefore question whether the inn is haunted by the thirsty shade of Billy Buttress seeking one of his favourite pints.[76]

According to Richard Daft, a contemporary of Billy,

> Buttress .... was a great amateur ventriloquist. He could imitate a cat mewing to the life, and used, it is said, often to carry a stuffed kitten about with him to which was attached a piece of string. This animal he would often place under a railway carriage seat before any passengers entered, and when the compartment was filled would begin to imitate the cries of a kitten, jerking the string at the same time to cause the stuffed one under the seat to knock against the passenger's legs, causing a great amount of confusion. Billy used to prefer playing these tricks when the compartment happened to be full of old women who were going to market. On these occasions he often escaped detection by making the cat hiss and 'swear' in the most alarming manner when the old ladies tried to drive it out from under the seat.[77]

As with most other local professional cricketers, Billy did not earn enough through cricket to support himself, which is why both Town and Gown often came to their aid. For example, Billy wrote the following letter in his early 30s, published in the Cambridge Independent Press:[78]

> THE CAMBRIDGE CRICKETERS. Sir, — Allow me, on the part of myself and brother cricketers residing in Cambridge, to return our most grateful thanks to the gentlemen of the University for their liberality and kindness in patronizing and playing a match with us, for our benefit, Monday and Tuesday last; in return we shall feel truly happy, at any time, and upon every occasion (if at liberty), to render them our services when required. We also beg to tender our sincere acknowledgments to Mr. F. P. Fenner for his gentlemanly conduct and urbanity in allowing the match to be played on the private ground. I am, Sir, your very obedient servant, WM. BUTTRESS. 8. Eden-street, Cambridge, May 27, 1858.

John Walker (student at Trinity College, and later early stalwart of Middlesex County Cricket Club) was also a well-known benefactor of cricketers fallen on hard times.[79]

Buttress died at the age of 38 in 1866 and is buried nearby in Mill Road Cemetery, without the exact location being known.

A cricket 'ghetto'

As a result of the extraordinary success that town cricketers experienced in the middle of the nineteenth century, thanks in no small part to Parker's Piece, Frank Fenner's Red House, and Israel Haggis's New Inn, all being nearby, that this area of Cambridge should develop into a cricket 'ghetto'. It not only attracted professional cricketers, but umpires and cricket equipment providers all declared as 'professions' by 21 individuals in the 1861 census living in the local parish.[80]

Stop 4: Reality Checkpoint – Town and Gown

The cast iron lamp located in the middle of Parker's Piece was first installed at the end of the nineteenth century. It was referred to as 'Reality Checkpoint' by students in the 1960s, given it marked the imaginary crossover from the intellectual 'bubble' of the University to the 'real world' found in the Mill Road / Barnwell area of town.

Over many centuries, since the University was founded in 1209, the tensions between Town and Gown have been challenging, sometimes violent, with Parker's Piece representing perhaps something of a buffer zone or *level-playing-field*. Since at least the eighteenth century, both Town and Gown have

Gas light in the centre of Parker's Piece circa 1900, today called 'Reality Checkpoint' (looking towards Park Terrace, and Parkside on the right)
From the collection of David Gent.

played and watched sport, side-by-side, against each other, and sometimes in the same team.

In 1940 Bernard Darwin (Eton and Trinity College, and grandson of the British naturalist Charles Darwin) wrote a pamphlet for a series on British life, claiming:

> Sport, to use the term in its widest sense, is an older thing here than elsewhere with a more settled custom and more generally accepted place in the national life ... In fact sport is one of the most obvious features in the general background of life, and of all interests it is perhaps the one which is common to the greatest number of people of all classes.[81]

Opportunities in Cambridge for such relative inclusivity also occurred on the River Cam, for rowing, swimming and fishing, and the Fens for walking, skating and bandy (or ice hockey), however Town versus Gown tensions have been played out much more overtly on Parker's Piece, given its location right in the heart of Cambridge, especially with cricket.

Cricket

In the eighteenth century 'it seems likely that some townspeople watched the students at play ... perhaps being influenced to take up the game ... (with) the students encouraging its growth in the surrounding town and county'.[82]

Later, 'the townsfolk, while welcoming the employment and commercial opportunities provided by the institution, resented the overbearing attitude and sense of entitlement of its students. Nevertheless, the annual early season fixture, Cambridge Town Cricket Club v Undergraduates of Cambridge - or 'Town versus Gown', as it was popularly known – dating from 1817, did much to bring the two communities together'.[83] This developed into 'their respective cricket clubs (having) a close, symbiotic relationship, especially in the period 1822–1848'.[84]

Frank Fenner can take most of the credit for this. It was through 'being an able communicator and networker, writing letters, addressing meetings and building good relationships, especially between the town and university',[85] Frank was able to access 'a regular supply of experienced (University) players.'[86]

Town and Gown players feature in same painting

This extraordinary feat resulted in Nicholas Felix[87] being commissioned to paint 'The Town and University of Cambridge' cricket teams mixed in 1847. This is believed to be, alongside Clarke's 'Eleven of England' (painted in the same year) the first two group paintings of any cricket teams in the country, in the history of the game.[88]

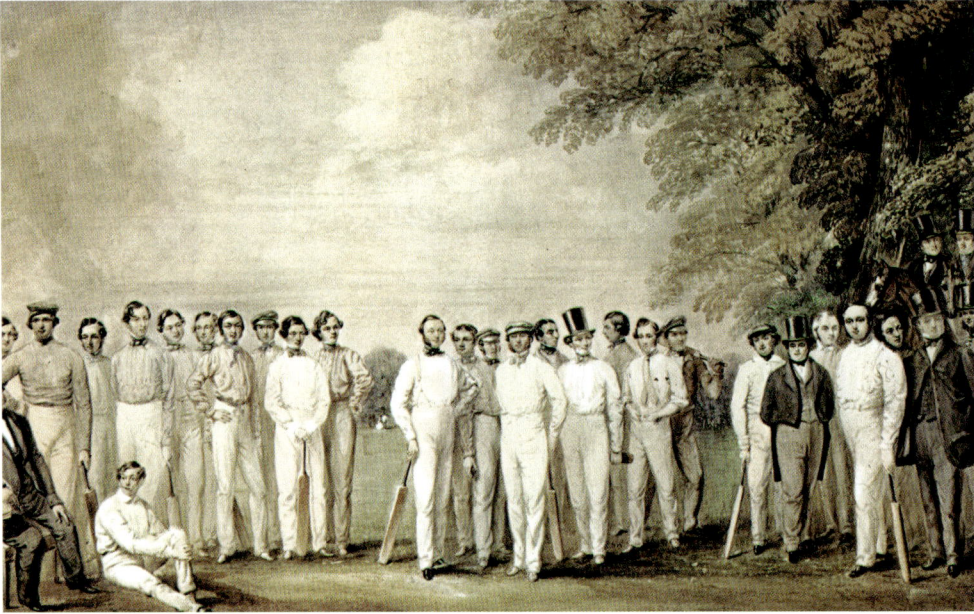

'The Town and University of Cambridge' cricket teams in 1847 painted by Nicholas Felix

The Roger Mann Collection.

The painting does portray the true likenesses of the thirty people featured, thanks to Felix writing to a friend earlier in 1847 and describing the commission:

The Roger Mann Collection.

'I have plenty of work on hand thank God - a large picture of Town and Gown of Cambridge - on hand consisting of 30 portraits'.

As far as the finished painting is concerned, given that in the Victorian era, class lines and status in cricket were so inflexibly drawn,[89] having Frank, a local tobacconist take centre stage in the painting, and that he is holding a bat, must have been considered astonishing. This is because at that time batting was very definitely 'a suitable occupation for gentlemen, while bowling was a trade fit for professionals'.[90]

University players

Frank is surrounded by those from the University cricket team who also played for the town under his captaincy, such as:

- William Hammersley (left group standing – second from right), who later emigrated to Australia, captaining the Victoria State Cricket team, and being jointly responsible for creating Australian Rules Football,

- John Morley Lee (middle group third from left) who graduated from St John's College in 1848, later becoming a clergyman,

- Robert Turner King (middle group fourth from left) a student at Emmanuel College from 1845, later a clergyman in the Fens for nearly 15 years,

- Arthur Malortie Hoare (middle group sixth from left with top hat) who at the time of this painting was a Fellow at St John's College having also been a student there. Later also a clergyman,

- Oliver Claude Pell (middle group second from right) student at Trinity College from 1843, later a member of William Clarke's All-England XI cricket team. His older brother Albert Pell, also at Trinity College, was involved in the creation of the laws of football on Parker's Piece, and

- Thomas M Townley (on horseback back right, rider second in from the right) who also finished second in the 1860 Grand National steeplechase, later becoming President of the Cambridge Town & County Cricket Club.

Whilst there is no record of John Walker (fourth from left - standing) playing for the Town Cricket Club, he benefitted from the coaching he received from Town players so that later in life he became a well-known benefactor of cricketers fallen on hard times, such as Billy Buttress, too young to feature in the painting.

The Walker brothers (John and Alfred, seated on grass front row) were responsible for later establishing Middlesex County Cricket Club.

Town players – employment by the University

Although the painting presents all players as equals, 'on a level playing field', it is no surprise many of the Town players were employed as cricket professionals by the university club and / or as college servants such as John Crouch (seated extreme left with top hat), Charles Arnold (standing extreme left), Henry Cornwell (standing second from left) and probably A J D or 'Ducky' Diver (standing third from left).

Other University support of Town cricket

In addition to the University players featured in this painting, there were over twenty others at this time,[91] who played cricket for the town and / or had a role in its management and / or played with Frank Fenner. These included:

The best players in the country

- Thomas Anchitel Anson, a student at Jesus College described later by Frank Fenner as 'an excellent wicket keeper … altogether a noble specimen of a well-trained athlete. He was tall, well proportioned, and muscular – every inch a man – and if that were doubted, a few minutes' practice before him would undeceive the most sceptical'[92]

- Charles George Taylor, said to be 'the most graceful batsman of them all', having been a student at Emmanuel College.

Significant administrators and promoters of the game

- Henry Perkins (Trinity College) – later secretary of the MCC from 1876 to 1898,

- William Percival 'Bull' Pickering (Trinity Hall from 1840) – who played a significant role in the beginnings of international cricket.

Those linked with the arts

- Frederick Ponsonby (Trinity College) – also founder of The Old Stagers, the oldest amateur dramatic society in the world today (chapter 5).

These players chose to play for the town cricket team because of 'the high standing of Cambridge town cricket which these talented cricket players wanted to be part of'.[93]

Frank's motives

Despite the centuries-old tensions and violence between Town and Gown, Frank believed cricket 'produces that happy concord of social enjoyment,' that could 'strengthen the links of society...' This spirited defence of 'this truly English game' was shared in a letter the 25-year-old Frank wrote to the press in 1836 complaining about horses damaging Parker's Piece.

Frank believed, before opening his 'own' cricket ground, 'we have a ground [Parker's Piece] the most advantageously situated, and I think the best public ground in England; as such we ought to consider it inestimable, and use every effort to preserve and improve it'.[94]

He was an ardent defender of the game, insisting that 'in cricketing matters there was an entire absence of political feeling' and as late as 1880 nostalgically recalling the cross-class sociability in cricket during his playing days.[95]

Top three teams in the country

In bringing Town and Gown together, the local club became one of the top three teams in the country, with Frank Fenner taking most of the credit for this.

He combined his skills as a player (the first locally to gain national recognition), club captain and secretary, to transform 'an unconstituted group of talented pub club veterans into a "far-famed" provincial club capable of taking on the Gentlemen of England and challenging for county club status'.[96]

William Denison, the noted cricket chronicler in the 1840s, rated the Cambridge Town and County Club second only to the East Kent Club of Mynn, Wenman and Hillyer.[97]

Others believed the top four teams in the country at the time were Sussex, Nottingham Old Club and Cambridge Town, followed by Surrey. Up until then teams were dependent on conspicuous patronage by the aristocracy but both Nottingham and Cambridge were reliant on the new and growing influence of the entrepreneur. In Nottingham's case this was William Clarke, a bricklayer turned innkeeper, who set up an enclosed money-taking ground beside the Trent Bridge Inn, and in Cambridge this role was largely fulfilled by Francis Fenner, a local tobacconist.

It was no surprise in 1846 Cambridge Town and County Club beat a Gentlemen of England side including Mynn, Pilch and Dean (the cricketing stars of the day). The local press reported:[98]

> It is absolutely impossible to depict the excitement which prevailed for many minutes. Old men were transformed into young ones, cripples were made sound and active by the electrical effect of victory, and nothing but congratulations could be heard above the coarse but mighty din of the joyous population.

There was even a presentation of the team at the local theatre (the Theatre Royal, Barnwell opened in 1815), complete with tent, toasts and cricket songs with 'deafening reiterations' calling the club captain to the front of the stage:

> The Cambridge lads, so spruce and neat
> To see them turn out is a treat,
> A strongish team 'twill take to beat,
> The jolly Cambridge cricketers.'[99]

Such success continued into the 1850s and 1860s with Christopher Martin-Jenkins (Fitzwilliam College), commentator on BBC Radio's Test Match Special, and cricket journalist believing 'for about ten seasons during the 1850s and 1860s Cambridgeshire ranked with the strongest counties'.[100]

It was therefore no surprise the Cambridge players Robert Carpenter, Thomas Hayward, Alfred 'Ducky' Diver and George Tarrant toured abroad with England sides. Alongside them were professional stalwarts Fred Bell, also known for coaching the Queen's sons, Fred Reynolds later of Lancashire, and Billy Buttress.[101] All these individuals were local men from Cambridge learning their cricketing trade on Parker's Piece.

Ranjitsinhji's success

As already mentioned, Ranjitsinhji was probably not only an inspiration to the 10-year-old Jack Hobbs, but also an example of a student at the University playing town cricket, towards the end of the nineteenth century.

Stop 5: Prince Regent Pub – Hayward family dynasty

The Prince Regent Pub or Inn on Regent Street, with a rear entrance onto Regent Terrace and Parker's Piece, had an unremarkable history until its association with the Hayward family.

Cricketing success – in summary

The Haywards were a famous local cricketing family spread over three generations, producing four outstanding players. Together they featured in nearly 900 first-class matches, scored nearly 50,000 runs and took over 750 wickets. They were on the first overseas cricket tour, drove the rise of county cricket and battled for the Ashes. 'Some believe therefore, the Haywards should rank alongside the Graces and Lillywhites as one of cricket's foremost families'.[102]

Their association with the Prince Regent Pub started in 1869 however their involvement with local cricket started earlier.

Daniel Haywood – 'the Elder' (1807 to 1852)

Daniel first started playing for Chatteris alongside Frank Fenner in 1830. Daniel later played for England v Kent in 1836, Cambridge Town, and St Ives, where he was landlord of the Three Tuns pub, now called the Nelson's Head, competing against 54 other hostelries in this small town on the Great Ouse river. St Ives is 12 miles (20km) northwest from Cambridge.

Daniel Hayward (1807 - 1852) married **Eliza Franklin** (1808-1886)

Martha (1827 -) married **William Baker**

Jane (1828 -) married **William Arnold**

Eliza* (1830 - 1907) married **Alfred Brocker**

Daniel Hayward* (1832 - 1910) married **Emma Martin** (1837-1903)

Thomas Hayward* (1835 - 1876) married **Lizzie Dell** (1836-)

Mary Ann (1837 -)

Emma* (1847 - 1909) married **William Pont**

Caroline (1850 -)

Arthur* (1864 - 1904) married **Laura Moulton**

Daniel Martin* (1866 - 1953) married **Mary Ann Dent**

Emma Martin* (1867 - 1925) married **Ernest Stubbings***

Alice* (1869 - 1925)

Thomas Walter* (1871 - 1939) married **Matilda Mitchell**

Frank* (1881 - 1929)

Emma (1855 -)

Lizzie (1857 - 1920) married **Edward Henri Balfe**

Fannie (1859 -)

Thomas (1860 - 1861)

Maude (1862 -)

Nora (1865 -) married **Ernest Bowden**

Clara (1867 -)

Edith (1870 -)

KEY

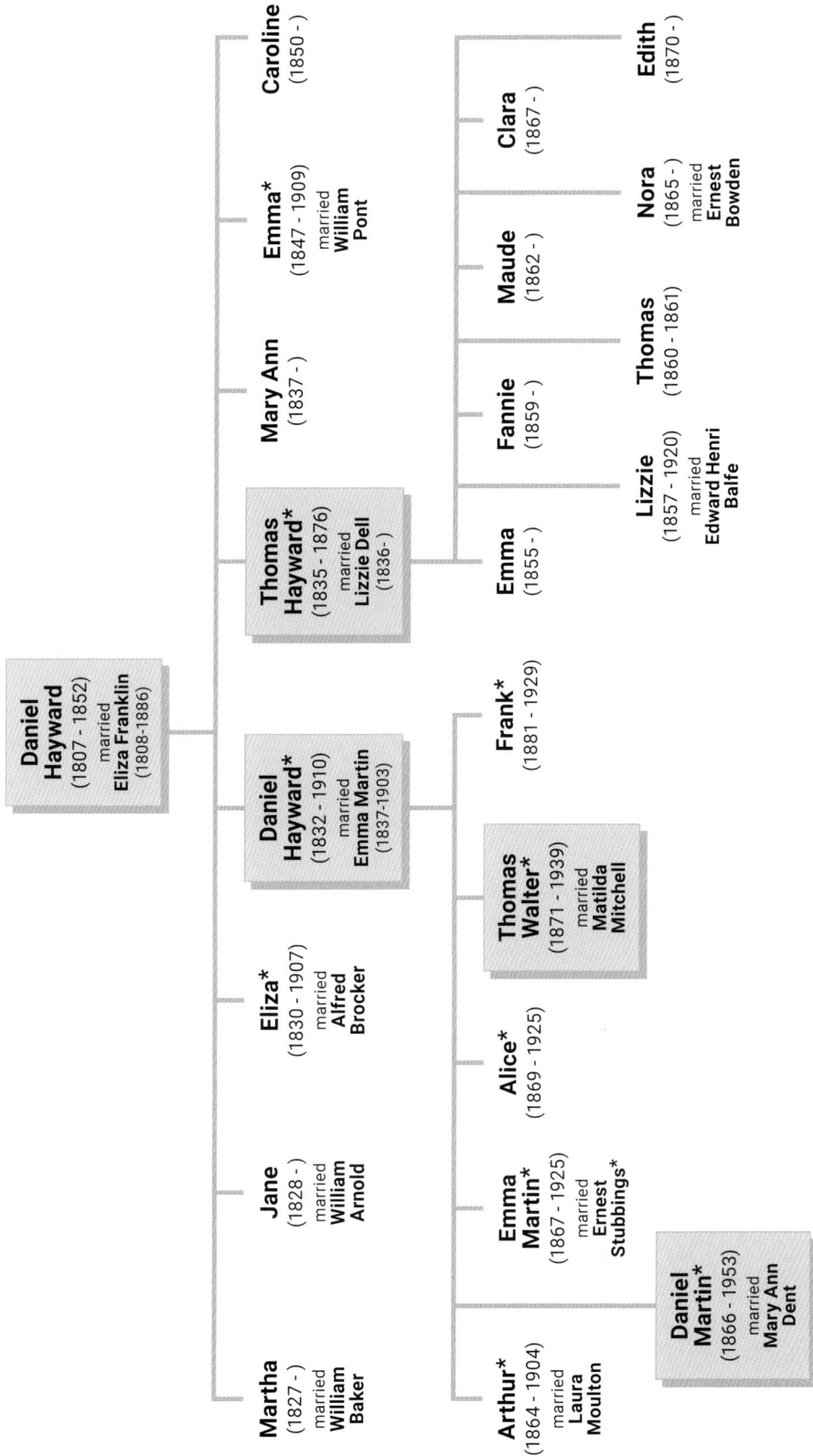

* buried in Mill Road Cemetery

Source: Keith and Jennifer Book (2018). The Haywards. The biography of a cricket dynasty. Chequered Flag Publishing, and Mill Road Cemetery website.

By trade Daniel was a gardener and groundsman and it is likely, given the close long-term relationship he had with Frank, that these skills were used in establishing Fenner's Cricket Ground in 1848 (chapter 22).

In the Felix painting of Town and Gown players of 1847 Daniel is in the right-hand group on the extreme left holding a cricket bat in his right hand.

Daniel had eight children including Daniel (referred to as 'the younger'), and Thomas – already featured at the Senate House (chapter 13).

Daniel Hayward – 'the Younger' (1832 to 1910)

Daniel Hayward was Thomas's older brother and was more of a businessman than player. Nevertheless, he still played 43 first-class and 80 other matches, mostly for Cambridge Town and Cambridgeshire. His business interests included

- o Landlord of the Prince Regent Inn starting 1869, a post he held for 42 years,[103]

- o Groundsman at 'the Rugger and Soccer pitches on Parker's Piece where (the University) played until the Grange Road ground opened in 1896 and the two clubs amalgamated',[104]

- o Tent hirer – for use on Parker's Piece and elsewhere, providing for players and spectators offering the essentials of a changing facility and shelter, equipment, food and drink,

- o Cricket coach and player – including being paid by the University of Cambridge to bowl at the University students in the nets, a role he shared with his brother Thomas. This included in the depths of winter, which was not uncommon. In 1855 the local press reported two gentlemen of Pembroke College playing cricket in frost on Parker's Piece with Daniel Hayward as the bowler,

- o 'Cricket, Lawn Tennis & Football Outfitter' advertised as being available at the Prince Regent in 1889, and

- o Landlord to the newly formed Cambridgeshire Football Association in 1884 who rented rooms in his pub, when

'The affiliation fee (for the Cambs FA) was to be 5 shillings and the county colours cerise and white. A county XI was to be formed to play the University and other counties. Mr F.C. Barrett of Girton notes that those who attended the first meeting included Arthur Dunn (Trinity College) who played for England five times between 1882 and 1887, eventually as captain; he also played for Granta - locally, and John Rawlinson (Trinity College and later MP for Cambridge University 1906 - 1926), the England goalkeeper who became Cambridgeshire FA president, a QC and the Cambridge Recorder'.[105]

Mr Barrett continues, 'in 1883 there were eight [football] clubs playing on the [Parker's] Piece, mixtures of Town and Gown players. They were Albert, Camden, Cassandra, Granta, Old Perseans, Printers, and Rovers.'

The image below is of football played on Parker's Piece in 1887, three years after the Cambridgeshire FA was formed. Its headquarters in the Prince Regent Pub, is just off to the right of this image.

A FOOTBALL MATCH ON PARKER'S PIECE

'A football match on Parker's Piece' in 1887
This is looking towards Gonville Place and today's Kelsey Kerridge sports hall
Source: The Graphic 8 Oct 1887.

Daniel Hayward 'the younger' had six children including Daniel Martin Hayward, and Thomas Walter Hayward (called Tom to distinguish him from Thomas).

Daniel Martin Hayward (1866 to 1953)

Whilst not as talented a cricketer as the other Haywards, Daniel nevertheless played 65 matches in the Minor Counties Championship for Cambridgeshire between 1895 and 1906.

Daniel was also coach at Corpus Christi College, where his best-known pupil was Ranjitsinhji, whom he probably coached on Parker's Piece in 1892.[106]

From 1890 Daniel Martin Hayward was also curator of Parker's Piece following in his father's footsteps, and from 1908, groundsman at Fenner's Cricket Ground.

Tom Hayward (1871 to 1939)

Tom Hayward was born 29 March 1871 at the Prince Regent Inn.

He initially played cricket for Cambridge YMCA and Cambridgeshire, before signing for Surrey in 1891 and scoring 43,551 runs, including 104 centuries, taking 480 wickets (as a medium-pace off-break bowler) and 462 catches. He also played for England in 35 Test matches.

Ranjitsinhji was very grateful to Tom for bowling at him in the nets and because he saw exciting potential offered Tom, in 1895, a diamond ring when he scored his first century. Hayward had not long to wait.[107] Later when playing in Australia, Tom Hayward was compared by the press with Ranjitsinhji.

In 1906 Tom Hayward took a full-strength Surrey team to play against a Cambridge team of 16 players on Parker's Piece, as reported in the press:[108]

> Although Cambridge people are very backward in supporting their county club, or any outdoor event where a gate is charged, they always respond liberally to any charity match at the end of the season. These are now an annual occurrence in which Tom Hayward, who lives at Cambridge, is the pioneer.

The attendance was reported to be around 10,000 raising over £61 for charity, equivalent to over £7,000 today.

After retirement from first-class cricket, he served as a coach for Oxford University Cricket Club, eventually returning to Cambridge, living at 6 Glisson Road (off Mill Road). He was married later in life in 1914, to Matilda Emma Mitchell, but the couple had no children.

He died of lung cancer on 19 July 1939, aged 68. He is buried in Mill Road Cemetery, with the location of his grave being known.

The relationship between Tom Hayward and Jack Hobbs

Both the Hayward and Hobbs families were considered 'part of the professional cricket, college, Parker's Piece and Fenner's groundsmanship community'.[109]

When Jack Hobbs was growing up, his boyhood hero was Tom Hayward. Later, starting in 1905, they formed an effective opening partnership for Surrey County Cricket Club, putting on a hundred or more runs for the first wicket on 40 occasions. They only played together once for England, given Tom Hayward's retirement.

When Jack Hobb's father died in 1902, he was not yet 20 years old and the oldest of twelve children, so given the closeness of the two families, Tom played a major part in organising a benefit match for Jack's mother.

In 1923 Jack Hobbs became the third player ever in the world to score a hundred first-class centuries after WG Grace and Tom Hayward, however if their abilities were to be compared 'there was a sense in which (Tom) Hayward was John the Baptist to the Messianic Hobbs'.[110]

Frank's father living on Regent Terrace.

Just outside the rear of the Prince Regent Pub, towards Gonville Place is 1, Regent Terrace, where Frank Fenner's father, Joseph died aged 91 on the

3 October 1864. This was soon after Frank had moved to Cheltenham. It is not known where he was buried.

Stop 6: Gonville Place – cycling

Some consider Cambridge, 'Britain's cycle city',[111] thanks to its flatness, narrow streets and relatively large student population.

The only reason this part of Cambridge is best placed to look at cycling is that it was the start for Stage 3 of the 2014 Tour de France, as painted on the pavement bordering Parker's Piece opposite the Gonville Hotel. The prestart parade rode through the streets of Cambridge.

Howes Cycle Shop, Regents Street – one of the oldest in the country

In 2013 Howes Cycles on Regent Street (almost opposite the front of the Prince Regent Pub) closed after 173 years, claiming to be the oldest bicycle shop in the country. The original shop was established in 1840 by John Howes, a wheelwright and carriage maker, who was later joined by his son in 1869 when they started making, selling and maintaining bicycles. This included them supporting the Cambridge University Bicycle Club as mechanics in the 1870s.

John Howes was buried in the nearby Mill Road Cemetery.[112]

University Cycle Club

One of the first to ride a 'penny-farthing' bicycle in the streets of Cambridge was believed to be Andrew Graham Murray who was a student from 1868 at Trinity College.

Six years later in 1874, the Cambridge University Bicycle Club (CUBiC) was founded, growing to 260 members within five years of opening. The first varsity race was also held in 1874, consisting of an 80-mile course between Oxford and Cambridge. Cambridge won.

In 1877, CUBiC built their own gravel racing track on what is now the northern part of Robinson College, Grange Road.[113]

By the late 1870s, one of the members of CUBiC, the Hon. Ion Keith-Falconer was the amateur champion of Great Britain. Ion also opened a mission in Barnwell in 1875, a year after he started at Trinity College. In an effort to reduce poverty in the area, in 1878 he together with others, bought the failing Theatre Royal on Newmarket Road to serve as a permanent mission hall.[114]

The University Cycle Club went from strength to strength, however in the early twentieth century the club was temporarily dissolved, probably because of the advent of the motor car.

Cycling and physical liberation for women

According to Kathleen McCrone, 'no history of sport at Girton (College) would be complete without mention of the activity which, although not strictly speaking a sport at all, made the greatest contribution to the physical liberation of women. This was bicycling. Like women everywhere during the 1890s, few Girtonians could resist its lure. Promises to parents to do nothing so 'fast' as ride a cycle were quickly forgotten.'[115]

Progress was slow though, not helped when a protest against granting full degrees to female graduates in 1897 hung an effigy of a woman on a bicycle, opposite the Senate House (chapter 13).

Whilst women kept on cycling, it nevertheless took until 1947 before women were accepted alongside men as equal members of the University.

Stop 7: Cambridge YMCA

There has been a YMCA in Cambridge since 1852, six years after the organisation was founded in London. It moved to its current premises on Gonville Place, facing Parker's Piece in 1972.

The YMCA movement has a reputation for sport. In the late nineteenth century both basketball and volleyball were invented in YMCAs based in America.[116]

At this time Tom Hayward played his cricket for his local YMCA before his career took off. This was when the YMCA was located at 1, Alexandra Street, now buried under the Lion Yard Shopping Centre.

In addition to playing cricket, the YMCA Rowing Club was one of the first members of the newly formed Cambridgeshire Rowing Association in 1868.[117]

Lord Kinnaird, a student at Trinity College from 1864, in addition to becoming football's first superstar playing in nine FA Cup Finals (chapter 9), was also President of the National YMCA and YWCA (the equivalent organisation for women) for many years.[118]

Stop 8: Cambridge Rules 1848 Sculpture – football

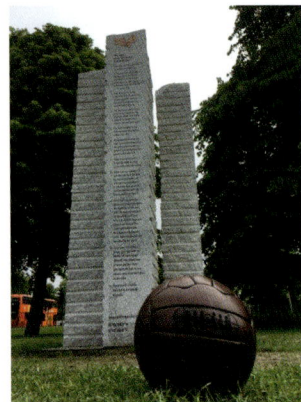

The governing body of world football, FIFA, have reported Cambridge as 'the birthplace of the laws of football',[119] today recognised by a sculpture on Parker's Piece. This is where students at the University 'played out' the rules they had codified in their college rooms, mostly at Trinity, and St John's Colleges (chapters 8 and 9), between 1837 and 1863.

On the front of the sculpture are written these 11 rules, translated into other languages on the remaining four columns. Before looking more closely at these 'Cambridge Rules', this section now explores over 650 years of local football,[b] often referred to as camp ball.

Clergy 'loose habits', and early references in literature

The golden era for play and games in general (before the twentieth century), may be considered the medieval period,[120] when even the local clergy took part. However, this attracted the attention of the Synod of Ely (the local governing body of the Church of England) concerned at the 'loose habits' of its junior clergy resulting in them being forbidden from playing games in 1364.[121]

In the early fifteenth century John Lydgate, 'the most important and most sought-after poet of his time',[122] wrote a satirical poem about the attractions of 'my fair lady' wearing a green hood and breasts like a 'camping ball'.[123] Having studied at Oxford and Cambridge, Lydgate was a monk based at Bury St Edmunds, Suffolk.[124]

In 1514, Andrew Barclay, a Scottish Benedictine based at Ely, offered this tribute (including how a football was made, and its surprising contents):

> The sturdie plowman, lustie, strong and bold
> O'ercometh the winter with driving the football
> Forgetting labour and many a grievous fall ...
> In the Winter, when men kill the fat swine,
> They get the bladder and blow it great and thin,
> With many beans and peasen put within.
> It ratleth, soundeth, and shineth clear and fayre.
> When it is thrown and cast upon the ayre,
> Each one contendeth and hath a great delite
> With foote and with hande the bladder for to smite.[125]

---

[a]   For the reader's information, 'football' is used here as a generic term, understood as the forerunner to Association Football, Rugby Union, Rugby League, Australian Rules, Gaelic Football, American Football and so on. In addition, the term 'camp ball' is used as the local, or East Anglian name for football, when in other regions it is more generally referred to as 'folk football'.

Camping Land

Camp ball was often played on a dedicated Camping Field, Close or Land and because it was invariably next to the local church, was usually endorsed by the local priest and gentry. There are over 100 known sites across East Anglia[126] including a number close to Cambridge. The author continues to identify sites so that now eight have been identified within 5 miles of the centre of Cambridge, and a further sixteen within 10 miles.

One piece of Camping Land, adjacent to Swaffham Church (40 miles (70 km) northeast from Cambridge), was donated in 1474 by Dr John Botwright, Master of Corpus Christi College, and Rector of this church.

One game however, almost certainly played nearby on the Camping Close adjacent to Chesterton Church, between the village team and some University students in 1579, resulted in 'heads being broken' and 'students escaping by swimming across the River Cam'.[127]

The Chesterton game, and probably others resulted in the University Vice-Chancellor issuing the following ban in 1595. 'Hurtful and unscholerlike exercise of Football' is prohibited 'except within places severall to the Colledges, and that for them only that be of the same Colledge'.[128]

A sixteenth century advocate

Richard Mulcaster (student at King's College, and Peterhouse, later headteacher at Merchant Taylor's School and St Paul's School, both in London) publicly declared that football had many educational benefits as well as improving health and strength.

His understanding of the game was closer to modern football because he differentiated it from those games involving other parts of the body, namely 'the hand ball' and 'the armeball'. These views were published in English in 1581 in 'Positions Wherein Those Primitive Circumstances Be Examined, Which Are Necessarie for the Training up of Children'.[129]

Later in 1612 Henry Peacham, who had been a student at Trinity College wrote and illustrated a poem on 'footeball' in Minerva Brittana which combined pictures and verse on matters of morality and manners. Peacham's theme was that life is like football, that our worldly wealth 'is tossed too and fro', and in the game of life there are winners and losers.

Oliver Cromwell

It is difficult to disentangle Royalist propaganda from the truth about Oliver Cromwell's participation in sport, however he himself was quoted as 'remembering the time when he was more afraid of meeting Wheelwright (a fellow student whilst in Cambridge in 1616) at football, than of meeting an army in the field'.[130]

If Parker's Piece was probably not suitable, there are two other possible sites in the town that Cromwell, and Wheelwright may have played on.

Football on Sheep's Green, the 'Campus Martius' and the Fens

Symonds D'Ewes, a student at St John's College from 1618, went out after supper to a spacious field at the back of Queens' College, called Sheep's Green, having heard that there was a game of foot-ball to be played there.[131]

A few years later in 1632, ground where Downing College now stands was referred to as the Campus Martius, and was being used for football, and presumably other sports.[132] This translates as 'Field of Mars', with the original in Rome used for centuries as the playground for Romans to practice their athletic games.[133] In Cambridge, this field was split into what was known as the Marsh, and St Thomas Leys for use by separate colleges, to stop them from playing against each other.

Local authorities were always nervous of large crowds. For example, in 1638 a game of camp ball was advertised as a mask for bringing 200 people together to destroy the new drainage ditches in the Fens which they believed were destroying their livelihoods. Six people were jailed.[134]

How a football was constructed, and rules of the game

Francis Willughby, a student at Trinity College (chapter 9) from 1652 later wrote 'The Book of Games', a compendium listing dozens of games and sports, including cards, cockfighting, word games, and football.[135] He was the first to describe and draw a diagram for football goals and a pitch, referring also to tactics, how to score, the way teams were selected, and a law of football, in not striking an opponent's leg above the ball.

He also describes the construction of the ball: 'they blow a strong bladder and tie the neck of it as fast as they can, and then put it into the skin of a bull's cod [bull's scrotal sack] and sew it fast in'. Sometimes it was filled with quicksilver [mercury] to keep it from lying still.

Mixing of the classes - as children only

In the village of Kirtling (15 miles (24km) east of Cambridge), work in the tillage farms and dairies:

> was usually done by noon ... and it was always the custom for the youth ... to assemble ... either upon the green or in a close accustomed to be so used, and there all to play till milking time, and supper at night. The men to football, and the maids with who we children commonly mixed ... to stoolball and such running games as they knew.[136]

This experience of childhood was shared by Roger North, later a student at Jesus College, Cambridge from 1667, where his experience was quite different. For example because North was admitted as a Fellow Commoner [indicating that he was from an aristocratic or wealthy background] he was unable to mix with the 'common scollers for the joy they had at foot ball'.[137]

The mixing of children from different classes for sport was an experience also later shared by Thomas Hughes (born 1822 died 1896) in his semi-autobiographical novel *Tom Brown's Schooldays*, first published in 1857:

> Squire Brown [presumably Thomas Hughes's father] held further that it didn't matter a straw whether his son associated with lords' sons or ploughmen's sons, provided they were brave and honest. He himself had played football and gone bird-nesting with the farmers whom he met at vestry and the labourers who tilled their fields, and so had his father and grandfather, with their progenitors. So he encouraged Tom in his intimacy with the boys of the village, and forwarded it by all means in his power, and gave them the run of a close for a playground, and provided bats and balls and a football for their sports.[138]

Camping balls available in every college

The same Roger North referred to above later wrote to his son in 1730, when also a student at Jesus College, claiming that 'as for camping-balls, that bubble-boy hath a shop in every college in Cambridge'.[139] It is not known who or what a bubble-boy was but this reference implies, that the game of camp ball was popular in the colleges at this time.

Students leaving dinner early for football or cricket

Richard Bentley was Master of Trinity College from 1700 to 1738 with a poor relationship with his Fellows or staff. One of their many grievances was Bentley allowing students to leave dinner early 'to run home to their studies, others to try a fair fall upon the grass, and others a match at Football or Cricket.'[140]

Camp ball more popular than cricket (before the 1800s)

When Robert Forby, a past student at Gonville & Caius College from 1777, was Rector of St Martin's Church, Fincham (10 miles south of King's Lynn, Norfolk) for over 25 years, he compiled a book on 'The Vocabulary of East Anglia'.

This included a lengthy entry for 'CAMP, an ancient athletic game at ball, now almost superseded by cricket, a less hardy and dangerous sport'. Forby adds camp ball was endorsed locally by William Windham, a Norfolk MP, Lord Rochford, who owned estates in Suffolk and Essex, and others from the titled classes.

He identifies two varieties of camp ball, 'rough-play, and civil-play. In the latter, there is no boxing'.

He also describes the pitch, the use of club colours when playing, and the time for each game, 'two or three hours', but sometimes 'the game is placed against time, as the phrase is. It is common to limit it to half an hour; and most campers, now-a-days, have in that time got enough of so hardy a contest'. Prizes are commonly hats, gloves, shoes, or small sums of money.

Forby describes Camping as an 'ancient game' rueing the fact 'it is now degenerated, and some meaner exercises unworthily usurp its name'.[141]

In a later supplement to Forby's book[142] it is reported a match at Diss Common in the early nineteenth century between Norfolk and Suffolk was so brutal that nine men were killed or died from their injuries. Apparently, there were about 300 on each team, with Suffolk victors after 14 hours of play.

Preparation for war

Camp ball survived well into the nineteenth century including being consciously revived after the Napoleonic Wars, from 1820,[143] as one means of keeping men fighting fit.

Thereafter little is known about camp ball across East Anglia, being superseded (gentrified?) by the public schools, alongside Oxford and Cambridge universities.

The public schools

Public school reforms in the 1830s and 1840s led to a recognition that sport was an important component of a young man's education, however it was largely organised and run by the students themselves. Understandably each school developed their own unique brand of football, given their traditions and the space and type of surface they played on, so that when they came together as undergraduate students at Cambridge University, there was need for compromise. It has been suggested the original reason for having a half time was that a game would, for example be played to Eton rules in the first half, and Rugby rules, in the second.[144]

The eight most prestigious public schools at this time were Charterhouse, Eton, Harrow, Rugby, Shrewsbury, Uppingham, Westminster and Winchester.[145]

University football in nineteenth century Cambridge

Given the 100-year anniversary since 'rugby football was initiated'[146] it was reported in the local press that this was to be celebrated on the Cambridge Market Square in 1923 (chapter 16). It is possible that rugby might have been played in Cambridge using 'Rugby rules' by students from Rugby, arriving at the university from as early as 1823.

The novelty of football

'In walking with Willis we passed by Parker's Piece, and there saw some forty gownsmen playing at football. The novelty and liveliness of the scene was very amusing', so wrote Dr George Corrie in his diary of 1838.[147] Corrie was later master of Jesus College in 1849, and vice chancellor of the University in 1850.

Rugby 'puntabout'

Cambridge University Rugby Union Football Club credit Albert Pell (Rugby School and Trinity College) and Edgar Montagu (Gonville & Caius College) with organising the earliest game of rugby union in Cambridge.[148] Albert however had difficulty finding players, claiming the Rugby School rules he was familiar with were 'unknown in Cambridge'.

The players and their 'puntabout' game played on Parker's Piece in 1839 became 'objects of wonder and at first of contempt. In time curiosity … attracting quite a little circle of onlookers'. As a result, Albert Pell later claimed 'we established football at Cambridge'.[149]

The curiosity people had for rugby being played on Parker's Piece sometimes led to misunderstandings. For example,

> A few old Rugby boys started their favourite game at Cambridge, [they] were looked upon as little less than madmen by the majority of Cantabs [University staff and students] of that day…... The great athletic revival was then beginning to spread over the kingdom, and in spite of the ridicule bestowed on it at Cambridge as being only fit for boys (the same argument, by the way, was urged against having Inter-' Varsity athletic sports), football made considerable headway and the number of players increased. In some of the first games played on Parker's Piece the spectators, from a misapprehension that the players were fighting, rushed on the ground to part the contestants.[150]

These games however prompted some students to take rugby as played on Parker's Piece across the world.

Rugby across the world

Whilst Thomas Wentworth Wills had played the Rugby School version before coming (briefly) to Cambridge in 1855, the two other founders of Australian Rules Football in 1859, James Bogue Thompson and William Josiah Hammersley (both students at Trinity College from 1845), almost certainly did not. Their first experience therefore, was probably on Parker's Piece.

Rowland Williams was a student at Eton College, then King's College, Cambridge from 1836 later also becoming a Fellow there from 1839 to 1850 (including a year or more teaching at Eton College from 1841),[151] and so would have been aware of these early attempts to play Rugby on Parker's Piece. In 1850 he became vice principal of St David's, Lampeter where he was responsible for introducing cricket, croquet and rugby football. The first recorded rugby match in Wales took place between St David's and nearby Llandovery College in 1866.[152]

Second Varsity Rugby Match on Parker's Piece

The first ever varsity rugby union match between Oxford and Cambridge was played in February 1872 in Oxford's University Parks. In that first match Oxford wore dark blue jerseys (the same as today, though on some occasions they have worn white), and Cambridge played in pink. The following year (February 1873) the return match was played in Cambridge on Parker's Piece.[153] So far, in the nineteenth century, most of the reports refer to Rugby rules being played on Parker's Piece, but with other University students arriving from their own public schools where the rules were different, something had to give.

Creation of the Cambridge Rules

There were at least five attempts by students at Cambridge University to codify The Cambridge Rules, from 1837 / 1838 to 1863.

The first attempt can be dated to 1838, thanks to the efforts of Pell and Montagu, described above, followed in 1846 by John Charles Thring (St John's College) and Henry de Winton (Trinity College) together with some Old Etonians who played on Parker's Piece.

Two years later in 1848 Henry James Malden wrote about a further set of rules being drafted by 14 Trinity College students in room F7 New Court:

> We met in my rooms ... at 4pm, anticipating a long meeting. I cleared the tables and provided pens, ink and paper. Several asked me on coming in whether an exam was on! Our progress in framing new rules was slow

… We broke up five minutes before midnight. The new rules were printed as the 'Cambridge Rules', copies were distributed and pasted up on the Parker's Piece, and very satisfactorily they worked.'[154]

De Winton and Thring: the rules of Football 1848
© Quentin Blake – with permission of A P Watt at United Agents on behalf of Quentin Blake.

Copies of these rules do not exist, but it is believed they are very similar to the version drafted in 1856, a copy of which is today found in the Shrewsbury School Library archive. These were:

The Laws of the University Foot Ball Club.

1. This club shall be called the University Foot Ball Club.

2. At the commencement of the play, the ball shall be kicked off from the middle of the ground: after every goal there shall be a kick-off in the same way.

3. After goal, the losing side shall kick off; the sides changing goals, unless a previous arrangement be made to the contrary.

4. The ball is out when it has passed the line of the flag-posts on either side of the ground, in which case it shall be thrown in straight.

5. The ball is behind when it has passed the goal on either side of it.

6. When the ball is behind it shall be brought forward at the place where it left the ground, not more than ten paces, and kicked off.

7. Goal is when the ball is kicked through the flag-posts and under the string.

8. When a player catches the ball directly from the foot, he may kick it as he can without running with it. In no other case may the ball be touched with the hands, except to stop it.

9. If the ball has passed a player, and has come from the direction of his own goal, he may not touch it till the other side have kicked it, unless there are more than three of the other side before him. No player is allowed to loiter between the ball and the adversaries' goal.

10. In no case is holding a player, pushing with the hands, or tripping up allowed. Any player may prevent another from getting to the ball by any means consistent with the above rules.

11. Every match shall be decided by a majority of goals.

Comments on these rules / laws

Law 7. Legend has it that the distance between the trees on Parker's Piece at the time became the standard width of a football goal at 8 yards (7.32 metres),[155] later replaced with 'flag-posts and string'.

Law 8. Most of these rules will be familiar to those who watch or play Association Football today, apart from Law 8. This catching of the ball is outlawed in Association Football (apart from the goalkeeper), but not so in today's Rugby Union, Gaelic Football, and Australian Rules.

Law 10. Agreeing Law 10 will have caused the greatest disagreements because it was designed as a move away from the much more physical Rugby rules.

Cambridge's preference for football, away from rugby

At Cambridge University students from Eton, with their bias towards use of the feet rather than hands, and a less physical encounter, were keen 'to put the "upstart" Rugbeians in their place and to "see off" this challenge to Eton's status as *the* leading public school in *all respects*.'[156] In fact Michael McCrum (Master of Corpus Christi College, vice chancellor of Cambridge University) writing in 1989 states the public schools (at the time) 'never admitted Thomas Arnold's [famous headteacher at Rugby School] influence. Indeed Eton, for example, prided itself on escaping it'.[157]

As a means of promoting their version of the game, for example, Etonians required the working class to play holding a shilling or other coin, being allowed to keep it, if they succeeded in not using their hands.[158] It is not known whether this took place on Parker's Piece, but probably not.

The reason that Cambridge University preferred Association Football was that the more academic students from Eton College were more likely to play the 'Wall Game' (a cross between football and rugby) before entry to King's College, Cambridge. However, the less gifted at Eton, called oppidans, or 'townboys' played the 'Field Game' (more like football), before going on to Trinity College where most of the signatories to the 'Cambridge Rules' were students.

There is also some evidence that suggests Oxford undergraduate students favoured the Rugby form of football.[159]

Popularising Association Football

Arthur Kinnaird (student at Trinity College from 1864) may be considered football's first superstar[160] who played in nine FA Cup Finals. He was also on the FA Committee at the age of 21 in 1868, followed by its treasurer, then president, a post he held for 33 years. In his time and under his leadership, football rose from obscurity, to become Britain's national sport, so it is no surprise he has been credited as doing 'more to popularise soccer than any man who ever lived.[161]

The national and global reach of football

… but not in Cambridge. The Jesus College magazine of 1889 reported

> There is little other evidence the University worked with Cambridge Town to promote its more codified and non-violent version of the game of football. Probably the greatest promoters of football and sports were graduates who entered teaching or the church. Teachers mostly returned to Public Schools, whilst some clergy worked in Missions in London, such as those sponsored by Trinity College, or Jesus College, or by taking sport across the world as missionaries.[162]

One possible reason might have been that when the 'Cambridge Rules' of football were being codified, across the middle of the nineteenth century, the relationship between Town and Gown was so poor as to rule out any form of local sharing or collaboration.

Whilst the newly formed Football Association (FA), founded in 1863, appreciated the value of the 'Cambridge Rules', they were clearly unimpressed with how the game was being rolled out locally for everyone's benefit. Instead, the FA looked to Sheffield.

Sheffield's contribution

Whilst the game in Cambridge was apparently only played by students, Sheffield is credited with creating 'the world's first football culture', having eight teams in 1861 and eleven in 1862, so that football became one of the areas most practiced sports – the 'now popular game', as reported in the local press.[163]

Cricket's role in Sheffield

One further possible reason why Sheffield was chosen was because it was already the major centre of cricket in the county of Yorkshire.

> Surely the strongest hint that cricketers played an important part in these early developments of football was the fact that two leading members of the nascent Sheffield FC [considered one of the oldest football clubs in the world] were clearly linked with the evolution of the summer game in the city and ... belonged to Sheffield's sporting elite.[164]

Football and cricket in Cambridge

One might have hoped that because Cambridge was one of the best three cricket teams in the country in the middle of the nineteenth century (combining the strengths of both Town and Gown cricketers, despite the heightened tensions in general, between them) that it might have had a similar impact rolling out football in Cambridge? However, there is no record of Frank Fenner ever referring to football, including establishing a partnership with it.

With the FA looking more to Sheffield, this did not stop those committed to the 'Cambridge Rules' from influencing others, beyond the University. Probably the best example was the Corinthian Football Club, founded in 1882 on the principles of amateurism, fair play, sportsmanship, collectively known as the 'Corinthian Spirit'.[165] Almost the whole membership of the club was made up of an equal share of 'gentlemen amateurs' who had attended either Oxford or Cambridge universities.[166]

Within twenty-five years the club believed they were the 'missionaries of Empire' regarding their brand of the game, as well as touring on continental Europe.[167]

This all came about however more by accident than design. At the start of the 1907 season, troubled by what they perceived to be the growing strength of professionalism, the club had broken away from the FA to form the Amateur FA. This split the amateur ranks, reducing the number of teams, their quality, and consequently the number of high-class, competitive matches, compounded by the FA banning its clubs from having anything to do with the Amateur FA.[168]

This drove Corinthian FC to look abroad for teams to play which is why they toured South Africa (three times), Brazil (twice), Hungary, Germany, Czechoslovakia, Sweden, France, Holland, Denmark, Canada, USA, Switzerland, Spain and Bohemia.[169]

Consequently, the club is credited with having popularised football around the world,[170] outcomes including Real Madrid adopting Corinthian FC's white strip, and inspiring the creation of 'Sport Club Corinthians Paulista', today one of the most successful, and well-supported teams in Brazil.

Today's symbol of this global reach

On the front of the 'Cambridge Rules' sculpture on Parker's Piece are written these 11 rules, translated into other languages on the remaining four columns. In addition to these different languages communicating very powerfully the game's global reach, the 'missing' five columns (the sculpture started as a single piece of granite split into nine columns), are located around the globe.

The choice as to where these five columns would be located was made by Street Child United, a Cambridge charity founded before the FIFA World Cup in Brazil in 2010, and who today 'use the power of sport to change the way the world sees and treats street children'.[171]

1   Roland Parker (1983). Town and Gown. The 700 years' war in Cambridge. Patrick Stephens, Cambridge. Page 123.

2   The colleges and halls: Downing. Pages 487-490. A History of the County of Cambridge and the Isle of Ely: Volume 3, the City and University of Cambridge. Originally published by Victoria County History, London, 1959.

3   Nicholas Chrimes (2017). Cambridge. Treasure Island of the Fens. Hobsaerie Publications. Page 169.

4   Henry Payne Stokes (1915). Outside the Barnwell Gate. Printed for the Cambridge Antiquarian Society. Pages 44 and 45.

5   S P Widnall's reminiscences, Gossiping Stroll through the Streets of Cambridge (1892) off Capturing Cambridge website: https://capturingcambridge.org

6   Cambridge Town gaol on Capturing Cambridge website: https://capturingcambridge.org

7   John Durrant (1984) Portrait of a hotel. The University Arms, Cambridge. 1834 – 1984. (Unnumbered page just before Acknowledgements).

8   Willie Sugg (2009). Fenner's Men. Cambridgeshire Cricket 1822-1848. Part 3 of A Tradition Unshared. Real Work Publishing. Page 47.

9   Willie Sugg (2009). Fenner's Men. Cambridgeshire Cricket 1822-1848. Part 3 of A Tradition Unshared. Real Work Publishing. Page 41.

10   Richard Gray (unpublished document - emailed 27 Dec 2019). Grays of Cambridge. A short history.

11   Entry 30 09 18b-c in Mike Petty (2018). Cambridge SPORT Chronicle. Chronology of Cambridge Sport 1888 to 1990 at https://archive.org/details/CambridgeSPORTSChronicle

12   Leo McKinstry (2012). Jack Hobbs. England's greatest cricketer. Yellow Jersey Press, London. Page 26.

13   Leo McKinstry (2012). Jack Hobbs. England's greatest cricketer. Yellow Jersey Press, London. Pages 23 and 24.

14   G.D. Martineau (1956). They made cricket. Museum Press, London. Page 181.

15   Leo McKinstry (2012). Jack Hobbs. England's greatest cricketer. Yellow Jersey Press, London. Page 31.

16   Cambridge Chronicle quoted in Leo McKinstry (2012) Jack Hobbs. Pages 42 and 43.

17   Keith and Jennifer Booth (2018). The Haywards. The biography of a cricket dynasty. Chequered Flag Publishing. Page 310.

18   1935 02 26 entry in Mike Petty (2018). Cambridge SPORT Chronicle. Chronology of Cambridge Sport 1888 to 1990 at https://archive.org/details/CambridgeSPORTSChronicle

19   Leo McKinstry (2012). Jack Hobbs. Pages 19 and 20.

20   Leo McKinstry (2012). Jack Hobbs. Yellow Jersey Press. Page 13.

21 Parker's Piece entry in Creating my Cambridge public art project at http://www. creatingmycambridge.com/history-stories/7-parkers-piece/

22 A Public Health report of 1849 presented to the Cambridge town council. Willie Sugg 'local context' article confirmed in 16 Dec 2021 email https://www.cambscrickethistory.co.uk/local-context/

23 Charles Astor Bristed (1873) Five years in an English University.

24 Walsh, Joan (2008). Aspects of Infant Mortality in a University Town, Cambridge 1875-1911. PhD thesis. The Open University.

25 H.D. Rawnsley (1896). Harvey Goodwin. Bishop of Carlisle. London, John Murray, Pages 66 to 69.

26 Walsh, Joan (2008). Aspects of Infant Mortality in a University Town, Cambridge 1875-1911. PhD thesis. The Open University.

27 Eglantyne Jebb (1906). Cambridge. A brief study in social questions.

28 Malcolm Tozer (2015). The ideal of manliness. The legacy of Thring's Uppingham. Sunnyrest Books. Ref 13 on page 47.

29 Eglantyne Jebb (1906). Cambridge. A brief study in social questions.

30 Rowland Parker (1983). Town and Gown. The 700 years' war in Cambridge. Patrick Stephens, Cambridge. Page 143.

31 Daniel Defoe (1724) Tour through the Eastern Counties in page 11 ' In Praise of Cambridge. An Anthology for Friends compiled by Lord Mervyn Horder (1952).

32 Enid Porter (1975) Victorian Cambridge. Josiah Chater's Diaries. Phillimore. Pages 30-31.

33 Rowland Parker (1983). Town and Gown. The 700 years' war in Cambridge. Patrick Stephens, Cambridge. Page 144.

34 Cambridge Chronicle and University Journal 9 Nov 1850.

35 Robert Kenny (1990). This College-Studded Marsh. A humorous history of the Cambridge Colleges. (Entry under Corpus Christi.)

36 38 Newmarket Road entry on Capturing Cambridge website https://capturingcambridge.org

37 Enid Porter (1975). Victorian Cambridge. Josiah Chater's diaries. Phillimore. Page 90.

38 Keith and Jennifer Booth (2018). The Haywards. The biography of a cricket dynasty. Chequered Flag Publishing. Page 18.

39 Willie Sugg (2009). Fenner's Men. Cambridgeshire Cricket 1822-1848. Part 3 of A Tradition Unshared. Real Work Publishing. Pages 46 and 47.

40 Willie Sugg (2002). A tradition unshared. A history of Cambridge Town & County Cricket 1700-1890. Part 1. Real Work Publishing, Cambridge. Page 57.

41 Alfred D Taylor (1923 and republished 1972). The Story of a Cricket Picture. Pages 36 and 37.

42 Willie Sugg (2009). Fenner's Men. Cambridgeshire Cricket 1822-1848. Part 3 of A Tradition Unshared. Real Work Publishing. Pages 44 and 45.

43 Alfred D Taylor (1923). The Story of a Cricket Picture.

44 Denison, W. 'Sketches of Players' in Arlott p 92 in Willie Sugg (2009). Fenner's Men. Cambridgeshire Cricket 1822-1848. Part 3 of A Tradition Unshared. Real Work Publishing. Real Work Publishing. Page 44.

45 Willie Sugg (2009). Fenner's Men. Cambridgeshire Cricket 1822-1848. Part 3 of A Tradition Unshared. Real Work Publishing. Pages 44 and 45.

46 Willie Sugg (email 24 Aug 2021) adds that "the 95 matches were not just for first class matches. Many of the matches from that time were made first-class retrospectively, not always for obvious reasons, so I prefer to put all the matches I know of in together".

47 Willie Sugg (2009). Fenner's Men. Cambridgeshire Cricket 1822-1848. Part 3 of A Tradition Unshared. Real Work Publishing. Page 54.

48 St James's Gazette. Politics and Persons. Wednesday 27 May 1896.

49 Weston Mercury 30 May 1896 page 3.

50 Cambridge Chronicle and Journal 30 August 1834 page 2.

51 Willie Sugg. F P Fenner. Seminar Sixteen (unpublished). Page 3.

52 Sketch. A veteran cricketer. 13 Sept 1893. Page 361.

53 Matches played 12 Sept in Saffron Walden, and 18 Sept 1838 on Parker's Piece. Frederick Lillywhite's Scores and Biographies of Celebrated Cricketers, from 1827 to 1840 (originally published 1862), facsimile edition published by Roger Heavens (1997).

54 Sketch. A veteran cricketer. 13 Sept 1893. Page 361.

55 F.P. Fenner (July and Sept 1893). Cricket jottings. Article II of VI published in Bath Chronicle.

56 Willie Sugg (2009). Fenner's Men. Cambridgeshire Cricket 1822-1848. Part 3 of A Tradition Unshared. Real Work Publishing. Page 47.

57 F.P. Fenner (July and Sept 1893). Cricket jottings. Article II of VI published in Bath Chronicle.

58 William Bolland (1851). Cricket Notes. With a letter containing practical hints by William Clark. Trelawney Sanders. Pages 32 and 33.

59 Sketch. A veteran cricketer. 13 Sept 1893. Page 361.

60 W.K.R. Bedford (the first Free Forester) in 'A Chat about Cricket' in The English illustrated magazine. v.10 Oct.1892-Sept.1893. Page 680.

61 Most wickets in a match on cricinfo https://i.imgci.com

62 Israel Haggis entry on a history of Cambridgeshire cricket website https://www.cambscrickethistory.co.uk

63 Israel Haggis entry on a history of Cambridgeshire cricket website https://www.cambscrickethistory.co.uk

64 Willie Sugg's new writing Israel Haggis – in the news. on a history of Cambridgeshire cricket website https://www.cambscrickethistory.co.uk

65 Advert for New Inn. Cambridge Chronicle and Journal. 9 and 20 April 1844.

66 Willie Sugg's new writing website. Israel Haggis – in the news. on a history of Cambridgeshire cricket website https://www.cambscrickethistory.co.uk

67 Willie Sugg (2009). Fenner's Men. Cambridgeshire Cricket 1822-1848. Part 3 of A Tradition Unshared. Real Work Publishing. Page Page 36.

68 Willie Sugg (2009). Fenner's Men. Cambridgeshire Cricket 1822-1848. Part 3 of A Tradition Unshared. Real Work Publishing. Page 36.

69 Willie Sugg (2009). Fenner's Men. Page 37.

70 Willie Sugg (2009). Fenner's Men. Page 12.

71 Mill Road Cemetery website: https://millroadcemetery.org.uk/arnold-charles/

72 Cambridge Chronicle and Journal 7 June 1933 p 9.

73 Bailey, Thorn, Wynne-Thomas (1984). Who's Who of Cricketers. Page 990.

74 Richard Daft (1893). Kings of Cricket. Published by J W Arrowsmith. Willie Sugg website: https://www.cambscrickethistory.co.uk/george-tarrant/

75 A A Thomson (1985) Odd Men In. Pavilion Books. Also personal communication from Willie Sugg 27 Oct 2019.

76 G Derek West (1989). Twelve days of Grace. Darf Publishers Ltd. Page 16.

77 Richard Daft (1926) A Cricketer's Yarns at http://www.cambscrickethistory.co.uk/Billy%20Buttress.shtml

78 Cambridge Independent Press 29 May 1858.

79 G Derek West (1989). Twelve days of Grace. Darf Publishers Ltd. Page 16.

80 Willie Sugg. Cricket ghetto shock in http://www.cambscrickethistory.co.uk

81 Historiography of Sport in Britain by Martin Johnes, 'Great Britain', in S.W. Pope and John Nauright (eds), Routledge Companion to Sports History (London, 2010), pp. 444-60.

[82] Willie Sugg (2002). A tradition unshared. A history of Cambridge Town and County Cricket 1700-1890. Part 1. Real Work Publishing. Page 37.

[83] Keith and Jennifer Booth (2018). The Haywards. The biography of a cricket dynasty. Chequered Flag Publishing. Page 18.

[84] Willie Sugg (2009). Fenner's Men. Page 39.

[85] Willie Sugg (2009). Fenner's Men. Pages 44 and 45.

[86] Willie Sugg (2009). Fenner's Men. Page 40.

[87] Felix was the pseudonym of Nicholas Wanostrocht an English amateur 'gentleman' cricketer, inventor of the catapulta (bowling machine), India-rubber batting gloves, cricket trousers with removable strips of india-rubber for use as batting pads, as well as being a painter. Simon Burnton (2019) Guardian 3rd Dec. Cricketer, comic, artist, innovator: 'Felix', the ultimate all-rounder.

[88] Willie Sugg article '1847 – Two of a kind?' under 'New writing' on website: https://www.cambscrickethistory.co.uk/new-writing/

[89] Sandiford, Keith A. P. 'Cricket and the Victorians: A Historiographical Essay.' Historical Reflections / Réflexions Historiques, vol. 9, no. 3, Berghahn Books, 1982, pp. 421–36, http://www.jstor.org/stable/41298796.

[90] Allison, Lincoln. 'Batsman and Bowler: The Key Relation of Victorian England.' Journal of Sport History, vol. 7, no. 2, University of Illinois Press, 1980, pp. 5–20, http://www.jstor.org/stable/43610351.

[91] Willie Sugg personal communication 13 Sept 2022.

[92] F.P. Fenner (July and Sept 1893). Cricket jottings. Article 5 of 6 articles published in Bath Chronicle.

[93] Willie Sugg (2009). Fenner's Men. Pages 46 and 47.

[94] Willie Sugg (2009). Fenner's Men. Pages 46 and 47.

[95] Willie Sugg. Francis Phillips Fenner. Unpublished Seminar 16. Page 4.

[96] Willie Sugg (2009). Fenner's Men. Page 43.

[97] Willie Sugg (2009). Fenner's Men. Page 1.

[98] Willie Sugg (2009). Fenner's Men. Page 11 and 12.

[99] Poem by James Martin - committee member, tobacconist, comedian and reporter published in the 1846 Cambridge Town and County Club Annual Report.

[100] Keith and Jennifer Booth (2018). The Haywards. The biography of a cricket dynasty. Chequered Flag Publishing. Page 41.

[101] Willie Sugg unpublished article 'What's in a name - the town that took on a county'. Page 2.

[102] Keith and Jennifer Booth (2018). The Haywards. The biography of a cricket dynasty. Chequered Flag Publishing. Book blurb.

[103] Keith and Jennifer Booth (2018). The Haywards. The biography of a cricket dynasty. Chequered Flag Publishing. Page 124.

[104] Mike Petty (2018). Cambridge SPORT Chronicle. Chronology of Cambridge Sport 1888 to 1990 at https://archive.org/details/CambridgeSPORTSChronicle

[105] Sara Payne (1984). Down your street. Cambridge Past and Present II East Cambridge. The Pevensey Press. Page 47.

[106] Keith and Jennifer Booth (2018). The Haywards. The biography of a cricket dynasty. Chequered Flag Publishing. Page 175.

[107] Keith and Jennifer Booth (2018). The Haywards. Page 188.

[108] Keith and Jennifer Booth (2018). The Haywards. Page 271.

[109] Keith and Jennifer Booth (2018). The Haywards. Page 262.

[110] Keith and Jennifer Booth (2018). The Haywards. Page 262.

[111] Chris Elliott. Why is Cambridge such a big cycling city? Cambridge News. 1 April 2018.

[112] Mill Road Cemetery website. http://millroadcemetery.org.uk/howes-arthur-james/

113 Cambridge University Cycling Club website: https://cucc.co.uk/the-club/history/

114 Barnwell Theatre at 38 Newmarket Road on Capturing Cambridge website: https://capturingcambridge.org

115 Kathleen McCrone. Page 161 in The 'lady blue'. Sport at the Oxbridge women's colleges from their foundation to 1914. Chapter 6 in J.A. Mangan - ed (2006). A sport-loving society. Routledge.

116 World YMCA website: https://www.ymca.int/about-us/ymca-history/the-ymcas-contribution-to-sports-and-physical-education/

117 Cambridgeshire Rowing Association website: https://www.crarowing.co.uk/about/about-the-cra/early-cra-history

118 Scottish Sport History website: https://www.scottishsporthistory.com/arthur-kinnaird-first-lord-of-football.html

119 FIFA (1997). Cambridge, the birthplace of the laws. FIFA website.

120 Peter Borsay (2006). A history of leisure. Palgrave Macmillan. Page 10

121 Graham Curry and Eric Dunning (2015). Association Football. A study in figurational sociology. Routledge. Page 15.

122 Poetry Foundation website: https://www.poetryfoundation.org/poets/john-lydgate

123 From Mary, Queen of Scots to the FIFA Women's World Cup: a brief history of women's football post https://www.historyextra.com website

124 The Middle Ages St Edmundsbury from 1216 to 1539 article on website http://www.stedmundsburychronicle.co.uk

125 Derek Birley (1993). Sport and the making of Britain. Manchester University Press. Pages 61 and 62.

126 David Dymond. A lost social institution: the Camping Close. Rural History (1990) 1, 2, 165-192.

127 David Dymond. A lost social institution: the Camping Close. Rural History (1990) 1, 2, 165-192.

128 The way things were article on Queens' College website https://www.queens.cam.ac.uk

129 Derek Birley (1993). Sport and the making of Britain. Manchester University Press. Page 69.

130 Reverend John Wheelwright entry on website http://freepages.rootsweb.com

131 Cambridge Chronicle and Journal 31 May 1851.

132 Henry Payne Stokes (1915). Outside the Barnwell Gate. Printed for the Cambridge Antiquarian Society. Pages 44 and 45.

133 Harold Whetstone Johnston, revised by Mary Johnston (1903, 1932). The Private Life of the Romans. Scott, Foresman and Co.

134 T D Atkinson, Ethel M Hampson, E T Long, C A F Meekings, Edward Miller, H B Wells and G M G Woodgate, 'Ely Hundred: Littleport', in A History of the County of Cambridge and the Isle of Ely: Volume 4, City of Ely; Ely, N. and S. Witchford and Wisbech Hundreds, ed. R B Pugh (London, 2002), pp. 95-102. British History Online http://www.british-history.ac.uk/vch/cambs/vol4/pp95-102 [accessed 13 September 2022].

135 David Cram et al (2003). Francis Willughby's Book of Games. Ashgate.

136 Paul Griffiths (1996). Youth and Authority: Formative Experiences in England 1560 - 1640. Oxford University Press. Pages 133 - 134.

137 Roger North's autobiography quoted on Jesus College website https://www.jesus.cam.ac.uk/articles/archive-month-mr-norths-instruments

138 Thomas Hughes (1911). Tom Brown's Schooldays (6th edition). Thames Publishing Co. Chapter III page 51.

139 Arthur Gray (1902). Cambridge University College Histories. Jesus College. London: F.E. Robinson & Co. Pages 147 and 148.

140 Willie Sugg (2002). A tradition unshared. A history of Cambridge Town and County Cricket 1700-1890. Part 1. Real Work Publishing. Page 50.

141 The Vocabulary of East Anglia (an attempt to record the Vulgar Tongue of the twin sister counties, Norfolk and Suffolk, as it existed in the last twenty years of the Eighteenth Century) - Volume 1 - by Rev Robert Forby, published in 1830 by J.B. Nichols & Son - in Bill Atkins. References to the East Anglian Sport of Camping (updated 7 March 2013). http://www.oldshuck.info/pdf/camping.pdf

142 Rev. William Tylney Spurdens (1858) Supplement to 'The Vocabulary of East Anglia'.

143 David Dymond. A lost social institution: the Camping Close. Rural History (1990) 1, 2, 165-192.

144 Melvyn Bragg quoted in The Telegraph 15 April 2006 'How a book of golden rules claimed Bragging rights'.

145 Graham Curry and Eric Dunning (2015). Association Football. A study in figurational sociology. Routledge. Page 40.

146 Mike Petty (2018). Cambridge SPORT Chronicle. Chronology of Cambridge Sport 1888 to 1990 at https://archive.org/details/CambridgeSPORTSChronicle

147 Graham Curry and Eric Dunning (2015). Association Football. A study in figurational sociology. Routledge. Page 63.

148 Cambridge University Rugby Union Football Club website: http://www.curufc.com/History.aspx

149 Albert Pell (1908) The reminiscences of Albert Pell: London: John Murray.

150 C. J. B. Marriott. Rugby Football at Cambridge chapter in Football. The Rugby Union Game edited by Rev F Marshall (1892).

151 Venn Cambridge Alumni Database. https://venn.lib.cam.ac.uk/

152 Selwyn Walters. Memorial to first Welsh rugby match article on historypoints.com website.

153 The Varsity match history at https://thevarsitymatches.com/history/

154 H. C. Malden (Trinity 1847). Contents of letter written in 1897 reported in The Fountain. Trinity College Newsletter. Issue 7. Autumn 2008.

155 Nicholas Chrimes (2017). Cambridge. Treasure Island of the Fens. Hobsaerie Publications. Page 230.

156 Graham Curry and Eric Dunning (2015). Association Football. A study in figurational sociology. Routledge. Page 48.

157 Michael McCrum (1989) Thomas Arnold – Head Master. Oxford University Press. Page 116.

158 Graham Curry and Eric Dunning (2015). Association Football. A study in figurational sociology. Routledge. Page 51.

159 Graham Curry and Eric Dunning (2015). Association Football. A study in figurational sociology. Routledge. Page 77.

160 https://www.scottishsporthistory.com/arthur-kinnaird-first-lord-of-football.html

161 https://www.scottishsporthistory.com/arthur-kinnaird-first-lord-of-football.html

162 The Chanticleer (Jesus College magazine) No 13 Michaelmas Term 1889.

163 Adrian Harvey (2005). Football: the first hundred years – the untold story. Routledge. Page 103.

164 Graham Curry and Eric Dunning (2015). Association Football. A study in figurational sociology. Routledge. Pages 115 and 116.

165 Danny Lewis (2019). Corinthian Football Club: the legendary 19th century globetrotters. Article on These Football Times: https://thesefootballtimes.co/

166 4th April 2022 email from Chris Watney (Marketing Manager at Corinthian Casuals)

167 B.O.Corbett (1906). Annals of the Corinthian Football Club. Longmans, Green and Co.

168 Mick Collins (2006). All-round genius. The unknown story of Britain's greatest sportsman. Aurum. Page 49.

169 5th March 2022 email from Chris Watney (Marketing Manager at Corinthian Casuals)

170 Cavallini, R. (2007). Play up Corinth. Stroud: Stadia. Page 7.

171 Street Child United website: https://www.streetchildunited.org/

CHAPTER 21

Mortimer Road – ice skating

In 1879 the National Skating Association (NSA) was founded at the Guildhall (chapter 16), requiring a national office which was based at 4 Mortimer Villas, where it remained for over 15 years before moving to London. This was the home of local journalist James Drake Digby who took a lead role in the NSA.

HQ of the National Skating Association from 1879 - on the left at Number 4, with the entrance to Fenner's Cricket Ground at the bottom of Mortimer Road

Having the NSA headquarters here was logical, given the proximity of the flat and damp Fens, referred to as 'nature's ice rink', thanks largely to the Dutch engineers who not only drained the Fens in the seventeenth century, but also brought their skates with them'.[1]

Whilst most sports associated with Cambridge owe their success to being linked to the University, ice skating has a unique and proud local tradition.

Other people who have lived at 4 Mortimer Road include Ludvig Wittgenstein (the Austrian-British philosopher) who spent a short time here after returning to Cambridge from Austria in 1929.[2]

HISTORY OF SKATING

Whilst animal bones were used for hundreds of years for skates, they were replaced by bladed skates in the sixteenth century with the arrival of Dutch engineers to drain the Fens. Skates were vital to survive a harsh winter.

Increasingly skating was also used as recreation, for example in speed and distance races for men and women, attracting significant prizes, large crowds, the betting trade, and prestige for the winners and the villages they hailed from.

FROM BONE TO ALUMINIUM

Range of ice skates 'from bone to aluminium'
With thanks to the Norris Museum, St Ives.

SPEED SKATERS

William 'Turkey' Smart won £58 15s and a leg of mutton in February 1855, the equivalent of about 2 years' average earnings for him as an agricultural worker. He was given his nickname for inventing the modern way of racing, bent over to reduce wind resistance and swinging his arms – looking, apparently, like a turkey.

For his visit to Mepal (15 miles (25 km) north of Cambridge) during that February, the press reported:

> Cambridge, Ely, St Ives, Chatteris, and diverse other towns and villages were thinned of their population that day. The clergy and 'squires', gentry and tradesmen – hale ploughboys and rosy milkmaids – ladies parties in carriages, gigs and carts, made their way to the bank near the bridge, and took their respective positions, where the view was excellent, and all that could be wished for the 'St Ledger day on the ice'. A brass band of music from Chatteris was placed on the bridge, and played the most lively tunes: at the starting of a race, 'Cheer boys, cheer', and at the winning, 'See the conquering hero comes'. The number of persons present was stated at from five to eight thousand, and some said ten thousand. Punctually at the time appointed, half-past one, the racing commenced. The bold Fen-men soon appeared, whose iron frames, lion sinews, elasticity of action and body, astonished all beholders. They were a fine specimen of the bold peasantry of England.[3]

Another skating star from this time was William 'Gutta Percha' See, named after the very tough rubber used for the soles of shoes – and for golf balls.

Whilst most speed skaters understandably originated in the Fens, William Stutes was born and lived his short life close to Castle Hill, being known as 'The Pride of Cambridge' for his famous skating exploits. According to newspaper reports he was a happy waterman, but he died on the night of Boxing Day in 1848, having been 'turned out of the Pickerel Inn [almost on Magdalene Bridge] … for being rather intoxicated and obstreperous' and went out the back and fell into a ditch, being found dead the next morning. He was refused burial at his local church, St Peter's, given the suspicious nature of his death, which is why he was buried in Mill Road Cemetery, however the location of his grave is unknown.[4]

Other local speed skaters include Frederick Hiam who became the 220 yards world skating champion in 1895 in record time and was later president of Cambridge Town Football Club, and C.B. Fry, 'probably the most variously gifted Englishman of any age'.[5] He not only represented England at both cricket and football, equalled the world long jump record, but also, in the late nineteenth century, represented the Oxford University ice skating team against Cambridge University on the Fens.

BANDY – THE FORERUNNER TO ICE HOCKEY

The word bandy has been used for centuries to describe a bent stick, which is why it has been associated over this period with a range of 'ball and mallet' games such as golf, cricket, shinty, hockey and ice hockey.[6]

However, 'Bandy' was the word used for the sport of 'hockey on ice' on the Fens, for example at Bury Fen, located between Bluntisham and Earith (both 11 miles (17km) north of Cambridge), at the end of the eighteenth century, and probably a lot earlier. The local team remained unbeaten for decades, being also credited with introducing the game to Holland,[7] and formalising the rules.

Bandy played by two women in 1899
Source: Plate 34 in Enid Porter (1969). Cambridgeshire Customs and Folklore. Routledge & Kegan Paul.
Image reproduced with permission from Museum of Cambridge.

Three bandy sticks
With thanks to the Norris Museum, St Ives.

Rules

The National Skating Association, 'being desirous of setting rules of Hockey on the Ice' wrote to the Bury Fen Bandy Club requesting a copy of their rules, resulting in their approval in 1882 – see letter to right.

The oldest rivalry in ice hockey is believed to have started in 1885 in St Moritz between Oxford and Cambridge universities, probably played to Bandy rules. The Oxford University Ice Hockey Club concede the matches in the early twentieth century 'played according to the rules of bandy'.[8]

Bandy sticks were found locally as naturally curved sticks of ash or willow, and later produced commercially by Gray's of Cambridge in the second half of the nineteenth century.[9]

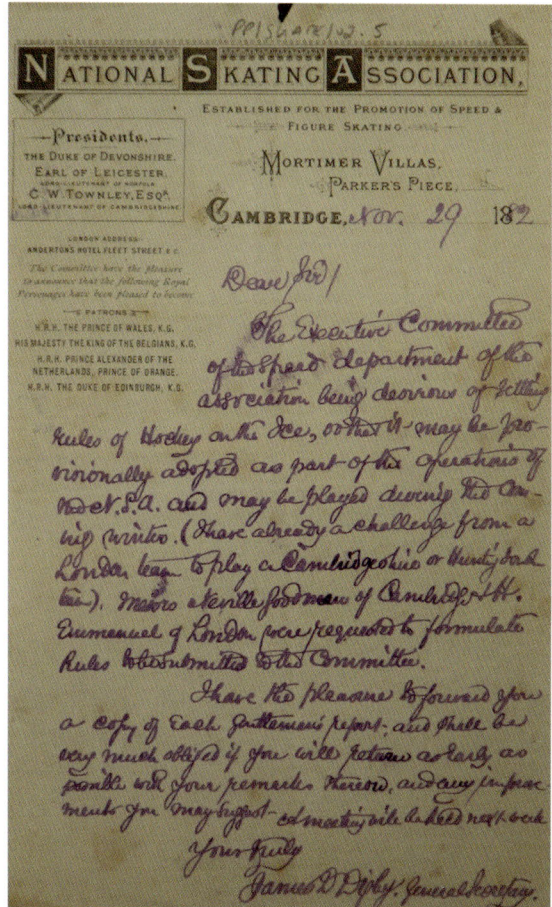

Letter from NSA asking the Bury Fen Bandy Club to provide its current Bandy Rules (1882)

With thanks to the Norris Museum, St Ives.

Charles Darwin 'On the Origin of Ice Hockey'

With ice hockey designated the national winter sport of Canada it is no surprise they claim to have played the first proper match in Montreal in 1875.

However, in a book entitled *On the Origin of Hockey*[10] (in a deliberate nod to Darwin's seminal work *On the Origin of Species*) the authors refer to a letter Charles Darwin wrote to his son in 1853, about his own experiences at Shrewsbury School between 1818 and 1825 enjoying 'hockey on ice'.

Darwin had later been a student from 1828 to 1831 at Christ's College, also returning to Cambridge in 1836 to organise his work following his five-year voyage on HMS Beagle. Because as a student he preferred outdoor sports to studying, it is possible he skated on the nearby Fens, especially after his earlier experiences at school.

Queen Victoria's 'hearty laughter'

A game of Bandy was played on the ice of the Windsor Castle pond in 1853, where Queen Victoria was a spectator watching 'the Prince Consort – who was a beautiful and graceful skater – (who) kept goal for the opposite side'.

John Astley, the writer, who also played in the match later referred to a tackle with a member of the opposition where:

> I lost my balance, and came down in a sitting posture, the impetus I had on carrying me right over to the Queen's feet, and the hearty laughter which greeted my unbidden arrival is still vividly impressed on my mind. It was altogether a glorious afternoon's sport.[11]

The Prince Consort, better known as Prince Albert, had already been appointed the chancellor of Cambridge University in 1847 (chapter 13).

SKATING AND OTHER SPORTS, AND FOR RECREATION

When the River Cam was frozen in 1879 the University Boat crew maintained their training by skating.

Samuel Pepys was well-known for skating with King Charles II's mistress Nell Gwynne on the River Thames when it froze for several weeks in 1683. Having been a student at Huntingdon Grammar School for a couple of years from the age of 11, and later a student at Magdalene College from 1651, it is possible he skated locally.

The Cambridge University rowing crew – winter training for the Boat Race in 1879
Source: The Graphic 15th Feb 1879.

In 1798 William Wordsworth (student at St John's College from 1787) wrote a letter to Samuel Taylor Coleridge about the importance of his experience skating as a child in the Lake District, which featured in *The Prelude*:[12]

> I wheeled about,
> Proud and exulting, like an untired horse,
> That cares not for its home. – All shod with steel,
> We hissed along the polish'd ice in games
> Confederate.... And oftentimes

When we had given our bodies to the wind,
     …..then at once
Have I, reclining back upon my heels,
Stopped short, yet still the solitary Cliffs
Wheeled by me, even as if the earth had rolled
With visible motion her diurnal round.
Behind me did they stretch in solemn train
Feebler and feebler, and I stood and watched
Till all was tranquil as a dreamless sleep.

It is not known whether Wordsworth skated in the Fens, however the weather was certainly cold enough in the winter of 1788/1789 to do so, given nearly two months of hard frost.[13]

In 1875 an ice-skating challenge was issued by a group of Littleport men claiming they could skate faster than the train travelling between Littleport and Ely.

They did, but not without some foul play by some 'railway supporters' who put cinder on the ice to slow the skaters. The skaters' response was to subsequently slow the train travelling to Sandringham with the Prince of Wales on board, by every few miles posting men with a red lamp, which when the train stopped, then turned to green. On the fifth occasion this happened the Prince of Wales demanded 'in loud tomes if the dammed train was going to be all night getting to Sandringham'.

Cricket on ice

There were a number of cricket matches played on ice in the second half of the nineteenth century, featuring England cricketers, students at the University and local people. In 1867, the Eleven of Cambridgeshire, including Daniel and Thomas Hayward and Robert Carpenter (the latter two being England cricketers) who beat the twenty-two of Swavesey on Mere Fen, a very popular Fenland winter sportsground.[15] In 1870, at the same 'ground', eleven members of an All-England and University team, captained by Robert Carpenter, again played Swavesey, who had sixteen players this time. There were a very large number of people watching the game 'whom were members of the University who travelled by special trains'. Swavesey scored 125, against the England team score of 280.[16]

In 1878 Charles Pigg, a student at Peterhouse, challenged Robert Carpenter to raise a side to play the University over three days on Grantchester Meadows. Cambridge Town scored 326 including Carpenter's 89 and in response the University were 274 for 4 when the two captains agreed on a draw.[17]

Sight-impaired skater

Henry Fawcett was a student and subsequently a professor at Trinity Hall, as well as a keen sportsman. However, in 1858 aged 25, he had a tragic accident with a shotgun that resulted in him losing his sight. This did not stop him rowing, swimming, diving and skating.

For example, Henry skated to Ely when the River Cam froze over, a distance of 16 miles, 'heedless of the dangers of a plunge into the icy waters'.[18]

Henry was married to Millicent Fawcett, a campaigner for women's suffrage and co-founder of Newnham College. They lived together on Brookside (near the Botanical Gardens,) where two blue plaques today list their achievements. Their only child, Philippa Fawcett, 'greatly enjoyed accompanying her father [skating], and whistling in order to guide him'.

In addition:

> Shortly after skating on rollers was introduced, Mrs. (Millicent) Fawcett went to a rink, and as she came in was told that a most extraordinary thing was going on—there was a blind man trying roller-skating. It was her husband, whizzing round delightedly. Fawcett was having a royal time, darting like a huge swallow in swift circles about the skating rink. He revelled in the motion and the exercise, which put him into a fine glow. The merry noise of many little wooden wheels rolling smoothly over the polished floor—the lifting and stumbling of awkard feet, and the skilful glide of the good skaters gave him a happy consciousness of the gay revolving spectacle through which he winged his way.[19]

Skating for people in Cambridge town

As a 15-year-old in 1844, apprentice Josiah Chater 'attached great importance to exercise, which he considered essential for his health', such as walking, swimming and skating. 'The nearest skating ground for the boys [apprentices] was the pond in the gardens of Emmanuel College'.[20] It is not known whether Frank Fenner skated.

[1] Guardian 4 April 2009.

[2] 4, Mortimer Road as featured on Capturing Cambridge website: https://capturingcambridge.org/

[3] Cambridge Chronicle and Journal 17 February 1855.

[4] William Stutes entry on Mill Road Cemetery website: http://millroadcemetery.org.uk/

[5] John Arlott quote - on Repton School website https://www.repton.org.uk/

[6] Joseph Strutt (1801). Sports and Pastimes of the People of England. Page 154 in 2008 edition.

[7] Diane K Bolton, G R Duncombe, R W Dunning, Jennifer I Kermode, A M Rowland, W B Stephens and A P M Wright, 'Sport', in A History of the County of Cambridge and the Isle of Ely: Volume 5, ed. C R Elrington (London, 1973), pp. 279-303. British History Online http://www.british-history.ac.uk/vch/cambs/vol5/pp279-303 [accessed 13 September 2022].

[8] Oldest Hockey Rivalry article on Oxford University Ice Hockey website: https://oxforduniversityicehockey.com/

[9] Enid Porter (1969). Cambridgeshire Customs and Folklore. Routledge & Kegan Paul. Page 227.

[10] Carl Gidén, Patrick Houda and Jean-Patrice Martel (2014). On the Origin Of Hockey. Hockey Origin Publishing.

[11] Arnold Tebbutt (1896). A Handbook of Bandy; or Hockey on the Ice. Page 2.

[12] 'Spots of time': ice skating poster, and original letter displayed in 2022 at William Wordsworth Museum, Grasmere.

[13] Martin Rowley. British Weather from 1700 to 1849. Website: https://www.pascalbonenfant.com/18c/geography/weather.html

[14] Enid Porter (1969). Cambridgeshire Customs and Folklore. Routledge & Kegan Paul. Pages 240 to 241.

[15] Cambridge Chronicle 26 Jan 1867 – in Keith and Jennifer Booth (2018). The Haywards. The biography of a cricket dynasty. Chequered Flag Publishing.

[16] Norwich Mercury, 19 Feb 1870 in Keith and Jennifer Booth (2018). The Haywards. The biography of a cricket dynasty. Chequered Flag Publishing.

[17] Andrew Ward (2018). Cricket's strangest matches. Pages 13 and 14.

[18] Henry Fawcett Blue Plaque further info on Cambridge, Past, Present & Future website: https://www.cambridgeppf.org

[19] Winifred Holt (1914). A Beacon for the Blind; Being a Life of Henry Fawcett, the Blind Postmaster-General. Boston, Houghton Mifflin.

[20] Enid Porter (1975). Victorian Cambridge. Josiah Chater's Diaries 1844 - 1884. Phillimore. Page 18.

CHAPTER 22

Fenner's Cricket Ground

The Cambridge University Cricket Club (CUCC), founded in 1820, made two known attempts to move off Parker's Piece to their own ground before finally settling at Fenner's in 1848. This had a substantial impact on University and town cricket, and Frank Fenner too, in very different ways. The chapter is therefore sub-divided into seven main sections that charts this story.

1. Early history of the Cambridge University Cricket Club, and their first dedicated cricket ground.

2. The need for the University to have their own private cricket ground.

3. Why Frank Fenner was engaged to provide it.

4. Why Frank took on the challenge, and what were his motives.

5. Cambridge cricket: in Fenner's hands:

   - Establishing the ground and the offer to town cricket,
   - The demise of town cricket,
   - Frank's ongoing support of the town, and
   - The town's own initiatives.

6. Other sports and community activities at Fenner's Ground.

7. University Cricket at Fenner's:

   - Frank falls out with the University, and
   - The University's extraordinary success.

1. EARLY HISTORY OF THE CAMBRIDGE UNIVERSITY CRICKET CLUB, AND GROUND

Whilst there were four references to cricket being played in Cambridge, (by William Goldwin in 1706; Richard Bentley in 1710; when it was banned for students between 9am and midday in 1750; and an advert in 1792 in the local press promoting a game at the 'Cambridge Cricket Ground'), it is not known precisely where such games were played. The options range from within the confines of a college's own grounds, to Midsummer Common, to Jesus Green, given their relative flatness compared with Parker's Piece.

What prompted the need for a dedicated ground was the formation of The Cambridge University Cricket Club in 1820, which is why from 1821 to at least 1831, they used a part of the current Mill Road Cemetery site, not far from Parker's Piece.

The ground was described by Herbert Jenner,[a] University cricket captain in 1827, as:

> An enclosed field of eight acres, near a newly built chapel in the parish of Barnwell, for which we paid £30 a-year [worth the equivalent of nearly £3,000 today]. After a couple of years two acres were taken off to increase the burial ground [for the newly built chapel]; rent however remained the same. Under such circumstances it was not to be expected that we could play many matches.[1]

In this same year Herbert Jenner accepted the challenge made by Charles Wordsworth (nephew of the poet) to instigate the first Oxford v Cambridge Cricket match on 4th June 1827. Given Herbert's view of his home ground, it was no surprise the match was played at Lord's Cricket Ground.

The cricket varsity match was the first in any sport, with the boat race following two years later in 1829.

As a teenager Frank Fenner probably saw Herbert Jenner play on this ground, as well as keeping an eye on his cricketing career, because he later penned this tribute[2] to him.

> 'The most notable all-round player of his time … It was as a wicket keeper that Mr Jenner first became distinguished, for he was especially classed as one of the best, if not the very best, of that day; but as a bowler and batsman he was also conspicuous for his skill, indeed for his general mastery in every department of the game. This position he indisputably held till his retirement some few years after, by which the cricket world suffered a loss long deplored by every true lover of the game.'

Herbert Jenner had been a student at Trinity Hall.

Cricket matches played at the University Cricket Ground

Frank Fenner recalled over 70 years later 'an extraordinary match played at Cambridge in 1820'.[3] Frank's memory had failed him because the match was actually played on 18 May 1827.[4]

This was the second of two games played on consecutive days between the University and Bury (St Edmunds), almost certainly on this University Cricket Ground. As a 16-year-old spectator, Frank would have no doubt paid close

---

[a]   Later changing his name to Herbert Jenner-Fust in 1864.

attention to the 24-year-old Fuller Pilch (playing for Bury), later described as 'the greatest batsman ever known until the appearance of W. G. Grace'.[5]

Frank later recalled the scores 'Bury, first innings 15; second innings 20. Total two innings, 35 runs. Cambridge UCC first innings 37 runs, thus winning the match in one innings and two runs to spare. This score is the smallest that has been known in the present century to have won a game in one innings.'[6] Frank selected this low-scoring game in 'wonderment' believing 'the cricketing palate is epicurean enough to relish all the 'bits' of cricket history'.

It is likely this low scoring game was influenced by the state of the pitch, a link that would have registered with Frank, given his later passion and commitment to preparing the best possible grounds for cricket on Parker's Piece, Fenner's and in both Gloucestershire and Somerset (chapter 23).

To support the increasing number of cricketers arriving from the public schools, there was growing demand for local groundsmen, bowlers, fielders and coaches. These included 'Murcutt of Cambridge' who worked at the new University Cricket Ground in 1823, if not earlier.[7]

University cricketer buried in the ground he played on

There is one University player who played his cricket on this ground who was later buried there.

William Hopkins (Peterhouse student from 1822) was known as the 'wrangler maker' given his success at tutoring mathematicians. From 1825 to 1828 he played first class cricket with the Cambridge University Cricket Club. One rare cricketing feat he achieved was as an opening batsman 'carrying his bat' not just through the first innings, but in the second too. The University were playing Bury (St Edmunds) which included the famous Fuller Pilch.[8]

He died in 1866, aged 73, being buried in Mill Road Cemetery, close to the chapel, now demolished.

2. THE NEED FOR THE UNIVERSITY TO HAVE THEIR OWN PRIVATE CRICKET GROUND

These first known attempts to play on their own ground ended for the University Cricket Club because it was not only too small but probably wet too,[9] but Parker's Piece was being improved through re-levelling, re-turfing 'for the use both of the university and town',[10] and the provision of a 'fence round'.[11]

However, it was not long before they wanted their own ground again.

The poor state of Parker's Piece

Despite these improvements the cricket pitches were not good enough, no doubt linked to cricket bowlers increasingly using a round-arm action (when underarm had been the norm). This made the quality of the pitch on which the bowled ball would bounce becoming increasingly important – not improved with horses riding over them. This prompted the young Frank Fenner, aged 25, to write a strikingly articulate letter to the press in 1836 complaining about the injury these horses caused to the cricket pitches.[12]

Later a local chimney sweep also spoke of 'the mean state of the grass – the town council spend so much money putting it right and getting it flat, and then people dig it up to lay drains from their houses to the new sewer!'.[13]

Too busy and too small

In addition to poor pitches, Parker's Piece was not big enough to cater for the very many games played there at any one time.

For example, Frederick Henry Norman (Trinity College, and University cricket captain in 1860) recalled that 'the fieldsmen of the different matches were all jumbled up together, long leg of one match somewhere near cover-point of another, and the hits of one game crossing those of another, which was both disconcerting and dangerous'.[14]

This prompted J L Roget to produce a suitable cartoon showing a gentleman crossing Parker's Piece protecting himself from 'raining cricket balls', as well as being asked to throw them back.

'Cricket on Parker's Piece.'

'Cricket on Parker's Piece' cartoon by J.L. Roget (1859) showing St Paul's Church, Hills Road in the background

Source: J.L. Roget (1859). A Cambridge scrap book, containing, in a pictorial form, a report on the manners [&c.], by a special commissioner appointed by himself [JL Roget]. University of Oxford.

It was not just cricket taking place on Parker's Piece, as the local press of 1842 reported, 'what with the cattle, the bows and arrows, the cricket balls etc it was really a wonder that some serious injury was not done'.[15]

The University's wish to separate themselves from 'the masses'

In addition, and undoubtedly the biggest reason for this second move off Parker's Piece was that many University cricketers, spectators and some of the University's opponents wanted to separate themselves from the hoi poloi, or 'the masses' because of the 'noisy and ill-mannered chaff'[16] (modern-day banter). Whilst the University would have always experienced this, it was probably more alarming, even frightening, given heightened Town versus Gown tensions in the 1840s (chapter 20).

Another reason was provided by Frank Fenner who remembered in 1893, nearly 50 years afterwards, that:

> I was constantly hearing complaints about the extortions of the men who had practically appropriated the Public Ground [Parker's Piece]. It became such a scandal that it was threatening the very existence of University cricket, for it was not to be expected that undergrads could long go on paying a half sovereign [worth £30 today] for an hour's practice, and it often amounted to that.'[17]

This was experienced as 'hard selling' by the University's Cricket Club historian.

> There also haunted 'The Piece' a class, which has perhaps died out, of rather seedy-looking professionals, provided with bat, ball, and stumps—no net—ready and anxious to bowl to any passer-by for a casual shilling … invited to stop and 'Ave a few balls,', even in March'.[18]

This continued even after Fenner's Ground was opened, given the large numbers of cricket professionals living in the town (chapter 20).

As a result of all these factors Oxford University did not want to play the early varsity matches in Cambridge for 'the want of a proper ground', nor allegedly, did the MCC, as Parker's Piece as 'an open public space, intersected with many paths, was scarcely suitable'.[19]

Frank Fenner also reported that 'at the close of last season (1847) several gentlemen of the University, of high standing as cricketers, and patrons of the game, called upon me, and declared their determination to retire from cricket in Cambridge, unless a private ground was secured, where they could play the game in safety and in comfort'.[20]

One of these gentlemen would probably have been Oliver Pell, who was not only captain of the University cricket team in 1847,[21] but who played with Frank for the Cambridge Town and County team.

When the University had their own ground for ten years (on the Mill Road Cemetery site) from 1821 it was considered 'a powerful status symbol', as well as providing 'sanctuary from the town'.[22]

Comparison with Oxford town and University

Whilst Oxford University were not prepared to play the early varsity matches on Parker's Piece, James Pycroft conceded:

> 'It is remarkable that no single professional [cricketer] of eminence ever came from Oxford, though Fenner, Buttress, Hayward, Carpenter, and Tarrant remind us of Cambridge practice on Parker's Piece.

Pycroft, writing his 'Oxford Memories'[23] in 1886, had played first-class cricket for Oxford University in 1836 and 1838.

An explanation in part, for the differences between Cambridge and Oxford comes from Professor Thomas Case who wrote the history of Oxford University Cricket Club,[24] which included asking the question 'why go so far as Bullingdon [approx. 3 miles southeast from the centre of Oxford] when in those days there were plenty of fields in the near vicinity of Oxford?'

> 'The answer' Case believed 'is to be found in the former life of Oxford, still reflected in the Bullingdon Club as it was when I was an undergraduate. Cricket was connected with riding, the amusement par excellence of those days. One must picture to oneself undergraduates riding or driving out across the Cowley Common undeterred by fences and on their arrival at Bullingdon Green partly playing cricket in the middle, partly riding races round the match, and finally eating and drinking in a manner adapted to youth, health and exercise'.

Of course, cricket was a priority game for many other students, such as Lord Harris, who captained both Kent and England. He later became the President of the MCC, who in sharing his 'Oxford Memories' in Wisden in 1928, stated 'he preferred playing for his college, Christchurch, more than Oxford, mostly because there were more of his Eton chums in the side', adding 'For Bullingdon cricket I cared not a jot: it was not business-like for my temperament. To start cricket at one o'clock and go to lunch - and a very elaborate one - at 1.15 did not appeal to me'.[25]

However, there was nothing to compare with Parker's Piece, nor apparently nearly as much mixing of Town and Gown (side by side, or in the same team) in Oxford. In addition, even when Oxford University Cricket Club secured their settled home at 'The Parks', they shared it with a museum, arboretum and other sports. Even Lewis Carroll wrote a poem as protesting The Parks being 'sacrificed to cricket'.[b]

3. WHY FRANK FENNER WAS ENGAGED TO PROVIDE A PRIVATE GROUND

In 1846 the Earl of Stamford and Lord Burghley (both students) were reported to have 'engaged a field behind the Gaol[26] ... at a very handsome sum as a private ground, where a quantity of men are engaged in preparing it under the superintendence of Lillywhite, presumably the University's cricket professional'.[27]

CAMBRIDGE UNIVERSITY STUDENTS PLAYING CRICKET, 1842.

'Cambridge University students playing cricket - 1842'

The view across Parker's Piece from outside the University Arms towards the Gaol (where the current Kelsey Kerridge Sports Centre is located). The new ground, from 1846, was located behind the gaol from this view.

Permission from Cambridgeshire Collection, Cambridge Central Library.

[b] Amidst they bowers the tyrant's hand is soon / and rude pavilions sadden all they green / one selfish pasture grasps the whole domain / And half a faction swallows up the plain, / Adown they glades all sacrificed to cricket......(from The Deserted Parks).

It is not known why Lillywhite only lasted a few months, however he was replaced by 'S Haggis' (which is possibly either Israel Haggis or a close relative – chapter 20) who probably acted as groundsman of this new ground, and later its manager,[28] when Lillywhite left.

A small number of games were played on the ground including appearances by I Zingari (a year after it was formed), Haileybury College, and invitation teams assembled by Stamford and Burghley. However, it is believed this scheme did not go on to establish itself because the Earl of Stamford had to leave the University immediately, having married the daughter of a college servant.[29]

It was possibly Thomas Townley and Lord Fitzwilliam, as the new custodiams of the private ground,[30] who then approached Frank Fenner to complete the project; both were in their early twenties having started together as students at Trinity College in 1844.

At such a young age, these students would have considered Frank given these credentials as:

- **Professional bowler / coach – and 'known about town'.** Frank had had a long association with the University starting from 1836, when aged 25 he was engaged as the University's professional cricket bowler / coach.[31] That same year he also opened a tobacco shop on Sidney Street, in the centre of Cambridge, where many of his customers would invariably have been members of the University.

- **Exclusive supplier of cricket equipment.** From at least 1844 he was the exclusive supplier of cricket equipment to the University, according to an advert placed in the local press (chapter 20).

- **Frank as secretary of the University Club.** Frank also claimed, admittedly over 40 years later, he had been secretary to the University Cricket Club for a period of 25 years, presumably from the mid 1830s to the early 1860s, when he left Cambridge.[32] Whilst he clearly did not hold the formal role, he would have made a significant contribution towards organising the University club including arranging its fixtures, given his successful secretaryship of the Cambridge Town & County Club, which was a mix of Town and Gown anyway. In 1837 Frank was appointed as the assistant to the secretary, Frederick Thackeray (student at Gonville & Caius College), but 'soon took on the post for himself',[33] confirmed in 1840.[34]

- **Perfect gentleman.** It is clear Frank was considered a perfect gentleman,[35] 'much respected by all classes, especially Cambridge [University] men, hundreds of whom were his pupils',[36] often 'seen surrounded by a posse of college dons … eager to hear his manly and generous deductions'.[37] Frank also held many important civic and church roles (chapter 16).

- **'One of the games brightest ornaments'.** The London Press were also clearly impressed with Fenner being engaged to create a new ground:

  'Setting aside the fact of Fenner being a Cambridge man, and a cricketer of a high standing, we know of no one better qualified to conduct such an undertaking in a respectable and satisfactory manner, so far as appertains to himself, or so as shall meet the wishes of his patrons to the fullest extent; with a view, also, to the welfare of that 'national game', of which he has for several years been one of the brightest ornaments.'[38]

4. WHY FRANK TOOK ON THE CHALLENGE

Frank later explained the reasoning behind his actions in 'establishing this private ground', as 'promoting cricket to prevent its decay in Cambridge – in fact, to make cricket a game that could be followed by all, the sensitive as well as the sturdy and indifferent'.[39]

But important too was the 'potential profit for the businessman Fenner'.[40]

It is likely, given Frank's experience in business as a tobacconist, cricket coach/professional and cricket equipment supplier, that he would have weighed up the following pros and cons to reassure himself that establishing a private ground was viable:

1. **Demand from University cricket.** This was already known, given Frank's very close relationship with university cricket for at least 10 years.

2. **Demand from Town cricket.** Again, Frank would have known exactly what demand there was, having been associated with town cricket as Secretary and Player for many years. Judging from newspaper reports in 1848, Frank would also have been aware of their being a 'lack of tent seats, lack of manners and conduct … and a ground infringed upon'[41] regarding town cricket played on Parker's Piece.

Whilst he might have hoped for town cricket to use his new ground, he publicly reported that 'I made my calculations without asking for any other patronage',[42] than that from the University.

3. **Gate money through paying spectators.** The norm for local cricket clubs was to be sustained by regular membership subscriptions, plus a 'call for subscriptions' advertised in the local press whenever there was a high-profile game to be played on Parker's Piece and the opposition's travel and professional player expenses had to be covered.

Given there was little aristocratic sponsorship supporting Cambridge cricket, their being a relative shortage of large local landowners, Frank would in all likelihood have explored examples elsewhere of gate money being taken.

For example, in the middle of the eighteenth century, London's premier cricket venue the Artillery Ground was fenced in and admission charged, though there were ambivalent attitudes towards the presence of paying spectators.

By contrast, when Thomas Lord opened his first cricket ground in 1787, with its 'high batten fence' to prevent free viewing, he was soon reaping the benefits, such as £500 (worth nearly £80,000 today) from the takings of one three-day match, and that after the professionals had been paid, including their travelling expenses.[43]

4. Growing influence of the entrepreneur. Frank would have experienced paying spectators when he played at Lord's Cricket Ground, including discussing this issue presumably with William Clarke who was playing at Lord's for the MCC against Fenner's Cambridge Town side in 1847. Frank had also played against William in July 1834 when Nottingham Old Club played Cambridge on Parker's Piece, and probably on other occasions too.

William would have had plenty of valuable experience to share with Frank, having established Nottingham's first pay-to-enter cricket stadium, in the late 1830s, and in 1846 forming the All-England Eleven (AEE) as a touring team of leading professional players to play matches at big city venues, from which he made a fortune.

With Frank a tobacconist, and William Clarke, a bricklayer-turned-innkeeper, they represented the new breed of entrepreneur entering the cricket business, where 'shopocracy' replaced the norm of conspicuous patronage by the aristocracy.[44]

5. Reluctance to pay an entrance fee. However, Trent Bridge as 'Nottingham's first pay-to-enter cricket stadium' was initially abandoned as a loss-making venture.

> He [William Clarke] miscalculated the demeanour of his fellow townsfolk who failed to appreciate the idea of paying to watch cricket, since they had hitherto viewed matches free of charge on The Forest [ground in Nottingham].[45]

This same attitude was prevalent in Cambridge too, still evident much later in the early twentieth century when the great Tom Hayward (the Surrey and England cricketer born at the Prince Regent pub on Parker's Piece) remarked 'Cambridge people are very backward in supporting their county club, or any outdoor event where a gate is charged'.[46]

Whilst Frank was to experience this same attitude, at least he could rely on university cricket (not yet available in Nottingham), and perhaps other up-and-coming sports to make his ground in Cambridge viable.

6. Other sources of gate money beyond cricket. 'Even the august precincts of Lord's [Cricket Ground] saw … in 1844 exhibitions of archery and dancing from a group of Iowa Indians who camped on the now hallowed turf',[47] and pedestrianism, later to include lacrosse, baseball, hockey and a balloon ascent.

Frank would have been aware of the growth of athletics as a spectator sport probably as early as 1838, when *Bell's Life* (the national sports paper) published its first annual 'Chronology of Pedestrianism', listing several enclosed grounds, some of them primarily cricket venues, also given over to athletics.[48]

Frank would also have been greatly encouraged by a number of other developments resulting out of the Industrial Revolution.

7. Importance of the railways.

Frank himself later wrote:

> As a cricketer of the almost forgotten past, I delight in seeing districts, so long overlooked becoming claimants for distinction; shewing their front, and by the force of their innate strength overcoming the prejudice, which for many years limited to a few counties all notice of that excellence which has of late been so widely developed. This magic circle was first broken through by the introduction of railways.'[49]

For example, in Cambridge, the first trains arrived from both London and Norwich in 1845 and two years later the line from Peterborough was built, with stops at both March and Ely, as well as another line, going west towards St. Ives and Huntington.[50]

The direct impact 'enabled the arrangement of [cricket] fixtures hitherto undreamed of when a day's travelling by stagecoach covered about five miles per hour. Journeys previously measured in days could now be undertaken in hours'.[51] This would have been a vital development to any cricket ground in Cambridge, with the new railway station only half a mile (0.6km) away.

5. CAMBRIDGE CRICKET: IN FENNER'S HANDS

Having been engaged to create this new ground, it would appear the future of cricket in Cambridge for both Town and Gown, together and separately, was in Frank Fenner's hands.

Creating the ground

When the first effort to create a cricket ground behind the gaol came to an end, Lord Charles Fitzwilliam and Thomas Townley took over responsibility, which, it can be inferred, included engaging Frank Fenner, whose brief according to *Bell's Life* was to provide a private ground, to create 'a sort of Lord's in miniature'. Later, Frank described how he achieved this:

There was a piece of ground adjoining John's, which was of very little use to the tenant, being almost a morass. I soon came to terms with him and got the tenancy made over to me. During the winter I had fifty navvies draining, levelling, and turfing the ground, every bit of turf was brought ten miles from a common which was being enclosed – and by the spring it was ready for use. It cost me about £1,200 to do it [equivalent to £100,000 today], but as secretary of the University Cricket Club for a quarter of a century I saw what an impetus it gave to the game.[53]

Given Frank was recalling these events nearly 50 years after they happened it is no surprise some of the details are incorrect. The land belonged to Gonville & Caius College and not St John's College, although there is a chance Frank was referring to John as an individual who held the tenancy. The land was understood to be a cherry orchard, possibly linked to the adjacent Covent Garden.[54]

Frank says nothing about where he secured £1,200, which was a huge amount for a 37-year-old tobacconist / professional cricketer. Soon after he opened the ground in 1848, Frank claimed it was 'speculation entirely my own', having 'made my calculations without asking for any other patronage',[55] for example from the town cricket club.

An explanation is provided by Alfred D Taylor who in 1923 reported that:

Tradition has it that the money (Frank) accumulated from his business – he was a grocer[c] and tobacconist – was expended in securing and preparing a cricket ground at Cambridge, known to this day as 'Fenner's', and which was purchased at the express wish, and under the direct patronage, of the Earl of Stamford and Lord Burghley.[56]

If Frank did use his own funds, it is unclear what role or contribution was made by the subsequent patrons, Charles Fitzwilliam and Thomas Townley.[57]

Frank's work extended the students' private ground by about a third[58] as well as improving it overall.

Frank had known Daniel Hayward (the 'father' of the famous cricketing dynasty) since they both played cricket for Chatteris over three years from 1830. Given Daniel now lived at 14 Covent Garden, next door to Frank's planned new ground, and possessed gardening and groundsmanship skills, there is every possibility he helped directly.[59]

Initially the land on which Frank created his ground was leased on a yearly basis from Gonville & Caius College,[60] apparently extended to a 25-year lease as Frank's ground became more established, but that this is not clear.[61]

---

[c] Frank was never a grocer. However, he went into partnership with John Bowles in 1859, who shared his tobacco shop on the market, which only lasted for 18 months.

Reactions to the new ground

'For the most part the Cambridge Town and County Cricket Club's opening general meeting for 1848 appeared to be business as usual, electing officers, optimistically planning a match against Kent and boasting a "delightful momento" to the Club in the shape of Felix's painting. At the foot of the press report, however, sat the following statement:

> A private ground situate at the back of the Town Gaol has been engaged by Mr Fenner, and during the whole winter men have been employed levelling and re-laying to the extent of 6 ½ acres. The ground is now completed, and promises to be one of the best private grounds in the country. The University club has arranged to play all their matches there and the advantages of a well-conducted private ground most people, we think, will be ready to appreciate.[62]

Frank had offered the Town cricket club opportunity to use the new ground for £21 per year (equivalent to £2,500 today), which was less than the average annual cost of using Parker's Piece over each of the previous four years.[63] For payment of this fee, 'every subscriber [member of the Town cricket club] to receive a ticket for gratuitous admission'.[64] Non-members would pay sixpence (or £2 today) for entry to each game.[65]

This prompted the town to hold the first of several general meetings for the subscribers of Town cricket 'to dispose finally of the question ... of playing matches on Fenner's new private ground'.[66] Their response entailed 'considerable discussion, in which the most kind feelings was expressed towards Mr Fenner', including an offer to get up a Benefit match for him, played on his ground.

Yet they rejected Frank's offer, reasoning that:

> The use of a private ground ... ought not to be entertained where there was so splendid and spacious a public ground as Parker's Piece. The amusement and comfort of the few subscribers should not alone be considered, said they, we contribute our money for the general welfare and enjoyment [of] many hundreds who cannot afford to pay to see the game; and what sight more pleasing than the ring of thousands on a fine summer's day, watching the exertions of two elevens, 'cricket for the million' should be the general cry.[67]

Frank was clearly in attendance at this meeting because the newspaper then reports 'Mr Fenner explained that he did not wish to urge the use of the ground by the club; but having been persuaded by the members of the university to establish such a convenience, thought it right to make the offer if the Town and County [Cricket] Club chose to avail themselves of it'.[68]

At this same meeting, characterised by a 'want of energy and support', there was a call for membership subscriptions to be paid up immediately,[69] and a report that Parker's Piece was 'not ... touched well into May',[70] regarding its preparation for cricket.

Whilst the public meetings held were initially supportive of Frank and his ground, a number of anonymous letters soon published in the press, were less so.

One argued if the University had their own ground, they should practice there too, rather than on Parker's Piece, 'the common right of the Piece would then be much improved and of much more use to the inhabitants'.[71]

Another letter,[72] signed 'Argus', claimed Parker's Piece was the envy of surrounding towns.

> Why therefore are all matches to be played in some private field, with a charge for admission? I should have thought that Fenner, our own pet, whose cricketing qualities we all admire, and whose frank and courteous bearing we all respect, would have protested against this selfish scheme'.[73]

Argus also picked up on the 'cricket for the million' slogan, believing:

> The days of exclusiveness are passed, and therefore, when we see everything now done for 'the million', the attempt to establish 'hole and corner' cricket, lest some 'slovenly and unhandsome' person should intrude, is neither characteristic of the noble game, nor, in accordance with the fraternising qualities of the true cricketer'.

A third letter believed 'a house divided against itself cannot stand,' making the very valid point that Cambridge would struggle to sustain two first class sides (a University club and separate Town club), which is why the writer called for another general meeting 'to decide the future of the Town and County Cricket Club which had apparently done nothing further to prepare Parker's Piece or arrange matches well into June'.[74]

The end of Town and Gown collaboration?

With another meeting arranged, Frank felt it necessary to respond in a lengthy letter, to the 'idle tales ... the utter fallacy of much that has been said' and to invite 'the honest expression of legitimate complaint, rather than the looseness which most people are apt to indulge in when descending to anonymous attack'.[75]

Frank believed his new ground was to 'promote cricket and prevent its decay', given the 'many grievous annoyances attending practice on Parker's Piece, the extortions and abuse to which (several gentlemen cricketers of the University) were victims, and 'to make cricket a game that could be followed by all, the sensitive as well as the sturdy and indifferent, without risk of having their feelings offended', referring here also to visiting teams and spectators.

However, for reasons probably connected to 'the business' of the new ground, Frank was sadly in danger of betraying his strongly held commitment to Town and Gown collaboration, when he wrote:

> I did not dream of *thrusting* the private ground upon the notice of parties who might with *apparent* justice, entertain a dislike to it; on the contrary, I did it to promote cricket; and must take it upon myself to say that, in my opinion, the Town and County Club have no more to do with the University Club in such a matter than the University Cricket Club could possibly have with the Marylebone Club [MCC] —and dictations from either to the other would be equally preposterous. The Town and County Club contribute in no way to the University Club, either to its funds or its strength of play; they are perfectly distinct bodies. What, then, can justify dictation? On the other hand, many of the members of the University Club are members of and contribute to the funds of the Town and County Club, besides lending powerful assistance to its playing strength; but have they offered to offend the taste of parties by requiring the Town and County Club matches to be played on their ground? ... I made the ground entirely for and at the suggestion of the University Club, and made my calculations without asking for any other patronage'.[76]

As Willie Sugg quite rightly points out, 'this was a debatable statement' made by Frank.

> During his tenure as secretary of the Town and County Club, Fenner had appeared previously to actively encourage co-operation between the two. Separate clubs they may have been, but certainly not unrelated. This was Fenner in his characteristically bullish letter writing mode and sounding like a businessman defending his pragmatism. Perhaps most significantly Fenner appeared insensitive to the emotions his move had stirred'.[77]

Nevertheless, Frank ended his letter with a rallying call:

> Let the Town and County Club rouse itself—let it shake off that apathy which has been induced by what some of its members look upon as a 'rival establishment.' Let it move independently, seeking no more to cramp my actions as an individual than I shall attempt to control theirs as a body. Then again shall we see cricket; and I shall be just as ready to hail the hard won successes of the Town and County Club, as I have been happy in times past to assist in the achievement of them.

Frank's letter drew another anonymous response, this time from an 'Old Cricketer', who in his letter to the press[78] started by flagging two key issues Frank had chosen to avoid:

> At a time when all persons in Cambridge are disengaged and naturally seek for amusement, the sixpences each non-member would have paid, would have been *rather* a desirable adjunct to the receipts of the *year* for admission.

This was not just the writer flagging the additional funds Frank would take on the gate from non-members, but that secondly the loss of Parker's Piece as a free venue for a significant number of the University's most popular cricket matches would further disengage local people, many of whom would be the town's poorest. This was at a time when the University, in endeavouring to maximise the learning environment for their students, banned or severely curtailed many local amusements, for example in theatres, public houses and local fairs.

'Old Cricketer' went on to ask two questions, firstly 'why Mr Fenner should put himself forward as the self-constituted and uncalled-for champion of the University Club?', and secondly, given 'the most perfect harmony has at all times existed between the University cricketers and the Town and County Club: why then attempt to disturb such perfect concord?'

It appears that Frank did not respond, but nor apparently did anyone from the University.

Unfortunately, the cumulative effect of all these meetings and letters was sadly a growing sense in the town that 'years of hard-won co-operation were being undermined by a traditional mistrust' of the University.[79]

The demise of local cricket

Whilst there were several immediate initiatives to get regular cricket played on Parker's Piece, these were mostly piecemeal. For example, a meeting of town players held at the New Inn resulted in a number of games being played but the sides put out were not as strong as they might have been.[80]

A further general meeting was held by the Town and County Cricket Club where 'it was resolved to continue the [Club] for at least another year, to see what will be the effect of the private ground on the interests of the [Club]'.[81] Frank also resigned as secretary.

The Town and County Club never did re-establish itself successfully. One immediate impact was that local professional cricketers resorted to advertising their individual services in the press, including travelling across the country to secure work, such as in the following example:

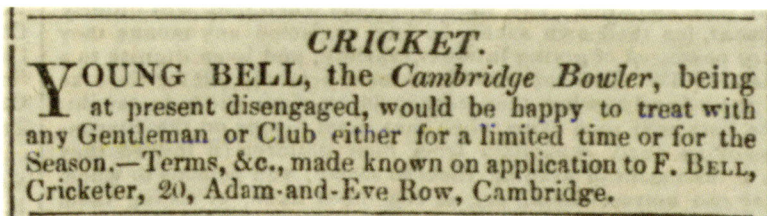

> **CRICKET.**
> YOUNG BELL, the *Cambridge Bowler*, being at present disengaged, would be happy to treat with any Gentleman or Club either for a limited time or for the Season.—Terms, &c., made known on application to F. Bell, Cricketer, 20, Adam-and-Eve Row, Cambridge.

Source: Cambridge Chronicle and Journal Saturday 24 June 1848.

Such an advertisement worked, as the 18-year-old Frederick Bell secured various engagements, leading to him later playing for the United England Eleven, as well as coaching at Eton, and Queen Victoria's sons.[82]

Town cricket's ongoing reliance on Frank Fenner

It would appear that town cricket had about five indifferent years after Frank had opened his private ground demonstrating they could not do without his skills and experience. For example, in April 1855, the local press[83] reported they were constantly being asked 'what is Cambridge doing?', resulting in 'a meeting of those desirous of re-establishing the Town and County Cricket Club'. This included voting in Frank Fenner as secretary.[84]

In 1856 an article in the press reported Frank was on the committee of the Cambridge Britannia Cricket Club (a small local club), and in an adjoining article publishing an invitation to those interested in local cricket to attend a meeting 'for the purpose of reviving matches on Parker's Piece … (and) to send in their names … to Mr. F. Fenner'.[85]

Fenner's Ground only for the University

Before the start of the 1856 season Frank had written a letter,[86] in response to one from London 'inviting local attention to the desirability of Cambridge once more taking its deserved rank in the cricketing world'. In it Frank stated:

> To those who suppose my private ground would interfere with the prospects of a Town and County Club—and some, probably, there are—I will just say, the contrary would be the fact. That ground is *expressly* for the *University*, and therefore is not to be appropriated to the use of other clubs.

In the same letter Frank added:

> The annual match between the University and Town will be played this year on Parker's Piece. Here then will be an opportunity for welding together all the disjointed materials of which Cambridge cricket is composed, which—vigorous as ever—will be found, in combination and discipline, equal to anything its best friends may say of its past, and successful, history. Old associations will be awakened—a spirit of emulation encouraged—and nothing will be required to ensure for it a worthy career but the judicious appliance of means—those wondrous sinews— without which, professions in cricket, as in all else, lead to certain disappointment, and sink to the level of imposing 'shams.' Meetings will shortly be held to test these probabilities, the particulars and success of which will be matter for future notice. I am, Sir, your obedient servant, F.P. FENNER - 6, Market Hill.

Cambridgeshire County Cricket

In response to Frank's letter the press received a reply[87] flagging the success of Surrey County Cricket Club as an example for Town and County cricket in Cambridge to follow.

This was certainly of interest to Frank because together with Henry Perkins (student at Trinity College from 1850 to 1854, later MCC secretary for over 20 years) and H J Adeane of Babraham they established Cambridgeshire County Cricket Club in 1858, which involved a number of meetings at Frank's tobacco shop on Market Hill (chapter 16). This initiative was supported by Robert Carpenter, the England cricketer, who pledged his assistance to such a venture.[88]

Whilst Frank was paid a fitting tribute in 1860 for creating an effective model for organising cricket clubs,[89] the County club did not last long, possibly linked to Frank leaving Cambridge in 1862 / 1863.

Town cricket on Parker's Piece

Frank was initially the Honorary Treasurer for the visit of the 'Eleven of All-England' to play against the 22 Amateurs of Cambridge in 1859 on Parker's Piece.[90] This involved raising £90 to cover expenses, equivalent to £11,000 today.

A match report[91] of the game claimed:

> Cambridge is not only proverbial as the seat of learning, but distinguished as the seat also of cricket; and on Parker's Piece and Fenner's unique and beautiful ground, as fine cricketing has been displayed the world ere saw.

The game on Parker's Piece was encircled by about twenty-five booths and an:

> Excellent and substantial stand … which for sight-seers, was an improvement upon tents, because, from its elevation, the spectators were not annoyed by those peripatetic strollers, or restless mortals, that are continually wandering from place to place, and therefore obscuring the views of more satisfied mortals.

The press also reported after the game:

> Mr. BLAINE, one of the All-England Eleven, rose to propose the next toast … He went to see Fenner's ground that morning, and on asking why the match was not played on there, he was told that it was desired that all might see and profit by it, whereas, if it had been played there every one would have had to pay an admission fee. He must say that he cordially agreed with the Cambridge Cricket Club in that noble purpose of allowing all to read a lesson free of any expense whatever.

Legacy of the Town's commitment to remaining on Parker's Piece

Whilst the stand the town took in not moving to Fenner's damaged their prospects of the county becoming a first-class cricket side, it could be argued that their ongoing commitment to Parker's Piece later provided the best of opportunities for three of the world's greatest cricketers to establish themselves. These were Ranjitsinhji, whose race, probably, and playing style, certainly, kept him out of University cricket until he proved himself on Parker's Piece playing for local teams.

The other two players were Tom Hayward and Sir Jack Hobbs,[92] both local men born very close to Parker's Piece, later to become two of the three best batsmen in the world, alongside W.G. Grace.

What if the Town Cricket Club had moved to Fenner's Ground in 1848?

Willie Sugg believes today:

> The fact that the cricket prowess of Cambridgeshire (County Cricket Club) is now reduced to a very minor footnote in cricket's history whilst Fenner, 'the Pride of Cambridge' is still celebrated for his founding of the Cambridge University cricket ground seems to sum up the Cambridgeshire cricket conundrum. Despite many fine achievements - great matches, teams and players - the main way in which nineteenth century Cambridgeshire cricket has been remembered over the years is as the provider of a cricket ground for a private club. Had the Cambridge Town and County Club committee of 1848 made a decision more in touch with the times by accepting Fenner's offer the Club may well have continued to flourish. With Fenner as secretary, a combination of subscription and gate money, and a promising crop of new players, it would have been hard for it not to. With the addition of players and spectators from the rest of the county with likely additions from the university it might even have become a fully recognised County Club both better financed and organised than the eventual County teams were ever to be. In helping to put Cambridge University Cricket Club, along with its Oxford counterpart, in the anomalous but welcome position of being virtual equals in standing to first-class counties, Cambridgeshire had ironically condemned itself to relative obscurity. This was a sad outcome.[93]

6. OTHER SPORTS AND COMMUNITY ACTIVITIES AT FENNER'S GROUND

Whilst Frank had made it explicitly clear in 1856 that Fenner's Ground was '*expressly* for the *University* [cricket club] and therefore is not to be appropriated to the use of other clubs' he always had plans to use it for other sports and community events. This is no surprise given the length of the University terms meant the majority of students were only resident in Cambridge for about half the year.

In fact, the ground was once named in 1861 in the press as 'Fenner's Cricket and Recreation Ground',[94] with Frank, towards the end of his life, believing that beyond cricket, 'Fenner's Ground has played no unimportant part in Town and Gown life generally'.[95]

Examples of such activities included:

- Downing Street Sunday School treat in 1853
- A Wedding on 29 June 1854, where 'great praise is due to …
  Mr. Fenner for the generous manner in which he not only granted the use of his admirable ground, but also for the way in which it was laid out for the amusement of the day'[96]
- Bat and trap matches, both for the Mutual Improvement Society,[97] and in 1856 as part of a festival on Parker's Piece celebrating the end of the Crimean War, for which Frank was one of the organising secretaries
- A planned sermon by Rev C H Spurgeon in 1857, cancelled because the famous preacher felt it would be too damp
- Promenade concerts by the Cambridge Cornet Society in 1858, 1859 and 1860, with 700 persons attending in 1858,[98] where it appears spectators paid, 'a moderate charge' for entry.

Interestingly whilst many local cricket supporters believed Fenner's, as an enclosed ground charging entry, would not serve the cause of 'cricket for the million', these promenade concerts were advertised in the local press under the banner headline 'music for the million'.[99]

- 'Grand Vocal & Instrumental Al Fresco Concerts and Fete Champetre' on 25th July 1859.[100] Attractions included Madame Geneive performing on the tight rope, the band of the Coldstream Guards, a Grand Ascent in the 'Aurora' balloon, and fireworks.

The advert advised Fenner's Cricket Ground 'will be enclosed on this occasion' with charge for admission starting at 2 shillings (£6 today). This probably meant some sort of temporary fencing was erected to obscure the view from outside.[101]

- Parades, inspections, training and drills for the Cambridgeshire First Rifle Volunteers, otherwise known as 'the Pensioners' from 1859

- Cambridge Temperance Band of Hope tea for children 1860, and

- A 'Monster Fete and Fancy Fair' in July 1860,[102] featuring a military band, the Zeleski Family acrobats, comic singing, a Chinese magician, the Austrian Salamander, or Fire King, and alfresco games. Whilst

By Permission of the Right Worshipful the Vice-Chancellor and under the patronage of Chas. Balls, Esq., Mayor.

GRAND VOCAL & INSTRUMENTAL AL FRESCO CONCERTS,
And **FETE CHAMPETRE,**
FENNER'S CRICKET GROUND,
(Which will be Enclosed on this occasion),
PARKER'S PIECE, CAMBRIDGE,
MONDAY NEXT (AFTERNOON & EVENING),
July 25th, 1859.

Marvellous EVOLUTIONS on the CORDE TENISON, by
THE INFANT CELINE!!
CHARACTERISTIC DANCING BY
LA PETIT ELIZA!
MADAME GENEIVE
Will display her graceful performance upon the
TIGHT ROPE!

By Permission of Colonel Lord FREDERIC PAULET, C.B., the celebrated
Band of the Coldstream Guards
Will attend, and play their most celebrated pieces; Conductor, C. GODFREY, Esq.

Mr. J. E. GODDARD, the celebrated Aeronaut of London, will make a **GRAND ASCENT** in his magnificent
"AURORA" BALLOON.
Wonderful Performance of the
GENEIVE FAMILY!
Mr. FENWICK, of London, Pyrotechnist to the Queen,
Will give a
BRILLIANT DISPLAY of FIREWORKS.
The whole to conclude with MADAME GENEIVE'S
TERRIFIC ASCENT on the **FIERY ROPE!**

With a desire to popularise this Monstre Fête, the Management has determined on the following terms of admission :—Tickets purchased before the 25th, 2s. each for the whole day, and to enable the holder to witness the inflation and partial ascents of the Balloon. After six o'clock, 1s. each. On the day of the Fête, Tickets 2s. 6d. and 1s. 6d each. Tickets to be had at the various Music Warehouses; Mr. Martin's, Sidney-street; and Mr. Fenner's, Market-hill.
N.B.—The Balloon Ascent will take place before the departure of the Trains to neighbouring towns.

Source: Cambridge Independent Press Saturday 23 July 1859.

there was a crowd of 2,000 the event made a loss, with Frank Fenner writing a letter in 1862[103] wondering whether he would receive any payments from Mr Poole who had put on the event, and yet had later filed for bankruptcy.

ATHLETICS

As mentioned earlier, in Frank's likely 'research' as to the ground's viability, he would have been aware of the growing popularity of pedestrianism or athletics featured at enclosed grounds across Britain, many being already used for cricket. As early as 1851 Frank held pedestrian races and demonstrations, soon realising that athletics provided a greater supply of gate money than cricket.[104]

College athletics

Records show that it was in 1855 that some colleges, the first being St Johns and Emmanuel, held their sports (often called 'foot races') on grass tracks, either on their own land, or at Fenner's.[105]

At the Emmanuel College's sports Thomas Bury was the first person in the world ever to run 10 seconds for 100 yards (just over 90 metres) on 29 November 1855. Thomas had also been a Cricket Blue that same year.[106]

In addition to the 100 yards, there was the 200 yards, 440 yards, 880 yards and mile races, 200 yards hurdles (using real sheep hurdles stuck in the ground), high jump, standing high jump, long jump, standing long jump, 15 or 16 hops, putting the stone (shot, 14lbs), throwing the cricket ball, sack race and trouser race (believed to involve two runners, one leg each in the same shared pair of trousers).

According to Chris Thorne[107] the driving force for inter College competition was probably John Russell Jackson of St. Johns (student from 1853 to 1857) given he 'induced athletes from the various Colleges to gather on Fenner's ground, to try their speed at various competitions'. These were initially within-College affairs, but Jackson soon realised that inter-College events would draw better competition. He was then responsible for initiating the first 'University foot races', held on 16, 17 and 18 March 1857.

He was supported by Anthony Wilkinson (St. Johns 1854–59) and Robert Barclay (Trinity 1855–59). In sharing the results of the races, the University reported[108] 'Mr Fenner acted as judge on the occasion and gave universal satisfaction'.

At the 1861 University Foot Races 'Fenner's ground was thronged and amongst the spectators we noticed His Royal Highness the Prince of Wales'. The events included 2 miles, 100 yards, hurdles, throwing the cricket ball, and running high jump.

> 'So much for the athletic part of the sports. Now succeeded the comic part, namely, running in sacks. For this race there were twelve entries. Immense excitement was caused by these races and great was the downfall of many a competitor too eager for sudden gains.... This ended the University sports for 1861.... Mr Fenner very ably, and much to the gratification of everyone, officiated as referee'.[109]

Oldest athletics club in the world?

Establishing these first University foot races is considered the beginnings of the Cambridge University Athletic Club (CUAC), believed to be the world's oldest athletics club,[110] a claim matched by the athletics club at Oxford University.[111]

Varsity matches

The first Oxford v Cambridge varsity athletics match took place in Oxford in 1864, with the second taking place the following year at Fenner's Ground, the only time Cambridge has hosted the match (except during the 1939–45 WW2 period) until the advent of the Wilberforce Road track in 1995.

This was despite Cambridge wanting to host the 1867 varsity athletics match at Fenner's, but apparently being prevented from doing so by 'heads of houses and tutors' (the University and College authorities),[112] given 'suspicions about gambling and also damage done to railway carriages by jubilant Cambridge supporters returning' from the first Cambridge and Oxford Games in Oxford.

> The University authorities decided that Varsity matches should no longer be held at the home Universities, but banished to London, where sin was sufficiently widespread, that a little more would not be noticed.[113]

Frank's wide ranging role

Frank Fenner contributed more than just providing a venue for these athletic events. For example, as a promoter and innovator his achievements ranged from putting on demonstration athletic events as early as 1851,[114] (four years before the first university colleges held their own athletic events there), to travelling to America to book Deerfoot (the Seneca Native American) to run at Fenner's in 1861, to laying down a cinder track at Fenner's in 1866 / 1867: 'the enterprising Fenner reckoned he could make more money by adding a cinder path for running'.[115]

In addition, he promoted these athletic events in his shop on Market Hill, where he also took entry fees both from spectators (subscribers) and athletes.

He also hosted and probably led planning meetings, for example in 1859 a notice was posted in the press that 'there will be a meeting of the gentlemen interested in these races at Mr. Fenner's, on Monday evening next, for the purpose of choosing a committee and making other arrangements'.[116]

Frank was often listed as the starter of races, and sometimes the referee 'much to the gratification of everyone',[117] and as host for the visit of dignitaries, such as HRH Prince of Wales who visited Fenner's twice in 1861 for the University foot races, and later, the appearance of Deerfoot, a Seneca Indian from the USA.

Deerfoot

Late in Frank's life he spoke to a reporter about his visit to the USA in about 1860 to meet with Deerfoot and invite him over to run at Fenner's Ground. He recalled:

> That visit to the States and Niagara, and laughing over the fears which beset him when he was deserted by his car-driver ['car' meaning: 2-wheeled wagon] close by a camp of hostile Indians during a terrible night storm.[117]

It is not known who or what had prompted Frank to go, but perhaps the three Cambridge cricketers who visited the USA on the England cricket team's first tour abroad in 1859, might have had an impact?[118]

Planning for Deerfoot's visit to Cambridge on 4 Dec 1861

The excitement of Deerfoot's visit prompted the creation of a committee including the Rev Leslie Stephen (Trinity Hall) and two other representatives from the University, and others from the town too.[119]

The press reported:

> The ground was laid out in the best possible manner, so that every one of the thousands expected to honour the scene with their presence could enjoy an uninterrupted view of the entire race. A spacious covered stand was erected for the especial use of the ladies. The course, which was 440 yards round, had been *accurately measured*, and flagged out by the members of the committees and it, although heavy for running on, is one of the finest bits of turf in the kingdom, and does Mr. Fenner great credit for the perfection to which he has brought it.'[120]

Additionally, it was also reported that:

> Shortly after two o'clock, his Royal Highness the Prince of Wales arrived on the ground ... joined by ... upwards of eight thousand ... comprised of the nobility and gentry of the town and county, heads of colleges, proctors, and upwards of two thousand of the 'fair sex' ... as well as famous jockeys from Newmarket, and Jem Mace,[d] later the heavyweight boxing champion of the world.

If this estimate of the crowd is correct Frank would have taken £2,000 on the gate, equivalent to £24,000 today. To the press's credit they also noted 'the efficient manner in which W. Price, R. Lewis, and W. Richards discharged their duties at the different entrance-gates'.[121]

---

[d] Jem Mace (1831 to 1910), heavyweight boxing champion of the world in 1870 served his apprenticeship with Nat Langham (based at the Ram Inn, chapter 5). Jem boxed with the 8th Marquess of Queensberry, whose son (the 9th Marquess) is credited with sponsoring the Queensberry Rules, which Jem actively promoted using exhibitions which helped to pave the way for the worldwide acceptance of gloved boxing.

Deerfoot meets HRH at Fenner's

In his own words Frank recalled:

> Twas there that the Prince of Wales and suite saw Deerfoot. When in the States I had visited Deerfoot's tribe, and he was delighted, when in England, to meet someone who was acquainted with his people. When I introduced him to the Prince, who affably chatted with him and shook him by the hand, his enthusiasm knew no bounds.[122]

Whilst there were a range of other events it was the six-mile race that attracted most attention, offering the winner 'a purse of gold, subscribed by the inhabitants of the vicinity, with £10 (£1,200 today) for the second man, £5 for the third, and £1 for the fourth'.

There were five participants from Newcastle, Middlesborough, Norwich, London and the USA started by Frank Fenner,[123] who had to recall the competitors, after a false start. Deerfoot ran in 'his fantastic skirt, head dress, and eagle's feather' and duly won by about four yards.

In addition to the official prizes 'His Royal Highness presented Deerfoot with a purse containing two Bank notes and to each of the others a golden token of his approbation, and having again graciously extended his hand to Deerfoot, left the ground'.[124]

Impact of Deerfoot's visit to Cambridge

The visit of Deerfoot to Cambridge, including his attending dinner at Trinity College, elicited two very different responses.

> In the evening, he [Deerfoot] dined with the Fellows of Trinity College. This honour—due to his birth rather than to his profession—will be less calculated to astonish the public, when it is borne in mind that the races were attended by Masters of Colleges, Professors of Divinity, and other distinguished dignitaries, who do not shrink from countenancing, by their presence, the revival of pedestrian and other athletic amusements in the University.[125]

By complete contrast the Cambridge Chronicle and Journal (the local paper much more aligned to the University) considered this a 'monstrous and absurd offence against all the laws of decency and good taste'.[126] For more on the Trinity College Fellow who invited him, see chapter 9.

In addition to the organising committee for the visit of Deerfoot being a mix of Town and Gown, so too were the other races that preceded the six-mile race won by Deerfoot.

There were also other 'open' athletic events featured at Fenner's Ground, for example the Cambridge Amateur Foot Races on 13 September 1861, apart from the one hundred yards, and quarter of a mile races, only 'open to Members of Rifle Corps, in full marching order only'.

The one-mile race for the 'The Cambridge Plate', was 'open to all comers', presumably meaning professional runners.

Layout of Fenner's ground for athletics

Whilst Frank had created a cricket ground it also evolved into a venue for all the athletics events.

First, a wooden sports pavilion was built in 1856, with water laid on in 1861. It was used by both the University cricket and athletic clubs.

Cambridge Amateur Foot Races

WILL be held on FENNER'S GROUND, Cambridge, on FRIDAY, September the 13th, 1861.

Committee :—

Captain W. PREST.   Mr. F. P. FENNER.
Mr. DENNIS ADAMS.   Mr. A. D. CLAYDON.
Mr. F. GRAIN.   Mr. F. R. HALL.
Mr. P. HUDSON.   M. P. BRALES, Junr.

Judge : Captain PREST; *Starter :* Mr. F. P. FENNER; *Secretary :* Mr. J. E. McDONALD.

Programme :—
100 Yards, First Heat.
Long Jump, Standing.
Hurdle Race, 200 yards, over 10 flights of Hurdles.
Quarter of a Mile Race.
High Jump, Running.
Quarter of a Mile Race, (open to Members of Rifle Corps, in full marching order only.)
Half a Mile Race.
"The Rifle Corps Plate," Quarter of a Mile, (open to Members of Rifle Corps only.)
100 Yards, remaining Heats.
Long Jump, Running.
Hurdle Race, 100 Yards, over 5 flights of Hurdles.
"The Cambridge Plate," One Mile. (open to all comers.)
100 Yards, (for Members of Rifle Corps only.)
High Jump, Standing.
Walking Race, One Mile.
Throwing the Cricket Ball.
Putting the Weight.   Sack Race.
The Start for the First Race at 2·30 p.m. precisely.
Entrance Fee :—One Shilling for each race entered for. Admission to the Ground, Non-Subscribers, 6d. each.

Source: Cambridge Independent Press 7 Sept 1861.

The Pavilion on Fenner's Ground from 1856 to 1877

Source: W.J. Ford (1902). The Cambridge University Cricket Club. William Blackwood and Sons, page 10.

The pavilion featured in the photo on the previous page does look the same as that featured in Roget's cartoon of cricket on Fenner's dated 1859 (next), however the cartoon also shows the high wall of the Borough Gaol located behind it. This implies the high gaol wall was built between 1856 and 1859. The Borough Gaol was built in 1829 next to Parker's Piece, later pulled down in 1878.

J.L. Roget's cartoon showing the calm of cricket on Fenner's Cricket Ground in 1859

Source: J.L. Roget (1859). A Cambridge scrap book, containing, in a pictorial form, a report on the manners [&c.], by a special commissioner appointed by himself [JL Roget]. University of Oxford.

Whilst the building of this pavilion was apparently 'masterminded by the three "treasurers" of the Cambridge University Cricket Club (Joe McCormick, Alfred Du Cane and Robert Fitzgerald, later the first secretary of the MCC)',[127] the debt of £433 was covered by takings at the gate, which implies that Frank was also directly involved.

Interestingly, Frank took more takings on the gate from athletics (then 'played' through the winter months), than cricket, which is why the pavilion was made available to all.

Running track

Frank would have been aware of one of the first purpose-built tracks around Lord's Cricket Ground in 1837, made of hard gravel, designed for two-man races,[128] which is why he had a track put down at Fenner's, made from cinder or black ash in 1866/1867.

This was 586 yards long to ensure it was located outside the boundary of the cricket pitch. Later the track was extended so that one complete circuit, was one-third of a mile long.[129]

How this was funded is unclear, however whilst Frank had left Cambridge he still held the lease on the ground, so presumably was still benefitting from takings on the gate / charging for use of his ground. Perhaps because of what this income might have been, and that 'the University' were beginning to understand that 'sports' were establishing a credibility, that Frank was given notice in Christmas 1867 to 'quit the land' by Gonville & Caius College, who held the freehold.[130]

Cambridge University athletics matches continued to be held at Fenner's until 1959 when the new track was opened on Milton Road. However, it was not until 1967 that the cinder track on Fenner's was done away with.[131] To understand the impact of the cinder track on Fenner's, look at the image on the front cover of this book.

TENNIS

It is not known when lawn tennis was first played at Fenner's Ground. However, because the game was only invented in the 1870s, Frank would not have been involved in welcoming the sport there. Nevertheless, tennis at Fenner's has an exceptional history.

Cambridge University Lawn Tennis Club (CULTC), is considered one of the oldest lawn tennis clubs in the world, founded in 1881,[132] seven years before the Lawn Tennis Association (LTA).

28 Grand Slam titles

When tennis was an amateur sport, five Grand Slam winners had been students at Cambridge University amassing 28 Grand Slam titles. Ten of these titles were won by the Doherty brothers, Reginald and Laurie (Trinity Hall). Other title winners were Anthony Wilding (Trinity College), Raymond Tuckey (Queens' College) and Max Woosnam (Trinity College), probably Cambridge University's greatest ever all-round sportsman.

Inventor of the tie-break

James Henry Van Alen II, an American, had been a student at Christ's College, graduating in 1924, having won his Blue for Lawn Tennis. His greatest legacy was as the inventor of the tie-break in tennis in 1954.[133]

7. CRICKET AT FENNER'S

As an entrepreneur Frank looked to community events and athletics to provide valuable income (with tennis at Fenner's coming after he had left Cambridge). Still, his first love was cricket.

Having opened the ground in 1848 hoping it might serve both Town and Gown cricket, it was in 1856 that he finally closed the door on this possibility, when he declared the ground 'is expressly for the University, and therefore is not to be appropriated to the use of other clubs'.[134]

This section therefore describes the early cricket games played on Fenner's ground, and its operation, and how, following the fallout between Frank and the University Cricket Club, it went on to achieve extraordinary success.

Early cricket matches

There were a range of matches played including past versus present students, such as in 1856 when a 'private marquee for the ladies' was provided, and, for students and staff remaining in Cambridge over the summer months playing for the Long Vacation Club against local teams such as Royston, as in 1857.

In addition, an 'Odd Match' as described by the local press 'was played on Fenner's Ground by members of the University, eleven playing with bats and eleven with sticks: the game concluded in one innings, the bats proving victors, they having scored upwards of 130, while the "poor sticks" could only manage about 80'.[135]

First college servants cricket match

Following the creation of the 'Cricket and Boating Club for College Servants' in August 1856 at the Castle Hotel (chapter 19), the St John's College Servants played their first game, against the Gentlemen of the College the following summer. This included 'a good substantial dinner … served in the Pavilion, to which all sat down and partook of with a zest that cricket can only give.'[136]

Although the first Cambridge College Servants versus Oxford College Servants varsity cricket match had taken place in 1850 at Fenner's Ground, it was not until 1863 that the next match was played.[137]

Frank scores 176 not out

Whilst Frank's highest score in first class games was only 80, he nevertheless would have greatly enjoyed scoring 176 runs on his own ground over two days in 1850, Frank being aged 39.

> A single wicket match – a curiosity in its way – came off on Fenner's Ground on Tuesday and Wednesday last, between the proprietor (Mr F.P. Fenner) and Mr Thomas Whittaker, the latter being allowed ten innings to the former's two. The match (which was for a stake) was got up in a spurt, and commenced immediately, Mr Whittaker taking the bat to receive his first five innings. Fenner commenced bowling at a fearful pace, and speedily floored his adversary, whose five innings shewed a total of two runs. Fenner then took the bat, and at the close of the evening's play had scored 50 runs. The game was resumed on Wednesday

afternoon, Fenner taking the bat and remaining at the wicket until the stumps were again drawn for the evening, when his score stood 176 runs, not out. Whittaker, who had throughout fagged very determinedly, now resigned the contest, evidently content with the gruelling, the pay and the experiment.[138]

Frank's last first-class match took place over two days in May 1856 when he was 45 years old, playing for the Town against the University on his ground. Frank made 5 and 4 runs in the 1st and 2nd innings, took one catch and does not appear to have bowled.

This must have been a difficult match for him to play in, not just because it was his last, but because of his failure to use his ground to broker a closer relationship between Town and Gown, following his success in bringing both sides together in the 1830s and 1840s.

High profile games, but never the varsity match

In 1854 the University (with two Cambridge Town bowlers, Buttress and Reynolds) played against the United All-England eleven at Fenner's Ground over three days in June.

'The attendance was good, a great number of the admirers of the manly game having arrived by rail'. However the England team run out winners, by 8 wickets. The local press finished their report by stating 'however extraordinary it may appear, it was generally remarked that Fenner's Ground was too good for cricket'.[139] This was a compliment after Fenner's Ground took a few years to bed down including in 1850 when the Cambridge University captain, William Deacon, certified 'the ground was pretty rough, for I was knocked down senseless by a ball in the eye from "young" Lillywhite.[140]

This may have been the reason why Oxford did not want to play early varsity matches at Fenner's, despite Frank's claim one could 'put a stump where you will, and where you will, measure twenty-two yards, and you can play a game'. [141]

As Fenner's ground improved, it reduced Cambridge's chance of hosting, and winning the Varsity match:

> The Oxford grounds had the reputation of being inferior both to Parker's Piece and to Fenner's, as far as the smoothness of the wickets provided were concerned. Indeed in comparatively late times, the early 'Seventies [1870s], when Lord's was regarded as a rough and difficult ground, it was considered that the Oxford men were much more at home when they appeared there than were the Cantabs [Cambridge University players]. It is certain that many famous scorers at Fenner's failed woefully on the hardened clay of the St John's Wood club [Lord's Cricket Ground].[142]

So, what might be the reasons why Fenner's Ground became 'too good for cricket'?

The running of Fenner's

Following the creation of the ground by Frank Fenner, supported probably by Daniel Hayward (Senior) in 1848, there were only four groundsmen spanning the next 130 years.

The first, Tom Parmenter, was succeeded by Walter Watts in 1861 who served for 47 years before handing over to Daniel Martin Hayward in 1908, then Cyril Coote in 1936 who retired 44 years later.

Over the years all these individuals were far more than groundsmen. For example, Cyril Coote's role was viewed as the 'Custodian of Fenner's … becoming in the eyes of most visitors, suppliers and spectators the normal spokesman for the club'. In addition, Cyril was coach on the back of his own experience of playing and captaining Cambridgeshire, and 'observing and analysing the methods of the top-class batsmen and bowlers who visited Fenner's'. Cyril also had 'an avuncular rôle, smoothing over tensions within the group of regular players'.[143]

Those who benefitted from Cyril's expertise included Mike Brearley (later captain of England) and Majid Khan (later captain of Pakistan), who described Cyril as a 'great man'.

With the majority of students only staying for three to four years at the University it is no surprise the success of University cricket relied heavily on this custodian role, held not just by Cyril Coote, but by all his predecessors going right back to Fenner. In addition, back in Frank's day, organising sport was entirely the responsibility of the students (as it was in the public schools) rather than any of the permanent staff at the University. This in many ways validates Frank's claim he was secretary to the University Cricket Club for a period of 25 years.[144]

Given the importance of the role, listed next are the life stories of both Walter Watts and Daniel Martin Hayward, who are also featured in the Anchor Cricket Team photo of 1892 in chapter 20.

Walter Watts

Walter was born in 1827 in Wimpole (8 miles or 13km southwest from Cambridge) to Robert, a glazier and plumber, and Ann. When Walter was a child they moved to Cambridge; by the 1851 census Walter was living on East Road and described himself as a master baker, and in 1852 he married Louisa Sandfield. He became a first-class cricketer by 1866 playing for the Cambridge

Town Club, having already started as the Custodian of Fenner's Cricket Ground in 1861, only retiring at the age of 81, after 47 years, when his wife Louisa died.

He is buried at the nearby Mill Road Cemetery, with his wife and their son Arthur, who died in 1875 aged 11 years, 'when the family were living at the university cricket ground'.[145]

Daniel Martin Hayward

Daniel was born in 1865 in Cambridge growing up at the Prince Regent pub on Regent Street.

His working life was primarily as a groundsman and cricket coach, but also included work as an athletic outfitter assistant.[146] Whilst he represented Cambridgeshire by playing 65 matches, he was not as talented as his brother Tom.[147]

Daniel was the curator of Parker's Piece from 1890, then groundsman and cricket coach at Corpus Christi, which coincided with him coaching Ranjitsinhji. From 1908 he became groundsman at Fenner's as well as being the coach for the University Cricket Club, which overlapped with his (much more famous) brother Tom being cricket coach at Oxford University.

Daniel Martin Hayward - 1931
Source: Caricature by Matt in Sunday Graphic 14 June 1931.
Cambridgeshire Collection, Cambridge Central Library.

Daniel retired from the Fenner's job in 1936 at the age of seventy. He was the last survivor of his generation of the Haywards, living on to 1953, surviving Tom by 14 years, born a Victorian and dying an Elizabethan.[148]

Daniel married Pollie Dent in 1901, and together they had two children, Hilda, and another child who died as an infant. Daniel died, aged 87 years old and is buried together with his wife in Mill Road Cemetery.

Despite excellent ground staff, there were unsurprisingly some operational challenges in the early days of Fenner's.

Early cricket professionals take 'French leave'

Henry Plowden (student at Trinity College from 1859) won four Cricket Blues and was captain of the University in 1862 and 1863. He reported:

> Some trouble with the Cambridgeshire professionals ... Hayward, Buttress, Tarrant, and Carpenter who were all engaged on [Fenner's] ground having on one occasion taken what is generally known as 'French leave' [taking leave without permission], and not being re-engaged in consequence. It was even said that they threatened to transfer their services to Oxford when their pay for the time of absence was stopped. Their value, however, to Cambridge cricket had been great, though they were an expensive luxury and were often absent –on leave – to fulfil first-class engagements elsewhere. Two finer batsmen than Hayward and Carpenter – in different styles – and two finer bowlers than Tarrant and Buttress – in different styles – it would have been hard to find.[149]

Bowling machine accident

Arthur Trollope, a student at St John's College, and University Cricket player from 1854 did not win his cricket Blue 'owing to a severe injury received from a catapult bowling-machine',[150] at Fenner's Ground:

> He got the lever back to the utmost point of the tension, when, through some inadvertency, it sprung up, and the end of it, which is covered with brass, hit him on the cheek. The effect of the blow was so severe, that his cheek was cut completely through.[151]

Ball collectors fined

Frank employed ball collectors to retrieve cricket balls hit onto the neighbouring properties next to his ground. However:

> John King and Henry Howes were charged with trespassing on land on the Hills-Road, belonging to Mr. Sayle, doing damage to the amount of 1s. They were looking after a cricket ball..... Mr. Sayle refused to throw any of the balls back, which is why, apparently, he had 'as many as nine cricket balls, worth at least £3'. Whilst Frank reported to the Bench the two defendants were in his service, they were 'fined 1s. each [worth £3 today], and expenses.....which Mr. Fenner paid for them'.[152]

As described earlier, Fenner's Ground had its first pavilion in 1856. However, 'the first tremor of what was to prove a great quake occurred in 1871 when "owing to the dilapidated state of the old pavilion and its smallness," it was proposed to build a new one....deferred.....till a long lease of the ground could be obtained from Caius College'.[153]

This was secured in 1873, resulting in the new pavilion being built at a cost of £3,780 and 9 shillings[154] (following an estimated cost of £1,500), thanks mostly to the letter-writing efforts of Rev Arthur Ward (chapter 5).[155]

Cambridge University Cricket Club pavilion (left of photo), **with Catholic Church spire behind Fenner's - view from Hughes Hall**
SOURCE: Peter May (1956). Peter May's Book of Cricket. Cassell and Co Ltd. Page 6.

Fenner and 'the first tremor of...a great quake'

For a range of possible reasons (explored later in chapter 23) Frank left Cambridge in the early 1860s, whilst continuing to hold the lease on Fenner's ground. This understandably led to problems, as both University cricket and athletics grew in popularity and status.

The first evidence we have is that 'Fenner was given notice to quit the land at Christmas 1867',[156] no doubt because he was behind on paying the rent. According to Montague Haslam Stow (captain, University Cricket Club) he reported in 1868 'on entering office ... we were confronted by a claim from Caius College for heavy arrears of rent for Fenner's (and a threat of ejection) which we had difficulty in satisfying'.[157] Presumably Frank paid up because he continued to hold the lease until 1873.

Following complaints in 1871 about 'the dilapidated state of the old pavilion and its smallness', in 1873, when the new pavilion was being constructed:

> Mr Ward requested Fenner to remove part of his property which the University Cricket Club declined to take over, the said property consisting of a bell, some quoits, trap-bats, targets, and two casks! For these Fenner, who seems to have been a little grasping, had lodged a claim.[158]

Not 'Fenner's' anymore

In 1873 the Cricket Club stipulated that 'Fenner's' be referred to as '"The Cambridge University Cricket Ground"', but according to W.J. Ford, author of the Cambridge University Cricket Club published in 1902, 'the new name never caught on, notwithstanding Mr Ward's strenuous efforts to make it popular, and it is sad to be compelled to record that as lately as 1900 the captain of the (CUCC) XI still alludes to the ground as 'Fenner's".[159]

Lastly, between 1886 and 1889. it was recorded in the minutes of the University Cricket Club that 'the veteran Fenner [he was 75 years old now], being in financial trouble at Bath, received a *douceur* of £10'[160] [worth £800 today, and defined in the dictionary as 'a gift or payment to enhance or 'sweeten' a deal'].

Multiple sports grounds

As Fenner's became established, the colleges of the University, and others appear to have followed its example. According to the Cambridge Independent Press of 1868 'formerly Cambridge possessed but one ground, and now the town can boast of six, namely, Parker's Piece, Fenner's, Trinity, St. John's, Jesus, and Corpus; and rumour says that a field is about to be prepared for Clare College. It will thus be seen that interest in the game is only divided'.[161] John Graham Chambers appears to have been inspired by the success of Fenner's Ground to establish a dedicated facility for the newly-formed Amateur Athletic Club (AAC) he had co-founded.

AFTER FENNER – THE RISE AND RISE OF UNIVERSITY CRICKET

Whilst the University Cricket Club had taken over the lease from Fenner they needed to purchase the freehold in 1892, to avoid the land being built on, as described in 'The Truth' published on 5 May 1892:

> It is proposed at Cambridge that the University Clubs shall purchase Fenner's famous cricket-ground, which is one of the best in England. This ground belongs to Caius, and the authorities of that College are willing to sell it for £12,000. it is tolerably certain that unless the Clubs can carry out the purchase, Fenner's will in a few years be devoted to building purposes. It will be necessary to raise a fund of at least £5,000 in order to buy the ground, and it may be hoped on all accounts that the attempt will be successful.[162]

Once achieved the University Cricket Club went from strength to strength. Others have written extensively about such success, so this section only refers to a suggested best XI, a few fun / interesting anecdotes, and the celebrations to mark the 150th anniversary of the founding of Fenner's.

21 test captains

Over the 200 years Cambridge University Cricket Club has been in existence it has produced 21 Test captains, including Gerry Alexander (West Indies), Deryck Murray (West Indies) and Majid Khan (Pakistan) and at least 62 other Test players.

A Cambridge University Best Cricket XI

It is often the task of sporting history books to share a 'best ever' team, so, thanks to Giles Phillips,[163] here is his Cambridge University XI given their impact and achievement at Cambridge, rather than what they went on to do. They are listed in batting order, the date they arrived in Cambridge and their college.

1. Majid Khan (1969 –Emmanuel College).

2. David Sheppard (1947 – Trinity Hall, then Ridley Hall Theological College).

3. Peter May (1949 – Pembroke College).

4. Hubert Ashton (1919 – Trinity College).

5. Kumor Shri Duleepsinhji (1924 – Clare College).

6. Stanley Jackson (Captain) (1889 – Trinity College).

7. Allan Steel (1878 – Trinity Hall).

8. Sammy Woods (1888 – Jesus College).

9. Gregor MacGregor (W/K) (1887 – Jesus College).

10. Ken Farnes (1929 – Pembroke College).

11. Charles Marriott (1919 – Peterhouse).

Best XIs always prompt alternative suggestions, and given the focus of the current book, especially on the relationship between Town and Gown, Ranjitsinijhi would certainly be included. Initially not given a chance by the University, Ranji proved himself by playing local cricket.

Here are some other University cricket highlights.

*   1870 was probably the most famous University varsity match, finished by Frank Cobden's hat-trick with the last three balls of the match resulting in a two-run victory.

*   The 1878 team was regarded as Cambridge's best ever, winning all their matches, the side featuring the brilliant all-rounder Allan Steel, and Ivo Bligh, both of Ashes fame.

*   The defeat of the all-powerful Australians in 1882.

- In 1890, Cambridge scored 703 for 9 declared against Sussex, still the University's top score.

- In 1896, the students chased 507 to win in the fourth innings against the MCC, still a world record.

- Duleepsinhji scored 254 not out against Middlesex in 1927, still a Cambridge record.[164]

- Donald Bradman the best-ever batsman scored 0 playing for the Australians against the University in 1934, out clean bowled, fourth ball by a slow leg-break from J.G.W. Davies of St John's.[165]

150th anniversary game

To celebrate 150 years since Frank Fenner opened Fenner's Ground, a match was played between the University and Fenner's XI on 13 June 1998, and a further one-day match the next day, against the MCC.

The Fenner's XI was brought together by Frank Fenner (another Frank), being made up of players he managed when in charge of cricket at Millfield School, and others he had invited, such as Derek Randall, Nick Cook, David Capel and Derek Pringle. Taking the field, and down to bat at number 11 was Nigel Fenner, the author, being the son of Frank Fenner. Unfortunately rain badly affected the game.

[1] WJ Ford (1902). The Cambridge University Cricket Club. William Blackwood and Sons. Page 3.

[2] F.P. Fenner (July and Sept 1893). Cricket jottings. Article 5 of 6 published in Bath Chronicle.

[3] F.P. Fenner (July and Sept 1893). Cricket jottings. Article 5 of 6 published in Bath Chronicle.

[4] Personal communication from Willie Sugg. 'This match was played on 18 May 1827. The Cambridge Independent Press (19 May) called it the return of a match played the day before at the University Ground. Scores and Biographies give the venue of both matches as Parker's Piece, which certainly appears wrong for the first match. The Bury & Norwich Post (23 May) called it 'a second match'. Whilst one would expect the return to have been played at Bury, this is not referred to. It seems most likely to me that it was played, like the first, on the University Ground'.

[5] Fuller Pilch entry at https://www.espncricinfo.com/

[6] F.P. Fenner (July and Sept 1893). Cricket jottings. Article 5 of 6 published in Bath Chronicle.

[7] Willie Sugg (2009). Fenner's Men. Cambridgeshire Cricket 1822-1848. Part 3 of A Tradition Unshared. Real Work Publishing. Page 40.

[8] Cambridge Independent Press 2 May 1868. Page 8.

[9] Willie Sugg. 1821 – The CU conforms to type. New Writings on website https://www.cambscrickethistory.co.uk/

[10] Cambridge Chronicle, 11 Feb 1831 in Willie Sugg (2009). Fenner's Men. Cambridgeshire Cricket 1822-1848. Part 3 of A Tradition Unshared. Real Work Publishing. Page 39.

[11] Henry Payne Stokes (1915). Outside the Barnwell Gate. Printed for the Cambridge Antiquarian Society. Pages 44 and 45.

[12] Willie Sugg (2009). Fenner's Men. Cambridgeshire Cricket 1822-1848. Part 3 of A Tradition Unshared. Real Work Publishing. Pages 46 and 47.

[13] Cambridge Weekly News 20 May 1998. Mike Petty's Scrapbook. Page 6.

[14] W.J. Ford (1902). The Cambridge University Cricket Club. William Blackwood and Sons. Page 13.

[15] Cambridge Chronicle and Journal. 7 May 1842 Page 2.

[16] W.J. Ford (1902). The Cambridge University Cricket Club. William Blackwood and Sons. Pages 6 and 7.

[17] Sketch. A veteran cricketer. 13 Sept 1893. Page 361.

[18] K.S. Ranjitsinhji (1897 - 4th ed). The Jubilee Book of Cricket. William Blackwood and Sons. Page 343.

[19] W.J. Ford (1902). The Cambridge University Cricket Club. William Blackwood and Sons. Pages 6 and 7.

[20] Frank Fenner's letter to Cambridge Chronicle and Journal Saturday 3 June 1848.

[21] Cambridge University Cricket Club website: http://cucc.net/index.php/cucc-captains/

[22] Willie Sugg. 1821 – the CU conforms to type. New writings on WS website: https://www.cambscrickethistory.co.uk/

[23] James Pycroft (1886) 'Oxford Memories' in The Middle Ages of Cricket edited by John Arlott. Page 184.

[24] K.S. Ranjitsinhji (1897 - 4th ed). The Jubilee Book of Cricket. William Blackwood and Sons. Page 316.

[25] Personal email from Derek Pringle June 2020.

[26] The Borough Gaol was built in 1829 next to Parker's Piece, later pulled down in 1878. The County Gaol was located on Castle Hill.

[27] Willie Sugg (2009). Fenner's Men. Cambridgeshire Cricket 1822-1848. Part 3 of A Tradition Unshared. Real Work Publishing. Page 43.

[28] The Era 18 April 1847. Also personal email from Willie Sugg 2 March 2021.

[29] Willie Sugg (2009). Fenner's Men. Cambridgeshire Cricket 1822-1848. Part 3 of A Tradition Unshared. Real Work Publishing. Page 43.

[30] Willie Sugg (2009). Fenner's Men. Page 43.

[31] Willie Sugg (2009). Fenner's Men. Page 46.

[32] Sketch. A veteran cricketer. 13 Sept 1893. Page 361.

[33] Willie Sugg (2009). Fenner's Men. Page 47.

[34] Cambridge General Advertiser 12 Feb 1840.

[35] Cricket magazine 1896 page 188 in Willie Sugg (2009). Fenner's Men. Cambridgeshire Cricket 1822-1848. Part 3 of A Tradition Unshared. Real Work Publishing. Page 54.

[36] Willie Sugg (2009). Fenner's Men. Cambridgeshire Cricket 1822-1848. Part 3 of A Tradition Unshared. Real Work Publishing. Page 46.

[37] Willie Sugg (2009). Fenner's Men. Page 54.

[38] Willie Sugg '1848 – Fenner's ground opens' New writings on WS website https://www.cambscrickethistory.co.uk/

[39] Frank Fenner's letter to Cambridge Chronicle and Journal Saturday 3 June 1848.

[40] Willie Sugg '1848 - Fenner's Ground opens'. New writings on WS website https://www.cambscrickethistory.co.uk/

[41] Views expressed at the first general meeting of the Town and County Cricket Club for the 1848 season – from 'Fenner's ground opens' on Willie Sugg's website https://www.cambscrickethistory.co.uk/

[42] Frank Fenner letter dated 1st June and published in the Cambridge Chronicle and Journal 3 June 1848.

[43] Dennis Brailsford (2014). Sport, Time and Society: The British at Play. Routledge Library Editions. Page 61.

[44] Derek Birley (1993). Sport and the making of Britain. Manchester University Press. Page 83.

[45] William Clarke, the father of Trent Bridge article on Trent Bridge website: https://www.trentbridge.co.uk/

[46] Keith and Jennifer Booth (2018). The Haywards. The biography of a cricket dynasty. Chequered Flag Publishing. Page 262.

[47] Robert M. Lewis (Spring 2008). Wild American Savages and the Civilized English: Catlin's Indian Gallery and the Shows of London. European Journal of American Studies. Paragraph 40.

[48] Dennis Brailsford (2014). Sport, Time and Society: The British at Play. Routledge Library Editions. Pages 64 and 65.

[49] F.P. Fenner (July and Sept 1893). Cricket jottings. Article 1 of 6 articles published in Bath Chronicle.

50 The coming of the railway article on Creating my Cambridge / History Works website: http://www.creatingmycambridge.com/

51 Keith and Jennifer Booth (2018). The Haywards. The biography of a cricket dynasty. Chequered Flag Publishing. Page 14.

52 Willie Sugg (2009). Fenner's Men. Cambridgeshire Cricket 1822-1848. Part 3 of A Tradition Unshared. Real Work Publishing. Page 52.

53 Sketch. A veteran cricketer. 13 Sept 1893. Page 361.

54 'Memoirs of a King's College Chorister' by Thomas Henry Case, page 45, in personal communication from Willie Sugg 13 May 2020.

55 Cambridge Chronicle and Journal 3 June 1848.

56 Alfred D Taylor (1972). The Story of a Cricket Picture. S.R. Publishers Ltd.

57 Willie Sugg '1848 - Fenner's Ground opens'. New writings on WS website https://www.cambscrickethistory.co.uk/

58 Willie Sugg (2009). Fenner's Men. Cambridgeshire Cricket 1822-1848. Part 3 of A Tradition Unshared. Real Work Publishing. Page 43.

59 Keith and Jennifer Booth (2018). The Haywards. The biography of a cricket dynasty. Chequered Flag Publishing. Page 35.

60 J.D.A Lander (1982). The Caius Building Estate in Barnwell. Part 1 Diploma in Architecture dissertation. Page 11 – from Capturing Cambridge website: https://capturingcambridge.org/

61 W.J. Ford (1902). The Cambridge University Cricket Club. William Blackwood and Sons. Page 16.

62 Cambridge Chronicle and Journal 1 April 1848 report in Willie Sugg (2009). Fenner's Men. Cambridgeshire Cricket 1822-1848. Part 3 of A Tradition Unshared. Real Work Publishing. Page 52.

63 Willie Sugg '1848 - Fenner's Ground opens'. New writings on WS website https://www.cambscrickethistory.co.uk/

64 Cambridge Chronicle and Journal 22 April 1848.

65 Cambridge Chronicle and Journal 17 June 1848.

66 Advertised in Cambridge Advertiser 19 April 1848 and held on 22 April, proceedings reported in Cambridge Chronicle and Journal.

67 Cambridge Chronicle and Journal 22 April 1848.

68 Cambridge Chronicle and Journal 22 April 1848.

69 Willie Sugg '1848 - Fenner's Ground opens'. New writings on WS website https://www.cambscrickethistory.co.uk/

70 Willie Sugg '1848 - Fenner's Ground opens'. New writings on WS website https://www.cambscrickethistory.co.uk/

71 Willie Sugg '1848 - Fenner's Ground opens'. New writings on WS website https://www.cambscrickethistory.co.uk/

72 Cambridge Independent Press 27th May 1848 page 3.

73 Willie Sugg '1848 - Fenner's Ground opens'. New writings on WS website https://www.cambscrickethistory.co.uk/

74 Willie Sugg '1848 - Fenner's Ground opens'. New writings on WS website https://www.cambscrickethistory.co.uk/

75 Frank Fenner letter dated 1st June and published in the Cambridge Chronicle and Journal 3rd June 1848.

76 Frank Fenner letter published in Cambridge Chronicle and Journal Saturday 3 June 1848.

77 Willie Sugg '1848 - Fenner's Ground opens'. New writings on WS website https://www.cambscrickethistory.co.uk/

78 Cambridge Chronicle and Journal 17 June 1848.

79 Willie Sugg (2009). Fenner's Men. Cambridgeshire Cricket 1822-1848. Part 3 of A Tradition Unshared. Real Work Publishing. Page 52.

80 Willie Sugg '1848 - Fenner's Ground opens'. New writings on WS website https://www.cambscrickethistory.co.uk/

81 Willie Sugg '1848 - Fenner's Ground opens'. New writings on WS website https://www.cambscrickethistory.co.uk/

82 Two generations sub head in 1847 – Two of a kind? article under New Writing on Willie Sugg website https://www.cambscrickethistory.co.uk/

83 Cambridge Independent Press 07 April 1855.

84 Cambridge Independent Press 19 May 1855.

85 Cambridge Independent Press 05 April 1856.

86 Cambridge Independent Press 15 March 1856.

87 Cambridge Independent Press 29 March 1856.

88 Robert Pearson Carpenter article on Willie Sugg website https://www.cambscrickethistory.co.uk/

89 Willie Sugg (2009). Fenner's Men. Cambridgeshire Cricket 1822-1848. Part 3 of A Tradition Unshared. Real Work Publishing. Page 54.

90 Cambridge Independent Press 05 March 1859.

91 Cambridge Independent Press 13 August 1859.

92 Ronald Mason. WG Grace and his Times, 1865-1899 in EW Swanton – editor (1980). Barclays World of Cricket. The game from A to Z. Collins Publishers.

93 Willie Sugg (2009). Fenner's Men. Cambridgeshire Cricket 1822-1848. Part 3 of A Tradition Unshared. Real Work Publishing. Pages 55 and 56.

94 Sporting Life Saturday 07 December 1861.

95 Sketch. A veteran cricketer. 13 Sept 1893. Page 361.

96 Cambridge Independent Press 8 July 1854.

97 Cambridge Independent Press 8 Sept 1855.

98 Cambridge Independent Press 28 August 1858.

99 Cambridge Independent Press 12 June 1858.

100 Cambridge Independent Press 23 July 1859.

101 W.J. Ford (1902). The Cambridge University Cricket Club. William Blackwood and Sons. Page 13.

102 Cambridge Independent Press 7 July 1860.

103 Cambridge Independent Press 30 Aug 1862.

104 Chris Thorne (2020). 1856 entry in History of athletics in Cambridge. Unpublished.

105 C.J.R. Thorne (February 2018). Cambridge University Athletic Club. 160th Anniversary Games.

106 Chris Thorne (2020). 1855 entry in History of athletics in Cambridge. Unpublished.

107 C.J.R. Thorne (February 2018). Cambridge University Athletic Club. 160th Anniversary Games.

108 Archive document UA SOC.XVIII.2.1 at Cambridge University Library.

109 Cambridge Chronicle and Journal 08 June 1861.

110 Cambridge University Athletic Club website: https://www.cuac.org.uk/history

111 Oxford University Athletic Club website: https://www.ouac.org/files/historypdf

112 Chris Thorne (2020). 1867 entry in History of athletics in Cambridge. Unpublished.

113 Chris Thorne (2020). 1866 entry in History of athletics in Cambridge. Unpublished.

114 Willie Sugg personal communication 1 Jan 2020.

115 Chris Thorne (2020). Hadgraft reference in History of athletics in Cambridge. Unpublished.

116 Cambridge Independent Press 19 February 1859.

117 Cambridge Chronicle and Journal 08 June 1861.

118 Sketch. A veteran cricketer. 13 Sept 1893. Page 361.

119 Cambridge Independent Press 1 December 1861.

120 Cambridge Independent Press 1 December 1861.

121 Cambridge Independent Press 1 December 1861.

122 Sketch. A veteran cricketer. 13 Sept 1893. Page 361.

123 Referred to as R Fenner in the press report.

124 Cambridge Independent Press 1 December 1861.

125 Cambridge Independent Press 14 December 1861.

126 Cambridge Chronicle and Journal 28 December 1861.

[127] Chris Thorne (2020). 1856 entry in History of athletics in Cambridge. Unpublished.

[128] Chris Thorne (2020). History of athletics in Cambridge. Unpublished.

[129] Chris Thorne. 150th Anniversary Oxford v Cambridge Varsity Sports from www.achilles.org

[130] J.D.A. Lander (1982) The Caius Building Estate in Barnwell. (Dissertation for Part 1. Dip in Architecture). Capturing Cambridge website: https://capturingcambridge.org/

[131] Mike Petty (2018). 1967 06 14 entry in Cambridge SPORT Chronicle. Chronology of Cambridge Sport 1888 to 1990 at https://archive.org/details/CambridgeSPORTSChronicle

[132] Cambridge University Lawn Tennis Club website: http://cultc.soc.srcf.net/

[133] History of the tie-break on Tennishead website: https://tennishead.net/the-history-of-the-tie-break/

[134] Cambridge Independent Press 15 March 1856.

[135] Cambridge Independent Press 10 May 1856.

[136] Cambridge Independent Press 5 September 1857.

[137] The Oxford Times 1 Aug 1863 page 6.

[138] Bell's Life in London and Sporting Chronicle 30 June 1850.

[139] Cambridge Independent Press 3 June 1854.

[140] Giles Phillips (2005). On Fenner's Sward. A history of Cambridge University Cricket Club. Tempus. Page 34.

[141] Giles Phillips (2005). On Fenner's Sward. A history of Cambridge University Cricket Club. Tempus. Page 34.

[142] W.J. Ford (1902). The Cambridge University Cricket Club. William Blackwood and Sons. Pages 6 and 7.

[143] Cyril Coote - a Cambridge legend. The man behind Fenner's peerless reputation (1982) John Wisden & Co. https://www.espncricinfo.com/wisdenalmanack/content/story/152208.html

[144] Sketch. A veteran cricketer. 13 Sept 1893. Page 361.

[145] Walter Watts entry on Mill Road Cemetery website: https://millroadcemetery.org.uk/

[146] Keith and Jennifer Booth (2018). The Haywards. The biography of a cricket dynasty. Chequered Flag Publishing. Page 125.

[147] Keith and Jennifer Booth (2018). The Haywards. The biography of a cricket dynasty. Chequered Flag Publishing. Page 174.

[148] Keith and Jennifer Booth (2018). The Haywards. The biography of a cricket dynasty. Chequered Flag Publishing. Page 315.

[149] W.J. Ford (1902). The Cambridge University Cricket Club. William Blackwood and Sons. Page 15 and 16.

[150] Venn Cambridge Alumni Database. https://venn.lib.cam.ac.uk/

[151] Cambridge Independent Press 9 June 1855.

[152] Cambridge Independent Press 24 July 1858.

[153] W.J. Ford (1902). The Cambridge University Cricket Club. William Blackwood and Sons. Pages 23 and 24.

[154] W.J. Ford (1902). The Cambridge University Cricket Club. William Blackwood and Sons. Page 25.

[155] W.J. Ford (1902). The Cambridge University Cricket Club. William Blackwood and Sons. Pages 23 and 24.

[156] Lander dissertation The Caius College Building estate in Barnwell. Page 11. Off Capturing Cambridge website: https://capturingcambridge.org/

[157] W.J. Ford (1902). The Cambridge University Cricket Club. William Blackwood and Sons. Page 20 and 21.

[158] W.J. Ford (1902). The Cambridge University Cricket Club. William Blackwood and Sons. Page 33.

[159] W.J. Ford (1902). The Cambridge University Cricket Club. William Blackwood and Sons.Page 26.

[160] W.J. Ford (1902). The Cambridge University Cricket Club. William Blackwood and Sons. Page 34.

[161] Cambridge Independent Press 2 May 1868. Page 8.

[162] The Truth 5 May 1892.

[163] Giles Phillips (2005). On Fenner's Sward. A history of Cambridge University Cricket Club. Tempus Publishing Ltd.

[164] Cambridge University Cricket Club website: http://cucc.net/index.php/history/

[165] Mike Petty (2018). 1934 05 09 [2.25] entry in Cambridge SPORT Chronicle. Chronology of Cambridge Sport 1888 to 1990 at https://archive.org/details/CambridgeSPORTSChronicle

After Cambridge, and Frank finally 'bowled out'

Frank left Cambridge in his early fifties in 1862 or 1863. Why he left is unclear; it was not an issue he ever fully alluded to, nor was it ever speculated about in the local or national press.

One reason perhaps why Frank leaving did not register as a significant event was that he continued to retain the lease on Fenner's Ground for at least a further 10 years, which would have required him to return regularly to manage it, as well as visit his elderly father.

WHY MIGHT FRANK HAVE LEFT?

In this section we will look at four areas: Frank's businesses, his family, his commitment and passion for establishing a county cricket club, and other possible reasons.

Fenner's businesses

It would appear his core businesses in Cambridge of a tobacco shop, gymnasium (both located on the same site on the market) and Fenner's Ground, as a venue for university cricket, athletics and community events were largely operating profitably. There were some challenges, including having a growing portfolio.

Athletics

The best evidence that this aspect of the business was thriving was the visit of Deerfoot to Fenner's Ground in front of the Prince of Wales watched by a large crowd in 1861, which was presumably a major reason why a (three laps to a mile) cinder track was later installed at Fenner's Ground in 1867.

Cricket – and managing Fenner's Ground from the West Country

Cricket did not attract the same numbers of paying spectators as the athletics, but the University Cricket Club became increasingly aware of the importance of Fenner's Ground. This is why they put pressure on Frank to improve the facilities there, particularly the pavilion.

Instead, it appears the priority for Frank was the installation of the cinder track, presumably because of the projected gate receipts.

Tobacco shop

Frank managed a tobacco shop in Cambridge for 25 years, with the last location on the market being in the best location of all for passing trade, including those visiting for more information on the cricket, athletics or gymnasium promoted through his shop. However, a tobacco / grocery partnership on this same site with John Bowles was soon dissolved, only after 18 months of operation, ending in April 1861.[1]

Gymnasium

The University Gymnasium appears to have had a good start, with the gymnastics display in 1855 attracting excellent reports in the press,[2] and its use by the Working Men's College, also situated behind his tobacco shop. However, Harvey Goodwin and Francis Vesey, two key drivers of the college, both left in 1858, marking the start of the college's decline in Cambridge.

Community events

It is likely the wide range of community events staged at Fenner's Ground generated goodwill more than any profit. However, Frank would have expected the fairs he hosted to generate significant profits, one exception being the 'Monster Fete and Fancy Fair' in July 1860 which resulted in the organiser / promoter filing for bankruptcy, thereby having a negative impact on Frank too.

New venture goes bust

Despite the relatively minor challenges relating to his businesses listed here, Frank must still have believed he had a future in Cambridge to grow his portfolio of sporting and leisure facilities. For example, in April 1861, at the same time as his partnership with Bowles was dissolved, he became the manager of the Roman Baths Company on Jesus Lane, with approval for such an appointment being registered in the local press (chapter 5). The company was soon in financial difficulty, with £4,000 (over £50,000 today) being unaccounted for.

At no stage was Fenner ever suspected of misappropriating this money, but its collapse may have harmed his reputation locally, and he did not have his tobacco shop on the Market to fall back on.

Fenner's family

It would appear that Frank and his family had a mostly settled family home. At some stage after the death in 1855 of their 18-month-old son, Frederick Augustus Fenner, when the family home was based on Regent Street,[3] they moved to 12 (today's 15) Emmanuel Road – opposite Christ's Pieces. In the 1861 census, Frank was listed as a cigar merchant, living with his wife Mary Williams Fenner and six of their children and two servants.

One family-related issue for Frank would have been whether Frank's elderly father, Joseph would follow the family to Cheltenham, or stay in Cambridge. Joseph remained at his home on Regent Terrace, near the Prince Regent pub, and about a year after Frank left, he died aged 91.

Fenner's commitment to establishing a county cricket club

Frank must have been very disappointed that town cricket did not buy into his plans for using Fenner's Ground in 1848, which might have been one reason for leaving, but for the fact he remained in Cambridge for a further 15 years.

Over these 15 years he continued to actively support local cricket including acting as first secretary for the Cambridge [Cambridgeshire] County Cricket Club in 1858, which because the club did not last long, was perhaps another reason for Frank to move to Gloucestershire and attempt to establish a county club there.

Other possible reasons

There is some circumstantial evidence that Frank's ill-health might have been a factor in him moving to the spa town of Cheltenham.

In June 1861 there was much discussion in the local press regarding the resignation of Sergeant Fenner from the Cambridgeshire Volunteer Rifles. Frank had a poor attendance record at drills 'because of illness and other important engagements'. It is not a lot of evidence to go on, however Alfred D Taylor reported in 1923[4] that:

> In middle life Fenner experienced frequent periods of indisposition, and this state of health was responsible for his removal to the West of England. He first experimented as mine host of the Royal Hotel, Cheltenham.

Interestingly when Frank gave an interview to the *Sketch*, and wrote six lengthy articles in the *Bath Chronicle* reflecting on cricket and his life, he never mentioned his own ill-health. This was a couple of years before he died at the age of 85, which given life expectancy was 47 years in England for a man, meant that Frank's ill-health was temporary, and / or a convenient reason for others to use in explaining why Frank left Cambridge.

Better opportunities in Cheltenham?

Given Frank was born and bred in Cambridge and lived the first fifty years of his life there, in the absence of clear and obvious reasons why he should leave, one would have expected Cheltenham to have offered something hugely attractive to lure him away.

It is known for certain Frank visited Cheltenham on Saturday 11 October 1862 because he was listed under 'hotel – arrivals' in the *Cheltenham Journal and Gloucestershire Fashionable Weekly Gazette*. This must have involved discussions on Frank's proprietorship of the Royal Hotel (a new career for him), and the potential for Cheltenham Cricket Club to grow into Gloucestershire County Cricket Club. Even before making the announcement of his move to Cheltenham in the Cambridge press, he was voted onto the Committee of Cheltenham Cricket Club in March 1863:

> Cheltenham Cricket Club Annual Meeting. Several new members were nominated and amongst them Mr J.B. [sic] Fenner, a gentleman formerly well known as one of the great players of the country, and who is about to become connected with the town as landlord of the Royal [Hotel].[5]

FRANK'S HOMES AND ACHIEVEMENTS AFTER CAMBRIDGE

With Frank living in the Royal Hotel, Cheltenham he did not require many of his home possessions from Cambridge, which is why he held an auction on 29 May 1862.

NEXT THURSDAY.
GOOD USEFUL HOUSEHOLD FURNITURE
Two Large Chimney Glasses, Pianoforte, China, Glass,
and numerous Miscellaneous Effects.
No. 12, EMMANUEL ROAD, CAMBRIDGE.

TO BE SOLD BY AUCTION, BY
CHARLES WISBEY,
On THURSDAY NEXT, the 29th day of May, 1862, at 11 o'clock, on the premises opposite Christ Pieces, by direction of Mr. F Fenner, who has left Cambridge.

Comprising 4 mahogany sideboards, telescope dining tables, loo, library, sofa, and card tables, cheffioneer, dumb waiters, bookcases, mahogany hair seated chairs, sofas in hair seating and damask, study chairs, mahogany, Arabian and other bedsteads, feather beds, and bedding, several mahogany chests of drawers, with other bedroom appendages, 2 large pier-shape chimney glasses, in gilt frames, a 6-octave pianoforte, by Broadwood; large Brussels carpets, damask window curtains, and a variety of china and glass, some plated and japanned ware, numerous culinary articles, and miscellaneous effects.

On View the morning of Sale, and Catalogues had of CHARLES WISBEY, Auctioneer, Valuer, and Estate Agent Cambridge.

Cheltenham

The month after being voted onto the local cricket committee, Frank posted the following advertisement in the Cambridge Independent Press on the 4 April 1863.

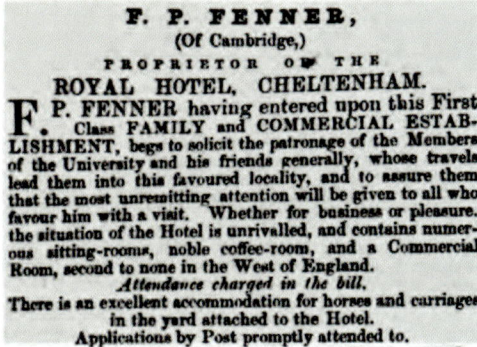

F. P. FENNER,
(Of Cambridge,)
PROPRIETOR OF THE
ROYAL HOTEL, CHELTENHAM.
F. P. FENNER having entered upon this First Class FAMILY and COMMERCIAL ESTAB-LISHMENT, begs to solicit the patronage of the Members of the University and his friends generally, whose travels lead them into this favoured locality, and to assure them that the most unremitting attention will be given to all who favour him with a visit. Whether for business or pleasure, the situation of the Hotel is unrivalled, and contains numerous sitting-rooms, noble coffee-room, and a Commercial Room, second to none in the West of England.
Attendance charged in the bill.
There is an excellent accommodation for horses and carriages in the yard attached to the Hotel.
Applications by Post promptly attended to.

It was accompanied by the following comment made by the newspaper:

> It will be seen by advertisement that Mr. Fenner has become the proprietor of the Royal Hotel, Cheltenham. We, in common with the whole town, wish Mr. Fenner all prosperity in his new undertaking; and we are quite sure that if business or pleasure should draw any Cambridge persons to Cheltenham, they will not forget Mr. Fenner, whose hotel offers every inducement for genuine comfort.

It is odd that whilst the newspaper wished Frank Fenner 'all prosperity in his new undertaking', no recognition of his contribution to Cambridge, and how this might be missed, accompanied this statement.

Royal Hotel, Cheltenham (painting by George Rowe, 1840s)
Courtesy of Jill Waller.

Frank as Secretary of the local cricket club

Having been voted in as a member of Cheltenham Cricket Club, it took only seven months before Frank became its secretary in November 1863. This included the club taking on a new name, and the creation of a new ground,[6] following acceptance of this resolution:

> 'That in the absence of any cricketing centre in the county of Gloucester, an attempt be made to supply the want by the formation of a new ground and the establishment of a club to be called the Cheltenham and County of Gloucester Cricket Club.'[7]

A few days later the *Cheltenham Chronicle*[8] provided more details on Mr F.P. Fenner's appointment as secretary:

> The gentleman has for many years been the proprietor of a ground at Cambridge, which has been one of the finest grounds in the kingdom, and late secretary to the Cambridgeshire C.C.,

It also included what the local aspirations for local and county cricket might be:

> That the county possesses the Messrs. Graces, Messrs. Hagarth, Sewell, Eccles and other promising players, we see no reason why Gloucestershire could not turn out an eleven which could compete with the far-famed Surrey or Kent elevens.

Members of the local cricket club committee making these decisions included C.H. Jessop, the previous secretary, and his brother, Dr Henry Edward Jessop, the local physician and surgeon,[9] whose son Gilbert Laird Jessop later attended Cambridge University from 1896, going on to great things as an England cricketer.

Fenner and the formation of the county club

The first attempts to establish a Gloucestershire County Cricket Club before Frank's arrival took place in 1839, and more formally in 1842, but because of 'the low standard of cricket played' it folded in 1846.[10]

The second 'county' club was formed with Fenner as its secretary in 1863 and 'seems to have flourished for a time, and certainly played other nearby counties; the ground used at Cheltenham was occasionally referred to as the county ground'.[11]

However, the national newspaper, *Sporting Life* had not listed the new county club, prompting Frank as its secretary to write on 2 April 1864:

> Perhaps I might be allowed to remark that the existence of a 'Cheltenham and County of Gloucester Cricket Club' seems to be ignored in your notice of county clubs. Whatever may be the success of the experiment, I think it right to say that a club has been started, intended, in the absence of

any other claim to a 'county club', to be 'The County of Gloucester Cricket Club'; and when I call attention to the list of officers – gentlemen who are taking a strong interest in the movement – you will, I think, agree with me that the existence of a county club is something more than a myth. You must not think I am blaming you, Sir, for any want of acknowledgement. I am merely giving you, in accordance with a suggestion from the members of our committee, some inkling of what was evidently being done without your knowledge. Officers of the Cheltenham and County of Gloucester Cricket Club: President: Colonel Berkeley, MP [local MP], Vice Presidents… [list including the Principal and Vice Principal of Cheltenham College, a number of local head teachers, and doctors, and members of the committee including the Jessops].

However, 'heightened by the formation by the Grace family of a more truly representative Gloucestershire XI'[12] in 1870, the Cheltenham and County of Gloucester Cricket Club folded in 1871'.[13]

There is no evidence that Frank and the Grace family explored the possibility of collaborating together; had they done so, their respective skills may have complimented each other.

It was probably anticipating this initiative by the Grace family that hastened Frank's departure from Cheltenham. Whilst Frank moved to Weston-Super-Mare in May 1867 having only stayed in Cheltenham for four years, his son (also called Frank) remained.

Frank's son remains in Cheltenham

In the 1871 census Frank's son, born in 1849 was lodging in Cheltenham as a wine merchant's clerk and by 1874 was managing the wine and spirits department of the local brewery where he continued to work until his retirement at the end of 1928, recognised in the local newspaper:[14]

> One of the best-known men in Cheltenham, ended a connection of over sixty years as manager of the Original Brewery Company's Wine Office in High Street Cheltenham. Mr Fenner is eighty years of age.

> He has been a very popular and much respected man, for we all like people who can be both shrewd and genial; and shrewdness and geniality are qualities possessed by our veteran townsman in a very high degree.

The newspaper added a lengthy reference to Frank's athletic ability:

> One cause of Mr Fenner's evergreen vigour of body and mind is, we imagine, to be traced to his early love of athletic exercises. In his 'teens [he would have left Cambridge aged about 12] he was 'hot stuff' at the hundred yards, the quarter mile flat, and the long jump, and like every

young man with a wholesome and manly heart in his bosom, he gloried in a bout with the gloves, for which he had a 'very useful' turn, as might be supposed by those who knew him at eighty, still stocky and straight, and looking very likely to be able to deal a good, sturdy straight one should it be demanded by any good cause.

The newspaper added he 'played a valuable part in assisting to found two of our most important sporting organisations, for he was one of the original members of the East Gloucestershire Cricket Club.....and a foundation member of the Cheltenham Race Club. He also served as a member of the committee of the Cheltenham Town Cricket Club.'

As far as his relationship with his father, it would appear they had fallen out. If this is true it is particularly sad, as Frank (senior) and Mary had two other sons named Frank, both dying in childhood in 1842 and 1843.[15] The evidence that their relationship was poor was that all Frank (senior's) valuable cricket memorabilia when he died was given to his brother's family, rather than to his son. (More details on what happened to this cricket memorabilia can be found in the Preface.)

Weston-super-Mare

Quite why Frank senior moved the 50 miles southwest from the Royal Hotel, Cheltenham to the coast at Weston-super-Mare is unknown. On 18 May 1867 the Weston-super-Mare Gazette reported:

> [The] Royal Pier Hotel ... being rapidly fitted up by the proprietor ... ready for occupation on the 5th of June, a circumstance coincident with the inauguration of the pier. The excellence of the management is guaranteed by the fact that it will be directed by Mr Fenner, a gentleman well known amongst cricketers.

The hotel had '17 bedrooms, 6 sitting-rooms, a billiard room, club rooms etc' declared when Frank Fenner applied for a public house license.[16]

**Royal Pier Hotel
c 1910**

Permission to use granted by WSM & District Family History Society.

Whilst the hotel was owned by Fred Harris, with Frank, as the licensee,[17] the Weston-super-Mare Gazette and General Advertiser of 8 June 1867 named it 'Fenner's Hotel'.

The only reference in the local press[18] to his other involvement in local affairs in Weston-super-Mare relates to Frank and his daughter winning prizes for producing the first and third best conundrums, respectively, judged by Professor Stone who had given lectures in electro biology, and the prizes for the competition.

Frank won a silver watch with 'If the Queen was disposed to confer dignity on a biologist, what part of Weston-super-Mare would suggest the honour? – Knight-stone.' (Knight Stone was an island off Weston-super-Mare.)

Miss Fenner obtained the third prize, consisting of a purse containing a sovereign, her conundrum being – 'Why is the Assembly-room [presumably where Professor Stone provided his entertainment] at the present moment the greatest of all anomalies? – Because there you may see an animated Stone, that not only laughs, talks, and walks, but has power to move an audience.'

Miss Fenner would be either Emma Louise, Frances Mary, or Ellen Julie, with Jeanette, Frank's fourth daughter being too young.

There are no direct references to Frank involving himself in local sport, however it is possible he was invited to contribute to strengthening local cricket by William Henry Davies who had been a student at Trinity College from 1856 to 1860, before going on to 'inject a lot of enthusiasm into Weston-super-Mare cricket'. This was suspended until 1869 given the death of William's father,[19] by which time Frank would have committed himself to moving to Bath.

It must also be remembered that Frank still held the lease on Fenner's Ground, which must have involved visits back to Cambridge. Live issues that needed addressing at this time, included Frank being 'given notice to quit the land at Christmas 1867',[20] no doubt because he was behind on paying the rent for Fenner's. Presumably Frank paid up because he continued to hold the lease until 1873.

Just over two years after arriving in Weston-super-Mare, Frank and his family moved to Bath.

Bath

In October 1869 a notice appeared in the *Bath Chronicle* reporting 'the White Lion Hotel in Bath had been bought by F.P. Fenner of the Royal Pier Hotel, Weston-super-Mare'. A later report[21] clarified that Frank had taken on the tenancy, from Bath Corporation.

This 'long-established coaching house in the centre of the city' was ideally situated next to the Guildhall, close to Bath Abbey.

The White Lion Hotel (foreground on the left), **next to the Guildhall and Abbey Church, Bath c.1856**
Permission to use granted by Bath in Time.

In advertising his hotel, for example in the *Western Mail*,[22] he would often describe himself as 'F P Fenner (of Cambridge)'.

It was not long after arriving in Bath that Frank became a Freemason, in 1870.

Sport and cricket in Somerset and Bath

Frank also joined the committee of the Bath 'New Improvement Society'[23] in 1874, which proposed 'a scheme involving in one comprehensive whole the establishment of a cricket ground, archery ground, gymnasium, aquarium and winter garden.' Frank would have been a huge asset to this society, given his experience creating and managing a gymnasium, and Fenner's Ground, not just for cricket and athletics, but community events too.

It is no surprise given Frank's experiences in both Cambridgeshire and Gloucestershire that he should want a ground for his new home county.

> It is unfortunate for the promoters of County Cricket that a ground could not be found locally, to assist, by position and capabilities, in

bringing together the known as well as the unknown strength of the county. Much energy and joint action are required to make any attempt to unite the slumbering talent of such a county as Somerset; but this ought not to be found a deterrent in the endeavour to accomplish what is thought to be possible.

This was written by Frank in 1893 after Somerset had recently beaten Surrey, the champion county.

Later in his 'Cricket Jottings' (article number 5 of 6 published in the Bath Chronicle in September 1893) he reported 'it is pleasing to find that the desire to make Bath a cricketing centre is spreading, and if the Press generally would throw the weight of its intelligence into the advocacy, the object, I think, would be considerably advanced.'

It took Frank and the New Improvement Society over 20 years before a ground was built, as the forerunner to the current Recreation Ground. Unfortunately, Frank did not get to see Somerset play their first match there in 1897, as he had died the year before.[25] Maybe the disappointment that Somerset County Cricket Club had chosen the County Ground in Taunton as their home in 1896,[26] hastened Frank's end?

Relationship with Cambridge University Cricket Club, and financial troubles

With Frank moving regularly (in 1863 from Cambridge to Cheltenham, in 1867 to Weston-super-Mare, and in 1869 to Bath), coupled with the challenges of running hotels, and local / county cricket clubs and grounds, it is no surprise he could not also adequately fulfil the responsibilities he still held as the leaseholder of Fenner's Ground in Cambridge.

Nevertheless, during this period of arms-length management, a cinder track for athletics was installed at Fenner's Ground in 1866. However, the complaints from the University Cricket Club started in 1871 regarding 'the dilapidated state of the old pavilion and its smallness',[27] and in 1873, when the new pavilion was being constructed (funded entirely by CUCC), Frank was asked to remove some of his property, which he had lodged a claim for.

In 1873 when Frank gave up the lease, the University Cricket Club stipulated that 'Fenner's' be referred to as 'The Cambridge University Cricket Ground',[28] which might have caused Frank some distress, until being made aware that students continued to use his name.

Lastly, between 1886 and 1889, just before Frank retired from his role at the hotel, he was given a payment of £10 by the University Cricket Club because of their belief he was in financial trouble.

In addition, according to Alfred D Taylor, writing in 1923.[29]

> Failure unfortunately dogged [Frank's] footsteps and his life's savings slipped steadily through his fingers like sand through a sieve. Eventually he fell upon evil days, but it is pleasing to record that the cricket clubs of Cambridge frequently assisted him and doubly pleasing to reflect in the knowledge that his pecuniary embarrassment did not hasten his end.

Other than the University, it is not known which other clubs provided such assistance.

Frank and his family retire to Pulteney Street

There are a number of possible reasons why Frank vacated the White Lion Hotel in 1891 in addition to being in financial trouble. For example, as a 75-year-old, he probably needed to retire.

There were also plans to demolish the hotel to allow for an extension to the Guildhall next door to create the Victoria Art Gallery.[30] Frank vacating the hotel accelerated this process.

Once Frank had left the hotel he held an auction of the belongings he did not need on 15 May 1891.[31] Frank and his family then moved to 34 Pulteney Street, Bath.

Eight months later on 15 Jan 1892, Mary Williams Fenner, Frank's wife, died aged 79 years.

Frank reflects on his lifetime in cricket

From July to September 1893 Frank wrote six lengthy pieces in the *Bath Chronicle* entitled 'cricket jottings & reminiscences by F. P. Fenner'. In September he was interviewed by a reporter from the *Sketch*, again on his reflections on cricket. The *Sketch* article also included a photograph of Frank, the only surviving photograph of him, used on the back cover of this book.

Many of these memories and insights have been included throughout this book.

FRANK FENNER DIES, AND A TRADITION GOES UNSHARED

Frank Fenner died on the 22 May 1896, at 34 Pulteney St, Bath aged 85, being 'bowled out by the grim player against whom none of us are able to stand'.[32] He was buried with his wife Mary in Bath Abbey Cemetery.

The local press also reported 'although an affection of the knee had prevented him getting about, his eye was undimmed until the last. Paralysis brought about the end, after only a fortnight's illness'.[33]

Later, Frank and Mary were joined by their daughter Mary Frances Fenner who died on 30 July 1927, aged 82 years.

Obituaries

Of all the obituaries written, the one shared below published in 'Cricket: a weekly record of the game' is chosen first because the writer 'F. G.' (probably Frederick Gale) declares knowing Frank.

Frank Fenner, Mary Williams Fenner and their daughter Mary Frances Fenner buried together at Bath Abbey Cemetery. The Gray Nicholls cricket bat belongs to the author's son

> MR. FRANCIS PHILLIPS FENNER. Exit at Pulteney Street, Bath, on May 22nd [1896], in his 86th year, one of the very front rank of the Old School of the Pilch and Mynn era. Mr. Fenner, who kept 'Fenner's Ground' at Cambridge, was undoubtedly one of the most finished all-round cricketers of his day, in proof whereof he was selected to play in the Jubilee Match at Lord's in 1837 — the North against the South; and in days when Lord Bessborough (then the Hon. F. Ponsonby) was entrusted to select the All-England XI. v. Kent, by the M.C.C., from 1840 onwards, Fenner was generally one. He was a very handsome man, and a perfect gentleman in manners and tone. He was a tobacconist at Cambridge, and also had the cricket ground. He was a very good bowler and very fine bat, and a celebrated single wicket player.

> I renewed my acquaintance with him some seven or eight years ago, when he was landlord of the White Lion Hotel at Bath, and received a most cordial welcome; and two years ago I was staying in Bath for a week, and on three consecutive evenings I passed two or three hours with him talking over the old days. He had then given up his hotel, and was living with his daughter, who had a first-rate lodging-house in a good part of Bath. When I last saw him he was very enthusiastic about a visit which Lord Bessborough had paid him, breaking his journey into the West of England for the sake of two or three hours' talk with him.

Well, eighty-six is not a bad innings, and sounds like one of the colossal scores, as they were called fifty years ago, when the leg before wicket was judged from bowler's hand to the wicket, and batsmen did not play with a pad as well as a bat to defend their wickets; and 50 runs was a grand innings. The last time I saw him he spoke very strongly on this point, and about men using their pads when wicket-keeping for deliberately stopping 'byes,' and stopping balls thrown in from the long field; and he was also very strong against the shouting at umpires, and all shabby tricks. Well, he had a long career, and lived honoured and respected, and so peace to his ashes ... F.G.[34]

Clearly F. G's. praise of Frank's cricketing ability was not enough for one reader, according to the editor of *Cricket* in which the obituary featured:

'Three days after the interesting notice by F. G. of the late Mr Francis Fenner had appeared an anonymous and unnecessary postcard arrived. It was worded as follows:

Not a word about Fenner who could have given many of the present 'cracks' [best players] points and beaten them. He had not the advantage of the monstrous 'boundaries', it is true, and the wickets he played on were difficult. But he will be remembered long after most of the 'cracks' of 1896 are forgotten. I believe you call yourselves a cricket paper!!![35]

Other obituaries added further tributes, across Frank's range of interests and skills.

From the field of athletics: 'Cricket, in common with athletics generally, was in a bad way, and a difficulty with regard to the practising fields [in Cambridge] threatened to make matters worse ... [Fenner's Ground] was, while under Mr Fenner's control, the scene of many athletic gatherings, and here the fleet-footed Deerfoot made his first appearance before the Prince of Wales. Mr Fenner used to tell with great gusto how he was the intermediary of an introduction of Deerfoot to the Prince, and of the former's almost childish delight at the Prince's urbanity'.[36]

On the subject of the gymnasium: 'A completely equipped gymnasium and constant round of athletic sports were also provided, for in those days athleticism was a plant which needed tender cultivation'.[37]

'At Cambridge he provided – in addition to Fenner's Ground, and despite much opposition from the dons – one of the most complete gymnasia of the day.'[38]

From sport in general: Frank was a 'friend and patron of all kinds of legitimate sport, especially cricket'.[39]

A pilgrimage destination

'In the days of his retirement, Mr Fenner's well-knit form, erect as of yore, and with his eye undimmed, was a familiar figure at Bath, whither many a pilgrimage was made by those who would fight again the old battles. He never lost his keen interest in all forms of athleticism, but more particularly in cricket, about which his store of reminiscences was unbounded ... [His passing] removes from our midst one of the best-known cricketers of the earlier lustres of the century.'[40]

From cricket, and Cambridge: 'For something like a quarter of a century he held a prominent position in the cricket world.'[41]

'... at Cambridge in connection with Varsity cricket, that he did his most useful work.'[42]

'... generations of Cambridge men have known ... 'Fenner's Ground,' and upon which [Frank] assisted for many years in training the best of the university cricketers ... a work for which thousands have blessed the name of Fenner.'[43]

Such appreciation of Frank's contribution to Cambridge University cricket was also made three years before he died by a reporter from the *Sketch* who visited him in Bath. 'I found the hale and hearty veteran cricketer whose figure was familiar to so many generations of Cambridge men, and whose name is still a household word among students by the banks of the Cam'.[44]

Such acclaim was however not evident in Cambridge, given the only reference[45] to Frank's death locally was:

> May 22, at 34, Pulteney Street, Bath. Francis Phillips Fenner, formerly of Cambridge, in his 86th year.

So why might Frank be only briefly recognised by the Cambridge press, when he died? Was there not a legacy Fenner left in Cambridge, good or bad, worthy of report? It took nearly one hundred years before the cricket history books recognised the extraordinary local cricketing tradition established in Cambridge, lamenting also, that it went unshared.

A tradition unshared

An early entry in the *World of Cricket* – the Game from A to Z, published in 1980 and edited by the renowned cricket journalist and author, E.W. Swanton,[46] started by plotting 'the history of the game in England'. In the section covering the key developments in the second half of the nineteenth century it reported:

> A curious fate was hanging over Cambridgeshire (cricket) ... of the 1860s (as) a powerful combination, ready and eager to be matched with any side in England, and they allied in their collective talents a most comprehensive variety of all-round skills. They had an admirable leg-spinner in Buttress

and a most terrifying fast bowler Tarrant, nicknamed rather ominously 'Tear 'em', who bowled with deadly effect from round the wicket on the line of the batsmen's legs. Balancing these were the neat and capable all-rounder, A.J. ('Ducky') Diver, and the memorable pair of batsmen, Tom Hayward and Robert Carpenter, the one frail and neurotic but a brilliantly adaptable stylist, the other a fierce, rapacious aggressor with a fine defence and great quickness of foot.

It is much to be regretted that this wonderfully promising county's cricket history ends where it begins. The county lost its leeway among its first-class rivals and never recovered it, relying for its fame upon its lost glories. It would perhaps not be fair to forget that it may be said to have continued its honourable service to the game vicariously and a little obscurely; for it was the great Tom Hayward's even more distinguished nephew and namesake who not only gave his own considerable talents to Surrey but fostered the promise of an even greater player, Jack Hobbs.

It was Cambridgeshire's honour to found a tradition without sharing it.

Regrettably the article ends as abruptly as Cambridgeshire cricket, with no mention of Frank Fenner's contribution either on the field, or off it. So how might he be judged today?

---

[1] Cambridge Chronicle and Journal 06 April 1861.

[2] Cambridge Chronicle and Journal 15 Dec 1855. Page 5.

[3] Cambridge Independent Press 12 May 1855.

[4] Alfred D Taylor (1972). The Story of a Cricket Picture. S.R. Publishers Ltd. Pages 36 and 37.

[5] Cheltenham Examiner 18 March 1863.

[6] Stephen Chalke personal communication 16 Dec 2020.

[7] Cheltenham Journal 7 Nov 1863.

[8] Cheltenham Journal 10 Nov 1863.

[9] Cheltenham Examiner 18 March 1863.

[10] Grahame Parker (1983) Gloucestershire Road. Page 25.

[11] Roland Bowen (1970). Cricket: History of Its Growth and Development Throughout the World. Page 31.

[12] Roland Bowen (1970). Cricket: History of Its Growth and Development Throughout the World. Page 31.

[13] Roland Bowen (1970). Cricket: History of Its Growth and Development Throughout the World. Page 31.

[14] Cheltenham Chronicle 5 Jan 1929.

[15] Fenner family tree: http://www.fennerfamilytree.me.uk/

[16] Weston-super-Mare Gazette 7 Sept 1867.

[17] Stan & Joan Rendell (2003). Steep Holm's Pioneers. Page 67.

[18] Weston-super-Mare Gazette 11 July 1867.

[19] Ian Smith (member of Somerset County Cricket Club official Facebook page) personal message 28 Dec 2021.

[20] Lander dissertation: The Caius College Building estate in Barnwell page 11. Capturing Cambridge. website: https://capturingcambridge.org/

[21] Bath Chronicle 18 June 1891.

[22] Western Mail 8 Oct 1870.

[23] Bristol Mercury 25 July 1874.

[24] F.P. Fenner (July and Sept 1893). Cricket jottings. Article 1 of 6 published in Bath Chronicle.

[25] Stephen Chalke personal communication 16 Dec 2020.

[26] David Foot (1986). Sunshine, Sixes and Cider: The History of Somerset Cricket. David & Charles.

[27] W.J. Ford (1902). The Cambridge University Cricket Club. William Blackwood and Sons. Page 23.

[28] W.J. Ford (1902). The Cambridge University Cricket Club. William Blackwood and Sons. Page 21.

[29] Alfred D Taylor (1972). The Story of a Cricket Picture. S.R. Publishers Ltd. Pages 36 and 37.

[30] Bath Chronicle and Weekly Gazette 7 May and 18 June 1891.

[31] Bath Chronicle and Weekly Gazette 7 May 1891.

[32] Sporting Notes and News – Cricket in Pall Mall Gazette 25 May 25 1896. Page 6.

[33] Weston Mercury 30 May 1896. Page 3.

[34] Believed to be Frederick Gale. Francis Phillips Fenner Obituary in Cricket: a weekly record of the game. 4 June 1896 page 188.

[35] Cricket: a weekly record of the game 11 June 1896. Page 208.

[36] Weston Mercury 30 May 1896 page 3 also 'Sporting Notes and News – Cricket' in Pall Mall Gazette 25 May 1896. Page 6.

[37] St James's Gazette. Politics and Persons 27 May 1896.

[38] 'Sporting Notes and News – Cricket' in Pall Mall Gazette 25 May 1896). Page 6.

[39] Bath Chronicle and Weekly Gazette 28 May 1896.

[40] St James's Gazette. Politics and Persons 27 May 1896.

[41] Alfred D Taylor (1972). The Story of a Cricket Picture. S.R. Publishers Ltd. Pages 36 and 37.

[42] Weston Mercury 30 May 1896 Page 3.

[43] St James's Gazette. Politics and Persons 27 May 1896.

[44] Sketch. A veteran cricketer. 13 Sept 1893. Page 361.

[45] Cambridge Chronicle and Journal 29 May 1896.

[46] Ronald Mason. WG Grace and his Times, 1865-1899 in EW Swanton – editor (1980). Barclays World of Cricket. The game from A to Z. Collins Publishers. Page 13.

CHAPTER 24

Frank Fenner's legacy

The Frank Fenner who emerges from these pages was clearly a complex character whose loyalty, not just to the cricket he loved, meant he chose to keep his own counsel on many of the things that happened to him. There are gaps in our knowledge.

Beyond his obituaries, press reports and history books, his character and resilience can only be inferred through his achievements, and how he responded to the range of challenges and difficulties he faced.

ACHIEVEMENTS

A cricketing legend

No one can question his outstanding achievements as a cricket player and captain on the pitch, and off it as coach and administrator, all born out of an undying passion and love for the game, particularly its ethos. Not only was he one of the most finished all-round cricketers of his day but a perfect gentleman too.

A unique role in democratising the game?

In the 1840s Frank was largely responsible for creating one of the best cricket teams in the country because of his approach, or tradition to playing.

From a young age, as a 25-year-old, Frank had the belief that cricket 'produces that happy concord of social enjoyment,' that could 'strengthen the links of society', which by bringing Town and Gown together also enabled Frank to create a winning team. This is why Felix's painting of 1847, portrays the players from both Town and Gown 'as equals...', forging 'a socio-cricket alliance of considerable influence'.[1]

This was at a time when tensions in Cambridge between the town and University were particularly high, on the back of centuries of any activity that might interfere with students attending to their studies being repeatedly banned. It is no wonder Felix places Frank in the centre of his painting, 'chest out ... an imposing looking figure'[2] and holding a bat, the symbol of being a gentleman player. Remember it would take another hundred years or so before a professional, such as Frank, would hold a comparable leadership role in a mixed group including gentlemen amateurs.

Frank's sporting plans: a broad agenda

Frank Fenner's cricketing achievements 'off the field' are not just restricted to creating Fenner's Cricket Ground, as he also endeavoured to create two more in Cheltenham and Bath as 'county grounds', and launch two county cricket teams in Cambridgeshire, and Gloucestershire. Sadly, these schemes either failed or were picked up by others, but this did not deter him.

For example, his agenda or portfolio also grew beyond cricket, to include the hugely successful introduction of athletics onto Fenner's Ground, as well as opening a gymnasium behind his tobacco shop, right in the centre of Cambridge. Naturally these developments prompted 'much opposition from the dons'.[3] However, his skills of 'tender cultivation' were so successful the local press reported Frank would be 'seen surrounded by a posse of college dons … eager to hear his manly and generous deductions',[4] one possible outcome being the 'revival of pedestrian and other athletic amusements in the University',[5] perhaps a key precursor to the local sporting revolution that went global in the second half of the nineteenth century? (chapter 24).

Partners

Whilst keeping 'the dons' on-side was important, it must be remembered that sport in the University, as in the public schools, was organised at this time almost exclusively by the students themselves. Because their stay at university was limited to a few years, it is no surprise they were drawn to Frank's dependability year in, year out, but also his skills as player, coach, equipment provider, administrator, networker, leader and gentleman, and his dedicated 'state of the art' sporting facilities located close to the centre of town.

As a result, Frank worked with several students who later took up key roles in cricket, such as Robert Fitzgerald, Henry Perkins and Frederick Ponsonby, later Lord Bessborough. This is not to forget Frank would have worked closely with many very talented local cricketers such as Thomas Hayward and Robert Carpenter, both outstanding England players.

Frank also hosted, and actively supported the Working Men's College located behind his tobacco shop on the market from 1855, thereby mixing directly with some of the foremost social thinkers and reformers of the mid nineteenth century. In addition to promoting accessible education on the back of a Christian socialism agenda, Frederick Maurice and others from the University were also advocates of the new 'manliness' or Muscular Christianity agenda, actively fostered by Thomas Hughes who led the early classes held by the college in Frank's gymnasium.

The active involvement of HRH the Prince of Wales (later Edward VII) on Fenner's Ground, not just playing cricket on his own wicket,[6] but being a spectator at a number of athletic meetings. This includes the appearance of Deerfoot, the Seneca Native American in 1861, which must surely rank as the pinnacle of Frank's business career, given such royal patronage and up to 8,000 paying spectators.

CHALLENGES

In addition to Frank's achievements, he experienced a significant number of challenges only known about through reports in the press and / or by others, never directly from Frank. We can only guess at the pain these might have caused.

Relationship with the town

One of the biggest challenges must have been when the town rejected his business case for creating Fenner's. He believed a private ground would 'prevent the decay of cricket in Cambridge' given the abuse players were increasingly receiving on Parker's Piece. What Frank perhaps did not anticipate was that the town turned down his offer to play at his ground, believing instead cricket on Parker's Piece was 'for the million', especially the poor who would struggle to pay Frank's admission charge.

This is to the town's credit. However, the resultant dialogue, particularly in the press descended to anonymous criticism, including a reference to Frank as the 'uncalled-for champion of the University Club'.[7]

Whilst Frank's early responses were perhaps 'bullish … and insensitive to the emotions his move had stirred',[8] he nevertheless continued to be a loyal supporter of local cricket, even attempting to resurrect a Cambridgeshire Cricket Club in 1858, reflecting his passion for the game, alongside any business considerations.

Even so, 'years of hard-won co-operation' in pooling the strengths of town and University cricket, thanks largely to Frank, were now 'undermined by a traditional mistrust' by the town of the University.[9] With hindsight Frank might have invested more time in consolidating the cricketing tradition he, the town and the University had created, before the opening of Fenner's.

Whatever the case, the poor relationship he had with the town immediately, and later with the University, after opening his ground, must have been sources of great pain and disappointment.

Relationship with the University

Despite the fact Cambridge University had a long history of believing sport contributed little or nothing to a student's education, Frank's 'tender cultivation' appears to have suggested otherwise. Initially the relationship appears to have been very healthy, but cracks soon appeared.

The Deerfoot furore

Frank had travelled to the United States to book Deerfoot to visit England and appear in athletic races including at Fenner's, where Frank introduced him to the Prince of Wales. As positive as the visit of Deerfoot in 1861 had been, it nevertheless caused a furore, given his attendance at dinner at Trinity College, in the presence of the Prince.

Whilst Frank was not directly involved in this dinner incident, perhaps 'the University' realised, whilst sport was perhaps here to stay, it needed to be better managed? And not by a local tobacconist. Perhaps those members of the University on the Deerfoot organising committee, such as Leslie Stephen, were reprimanded, and / or tasked with taking more of a leadership role in future? Remember at this time, the University had suddenly lost its Chancellor, Prince Albert, responsible for 'reviving the spirit of learning' there, as well as more generally having an influence 'in the direction of humanitarianism including speaking out against slavery and child labour'.[10]

Whether the visit of Deerfoot, and the change in Chancellorship was the catalyst or not, there were an increasing number of University staff who took more of an active role in promoting and managing sport, in addition to Leslie Stephen. These included Arthur Ward (cricket), Edmund Morgan (athletics), and Henry Morgan (rowing), with these latter two (not related) leading the way in Jesus College championing the importance of sport in the 1870s and 1880s.[11]

Loss of Working Men's College backing

If there were moves to take over Frank's control of sport, he may have had fewer supporters in the University to advise and support him when the Working Men's College in Cambridge began to languish from 1858 when both the Principal and Secretary left, both being past students at Cambridge.

Handing over 'Fenner's'

Although Frank moved from Cambridge in the early 1860s, he still retained the lease on Fenner's Ground for a further ten years, which clearly placed additional strain on his relationship with the University.

Their records report on rent arrears, the poor state and size of the pavilion, and Frank making a 'grasping' claim on some property, all reflecting the tensions. But what would have perhaps saddened him most of all was the attempted change of name from 'Fenner's' to the 'Cambridge University Cricket Ground' as soon as they had taken over the lease from Frank.

The University Cricket Club's records refer to later making a £10 payment to 'the veteran Fenner', because he was in 'financial trouble'. Why it needed to be called a *douceur* is unclear, but if today's dictionary definition is anything to go by: 'gift or payment - sometimes, but not necessarily, considered a bribe - provided by someone to enhance or 'sweeten' a deal', then it probably caused Frank great sadness.

To his credit, throughout his life, Frank was never openly critical of the University, its staff or students.

Frank leaves Cambridge

It is not known precisely why Frank Fenner left Cambridge in 1862 / 1863 to start a new career, new home, and new cricket ground and county club one hundred miles away in the west country, at the age of fifty.

Whilst he had a relatively poor relationship with local people in Cambridge, surely this would not have been the only reason for leaving, especially so given his businesses, and his standing (then) with the University, appear to have been in good shape. This is a mystery to speculate upon.

Perhaps he was modelling to the University how sport might be managed, but that as a local tobacconist and 'sporting professional' he was not the right man for the job? If this were true, how might it relate to the origins of Cambridge's sporting revolution that went global?

[1] Willie Sugg '1847 – Two of a kind?' article on website: https://www.cambscrickethistory.co.uk/new-writing/

[2] Willie Sugg (2009). Fenner's Men. Cambridgeshire Cricket 1822-1848. Part 3 of A Tradition Unshared. Real Work Publishing. Page 44.

[3] 'Sporting Notes and News – Cricket' in Pall Mall Gazette 25 May 1896. Page 6.

[4] Cambridge Independent Press 2 May 1868. Page 8.

[5] Cambridge Independent Press 14 December 1861.

[6] W.J. Ford (1902). The Cambridge University Cricket Club. William Blackwood and Sons. Page 18.

[7] Cambridge Chronicle and Journal 17 June 1848.

[8] Willie Sugg '1848 - Fenner's Ground opens'. New writings on WS website https://www.cambscrickethistory.co.uk/

[9] Willie Sugg (2009). Fenner's Men. Cambridgeshire Cricket 1822-1848. Part 3 of A Tradition Unshared. Real Work Publishing. Page 52.

[10] The royal family's website (Sept 2022): https://www.royal.uk/prince-albert

[11] J.A. Mangan (2006). 'Oars and the man'. Pleasure and purpose in Victorian and Edwardian Cambridge. Ch 3 in J.A. Mangan (2006). A sport-loving society. Victorian and Edwardian middle-class England at play. Routledge.

CHAPTER 25

The sporting revolution

Ed Smith, one time student at Cambridge University, and England's national cricket selector, believes sporting dynasties (and revolutions?) 'emerge organically', using Welsh rugby in the 1970s and West Indies cricket in the 1980s, as examples:[1]

> Cricket in the Caribbean enjoyed a perfect storm scenario. You couldn't have drawn up a set of social and political circumstances more likely to promote sporting excellence. But planning had nothing to do with it.

So, was there a *perfect storm* in Cambridge in the middle of the nineteenth century?

The context for sport had not changed much for centuries as it was repeatedly banned by the University, being sustained by the more non-academic students, and the doggedness, courage and creativity of local people, all sharing local facilities. These included the river, Fens, Cambridge's four fairs and its commons, especially Parker's Piece.

Such a status quo was unsettled by perhaps two *storms* Frank helped to create, one that petered out relatively quickly, and another that followed, so large it had a global spread.

Frank Fenner must be credited with securing the achievements of the Cambridge Town Club and Town and County Club era of 1838-48, so that Cambridge had one of the best teams in the country, made up of members of both Town and Gown. This inclusive approach dovetailed with the Working Men's College, an initiative Frank was also directly involved in, that endeavoured to extend a Cambridge education beyond the University, driven by some of the foremost social thinkers and reformers of the mid nineteenth century. Unfortunately, both these initiatives, using a *sport, and education for all* ethos, ended abruptly, being lamented as a 'tradition unshared', blown away by a much bigger storm.

As a businessman Frank took full advantage of the increasing opportunities available to entrepreneurs in the Victorian era, beyond his tobacco business, cricket coaching and sale of cricket equipment. When those playing cricket on Parker's Piece complained the pitches were poor and too busy, including the 'noisy and ill-mannered chaff'[2] they experienced from local people, Frank created an enclosed ground. Later his portfolio grew so that this same ground was also used for athletics, and other events where an entry fee was charged, as well as providing a gymnasium behind his tobacco shop on the Market.

Maybe because of Fenner demonstrating that a dedicated, safe and enclosed sporting facility could succeed, the colleges of the University followed this example, each establishing playing fields of their own, on the edge or outside town?

This increasing physical separation from the town may have reinforced the increasing gap opening up in sport between the gentleman amateur and the professional player. With Frank making money out of his growing portfolio of sports facilities he would have lost the support of Thomas Hughes, one of the foremost and influential gentlemen amateurs Frank probably had most in common with, through the Working Men's College. Hughes, like other Christian socialists, were strongly opposed to the professionalisation of sport.

Also, whilst the visit of Deerfoot was perhaps the pinnacle of Frank's business career, not just in terms of takings on the gate, but also the Royal patronage he secured, the shock waves it produced was enough for the gentlemen amateurs in 'the University' to somehow plot a takeover?

Were all these unplanned factors, the *perfect storm*?

Whilst the era of the gentlemen amateur in sport is today understood as being largely self-serving, that included the exclusion of women, and the non-university population in Cambridge, the sporting outcomes they achieved across the globe may be considered extraordinary, many examples of which have been shared in this book. These include contributing towards 'the drawing up of rules'[4] for Association Football, Australian Rules Football and boxing, and 'the development of sporting philosophies'[5] such as Muscular Christianity. Together with sports promoters, sponsors, administrators, Christian missionaries, schoolteachers, civil servants and players, whilst students in Cambridge, or following their education, many of them also took sport across the world, from Brazil, South Africa, Kashmir, Sudan, Wales, Japan, Melanesia, to North America.

Through their efforts they largely promoted a sporting ethos or Corinthian spirit characterised by sportsmanship, fair play, playing for the love of the game – not for profit, *esprit de corps*, and respect for both authority and opponents.

Were these outcomes achieved thanks to Frank Fenner's achievements? Had Cambridge sport been in Fenner's hands?

---

[1]   Ed Smith (2008). What sport tells us about life. Viking. Page 155.

[2]   W.J. Ford (1902). The Cambridge University Cricket Club. William Blackwood and Sons. Pages 6 and 7.

[3]   J.A. Mangan - ed (2006). A sport-loving society. Victorian and Edwardian middle-class England at play Routledge. Page 3.

[4]   Johnes, M. (2005). 'United Kingdom', in D. Levinsen and K. Christensen (eds.), Encyclopaedia of World Sport. Great Barrington, USA: Berkshire Publishing.

[5]   Johnes, M. (2005). 'United Kingdom', in D. Levinsen and K. Christensen (eds.), Encyclopaedia of World Sport. Great Barrington, USA: Berkshire Publishing.

ABOUT THE AUTHOR

Having studied sport as an undergraduate in Liverpool, Nigel came to Cambridge University to train as a teacher, which naturally helped to spark his interest in Frank Fenner. The local press picked up on this, sending out a request to its readers for any information on who Frank was, on the back of Nigel playing University football on Fenner's Cricket Ground.

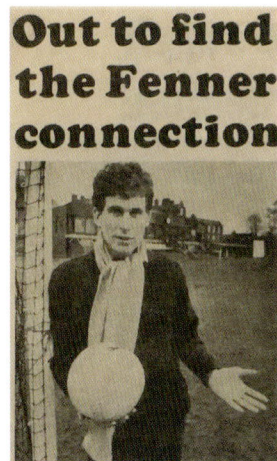

Source: Cambridge Evening News (December 1982).

Use of image granted by Reach Publishing Services Ltd.

Meanwhile, although very little became of this search, Nigel was busy winning a Cambridge University football Blue, playing in the annual Varsity match against Oxford University in 1982, and very soon after, starting work and a family.

After University Nigel continued to play some sport, the highlights being scoring a cricket hundred on Parker's Piece, and keeping wicket to Ian Botham's bowling, and batting with Martin Crowe (the best ranked batsmen in the world at the time), for Ian Botham's Benefit XI at the Perse School.

In addition, and without grasping the full significance of what he was doing in emulating Frank Fenner, Nigel was the Cambridge University Cricket Club's pre-season fitness trainer (the year Rob Andrew was captain, later a British Lions rugby player). Nigel also played cricket once on Fenner's, being the only family representative in the 'Fenner's XI' team playing against the University, when celebrating 150 years of Fenner's Cricket Ground opening in 1848.

Towards the end of Nigel's teaching career, spanning work with young offenders, adults with disabilities, and children excluded from school, did he decide to dig deeper to find out more about Frank Fenner. They are first cousins sharing Frank's grandfather, Andrew Fenner (born about 1730, died 1817), who is Nigel's great (x5) grandfather. This search was linked to establishing and running sports walking tours in Cambridge in 2017 as a retirement project, still operating today as 'Cambridge Sports Tours' (www.cambridgesportstours.co.uk).

Today Nigel lives with his wife not far from Cambridge, and his two children and their families, a source of extraordinary joy and happiness.

INDEX

NOTES